A HISTORY OF SOUTH.
THE SOUTH
BY

F. Marion Crawford

Scylla

The Earliest Time

Etna at sunrise

In very early times, when demigods made history and myth together, heroic beings moved upon the southern land and sea, in seasons of beauty and of strength, sometimes of terror, that pursued each other, changing and interchanging forms, appearing and disappearing, rising from the waters as a mirage and sinking into the bosom of the earth, then springing into life again elsewhere in the more vivid day of a nearer reality, half human still but already mortal, to die at the last, to be buried in tombs that endure, and to leave names behind them which history can neither quite accept nor wholly overlook.

First, ancient Kronos is the kindly god of the golden age in all Italy, but changes in Sicily to Baal-Moloch, grasping tyrant, devourer of human flesh, fortified against mankind in the high places of the earth; and he slays Ouranos, his father, whose blood falls as a fertilizing rain from heaven upon the burning Sicilian earth. Armed with the scythe, he rules in wrath, then fades from existence, and leaves his crooked weapon twice buried in the earth in Drepanon, the sickle of Western Trapani, and in Zancle, the wide reaping-hook of land that guards Messina from the southern storms.

Poseidon next, his son, god of the Mediterranean Sea, smites his trident deep into the uncertain land. He is the father of many heroes, of Trinakros and Sikelos, whose names stuck fast, of giant Polyphemus, of the man-eating Laestrygones, of Eryx, Aphrodite's son; he is the father, too, of great Demeter, who fights forever with fiery Hephaestos for possession of her rich inheritance, of Demeter, who first taught men to sow corn;° while the nymph Aetna, high on her mountain throne, watches the eternal strife, forever umpire of a never-ending war. Still the fight for bread against fire is raging, and in the wild burnt lands between Randazzo and Brontë, the 'thunder-town,' the myth of Hephaestos and Demeter is truth still.

From her springs the lovely fable-allegory of the seed hidden in the earth, dead half the year and half the year alive again. For of Demeter, by Zeus, was born Kore, the 'Maiden,' the girl Persephone, who played in Sicilian fields with maiden Athene and maiden Artemis, and each chose a playground of her own. Athene took Himera, on the west, for hers, and on the east Artemis chose Ortygia in the sea; but Kore loved best the fruitful land of Enna in the island's heart, where violets grew so close and sweet that the Huntress's own hounds could follow no scent there, and the chase ended among the flowers. There Kore wandered, gathering the violets to make a dark blue mantle for her father Zeus, the sky-king; but though the meadows were so fair, the gate of Hades was close at hand, among the trees at the foot of Enna's hill, and thence dark Pluton, master of hell, watched her with glowing eyes, and sprang forward at last and took her in his arms to bear her away. But when he was hard by Syracuse, the nymph Kyane, p4Kore's playmate, leapt lightly from the woods and stood in the way as he rushed along, and she prayed with all her heart for her friend's freedom, but could not move the raging god to mercy; so she sank to earth and was lost in her own tears, which made a deep translucent well, the most beautiful of all springs in the world to this day. After that Demeter went out to seek for her lost daughter, and lighted Aetna's fires for a torch, but could not find her, for Kore had eaten the seed of the pomegranate in Pluton's house, and was wedded, and could only come back for half the year. Therefore Zeus gave her Sicily for a wedding gift. By this is fabled the hiding of the seed in the earth, and its return to the upper world in leaf and flower.

Next came mysterious Daedalus, art and skill in person, flying before angry Minos, king of Crete, touching Sicily first and wandering from island to island, beautifying each and leaving in each some stable work to tell that he had passed there; while the Sicanians burned his enemies' ships, and drowned King Minos in the bath, burying him deep, and building above his grave their temple to Aphrodite. Daedalus built great reservoirs and impregnable cities, treasuries for kings and temples for gods, whose images he carved in rare wood, and set them moving with cunning devices hidden within. So, when bread had first been won, and when husbandry had grown strong in peace, thought and art came likewise, that Sicily might be a perfect home for men. The great legend of Troy embraced the island then. When old Laomedon had sacrificed his daughter

Hesione to atone for his broken word, many Trojans fled, or sent away their children secretly, lest like should befall them. Hippotes sent his child Egesta to Sicily, and she loved Crimisos and bore him Acestes, who went back when he was fully grown, and fought for Troy, but returned again and brought with him Elymos, son of Anchises; and this Elymos left his name to the children of Acestes, who were called Elymians. But some say that these were the Elamites of the Bible.

Soon after that came great Ulysses, wandering by sea, when he had dragged his unwilling companions from the shores of the Lotus land; and first he came to the eastern shore of Sicily, where Polyphemus dwelt p6among cliffs and caves, pasturing huge sheep, and he was taken with his companions by the giant; but he blinded him and escaped with those who still lived; and the Cyclops tore up great boulders, that were like hills, and sent them whirling after the Greeks, but could not hit them, being quite blind; so the rocks fell into the sea and became three islets, fast and firm to this day. One of them, moreover, is like a vast monster's head rising above the water, and where the eye should be there is a round aperture, through which the light shines brightly from side to side; for which reason it may well be that the Cyclops was made a one-eyed creature in the imagination of early men, as anyone who may understand who will go to Aci Castello or to Trezza and look at the rocks for himself.

Isles of the Cyclops, near Catania

Thence Ulysses sailed by the southern coast, round Sicily, touching here and there, and landing on islands where many advantages befell him, and along the Italian shore, so that his name and fame linked Sicily and Southern Italy with Greece.

Next, still from Troy, came Trojans with Aeneas and his fleet, wandering hither and thither, and founding the great temple of Idalian Venus, of Venus Erycina, on Mount Eryx, named after Aphrodite's son; and then Orestes came, crossing to Sicily when he had purged himself of his crime in Rhegium, and he built the temple of Artemis in Mylae, which is Milazzo, to hold the sacred image he had brought from far away.

So gods and heroes came and went, and left their names upon the south, and some of them found their last resting-places there; and tradition grew out of myth, and history was moulded upon tradition, till the legends would have filled volumes, and gradually concentrated themselves toward the point of transition at which fable becomes fact. Out of it all results clearly the main truth, that from very early times the rich south was a possession for which several races fought one with another, Orientals, Greeks, and peoples who p8had come down from Italy, and who were afterwards driven back by degrees into the inner country, the Sicanians and the Sicelians.

Isles of the Sirens, Gulf of Salerno

The most learned modern historian of Sicily, Adolf Holm, has proved almost conclusively that these two peoples were of common and Italian origin, and came in succession from their Latian home, somewhere near Anxur, which is now Terracina. The Sicanians came first, in small bands of wanderers, leaving many at home, whence afterwards arose the confusion of names, by which the stronger Sicelians were sometimes called Sicanians, but when the latter sailed down in force and took possession, the confusion ceased. The first comers had intrenched themselves in strong passes and had built fortresses on inaccessible heights, as men do who know that they may be easily destroyed. But the Sicelians came in hordes, driven from their homes by the vast immigration of the Pelasgian race when it moved westward and descended into Italy. They were Latins, speaking a Latin language, closely allied with that of the Romans, for they called a hare 'leporis'; and a basin 'katinon,' and they named a certain river 'Gela' because the hoar frost settled along the banks more thickly than elsewhere. And so, as Holm says, the Sicelians are proved by their language to have been closely connected with the Latins and the Oscans, and descended from the common Pelasgian stock; and it is clear that they had wandered from the Haemus p9to the Apennines, before they reached the island to which they gave their name, and that in their immigration they had overrun and filled the southern mainland of Italy. Once there, they built all those early cities of which remains exist that are not manifestly Greek; they built ships and sailed out on marauding expeditions, and some of them even attempted to plunder the Egyptians, joining themselves with Tyrrhenians and Sardinians, Achaeans and Lycians, as is proved by a hieroglyphic inscription found in Thebes, which tells how two hundred and fifty Sicelians were slain, under King Merenptah, and their hands were struck off and brought to him, twelve hundred years before our era began. It is sure, also, that even for centuries after the Greeks had settled in Sicily, the Sicelians dwelt there still, a flourishing and active race. They were therefore the first permanent element of a Sicilian population, and most probably of the south Italian people also; for Thucydides says that Italus, from whom Italy was supposed to have been named, was king of the Sicelians, and Aristotle states that he taught his pastoral people the more civilized arts of agriculture.

Three epochs stand out from the chaos of myth, legend, and history: the development of farming by the Sicelians, about 1200 B.C., the introduction of commerce with the Phoenicians after that time, and the gradual growth of a higher civilization under the Greeks, from the time of their landing in the eighth century before the Christian era, until the Carthaginian or Punic wars with Rome, and the subsequent wreck of Greek art and thought under the atrocious governorship of Verres, between 73 and 71 B.C., during which, with the connivance of his father, the senator, he pillaged all Sicily at his will.

The Roman rule became in the fourth century the rule of Constantinople, and next in history, when the Goths had ruled for a time, the Arabs began to take Sicily, in the year 827 A.D.; the Normans came after them, completing their conquest of the island in 1091, and through them the German Imperial house of Hohenstaufen, reigning from the fifth year before the preaching of the first Crusade, until the downfall of the Ghibellines in 1268. Then the French, under Charles of Anjou, during the few years that ended in the Sicilian Vespers, in 1282, after which the Sicilians chose for their king Peter of Aragon, and because both he and Charles of Anjou continued afterwards to call themselves kings of Sicily, the two kingdoms of Sicily and Naples became known from that time as the 'two Sicilies,' and were still so called under Ferdinand the Catholic, after Naples was annexed to Aragon, and both became Spanish monarchies. In 1700 began the war of the Spanish succession, after which Victor Amadeus of Savoy was king of Sicily for a time, until Sicily and Naples were again united under Charles the Third of the house of Bourbon. Last of all, in 1860, the two Sicilies were united to the modern Kingdom of Italy.

All these, through nearly three thousand years, were Rulers of the South in turn, Sicelians, Phoenicians, Greeks; Romans, Byzantines, Goths, and Arabs; Normans, German Emperors, and French; Spaniards of Aragon and of Bourbon, and Savoyard Kings of Italy. Every great race that has won rights on the shores of the Mediterranean Sea has, without an exception, sooner or later called the south its own, and has left the broad mark of full possession on the country, where it may still be seen, sometimes grotesque and sometimes grand, now rough, now beautiful; now vulgar, but always very strong and clear, as if the south had been a most cherished possession which each hoped to hold forever. There is no part of Europe which has been dominated by a greater number of different races, and none where each has left such deep traces of its domination. The Goths and Vandals are the only people who ever held the south for a time and left no sign of their presence; but their holding was short, and their occupation was followed by a disappearance so sudden that their brief rule never earned the designation of a kingdom.

The Italian south differs in one prime condition from all the other countries that open upon the Southern Sea. It has never at any time been the independent arbitrator of Europe or of civilization, and it has been held in succession by those powers that have ruled the rest, or most strongly influenced them, from very early times. Greece held it, and Imperial Rome, the wide-spreading Arab and Saracen domination, the all-grasping Normans, the Holy Roman Empire, and France and Spain. It has never been the source of an individual power that began in it, spread from it, and enveloped others. It has lacked strength of its own from the beginning, it has lacked the genius without which strength breeds monsters, it has been wanting in the original character which bears modification but resists extirpation, it has produced no race which another has not been able to enslave; one people after another has taken possession of it, each amalgamating in some degree with the last, but the welding of races has not become a great race, nor has any first element outlasted and outruled the others. It has been the prize of contending warriors, it has been the playground of magnificent civilizations, but it has neither acted the part of conqueror itself, nor has it ever produced a civilization of its own. It has resembled Greece and Rome, Arabia and Spain, in language, institutions, and manners, but its people have never gone forth in the flesh or in the spirit to impose upon others a resemblance to themselves. In the balance of the world's forces Sicily has been feminine and reproductive rather than masculine and creative; endowed with supreme natural beauty, she has been loved by all, she has favoured many, and she has borne sons to a few, sons such as Archimedes and Theocritus, Dionysius and Agathocles, King Roger and Frederick Second of Hohenstaufen, of Greek, Norman, and Norman-German blood. But if we ask for a great man whom we may call a Sicilian, we must ask what Sicilians were, and we shall receive different answers in different ages, — Greeks, Arabs, Normans, Spaniards, and Italians have all been Sicilians at one time or another.

At the first glance it might be thought that the result in history must be confusing and often disconnected, breaking off at a point to begin again at another with little or no apparent connexion, so as to present a series of detached episodes without logical sequence, and consequently without consecutive interest. But this is not at all the truth. That has been the case in some parts of the world, as in the plains of Central Asia, where one horde of invaders has succeeded and exterminated another of which it knew nothing, learned nothing, and desired nothing except plunder. The connexion between the Chinese Mongols and the Turanian Tartars, for instance, is not any closer, beyond the bounds of China, than that between white men and red Indians in America. But in the story of Sicily the continuous, reasonable cause of change lies in the unmatched attraction of Sicily, a charm so strong and lasting as to be a source of p14interest in itself, so that we may figure the island as the undying heroine of an unending romance, wooed, won, and lost by many lovers who have met and fought and have conquered, or have been vanquished in the struggle for the possession of her beauty. Sicily has been the Helen of a European Epos.

The southern mainland has for the most part served only as a stepping-stone to the conquest of the island. Pyrrhus, called over by the Greeks to help them, crossed the straits; Alaric meditated the passage, but withdrew, and Genseric took Sicily from Africa, but Roger the Norman and Charles of Anjou went over as conquerors of all the south. Yet in many respects Southern Italy has never been far behind the most coveted spot in the Mediterranean; there is great natural beauty in the mainland and great wealth of soil, and such climate as is hardly to be found elsewhere; there, too, the Greeks built marvellous temples to their gods, and there thinkers, philosophers, poets, and soldiers have been reared of successive races; Horace himself was of the south, and so was Zeno of Elea, founder of the great Eleatic school. Tarentum lost all manliness and vigour in a delicacy of thought and manners that outdid the refinements of Syracuse, and the civilization of Greece trained its growth of beauty like a climbing rose from tower to tower. But in spite of all, the mainland never rivalled Sicily in art or thought or war; in the vast construction of empires Lucania, Apulia, Calabria, were never names to conjure with, nor were they ever numbered among the kingdoms of fable, wherein godlike shapes of terror and of loveliness figured the drama of nature in immortal allegory. They were not divided from the p16world by the mystery of the moving sea nor hidden from it by the morning mist of the straits, nor brought to it in the magic mirage of the Fairy Morgana. There was no secret in them for men to learn at risk of life, there was no marvel in the thought of them; they were among the world's commonplaces, and every one might go to them and live in them who chose. It was not until the middle ages substituted romantic tragedy for classic myth that the inaccessible mountains of the south were filled with a sort of mysterious interest which they have not yet wholly lost.

The story of the Rulers of the South is as much a history of places as of the persons whose character marked them and left them as they are, since almost throughout history it was the nature of the places themselves which played so great a part in the lives of those who coveted them, grasped them, and ruled them, or who dwelt in them and made them famous. We cannot easily imagine Syracuse without Dionysius the Elder, nor Dionysius without Syracuse, nor would anyone ever think of Theocritus as a poet of the mainland. The great story of Roger the Norman moves towards Palermo as the sun to the splendour of its setting, and Charles of Anjou is better remembered by the awful Vespers of the Church of the Holy Ghost than by the long life of struggle, conquest, and murder which won him a kingdom and founded a long-lived dynasty.

It is true that in such a narrative it is necessary to return again and again to the same pieces, and to cross the same ground many times; but in successive ages the cities of the south, while many of them have kept their names, have so changed that it is hard to recognise them as the same; and each of them is therefore not one but many, all of which must be seen in imagination and understood, as far as possible, in order to form a clear and reasonable idea of the whole as it was and is.

Before going any further, however, it is necessary that the reader should have a general conception of the extraordinary country in which the events took place which are hereafter to be narrated.

Old Fortification in Manfredonia

Southern Italy is little more than a range of volcanic mountains which rise abruptly from the sea on the west side and descend on the east in a succession of fertile tablelands, the lowest of which is a vast foreshore only slightly raised above the level of the Adriatic. There is not a single natural harbour, really deserving the name, on the whole coast of the southern mainland, from the Gulf of Naples on the west to Manfredonia on the eastern side. The nearest approach to one is perhaps Tarentum, and it early owed its prosperity to the nature of the land, which there afforded tolerable shelter to large vessels before any harbour was constructed. Even at the present day there is no safe port for large ships between Naples, or Stabian Castellamare, close by it, and the straits. Messina, once called Zancle, the beautiful 'sickle' on the Sicilian side, was therefore the natural place for all vessels to put in that sailed round the coast.

Mare piccolo at Taranto, — the harbour of ancient Tarentum

At the extremity of the range which thus forms Southern Italy, and divided from it by a channel little more than two miles wide, lies Sicily, a mountainous, three-cornered island •over five hundred miles in circumference by straight lines, and over six hundred, if one closely follows the irregular coast. Viewed from the sea, the island appears almost everywhere as a vast assemblage of rocky peaks which often fall abruptly away in huge cliffs and bluffs. Only on parts of the eastern and southern side do the hills recede some distance so that rich plains open to the sea; but all round the coast the mountains are broken at intervals by deep valleys that lead to others at a higher level in the interior and there are more safe natural harbours on the northern and eastern sides of the island, from Trapani at the western extremity to Syracuse near the southeastern corner, than are to be found on an equal extent of coast line in any part of the world. The history of Sicily has been largely the history of those harbours and of those who held them; and as the size and draught of ships increased with the development of navigation under the Romans, after the Punic wars, the importance of the harbours grew likewise, while the cities on the southern side that possessed at most half-sheltered sandy beaches on which small vessels could be hauled up high and dry, steadily lost value, and did not recover until the construction of artificial harbours in modern times supplied what was deficient in nature.

Lighthouse at Colombaia, harbour of Trapani

The fertility of Sicily is proverbial, and seems incredible when one considers how large a part of the island consists of high mountains. It is hard for one bred in the north to realize that in southern latitudes a mountain •five thousand feet high may be richly cultivated to its very summit; it is even harder to understand that the climate and soil are such that certain plants bear two crops in the year without exhausting the land, after three thousand years of cultivation; it is hardest of all, perhaps, to believe that the old-fashioned methods of agriculture, originally introduced by the Greeks, are really the best adapted to the country, as well as to the genius of a people possessed of unbounded industry and vast traditional experience, but wholly unlearned in the ways of modern science.

Let it be considered that out of six millions of acres, barely one hundred and fifty thousand are barren; that the soil will bear anything, from wheat and barley to the orange, the lemon, the date palm, and the banana, from the papyrus to the manna-ash, from cotton and sumach to the carob and the Indian fig; that at a short distance below the surface lie the most valuable sulphur mines in the world, as well as excellent mines of rock salt; that the finest fisheries in the whole Mediterranean exist upon the coast; and finally that the most valuable coral is found in the same waters. Consider these few facts and it becomes plain that Sicily is one of the richest islands in the world, well worth the endless struggle for its possession that has been waged by a dozen different races since the beginning of all history. There is probably not to be found anywhere an equal area of land of the same value, not containing mines of diamonds, gold, or silver. The mainland opposite is very different. The plains to the eastward are indeed prosperous agricultural regions, but they are nowhere as fruitful as the island, nor do they produce any such variety of crops; and the mountains of Southern Calabria consist for the most part of barren rocks among which a few herds of goats can hardly find a precarious pasture. Sicily has been called the granary of Rome and the garden of the Mediterranean; no such epithets have ever been applied to Calabria or Apulia.

It is commonly said that the population of the eastern and southern portions of the island is of Greek descent, while the strongest traces of the Arab race are found in the central and western parts, and in a general way the statement is true. It is true also that the predominating type on the southern mainland is Greek rather than Latin. Both in Sicily and on the mainland there are still villages where only Greek is spoken and Italian is learned at school as a foreign language; and in the Maltese islands, only sixty miles south of Sicily, the modern tongue is Arabic, so far as it can be said to be anything definite. It is not more remarkable that Arabic should have wholly disappeared from Italian territory than that it should have been altogether lost in lower Spain. The absence of a social constitution in the Arab nation is the reason for the short endurance of its language, manners, and faith wherever it has become subject to a people more advanced in this respect. It has left us much of its art, and its profound genius laid the foundations of modern science, in mathematics, chemistry, and astronomy; but it has left nothing of itself behind it, and it is much harder for anyone who has not lived in the East to evoke even a faint picture of Arab life in Palermo, than it is to call up very vividly the sights of Greek Syracuse under Dionysius or Agathocles. The point is one that deserves the consideration of the student of ethics, but it is worth noticing that the same truth applies to the Semitic Phoenicians, who, perhaps, did more for civilization at large than all the Pharaohs together, but whose surviving image in the imagination of modern man is as vague as that of the Egyptians is bright and sharply defined. We may recall one more striking instance in the Goths, another people of whom it cannot be said that they had a definite social constitution, who held all Italy for a hundred years, and left few signs of their presence after them except the graves in which they were laid.

The main influences that have worked upon the south have been Greek, Roman, Arabic, and Norman, of which the Roman is the one least strongly noticeable at the present day, and even, perhaps, in earlier centuries. For, in the south, the Romans themselves lost character, and their decided taste for Greek art and manners hellenized them into insignificance. When their reign was over, the Goths dominated them and the Arabs made slaves of them. They had accepted and imitated all they had found, and they were themselves wiped out of social existence by those who conquered them; yet their works remain, of gigantic and sometimes not without a certain borrowed Greek grace, and we have no more difficulty in fancying how they lived and ruled and worked in Agrigentum, than in Rome itself. Yet, to speak figuratively and familiarly, we do not 'see' the Romans when we think of Sicily, excepting perhaps Verres and his train of satellites, and though we must follow their history, we do not wish to 'see' them more than is necessary to an understanding of their position in the succession of the rulers. We are chiefly concerned with the Greeks, the Arabs, and the Normans. That far-reaching Spanish domination which attained the height of its power in the sixteenth century was a part of modern history upon which the limits of this work will not allow us to dwell.

Spring called the "Fonte del Sole," in a grotto near Taranto

What has here been said by way of introduction shall not afterwards be repeated. The sum of it, in brief, is this: For three thousand years Sicily has been looked upon as the fairest among all the richly endowed lands that border on the Mediterranean Sea or lie as islands within it, a sort of earthly paradise, to obtain which no sacrifice could be thought too great; its claim to be so esteemed can be established by the short proof of any thoughtful man's first glance, even to the present day; its history is the narrative of fierce struggle fought by great and manly races for its possession, and is told in monuments and ruins still to be seen. It is of all lands the one in which the most enthralling romance is interwoven with the most stirring fact, for it has always been the debatable country where fact has met romance and vied with it for supremacy. It is much talked of, yet few travellers visit it, and those who do so see it through much misunderstanding and often at a great disadvantage. Its history is confused by an enormous number of small details, and by such endless accounts of insignificant personages and of minor actions, that the main stream of interest is diverted into a thousand channels where no single rivulet has much strength or beauty left; and sometimes all the channels are quite dry. For Sicily has been the favourite ground of the specialist for a long time, and in the specialist's minute work the smallest detail may possess for him the very highest importance.

It is the writer's aim, in this book, to give a simple and true account of the successive dominations by which Sicily and the south of Italy have sometimes prospered and sometimes suffered from the days of the early Greek settlers down to the establishment of the house of Aragon.

The Greeks

It is no wonder that the Greeks were seamen and wanderers on the sea. With little more than twice as much land as Sicily, Greece has a coast line equal to that of all Spain and Portugal together. Moreover, every strong race that has reached the sea in the migration of peoples has sooner or later attempted to sail westward, like Ulysses in his last voyage, beyond the baths of all the western stars, and the Greeks were almost driven from their own shore by the press of those behind them, when their little country was filled to overflowing. So they began to spread and multiply in the islands of the Mediterranean, and certain of the bolder among them reached Italy and passed the straits, whence, sailing up the dangerous western coast, they came to the safe waters of Cumae, protected from storms by the island of Ischia; and there they founded a colony which was the beginning of Naples. Some of them, it is said, turned pirates and found their way back to Sicily.

They were very perfect men, and could do all and bear all that could be done and borne by human flesh and blood. Taking them altogether they were the most faultlessly constructed human beings that ever lived, and they knew it, for they worshipped bodily beauty and strength, and they spent the lives of generations in the cultivation of both. They were p27fighting men, trained to use every weapon they knew, they were boxers and wrestlers, athletes, runners and jumpers, and drivers of chariots; but above all, they were seamen, skilled at the helm, quick at handling sails masters of the oar, and fearless navigators when half of all navigation led sooner or later to certain death. For though they loved life, as only the strong and the beautiful can love it, and though they looked forward to no condition of perpetual bliss beyond, but only to the shadowy place where regretful phantoms flitted in the gloom as in the twilight of the Hebrew Sheol, yet they faced dying as fighters always have and always will, with desperate hands and a quiet heart.

Their ships were small craft, much more like the little vessels in which the Greeks and Sicilians sail to-day, than those are like the vessels of the ocean. The first condition for safety was that their ships might be easily hauled up high and dry on any sandy beach, by means of such gear as they could carry with them; the second, that they should be very swift under the oar. The Norsemen who reached the Western Ocean needed the same qualities in their vessels; hence the resemblance between the old viking's ship and the southern felucca of our own time. Both are long, narrow, and of small draught, flat-bottomed amidships, yet sharp as a knife both fore and aft. The Greek ship, like the Norseman's, carried but one mast and one great sail that was furled whenever the wind was not free, so that the only means of motion lay in the sweeps, steadily swung and pulled by free men or slaves, as the case might be, sometimes from dawn to sunset.

Men rarely put to sea in one ship alone for any distant voyage. They sailed out in little fleets of ten, or even twenty sail, well knowing that some should not come home, and trusting in the number of their vessels to save some of their companions from death by drowning. As Holm quietly observes, when speaking of Ulysses, men did not travel for pleasure in those days.

When the Greek sailors were not pirates who got a living by robbing the Phoenician traders, they traded themselves, from Greece to Asia Minor and among all the rich Greek islands. They loaded their little ships on shore, covered the cargo with ox-hides battened down in the narrow waterways to keep the stuff dry, they launched their vessels with the cargo in them, and they lived on deck, sleeping as they could in the open air, or making awnings of skins when they could anchor for the night in some natural harbour, or when with infinite labour they were obliged to beach their vessels on lonely shores before a coming storm. It was a rough life, and often they had to fight in self-defence, when weather-bound in barbarous places; but most men carried their lives in their hands in those times, and few looked forward to dying of old age.

Cape Palinuro, Gulf of Policastro

A certain Theocles, whom some call Thucles, an Athenian, traded with Italy in the eighth century before Christ, and no doubt had been as far as Cumae, where the Greeks had settled. But neither he nor any other Greeks had landed in Sicily, for the Sicelians had a bad name in the south, and it was said that they devoured human flesh and destroyed everyone who tried to land upon their shores, so that other men left them in peace for a long time; and it is most likely that the Phoenicians, who traded with them, and even had settlements in Malta, and perhaps in Western Sicily, and who themselves offered up human sacrifices, spread this tale through the East to frighten off other trading folk.

But Theocles, the merchant, with his little fleet of vessels, was sailing near the straits one summer day, hugging the Italian shore, when the northeast wind came upon him, suddenly and violently, as it does in those waters, and he could not beat up against it to an anchorage under the land, but was obliged to run before it, towards Sicily; for it was wiser to take the risk of being eaten by the Sicelians than to face certain drowning in vessels that would not lie to in a gale. So he wore his ships to the wind under such sail as he dared carry and ran for the opposite land with a heavy sea following. It is very likely that two or three of his fleet were swamped and sank with all on board, though a felucca will run safely before weather that would be dangerous to many larger craft. Theocles offered prayers to Apollo, and kept the helm up.

Seeing that the wind was northeast, and that Sicily was a lee shore, he knew that his chance of safety and life lay in running under the only little headland that juts out from that part of the coast, and he succeeded in making the shelter in time, before the wind shifted to the eastward. The sea broke over him just as he rounded the point, but its force drove him on and into smooth water, where he came to and let go both anchors. One by one his companions followed him and anchored alongside, and the first Greeks proceeded to land, where they afterwards built Naxos and Tauromenium, on the soft beach of yellow sand below the little town now called Taormina, which many say is the most beautiful spot in the whole world.

It is not possible, as some traditions say, that Theocles should have landed in the sandy cove under Cape Schisò, and should have built his altar to Apollo on the spot where Saint Pancras's statue now stands; for the only storm which could have driven him across from Italy to the Sicilian shore was a northeaster; an easterly or southeasterly gale would have either swamped him or sent him up the straits, and when the wind is in the northeast, Cape Schisò affords no shelter, though there is smooth water a mile to the northward under Cape Sant' Andrea, and a little islet there protects the beach. So Theocles must have landed there, and there he doubtless proceeded to beach his vessels, heavy laden as they were, well knowing that the wind would shift to the dangerous southeast before the bad weather was over. It is most likely that he built his altar on the island, since he feared the Sicelians, and would feel safer if protected from them even by a narrow bit of shallow water; and on it he and his companions sacrificed with a little meal and wine, which was all they had, and they prayed that their lives might be spared, not dreaming that they should reach Greece again in safety, and return a second time, and build a city which should endure for ages, and be the near forerunner of a vast Greek colonization.

Instead of a race of cannibals, rushing down from the hills to kill them for food, the Greeks found a peaceable farmer folk, well satisfied with themselves and others, who sauntered down to the shore and eyed the weather-bound strangers with benevolent curiosity. From a distance they must have seen their ships, and understood at once that these were not of Phoenician build; and they could see too, before they descended to the shore, that the newcomers were neither pirates nor soldiers, but peaceable merchants driven in from the sea for shelter. It is easy to fancy the distrust of Theocles and his companions, and the simple plan they had followed; how they allured the Sicelians by holding up specimens of their merchandise, coloured stuffs, glass beads, and bits of tinsel-ware that caught the eye, just as English sailors made friends of South Sea islanders two thousand years later. The Greeks could not speak the Sicelian tongue, but they conversed in the universal dialect of all commercial enterprise, the language of exchange, and for their wares they obtained fresh supplies, and by and by the natives sat down by the Greek camp fires while the great storm lasted, and they ate and drank together and talked by signs.

On the Outskirts of Giardini, below Taormina

Sitting there on the beach below Taormina, and wandering along to the southward, the strangers saw the rich foreshore full of trees and running springs of good water; their eyes followed the stubble fields up the rising ground, where the plentiful corn° had last been harvested, to the vinelands beyond, where the scarlet leaves still clung to the gnarled vine-stocks after the vintage; further up there were silver-green olives, and higher still the rich, dark foliage of carob trees, and all was very fertile and good. They bought wine also of the Sicelians, which was strong and almost black, and had a flavour of its own, unlike all other wines. They sacrificed at sunrise and at evening, but not every day; and the Sicelians stood apart at a little distance and watched how the strangers dealt with their strange gods, and listened to the musical Greek voices when they sang a hymn to Phoebus Apollo. But the Greeks looked over at the vast smoking mountain to the southward and dared not wander far in that direction, lest the fire god should be angry with them, though the Sicelians smiled and tried to make them understand that there was no danger; for Ulysses seemed as real and well remembered to Theocles as Columbus seems to us; and the Athenians believed that blind Polyphemus still wandered, bellowing for light, about the foot of Etna, and that the smoke they saw still came from Vulcan's smithy, and that all manner of monstrous and half godlike beings dwelt in the little valleys round about. So Theocles would not let his companions wander far away. But in the evening, when the Sicelian farmers had gone to their dark huts, and the Greeks lay on skins around the blazing camp fire on the beach, while the southerly storm howled far overhead from over the mountains, they told each other that the land was good and the people mild, and that a few hundred Greeks could easily hold their own there, if only they could get possession of the first hill above the shore, and a little to the northward, on which Taormina now stands. There would be little difficulty about that, since the Sicelians dwelt mostly in the valleys. Their real danger was from Polyphemus and the Laestrygones, and Hephaestos, and they therefore sacrificed continually to Apollo, the protector of colonists and the giver of victory.

The storm may have lasted a week, and when it was over, and the sea rippled gently to the breeze under the quiet sunlight, Theocles launched his ships and sailed away, not without leaving gifts to the hospitable Sicelians. As soon as he reached Athens, he began to speak of the rich country he had seen, telling that the people were well disposed, and that it would be easy to get a broad strip of land, and hold it against all comers; but no one would listen to him, or if any noticed what he said, they answered that it would be unwise to disturb Polyphemus, or to run the risk of angering Hephaestos, and that moreover they did not believe anything that he said; which was a favourite refutation of argument among the Athenians. Then Theocles went over to Chalcis in Euboea, and told his story; and there he found hearers and men very restless with the spirit of the sea, who had sailed far, and wished to sail farther, and who preferred trading and wandering to staying at home, and liked fighting better than either. But they were not godless men, and before going upon the expedition they consulted the oracle of Apollo, and the god promised them his protection and a prosperous voyage and all good fortune. Then some other Ionians and certain Dorians joined themselves to the Chalcidians with more ships, and in the spring a whole fleet of vessels sailed westward, laden with all sorts of necessary things, and Theocles piloted them safely to the very point where he had found shelter the first time; but instead of waiting by the shore, he led his people up the hill by the easy declivities that are almost like artificial terraces, one above another, and took possession of the strong crest on which the theatre now stands. No doubt Theocles dealt in a friendly way with the Sicelians, especially at first; but they were a humble and peaceable folk who looked with admiration upon the Greeks and with mild covetousness on their possessions, and were quite willing to part with a little land in exchange for a few shining toys of glass and tinsel. Besides, it does not appear that the Greeks, who were after all but a few, had come with any idea of seizing a wide territory and enslaving the inhabitants to work for them. They had come, rather, to establish an outpost trading station whence they could export the produce of the rich island in the way of regular commerce, and the

Sicelians soon found that instead of being a thorn in their side, the young city of Naxos, which Theocles founded to the southward of the hill, was a profitable market for their corn and wine and oil.

Seeing how easy it was to settle and take possession of a site for a city, some of the Dorians who were with Theocles took courage to face the dangers of the fire mountain and the anger of Polyphemus, and they sailed farther southward, along the coast, til they came to the beautiful natural harbour which is now Augusta, but which they called Taurus, at the foot of the Hyblaean hills, and there they founded Megara Hyblaea, in remembrance of Megara in the Dorian country, between Attica and the isthmus of Corinth. There, from the end of a low promontory, a tongue of land runs due south and almost encloses a sheet of still water, where ships may lie in all weathers; and there the foreshore is deep and fertile, being that lower extremity of the great plain of Catania which sweeps round the base of Mount Thymbris and terminates in the jutting land at Trogilos, just north of Syracuse.

Swiftly the news went back to Greece that the colony was successful and that its wealth was already increasing, and within two years the great western movement of the Greeks had begun, and the fate of the Sicelians on the coasts of Sicily was decided forever. Archias, the rich Heraclid of Corinth, whose evil passion had brought about the riot in which beautiful Actaeon was killed, was a fugitive and an exile before gods and men, and he collected together his wealth, his people and his servants, and sailed forth to found lordly Syracuse; and within a few years the Chalcidians and Ionians got possession of Catania and Leontini — the broad meadow lands where the Laestrygones had been supposed to dwell; and Achaeans had come to the mainland and had founded Sybaris in the soft Italian gulf, and Crotona, which is now Cotrone, soon taking possession of all that is now Calabria and building Metapontum, Poseidonia, and Terina. The Messenians of the Peloponnesus also built Rhegium on the Italian side of the straits, and somehow their name afterwards crept across the narrow water, and Zancle came to be called Messana and then Messina. The Ionians also got round to the north side of Sicily and founded Himera, and after that came Dorians from the island of Rhodes and built Gela, which is Terranova on the Gela, the 'gelid' river of the Sicelians; and nearly a hundred years later the same people got possession of Akragas, which became Agrigentum, and which is Girgenti to-day. The Megarian Dorians also founded Selinus, near Western Lilybaeum, and there one may yet see the most unimaginable mass of ruins that exists in Europe, for the earthquake that destroyed it left not one stone upon another, and buried none.

In a hundred and fifty years the Greeks had got possession of the south, including all the mainland from Cumae near Naples, to the straits, and all the coast of Sicily from Himera on the north, not far from Palermo, round by the east and south sides to westward as far as Selinus. In Sicily the Phoenician traders had been gradually pushed to the west till their settlements only extended along about a hundred and fifty miles of the coast, though at that part of the island which was most convenient to them, as being nearest to Carthage. After they had got what they could of the south without very much fighting, the Greeks pushed further to the north and west, attempted to form a colony in Corsica and failed, and finally founded Massilia, now Marseilles.

Though the extent of territory which they occupied in a short time seems very great, it must be remembered that in reality they at first held only the coasts, and that both on the mainland and in Sicily they pushed the original people into the interior, where the Sicelians and Italians for a long time pursued their original rural occupations in peace and probably with profit, selling their produce to the Greeks, who consumed it in part, and in part exported it. The position of the Greeks in the south at that period was in one respect more like that which was held for a long time by the East India Company in India, than that of England's trading stations. It differed from it chiefly in that the majority of the Greek colonies were not only independent of each other, but also of the mother country, and had formed themselves into oligarchies, which had succeeded the first small monarchies of the founders, and were followed again by the despotisms of men who rose to the highest places through their own talents and the play of circumstances, like Gelon, Dionysius, and Agathocles. Another great difference lies in the fact that whereas the East India Company was never really a colony, in the ethnological sense, any more than it was politically one, and whereas the Englishmen who founded it, and the thousands who acted as its agents, officers, and fighting men, always looked forward to coming home to England, the Greek colonists settled permanently in new countries, and their cities became active and independent sources of genuine Greek thought, literature, and art.

Corinth alone seems to have kept some hold and influence upon the new settlements formed by her citizens, but in the end that connexion died away also, and at the time of the Athenian invasion all Sicily was entirely separated from the mother country. With regard to the relations between the Greeks and the natives, events followed their usual historical sequence. At first the newcomers spread round the coast, as p40they increased, seizing all places most desirable for trade, and driving out other traders as well as the indigenous population. But when the coast was fully occupied, they naturally began to take possession of the interior, enslaving the peaceable country people by degrees, till they were practically the masters through the length and breadth of Sicily and Southern Italy.

Ancient aqueduct at Solmona in the Abruzzi, the birthplace of Ovid

It would be a mistake to look upon the conquest of p41the south as a direct consequence of conditions in Greece. It was but an extension of the Hellenic westward movement from Asia Minor, which had settled Greece itself, and which filled all the eastern Mediterranean and ultimately spread into Spain. The whole race, continually fed by emigration from its place of origin in Asia, was moving towards the setting sun, as the Semite Phoenicians had moved before it, and it was with the latter people that it engaged in its first great struggle for existence in the west, at the very time when the mother country was fighting for life against the invasion of the Persian host. For the westward migration was itself caused by the awakening the Asian races, that culminated in the conquests of Nebuchadnezzar, Cambyses, Cyrus, and Darius, which was checked at Salamis, and was ultimately thrown back upon itself and annihilated by the Greek Alexander the Great.

We are too apt to think of those early times as barbarous and uncultivated compared with those of Pericles. We forget the vast civilization of Egypt, whose empire, in the seventh century before our era, was hastening to its decline, but whose culture was the model of all cultures then existing, and was looked up to by the Phoenician and the Babylonian alike, as well as by the Greeks themselves, who slavishly imitated Egyptian art for centuries, and surrounded with profoundest mystery the few poor secrets of nature they succeeded in stealing from the rich treasures of Egyptian learning. Many do not remember that Babylon was at that time the greatest city in the world, and was enclosed within walls that measured •thirty-six miles in circuit, the chief stronghold of a power that overshadowed all central and western Asia. One should recall the existence of enormous libraries of learning, of hundreds of thousands of books, written in Egypt on papyrus, in Assyria on clay tiles, which were afterwards hardened by baking and coloured with many tints, each of which was distinctive of some branch of learning and thus contributed to the easy classification of the whole. Nor should it be forgotten that in those days the magnificent monuments of the Egyptians were still in the glory of perfect preservation, in Memphis, Heliopolis, and in Thebes, or that in Babylon the legendary gardens of Semiramis still hung between earth and heaven, supported on a thousand arches, high above the city, but themselves overshadowed by the vast temple of Bel. The Greeks were familiar with Egypt through their trade, and many of them had wandered beyond Palestine to the banks of the Euphrates, and had written down careful accounts of their journeys. The men who settled Sicily and the south of Italy were adventurers, wanderers, and fighting men, but they were very far from uncivilized; more than half of their religion was the worship of beauty, and if the science they had obtained from Egypt was scanty, their own brilliant intelligence enlightened them in applying it. It is no wonder that within a few years of their settling in the south they became a new nation of artists, poets, and thinkers, actively creative in their own right, as it were, and immeasurably superior in cultivation to all the races with which they came into contact; it is not surprising that Sybaris should have outdone the East in refinement of luxury, nor that strong Crotona should have bred more winners of the Olympic Games than all Greece and all the Greek islands together. The Greek athlete was not the gladiator of later days, the mere 'swordsman,' as the word signifies; he was the result of the thoughtful worship of human beauty, brought to its final expression by natural selection and artificial training; and the winner of the Games was not merely a runner, a wrestler, or a boxer, he was the best man of his day at all bodily exercises whatsoever, and in the eyes of the people that brought him home in triumph he was a visible god, the living incarnation of the Greek spirit. Every race that has beaten the world has at the outset shown a physical as well as a characteristic superiority over its opponents, but in almost every case that superiority has been unconscious, or has asserted itself with loud boasting and overwhelming brutality. The Greek alone knew how to cultivate and perfect the gifts that placed him above other men, reverencing his own endowments as something divine within him, and analyzing the secret sources of his own strength, until he had almost found a formula for the production of great men.

After sunset on the shore of eastern Calabria

At this time appeared one of the most romantic figures in ancient history, the first that deserves especial mention in the story of the south, a man of almost superhuman genius, who, had he lived in more ordinary conditions than those which accompanied the first marvellous development of the Greek people, would have become in the west what his contemporaries, Zoroaster, Buddha, and Confucius, became in Persia, in India, and in China. This extraordinary person was Pythagoras, the Samian philosopher, the son of Mnesarchus, who was a very rich merchant and shipowner, and strange to say, in his moments of leisure, a sculptor of considerable talent.

It is neither a misuse of the term nor an exaggeration of fact to call the great thinker's career a romantic one; for in its original signification the romance was the tale of the 'romare,' of the pilgrim and wanderer; and from 'romare,' derived from, or very closely connected with Rome, as a chief place of pilgrimage, we have made our modern word 'roamer.' If ever a man earned that epithet it was the Samian seeker after knowledge, who, in a life that covered nearly a century, spent but the first eighteen years in his home, who lived twenty-two years in Egypt, twelve in Babylon, and thirty-nine in Italy, who was a pupil of Thales, the favoured guest of Pharaoh, the friend of Zoroaster, and the founder of the great Pythagorean brotherhoods that played so interesting a part in the political and civil history of Southern Italy.

The son of the rich man was taught by Hermodamas, and the tenderest affection grew up between the pupil and his master. The first instruction in those times consisted in the reading and recitation of poetry and in the art of music. Under the rule of Polycrates, Samos was the very centre of Greek art and thought. There lived Ibycus, the love poet born in Italian Rhegium, of whose works beautiful fragments have come down to us; there Anacreon spent his richest years, but of him little remains, for the Odes are not now believed to be all his work, though they have so long borne his name; there dwelt also Theodorus the younger, the Benvenuto Cellini of his day, famous for the statues he modelled and cast in bronze, and for his marvellous skill at engraving, who made the ring of Polycrates; and last, the great tyrant himself, cunning, cruel, fortunate, a lover of every beautiful art, the despot of the sea, the delight of poets, the friend of Pharaoh, fated to die on the cross at last, like a common malefactor. Such was the court in which the boy Pythagoras grew up to the age of eighteen years, beautiful beyond other youths and gifted of the gods above all his companions. It is a conspicuous fact and one that raises strange reflections concerning modern theories of education, that every supremely great man of antiquity, from myth to legend, from legend to fact, was first taught to recite poetry and make music, and was not instructed in mathematics till he had spent years in the study of both; for it was held that man who could not write in verse, could not write his own language at all, and that a being for whom musical sounds had no corresponding meaning was a barbarian unfit to associated with his fellows. So Pythagoras, whose famous proposition is the point of departure to which all trigonometry is referred, spent his first youth in playing on the seven-stringed lyre and in declaiming the Homeric poems, which Pisistratus, the wise ruler of Athens, had very lately collected and finally arranged. Without doubt he sat at the feet of Anacreon, and filled the poet's drinking-cup, listening to the voice that matched the words and to the words no age has ever matched, and doubtless he was beloved by Ibycus and saw Theodorus model gods of clay that were to be cast in bronze and set up in temples to be worshipped by the people; whence he began to understand that there was a faith above belief in idols, and that far beyond the earthly scenery of myth and the play of the beautiful little god-figures there was the All-Being in which all is contained that lives and dies and lives again. So when he was about eighteen years of age his mind was opened, and he began to desire absolute knowledge and to seek after it.

Now at this time Polycrates had not yet attained to the height of his power, and he was enriching himself by extorting money from his wealthy subjects and even by confiscating their goods with slight excuse. Therefore many writers have asserted that Pythagoras fled from Samos to escape from the tyrant's grasping hands, but this is a senseless story, since he was then but a boy and his father and mother remained in Samos and lived in riches for more than twenty years after his departure. It seems to me much more probable that Polycrates had made a law, as many modern despots have done, forbidding young men to leave their country until they had performed some stated service; and that Pythagoras was in such haste to increase his knowledge that he would not abide the ordained time. So he fled secretly by night with his teacher Hermodamas, who afterwards came back alone and appears to have suffered no penalty. It is very clear that Pythagoras feared pursuit and capture; for though Samos is close to the mainland, and not far from Miletus, where both Anaximander and Thales, or Theletas, as he is sometimes called, were famous philosophers, yet the young man preferred to sail all the way to Lesbos, far to northward, where at that time he was safe from the messengers of Polycrates. There he dwelt with an uncle, a brother of his father, and was taught by Pherecydes for some time; but when he had learned of him what he could, he journeyed southward by land to Miletus, and sat down beside the ancient Thales and began to be initiated into the secret wisdom of the priests.

The mysteries of the ancients were the truth, or the nearest approach to it then possible, as contrasted with the vast fictions of mythology in which the peoples believed. Without an exception, all the mysteries taught of a god who had died and had been buried on earth, and who had returned to life again in glory; most of them foretold a judgment of souls, and all looked forward to a future state, either as following directly upon death, or as the end of a series of migrations, in which the soul passed from one body to another, purifying itself by degrees, or sinking by steps of defilement to final perdition. All the mysteries were ultimately monotheistic in idea, though the one god of the secret faith was considered as containing two, three, or four principles in himself, according to the ethic and psychic schemes adopted by the initiated of different nations.

The early philosophers were all priests and mystics, most of them were poets, in the sense that they wrote down their thoughts in verse, and all were seekers after knowledge. The highest development, both of mysticism and of scientific inquiry, was considered to have been reached in Egypt, though it has been thought that the Magians of Assyria were better mathematicians than the Egyptian priests, and that the Chaldaeans were as good astronomers.

The true faith of those times was a profound secret in the hands of small communities of amazingly gifted men. It could never be popular, for the comprehension required to understand it was far beyond the gifts of the masses, and the consequence was that although initiation into the mysteries was not the exclusive privilege of the aristocratic class, it was nevertheless very closely associated with an aristocratic principle in the minds of the many, a fact which afterwards led directly to the violent destruction of the Pythagorean brotherhoods in Italy.

The intellectual grasp of the young Samian soon took possession of his master's knowledge, and when he had been initiated into the mysteries of Zeus in the temple on Mount Ida, Thales declared that if his pupil would learn more he must find a way to be received among the priests of Egypt. No foreign student had ever accomplished such an apparently impossible thing; but Pythagoras, who admitted no impossibilities, forthwith determined to possess himself of all the wisdom of the Egyptians, and of all learning possessed by men.

That was a period of peace and prosperity in the world. Under Croesus, Lydia had developed immeasurable wealth, Phoenicia, now under the lordship of Babylon, was recovering from the ravages of Nebuchadnezzar, and Persia had not yet started upon her long career of conquest. Egypt, after a revolution which had placed a man of plebeian extraction upon the throne of the Pharaohs, was enjoying the last years of her splendour under the wise rule of Amasis. In the west the Greeks were spreading mightily, and were quickly developing the strength which first repelled the Carthaginians and soon afterwards proved an impassable barrier to the advance of Xerxes. The known world was rich and at peace, and in the shadow of a hundred ancient temples, from the islands of the Mediterranean to Mount Ida, from Assyrian Babylon and Phoenician Sidon to Egyptian Thebes, the chosen company of the wise cherished what was wisdom in those days, and followed those patient investigations in mathematics and astronomy to which modern science is so deeply indebted.

It was in Sidon that Pythagoras first became a true mystic, and it was there that he first conceived the idea of uniting and simplifying the many forms of mysticism into one religion which should satisfy at the same time the highest aspirations of the soul and the widest speculations of the intellect, and which should be at once a faultless rule of spiritual life and a perfect guide to man's social existence. The thought was high and noble, for it was the thought which inspired Zoroaster, Buddha, and Confucius, and it foreran the teaching of Christ as the dawn the day.

In order to prepare himself for his mission, Pythagoras felt that he must withdraw himself from the world among the wisest men at that time living. After he had been initiated in Sidon, he wandered down through Phoenicia into Palestine; he gazed thoughtfully upon the ruins of Jerusalem that lay broken to pieces in the dust like a vessel of clay, and he came to Mount Carmel and looked towards Egypt, which was the goal of his desires. So he took ship for the Delta in a small Egyptian trading craft, and the merchant and the sailors saw that he was a Greek, well skilled in learning, and they agreed that they would sell him for a slave in Memphis, where he would fetch a good price. But he understood what was in their minds and showed no fear, and fixed his eyes upon them until they were afraid under the strength of his look, and gave over their evil designs; so he came safely to Memphis, where Pharaoh dwelt at that time, and where there were many wise priests. But these would have none of him, for he was a foreigner, and they thought that he wished to learn their secrets only to sell them for much wealth to the priests of Ida or of Delphi. So he abode among the Greeks, for there were many of these in Memphis, and he occupied himself in learning the Egyptian language.

Then he bethought himself of Polycrates, the tyrant of Samos, who was yet in close friendship with Amasis, and with whom his father Mnesarchus had much interest. After that time Pharaoh, seeing the marvellous good fortune of Polycrates, advised him to cast away what was dearest to him, lest the gods should be angry; and then the tyrant threw into the sea the ring which Theodorus had made for him, and which he prized above all his possessions; but it was found again in the belly of a fish and was brought back to him by the fisherman. So Amasis broke friendship with him, seeing that he was so highly favoured of the gods, because it was not good, being powerful, to be too closely intimate with one who was devouring the wealth of others and who never failed in an undertaking. But these things had not then happened, and Pythagoras wrote a letter to the tyrant, setting forth his desires, and speaking of his long studies, and showing that the Greeks might profit by the wisdom of the Egyptians if only Polycrates would persuade Amasis to command the admission of Pythagoras to the school of the Egyptian priesthood. Polycrates therefore wrote a very urgent letter to Pharaoh, which he sent to Pythagoras himself; and Amasis received the young man graciously, and sent him to the priests at Heliopolis, the city of the Sun. But these sent him back to the priests at Memphis, and these latter, not knowing what to do, sent him at last to the great high priest at Thebes, with the royal command. The high priest made it hard for him, and required a long period of purification, and a painful rite and ordeal, hoping perhaps to terrify the scholar. But Pythagoras was of those who are born without fear, and he despised pain, and was initiated.

Two and twenty years he lived in the temple in Thebes, and he mastered by degrees all the sciences, and the writings, and the mystic teaching of the Egyptians, and the religion which was afterwards called his teaching was a complete exposition of all that Egyptians both knew and believed, and had acquired laboriously in thousands of years. It was the wisdom of those to whom a hundred years were but a day, and to whom ten generations were but as the continuous life of one man, inasmuch as whatever was learned by each was wholly known to the next, without break nor interval of forgetfulness; and the whole was written down in a hard language that changed not in ten centuries, and was kept secret from the people. It is small wonder that Pythagoras should have spent a quarter of his life in acquiring what the wisest nation in the world had accumulated in more than a hundred generations. There, in the temple of Thebes, he dwelt and studied in peace, while the face of the earth was changed, while Cyrus grew greater and greater, till he seemed the greatest of men that had lived, and spread out the empire of Persia and gathered all into his hands, to the very borders of Egypt. Then he died, and Amasis died also, and Cambyses came victoriously to Egypt and dragged Pharaoh's embalmed body from its tomb in Sais to insult it shamefully; and he carried many away captive to Babylon, and Pythagoras the Samian was among the prisoners. Then Cambyses died too, and the pseudo-Smerdis, the Magian, and Atossa, the sister of the first and the wife of both, married Darius, the friend of Zoroaster, and became the mother of Xerxes who invaded Greece.

At the time when Pythagoras was taken to Babylon, he was forty-four years of age, and since he afterward lived to be almost a hundred years old, he had not then reached the middle of life. When he found himself a prisoner, and probably in the social condition of a slave, within the four walls of the greatest capital in existence, in the heart of Assyria and at least five hundred miles east of the Mediterranean, he can have had little hope of ever returning to the west again. Yet to his philosophic genius such a captivity may not have seemed irksome, and he was not cut off from intercourse with his own people, for a great number of Greeks were employed about the court of the Persian king, and though news travelled slowly, it was brought with much detail, if also with much exaggeration. He resigned himself to his fate, and set to work to study the religious reforms of Zoroaster, whom he undoubtedly knew, and the mathematical methods of the Assyrian and Chaldaean astronomers — of some of those very men, perhaps, whom Belshazzar had called in to interpret the writing on the wall. So he lived and studied in peace, being one of the wise men attached to the court of Darius.

Aqueduct at Taranto, formerly Tarentum

Then he regained his liberty by a most extraordinary train of circumstances. Before Cambyses died of his wound in Ecbatana, Oroetes, the governor of Sardis and satrap of Western Asia, who had long cherished a private quarrel with Polycrates of Samos, enticed him to land in Lydia as his guest, and then crucified him with circumstances of hideous cruelty. But Darius sent a single ambassador who came to the court of Sardis and read to Oroetes the king's commands, and the last command was that the satrap's own guards should smite off his head. And so they did, for Darius' name was great, and they hated Oroetes. The ambassador took back with him as slaves many of the friends and servants of the dead man, among whom was a very cunning physician of Crotona, who became the friend of Pythagoras in Babylon. One day Darius sprained his foot, and when his own physicians could do nothing for him, some one brought the skilled captive, who cured the king at once. So the king asked him what reward he desired, and he begged that he might return to his home. Darius yielded so far as to permit him to visit Crotona, if he would promise to come back, and not trusting him, he sent with him a Persian guard, and several men of learning, bidding them to write a description of the coast as they sailed, and he gave them a fine ship and many supplies. But it came to pass that as they sailed to Crotona they were driven into Tarentum under stress of weather, and the Tarentines took them all prisoners with their goods, and when the physician had told his story they let him go free and he returned to Crotona. Now there was at Crotona a rich man exiled from Tarentum. And learning what had happened, he sent thither, and ransomed the Persian captives and their ship, and sent them all back to Darius, asking two things; namely, that the King would use his power to make the Tarentines receive him again and also that he would set free the wise man Pythagoras whom Cambyses had taken captive in Egypt; this he asked at the request of the physician. Then Darius, being glad to receive his Persians safely again, promised both things, and the second, at least, he performed, for Pythagoras was set at liberty; and he came to Samos in time to see his father and his mother alive, and also Hermodamas his first teacher, who had helped him to escape in the days of Polycrates. But he stayed not long in his home, for he desired to work among men and to turn his learning to their good, and his thoughts went out westward to the great Greek colonies of Italy, so that at last he followed the instinct of his soul and took ship and came to Crotona and founded the Pythagorean brotherhood, which was mystic, philosophical, and aristocratic, after the model of this Egyptian priesthood from which Pythagoras had got his wisdom.

Hallam says somewhere that mankind has generally required some ceremonial follies to keep alive the wholesome spirit of association. It is hard to say now how many of the curious rules of life adopted by the Pythagorean brotherhood should be traced to this motive, and many of these contain more wisdom than appears in them at first sight. The brethren abstained from eating flesh, as most mystics have done, but they were as careful never to eat beans; they believed in the transmigration and immortality of souls, yet they prohibited the use of woollen grave-clothes; they had an elaborate system of degrees and initiations, they possessed most of the existing wisdom of their time, and they nevertheless followed rules for making a fire which seem utterly childish. Yet an inquiry into the origin and reason of some of these practices, if the facts could be sufficiently known, would throw a brilliant light upon the domestic customs of the early Greeks, and might not impossibly explain some of the peculiar superstitions of the south, such as that, for instance, with forbids a man to lay his hat upon a bed, or the universal southern belief that if a woman drinks from a new earthen jar, before a man has drunk from it, the water kept in it will ever afterwards taste of mould. In considering some of the extraordinary beliefs current among the Italians and Sicilians, it has often occurred to me that they may have had their origin in the fables about the Pythagorean brothers, to whom strange powers were imputed, of whom extraordinary tales were told, and some of whose visible practices may have been ignorantly imitated by the people in very early times.

Columns called the "tavole Paladine," at Metaponto, formerly Metapontum

The society founded by Pythagoras was as much a secret one as that of the modern Japanese Buddhists, and lovers of esoteric philosophy will find many points of close resemblance in the two religions, if the doctrine of the Greek philosopher deserves the name of religion, which he would undoubtedly have applied to it, if an equivalent word had existed in the Greek language. It taught that the soul is immortal, that the aim of man should be a virtuous life on earth and a state of peace hereafter, and that goodness, if not the fear of God, is the beginning of wisdom. Yet it limited by the strictest tests the number of those who were admitted to a full knowledge of its secrets, and its visited every betrayal with merciless severity; it professed to be a religion for the few, it was necessarily hieratic if not aristocratic, and it was fatally disposed by its exclusiveness to identify itself with a political party. It drew into itself, or its founder gathered round him, the noblest youth of Grecian Italy, at a time when the power of the democracy was increasing at an enormous rate; and in the first real conflict which took place its adherents died devoted deaths at the hands of a bloodthirsty proletariat, as more than one aristocracy has perished since. They had advised, directed, and morally ruled the people, and their general, the heroic Milo, had returned from a victorious war with Sybaris, once all-powerful, but then fast sinking to an inglorious decadence by degrees of aesthetic idleness and unmeasured luxury. They brought home great spoils to Crotona, and in the division, one Kylon, a brutal fellow whom the Pythagoreans had refused to receive on account of his evil life, stirred up a riot against them. In the house of Milo they made their last stand, and there most of them were slain; but a few escaped, and Pythagoras came to his end in Metapontum, and the brotherhoods were done away with forever. Their existence had endured twenty years; had it lasted longer they would have been led from their natural political sphere, by the dangerous paths of political expediency, down to the moral disgrace of a political necessity, which is wholly unreconcilable with any true philosophy, and they would have left behind them the tradition of a once pure faith degraded to the basest uses and expedients of politics. But they died in a whole and clean belief, and from their ashes arose something new, which was not the Pythagorean religion, but the Pythagorean philosophy; their leader left a name little less than saintly, he bequeathed the accumulated wisdom of the world to his surviving followers, and he left his memory to the veneration of mankind.

I have dwelt at great length upon his story because it combines in a wonderful degree the elements of fable, romance, and history, and is therefore a fitting link between myth and truth. I am aware that almost every incident in the tale has been held up to ridicule by someone scholar, but there is not one in which many others have not firmly believed. When learned authorities disagree, it is the right of the student of romantic history to choose from the confusion of discords those possible combinations which seem most harmonious. It is not his province to dissect the nerve of truth from the dead body of tradition, but rather by touch and thought and sympathy to make the old times live again in imagination. Therefore the godlike figure of this Pythagoras belongs among the Rulers of the South, as with the legends of his miracles, and the reality of his wisdom, with his profound learning, his untiring activity, and his unswerving belief in the soul's life to come, with his love of man and his love of beauty, his faith, his hope, and his almost Christian charity, he represented in its best conditions the highest type of the Aryan or Indo-Germanic people. It matters little that scholars should quarrel over the theories of numbers ascribed to him, that the one should deny his captivity in Babylon and the other his long residence in Egypt, that Bentley should tear the traditions of him to pieces, that Roeth should glorify him almost to sainthood, or that Ritter should make a laudable but ineffectual attempt to find a golden mean of sense between the extremes; the fact remains that he lived and laboured, that he dreamt of a world of brotherhoods in which all good was to be in common, and from which all evil was to be excluded, that when he was gone he left a philosophy behind him without which, as a beginning, it would be hard to imagine an Aristotle, a Socrates, or a Plato, and that both to his fellow-men and to those that came after him his name meant all that was best, whether possible or unattainable, in the struggle of inward civilization against outward darkness.

The place where Sybaris stood among gardens of roses and groves of fruit trees is a desolate plain, where not one hewn stone is to be seen above the storm-ploughed soil, and rotting trunks of trees and rain-bleached branches strew the sterile drift. There the soft Sybarites made it unlawful to rear a crowing cock in the city, or for braziers, smiths, and carpenters to work at their trades, lest any harsh sound should grate upon their delicate hearing; there even the children were clad in purple robes, and their hair was curled and braided with gold; there the idle reared witty dwarfs to jest for them, and bred little Maltese dogs with silky hair; and the five thousand horsemen of their cavalry rode in procession, wearing saffron-coloured robes over their corslets, and the people lived in luxuries beyond imagination, and in pleasures without a name, till Milo and the stern men of Crotona came and destroyed them all, and turned the waters of the river upon the city and swept it utterly away. The winter floods roar down the river bed where Sybaris was, and the spring freshets pile up brushwood and sand upon the barren stones, while overhead the southern hawk makes wide circles above the universal desolation, and his mournful note falls fitfully upon the lonely air. But Crotona flourished long and greatly, and its possessions extended from sea to sea; it has left in history the names of countless winners of the Olympic Games, and the reputation of its men and women for matchless strength and beauty; and though not a stone of its buildings remains in sight, yet there is a sort of logical satisfaction in knowing that the ancient ruins which were standing in the last century were finally destroyed in order that the stones might be used to build the mole of a safe harbour. For Crotona never disappeared from existence as Sybaris did, and where the ancient stronghold of Milo was reared upon a bold mass of seagirt rock, another fortress, strong in the middle ages, rebuilt by Charles the Fifth and still unruined, reflects its dark outline in the sea.

The site of Sybaris

Fortress of Charles the Fifth at Cotrone, formerly Crotona

A deserted corner of Italy now, Crotona is a land of farmers ignorant of all but farming, and it is hard to feel that it was once the heart of Greek strength, and beauty, and civilization in the west, and that where a single column rises in lonely beauty almost from the water's edge, at Capo Colonne, the great philosopher once lingered in the shade of Lacinian Hera's temple; that the picture of Lacedaemonian Helen hung upon the wall within, painted by Zeuxis from the five most lovely maidens of the city, and that the Greeks of all southern Italy came up thither every year in splendid procession, bearing gifts and offerings to the goddess and her shrine.

Temple of Hera, Capo Colonne, near Cotrone

It is generally said that the influence of Pythagoras and of the brotherhoods, which was dominant on the mainland and left distinct traces of itself there after the catastrophe in which the disciples and their master perished, had little influence upon Sicily. Some say indeed that a tyrant of Centoripa, one Simichus, became an adept and divided all his possessions between his sisters and his subjects, and others assert that the people of Akragas, and Tauromenium, and Himera threw off the yoke of their several tyrannies at last, not as common revolutionaries, but as true believers in the Pythagorean doctrines of individual freedom and common possessions; but these stories are gravely doubted, and Holm has shown that more than one wise despot was also accounted a Pythagorean. Yet to one who knows the south well, there is a striking resemblance between the organization of the original brotherhood, with its rigid tests of worthiness, its countless secret signs and pass words and peculiar practices, and its bloody vengeance upon unfaithfulness, and the rules and ordinances of secret societies that have ruled the south in later days. Were there no traces of such freemasonry among the slaves who twice rose against the Romans in Sicily and who seem to have connected themselves in some imaginative way with an Eastern tradition? Or among the people who destroyed Charles of Anjou's Frenchmen in the Sicilian Vespers? Or is the evil Camorra of Naples to-day wholly different from a brotherhood, so far as the laws that bind together its members are concerned, though the object be crime instead of good? Or, to go one step higher, is the modern Mafia of Sicily, which so strangely combines a mistaken idea of patriotism, or at least of independence, with the most nefarious notions of general lawlessness, so wholly different in its forms from the brotherhoods, as not to be perhaps a degenerate descendant of them? Answer the question as one will, the south has always been the natural home of widespread and secret unions of determined men for one end; and whereas in recent history political parties have made use of them and have risen to power by their help, no party and no government has ever been able to fight them to an issue nor to stamp them out.

The Greeks were an imaginative and a boastful people, prone to think well of themselves, like most highly gifted races, and it requires much good will to believe all the stories their historians have left us of their superhuman endurance and courage; but it is an undeniable proof of their extraordinary vitality and strength that they withstood victoriously the simultaneous attempts of two great powers to crush them out of existence at a very critical moment in their career. About the year 480 B.C. Xerxes and Carthage, apparently acting in concert, advanced from the east and west with vast armaments and enormous preparations, in the clear intention of annihilating the whole Greek nation in a single campaign. Xerxes came with all Persia and the north of India at his back; Carthage sent Hamilcar and three hundred thousand men.

At that time, except in Syracuse, despots ruled over the principal Greek cities of Sicily, Gela, Callipolis, Naxos, Leontini, and Zancle, the first of which had under Hippocrates acquired a sort of lordship over the rest; and he indeed attempted to conquer Syracuse also, but failed when on the point of success, and left the undertaking to his successor Gelon, the conqueror, and none could be compared with him excepting Theron of Akragas, who became his friend and gave him his daughter to wife; and Theron ruled through the midst of the land, from Akragas on the south to near Himera on the north, but the tyrant of Himera was his enemy and the friend of Anaxilas of Rhegium on the mainland. So there was war between the north and the south, and the south stood for a Greek Sicily and a Greek civilization, but the north was against both. But in Himera there was a division of parties, and the one asked help of Theron, who came and took the city and held it, while the tyrants of the north turned to the Phoenicians and to Carthage for aid. At that time the Phoenicians were powerful in Panormus and all the western° parts of the island, so that the Carthaginians were sure of being well received with all their forces and supplies in cities belonging to their own people, whence they could fight their way by land to a general conquest.

They saw that their opportunity was come at last, and they made great preparations during three years, and gathered together mercenaries from many lands, as was their custom in time of war, from Italy and Liguria and from Gaul and Spain and Corsica, and many from Africa, and weapons were made without number, and a vast provision was collected; then they set sail with two hundred galleys and three thousand transports, under Hamilcar, the son of Hanno, one of the two kings called Suffetes, a man of ancient Carthaginian lineage, though his mother was a Syracusan; and he was a devout person who neglected no service of the Phoenician gods, and continually sacrificed men and children to Ashtaroth on the altars of his house. Moreover, he had good surety that some of the most western Greek cities would help him, such as Selinus and others.

He set sail, therefore, with a good heart and dreaming of great spoil. But immediately a great storm arose, and the ships that bore the cavalry with their horses, and the war chariots also, were filled and sank with all on board; so that when he reached Panormus he had only the mercenary foot soldiers, a great host of fighting men of all nations, wearing strange dresses and armed with many sorts of weapons. In the wide bay of Panormus, the "All-harbour," where the Golden Shell stretches between the high mountain and the water's edge, he landed his men, and repaired his ships; and thence he marched along the narrow foreshore against Himera, where Theron awaited him, not without fear, for great rumours went before the armament.

The fleet sailed along close in shore, keeping the army in sight, and when they came to Himera and saw that the gates were shut against them, Hamilcar made two camps, the one for his land forces and the other for his ships, which he beached high and dry, surrounding them with a high stockade and a broad ditch. But the tents of the soldiers began from the enclosure and followed all the west side of the city and along the low heights to southward. When Theron saw how great a host was come against him, he was afraid, and he walled up the west gate of the city and sent messengers quickly and secretly to Gelon, the soldier king of Syracuse. But Hamilcar besieged the city, and when the defenders made sallies he drove them back with slaughter, making many of them prisoners; and the strange arms and wild dresses of the Carthaginian mercenaries frightened Theron's men even before they came to close quarters. Nevertheless Hamilcar did not press the siege overmuch, and while he was wasting his days in small engagements, thinking himself sure of taking the city without loss, Gelon was crossing over through the mountains by forced marches, day and night, with fifty thousand men-at-arms and five thousand horsemen, not mercenaries speaking many tongues and trained to many different kinds of warfare as Hamilcar's men were, but all Greeks of the Sicilian cities under Gelon's rule, well trained, speaking one tongue, and ready to die for their homes, their children, and their gods. They all encamped together and intrenched themselves in the plain to eastward of Himera, and Gelon began to harass the Carthaginians with his cavalry, for they had none, having lost both horses and men in the great storm. Then the face of things changed, and the Himerans took heart and opened the west gate again, tearing away the stones they had piled up, and Gelon took many prisoners and bethought him of some plan of striking a decisive blow. Now the Carthaginians had received promises of help from Selinus, the unfaithful city of the west, and the Selinuntians had agreed to send a body of horse to Hamilcar on a certain day which was also the feast of the Phoenicians; and a captive told his news to Gelon. He therefore waited until the feast day, and very early in the morning, before the sun was risen, he sent a chosen band of his own cavalry to the gate of Hamilcar's camp, bidding them say that they were the Greek horsemen from Selinus whom Hamilcar expected. He, being deceived, bade the gates be opened and the riders went in; but they rode past him and his men without drawing rein till they came to the ships that were beached upon the sand, and they set them on fire before the Carthaginians well understood what they were doing, and then drew their swords and began to slay.

Then, when Gelon saw the column of smoke rising up from the enemy's camp, he knew that his stratagem had succeeded, for he was ready and on the watch; and he marched down with all his fifty thousand men, and with all the Himeran soldiers also, and in that great day the Greeks slew of the Carthaginians outright one hundred and fifty thousand, and wounded many more; and the rest fled as they might, leaving all behind them. Hamilcar also perished, and some say that he died a strange death; for it is told that all day, while the battle ebbed and flowed in a tide of blood, he stood before the great altar in the midst of his camp, sacrificing human offerings to the gods, that by some miracle they might turn and save him from destruction; but when it was towards evening, and he saw that all was lost, he spread out his arms and prayed to the setting sun, and threw himself into the flames upon the altar, the last and noblest burnt-offering of his own sacrifice.

The few who fled intrenched themselves upon a mountain west of Himera, whither Gelon pursued them, and they were soon obliged to abandon their position for lack of water. Hastening to the shore with the Greeks in hot pursuit, they found the few vessels which had escaped the flames, launched them as best they could, and put to sea; yet the unappeased gods pursued them to the end, for the vessels were overladen and overwhelmed in the stormy waters of the Malta channel. Three thousand and two hundred ships had sailed from the harbour of Carthage with more than three hundred thousand men, to make the conquest of Sicily; a single skiff returned with scarce a dozen survivors to tell the tale.

Then the Carthaginians feared lest Gelon, having felt his strength and their weakness, should cross the water with his victorious Greeks to blot out their city and name, and take the rich coasts of Africa for his spoil, and so complete the circle of Greek possession round the central basin of the Mediterranean Sea. For, as some say, it was on the very day of Hamilcar's destruction that Xerxes was disgracefully beaten at Salamis; and if that be not so, it was at least soon afterwards; and the allied attempt of Persia and of Carthage to crush out the Greek power had utterly failed. Therefore the Carthaginians sent ambassadors to Gelon, who was now the greatest ruler in Sicily, to sue for peace on such terms as he could be induced to grant. But it is said that Damarete, Gelon's wife, advised him not to set the price of peace too high, lest at some future time he should need Carthaginian help for himself. He therefore exacted only three conditions; namely, that the Phoenicians should desist from offering human sacrifices in Sicily; that they should pay two thousand talents as indemnity for the cost of the war; and that they should build two temples to the memory of the peace; the one in Carthage, and the other at their expense in Syracuse. When the Carthaginians heard of such easy terms, they were overjoyed, and because they attributed their good fortune to Damarete, they presented her with a golden garland of one hundred talents' value, which may have been equal only to about seventy-five ounces of pure gold, if the Sicilian talent is meant, but if the Attic talent was the measure, the worth of the garland would have been near twenty-five thousand pounds sterling.

The power of Gelon grew vastly after these things, which happened about thirty years after Rome had become a republic, and more than two hundred years before Rome's first war with

Carthage. He was the first great ruler, for he brought under his dominion not only all Sicily but also a part of the mainland, and there is every reason to believe that he made Crotona and Rhegium, with all their possessions, tributary to him. In the first years of his lordship, he called a great meeting of the Syracusan people, and of all those to whom he had given the right of citizenship, bidding them come fully armed; but he himself, now that he trusted them, came alone and without armour or weapons, and stood up in their midst, and gave a true account of his actions in the war and afterwards. Then the people cried out and cheered, calling him their saviour, their benefactor, and their king; and so was, and he changed not till he died, for he was a brave and just man, and a glory to the Hellenic name. He died of a dropsy when he had ruled only seven years, and the Syracusans built him a tomb with nine towers; but long afterwards the Carthaginians destroyed the sepulchre, and at last Agathocles pulled down the towers in envy of Gelon's greatness, so that nothing remains to mark the spot to-day.

It is easy and generally unprofitable to construct imaginary history from the starting-point of an event which might have occurred, but did not. Yet one may ask not unreasonably what would have taken place if Gelon had followed up the victory of Himera by crossing over to Africa and destroying Carthage at once and forever. That he could have done so there is little doubt. At that time Carthage had few fighting men of her own, but was accustomed to raise mercenaries for her wars, and her whole army, consisting of a third of a million men, had just been utterly destroyed. Gelon had fifty thousand trained Greeks, he controlled vast wealth, and he had the prestige of victory. If he had pushed the war, the issue could hardly have been doubtful; Carthage would have sunk to the level of a province of Sicily, and two hundred years later Rome would not have had to fight the Punic Wars. But Gelon was a victor, a patriot, a wise ruler; he had not the instinct of the conqueror, and Carthage was left to recover from her defeat and to grow strong again within a few years. Yet what Gelon did contributed more directly to the growth of the beautiful civilization which blossomed in the reign of Hiero the First, and bore fruit long afterwards, than a career of foreign conquest could have done.

With the exception of Alexander, whose character was more Asiatic than Hellenic, no Greek appears to have conceived the idea of direct lordship over many states. The ruler of the dominant state controlled the rest, much as the German emperors controlled the Holy Roman Empire, leaving to each country its own ruler and its own laws, but without the tradition upon which the Holy Roman Empire rested, and from which it derived its authority. From the days of Gelon, Syracuse became the chief despotism in Sicily, and led the rest in civilization as well as in war; but the other tyrants continued to rule, each in his own place, both in the island and on the mainland, with very considerable authority; and Gelon's brother and successor Hiero, who usurped the power from Gelon's young heir, whose guardian he was jointly with another, had to sustain no insignificant struggle with Theron of Akragas, who had been Gelon's friend, and with Anaxilas of Rhegium, before he established his right to stand first among the despots of his day. Then, indeed, he pushed his influence northward on the mainland, and vanquished the Etruscans who had attacked Greek Cumae, planting colonies in the island of Ischia and elsewhere, some of which afterwards moved away, being terrified by earthquakes and volcanic eruptions, while others remained. So all the south became a harmonious, well-governed confederation of Greek states, a little empire — a great one for those days — under the guidance of Hiero.

But he having attained to greatness, not being by any means satisfied with the honour and glory achieved by his brother Gelon, nor being by nature of such simple and soldierly tastes, began to make his reign memorable for something higher and more enduring than conquest. Already the greatest ruler, he began to fill his court with the greatest men of the world, and to make Syracuse worthy, in beauty and grandeur, to be his home and theirs.

The Olympic Games held together all Greeks, throughout the civilized world, by a common bond; to be a winner was not only to win fame, sometimes undying — much glory was also shed upon the contestant's native city. Nor were the games only for those trained athletes who ran long races on the measured course, who wrestled desperately in the dust, or fought even to the death for the boxer's prize, or leapt with weights, or strove in mere feats of strength without skill; besides these were the chariot races, to which all the tyrants of the Greek states sent both chariots and priceless horses, vying with each other in the splendid show; and in these races the prize belonged not to him who drove, but to the owner of the steeds. Countless coins of exquisite design bear witness to the value the princes set upon a successful race, for it is now believed that these coins were only minted for such as had been winners; and has been pointed out by specialists, there are coins of Messina, Catania, Leontini, Syracuse, Akragas, and many other cities, some even with Phoenician inscriptions from Panormus, all of which have on the reverse the biga, triga, or quadriga, often with a figure of Victory flying in the air above the horses' heads. That racing with chariots was an almost universal sport throughout the Greek states we know, and the fact explains the immense importance attached to the great contests of Olympia, of Delphi, of the Isthmus of Corinth, and of Nemea. But their greatest value to the world lay in the fact that they gave opportunities of inspiration to the poets of the time, whose odes to the victors earned a greater immortality of their own, and enriched posterity with some of the most beautiful masterpieces of verse that have ever been produced.

The Greeks of Sicily and of the Italian mainland rivaled the rest and often outdid them in the number of winners they sent to Greece, and while Crotona surpassed all other cities in the foot races and in wrestling and boxing, Sicily was more often first with her chariots and horses. That was a sort of contest in which only the richest could compete, and more than once Hiero himself carried off the palm. Then in the train of Olympic victories came the Olympic poets, and Simonides of Ceos, and Bacchylides his nephew, and Pindar himself, all came to Sicily and spent years in Syracuse, being three lyric poets of strangely different genius, but reckoned almost equal in fame while they lived. We know something of the character of each. We can call up from the depth of five and twenty centuries the still living memory of Simonides, who enjoys the singular distinction of having for discovered that poetry is a marketable production of genius, for it is recorded that he was the first poet who not only received remuneration, but exacted payment for his verses, and he must therefore be looked upon as the direct literary ancestor of the modern author. Worldly, gifted, tactful and extravagant, he used to say that his poetry filled two chests, the one with thanks and the other with gold, but that when in need, he had always found the first empty. Once, when Anaxilas of Rhegium won the mule race at Olympia, — for there were mule races too, — he offered Simonides a sum of money to write an ode to him as victor. The poet thought the price too small and answered that he would not demean his genius by writing of mules. The tyrant determined to have what he wanted, increased his offer to a sum which he knew that the poet would not refuse, but wondered how the latter would extricate himself from the dilemma he had created by his first refusal. Simonides was equal to the occasion. His address to the mules began, 'All hail, ye daughters of wind-swift mares' — and the poem contained no further allusion to the hybrids. At another time he observed that it must be better to be rich than to be wise, since he always saw wise men knocking at rich men's doors. Filled with amazing vitality and love of large, age seemed to take no hold upon him; at eighty he was the winner of a poetic contest and led the Cyclic Chorus in Athens, which means that he not only composed the song and sang it, but danced round the altar with the chorus of fifty youths who sang with him; and this was in Athens, the very home of satire, where to be ridiculous for an instant was to be ruined forever. He lived to the age of ninety, and we do not hear that his faculties lost their vigour nor his genius its charm.

Bacchylides, his nephew, was of different temper, though he affected to imitate the worldly wisdom of his uncle. Nothing he wrote has come down to us, but at one time Hiero esteemed him above Pindar, and the blot upon his character is his mean jealousy of the latter and his low instinct of flattery. The evil that he did lived after him, but his good verses perished, like those of Simonides.

Last of the three, and unlike both, comes the greatest — 'as the rain-fed river overflows its banks and rushes from the mountains, immeasurable, deep-mouthed Pindar rages and rushes on' — the proud, the stern, the inspired, who 'lived not for the world but for himself,' scorning gold as Simonides loved it and despising flattery and backbiting alike. There must have been something about the man that imposed itself upon others, something not far from awe and much above the most sincere admiration — something that is in the Odes, which alone have come down to us, with a few fragments quoted by Athenaeus, something lofty, half divine, almost of the prophet; and all men recognized it and honoured the poet. Yet he would never make his home with Hiero, though he wrote four odes upon his victories, and in the end, being eighty years of age, he died in Argos, independent to the last, and leaving that rare and unrivalled fame which suggests neither comparison nor similarity with that of other men, the glory of those few who were not only first but last of their kind.

To the court of Syracuse there came not only lyric poets; Aeschylus was a favourite with Hiero also, and Epicharmus, the father of comedy, whose rough humour shocks the instinctive reverence we feel even for false gods, when they were grand or beautiful, who in the 'Marriage of Hebe' represented mighty Jove squabbling for the best fish at the feast of the gods, and introduced the divine Muses as glibly chattering fishwives, offering their wares for sale; a man of most irrepressible wit and impertinent humour, even in his ninetieth year.

Aeschylus was a younger and a stronger man. He may be called the father of tragedy as Epicharmus was of comedy. Rugged and vast of plan, his work is to that of Sophocles as a rock temple of India to a Gothic cathedral; dimly terrible with the unseen presence of fate, the horror of the final catastrophe overshadows the play from the first and speaks in every accent of predestined man and woman. The watchman sees evil coming from afar, the stamp of it is on Clytemnestra's brow, Cassandra in frenzied prophecy foretells the master's murder, and when it is accomplished, unseen, in the imagination of the horrified spectator, its effect is a hundred more times more terrible than if the king's blood were shed upon the stage. The weapons of Aeschylus are huge, and unwieldy to a common hand; but in his strong grasp they have a masterly precision and an appalling directness. Before his time there were playwrights and actors, there were wandering companies of Sicilian mimes who played from town to town, changing the action and the lines of their half-improvised dramas to suit the circumstances in which they found themselves; and there were genuine theatres also in the great cities, where graver plays were performed. But Aeschylus first made the stage what it has remained more or less ever since, by introducing machinery and accessories never heard of before, a god appearing through a trap-door — the original 'Deus ex machinâ,' — to put an end to a situation which had no natural conclusion; and rich costumes were also his invention, and sounds produced behind the scenes suggestive of deeds too atrocious to be seen by the audience.

Many tales are told to explain why the tragic poet left Greece. One writer says that he was dissatisfied with the honour he received in his own country; another, that during a great performance of one of his tragedies a platform broke down with its load, and that the poet feared the ridicule of the people; again, it is said that he left his home in anger, because in a contest of tragedy the young Sophocles obtained the prize against him, but the strangest reason of all is that the Athenians drove him out because their women were driven to frantic fear by the terrible chorus of the Furies, in his tragedy called the Eumenides. Whatever the cause may have been, and it seems useless to seek for a complicated one, he came twice to Sicily, and on the second visit, being nearly seventy years of age, he settled in the city of Gela, near which, as tradition says, he died a very extraordinary death. For it is said that an eagle, having taken a tortoise and meaning to drop it from a great height upon a rock, in order to break it and devour its flesh, looked down and saw the bald head of Aeschylus, who was walking in a meadow near the city; and taking it for a polished stone, the eagle dropped the tortoise directly upon it, whereby Aeschylus came to his end. The people of Gela buried him with great pomp, and raised a splendid monument to his memory.

Besides his other inventions in connexion with the stage, Aeschylus was the inventor of the tragic trilogy, which in its true and original form consisted of three complete tragedies, of which the subjects were closely dependent each upon the other and in each of which the unity of time, of place, and of action were maintained in the strictest manner. It had not entered the thoughts of Greek playwrights to give any play a greater scope of time than was required for its actual performance, by dividing it into acts, separated by an imaginary lapse of hours, days, or months; to produce such an illusion it seemed necessary to them to write as many different plays as the whole action required different times, and to present them on successive days in order that the spectators might the more easily imagine a longer interval of time to have passed. The modern play in three, four, or five acts is in substance a trilogy, a tetralogy, or a pentalogy on a small scale, and the Greeks would certainly not have admitted a Wagnerian trilogy to be a legitimate piece of play-writing.

During his splendid reign Hiero not only attracted to his court such men as this and many others besides, but he exerted also the great powers which had fallen to his lot in improving and beautifying his capital and it was largely due to his initiative that Syracuse soon afterwards became one of the most beautiful cities of the world. It was to be the privilege of others, notably of Dionysius the Elder and of Hiero the Second, to bring the work to full perfection, but the first and greatest merit is due to the first Hiero. To the end he was successful in all he understood, and victorious in every war. When Theron, the friend of Gelon, died at last after reigning sixteen years, his son Thrasydaeus succeeded him in the tyranny. Ambitious as he was cruel, and in all other respects different from his father, he conceived the idea of conquering Syracuse, and raised an army of twenty thousand men, almost all of whom were Greeks. But Hiero was before him, though he had to march his troops over a hundred miles through a difficult country, and Thrasydaeus, instead of invading his enemy's dominions, was forced to give battle within his own on the banks of the river Akragas. Hiero's army slew four thousand and put the rest to flight, including the young tyrant himself, who escaped to Megara in the hope of being received in a friendly manner; but the inhabitants feared him, for his name was associated with every sort of barbarity, and when they had taken counsel they put him to death. After that Hiero was supreme while he lived.

He died after reigning eleven years, probably in the city of Aetna, of which it is doubtful whether any trace remains. He had founded it himself, notwithstanding certain authorities which insist that it was only built after his death, and in the latter years of his life he probably preferred it as a residence during the cold weather, for it was situated on the southern slope of the volcano, partly protected from the east winds which, in the winter season, are the only drawback of the climate of Syracuse.

The first great development of art, as well as of literature, in Sicily dates from the victory of Himera which terminated the first Carthaginian invasion. It was between 480 B.C. and 409 B.C.

that the great temples of Selinus, of Segesta, and of Akragas were built, edifices which surpassed in size and solidity almost every building of the sort in the Greek world. The architecture was most magnificent; the art of sculpture, however, was still in its archaic infancy, and the large fragments of uncouthly sculptured metopes preserved in the museum at Palermo must have contrasted strangely, when whole and in their places, with the splendid proportions and finished workmanship of the temples they adorned. These stand, or lie in fragments, throughout the island from end to end, witnesses of an age of faith, of strength, and of warfare; of a primitive warfare that was but wholesale hand to hand strife, of physical strength deified and worshipped as the main requisite for victory, of a material faith which was little better than a glorified generalization of man's animal instincts and of nature's common phenomena. We modern men are more easily surprised by such monuments of material power than by the far more wonderful results which purely spiritual and ethic influences have brought about in more recent days. It seems more extraordinary to us that human hands should ever have piled one upon another the enormous masses of stone that composed the temples of Selinus, than that whole nations should have fought to the death for half a dozen more or less vague articles of religious belief.

Fragment of the ruins of Selinus, now Selinunto

There is nothing in Europe like the ruins of Selinus. Side by side, the one stone upon another, as they fell at the earthquake shock, the remains of four temples lie in the dust, within the city, and the still more gigantic fragments of three others lie without the ruined walls. At first sight the confusion looks so terrific that the whole seems as if it might have fallen from the sky to the world, from the homes of the gods to destruction on earth — as if Zeus might have hurled a city at mankind, to fall on Sicily in a wild wreck of senseless stone. Blocks that are Cyclopean lie like jackstraws one upon another, sections of columns •twenty-eight feet round are tossed together upon the ground like leaves from a basket, and fragments of cornice •fifteen feet long lie across them more stand half upright, or lean against the enormous steps. No words can explain to the mind the involuntary shock which the senses feel at the first sight of it all. One touches the stones in wonder, comparing one's small human stature with their mass, and the intellect strains hopelessly to recall their original position; one climbs in and out among them, sometimes mounting, sometimes descending, as one might pick one's way through an enormous quarry, scarcely understanding that the blocks one touches have all been hewn into shape by human hands and that the hills from which men brought them are but an outline in the distance. But as one reaches the highest fragment within the Acropolis, the plan of the whole begins to stand out from the confusion; the columns have all fallen in ranks, and in the same direction, and from the height one may count the round drums of stone which once composed each erect pillar. There is method in the ruin and a sort of natural order in the destruction. No earthly hands, bent on blotting out the glory of Selinus, could have done such work, neither the crowbar and lever of the Carthaginian, nor the giant-powder of the modern engineer. Nature herself did the deed. In the morning the seven temples of Selinus were standing whole and perfect against the pale and dazzling sky; at noonday the air grew sultry and full of a yellow glare, the sea lay still as liquid lead, and the sleeping beast in the field woke suddenly in terror of something far below, that could be felt rather than heard; an hour and more went by, and then the long, low sound that is like no other came up from the depths of the world, and the broad land heaved like the tidal swell of the ocean, once, twice, and thrice, and was still, and a great cloud of white dust hung where the seven temples had stood. As they fell, so they lie and will lie for all time, a very image of the abomination of desolation.

The Ruins of Selinus

The sculptured fragments have been almost all removed to the great museum in Palermo; they seem to have represented battles between goddesses and giants, and, while the treatment is of archaic simplicity, there are, here and there, a few figures in which the rising genius of sculpture foreshadows the great things it was soon to do. On the whole they almost reach the artistic level of the fragments from Aegina, and we may fairly take it for granted that this was the state of art throughout Sicily towards the end of the seventy years which elapsed between the two Carthaginian invasions. Of the same period is the great temple of Athene at Syracuse, crowning the island of Ortygia. Enclosed within high walls, it has been converted to the uses of a cathedral, but the columns of the temple stand intact within, and it is easy to fancy it as it was. High on its seaward side Athene's burnished shield was hung up of old to catch the rays of the noonday sun, a beacon to ships at sea; for mariners who were departing on a voyage used to go up thither before they weighed anchor, and when they had made offerings to the goddess they received from the priests little earthen vessels containing flowers and grains of incense; and when the burnished shield was lost to their view as they sailed away, they consigned the little jar and its contents to the sea with a final prayer for their safe return.

In widest contrast to the ruins of Selinus and to the church-temple at Ortygia, is the still almost perfect temple of Segesta.a At the western extremity of the island a lonely valley leads from the deep Gulf of Castellamare upwards to the mountains. Climbing the narrow path, the traveller looks in vain for ancient ruin or modern habitation until he pauses for breath upon the shoulder of a hill, and suddenly he sees over against him the faultless outline of one of the most beautiful temples in the world. Dark and symmetrical, it stands alone upon the waste, vividly perfect against the sky that is bright with the reflection from the sea beyond. Of all its forty Doric columns, only one is very slightly injured. Nothing more strangely impressive can be imagined, nothing more solid and more silently grand, more nobly done. It is as if the visible spirit of the Greeks had chosen that wild solitude for its last abiding-place.

Temple at Segesta

Yet of all the cities of Sicily, Segesta was the least Greek, if, indeed, it can be said to have been Greek at all. There is a sort of romantic uncertainty about its origin which was particularly attractive to the Romans, and they admitted the claim of the Segestans to Trojan descent as noble as that of Aeneas himself. It is certain that from very early times Segesta was in closer and more friendly relations with the Phoenicians than any other colony, and it was this circumstance which twice almost caused Segesta to be the ruin of all Greek Sicily: the first time when, finding itself isolated from the other Greek cities and hated by them owing to its former attachment to Phoenician interests, it sent out ambassadors to Athens and provoked the ill-fated Athenian expedition in which Alcibiades played so strange a part; the second, when it appealed to Carthage for help against Selinus and brought on directly another Carthaginian invasion.

But before describing those great events which took place when Sicily's power and influence were at their height, it is necessary to glance at the record of Hiero's successors, since Syracuse had, under him, become the commanding power of the island, and the chief centre of its civilization. Though Hiero was one of the great rulers, and, on the whole, a wise one, it must not be forgotten that he had in reality usurped the sovereignty which Gelon had intended to transmit to his own son, and had held it in spite of the other members of his own family, by the means usually adopted by usurpers. He employed numerous spies, both men and women, to detect his enemies, and he exiled or destroyed the latter without the slightest hesitation. At his death, he left one brother living, the eldest of all and the least gifted, Thrasybulus by name. He also believed that he was destined to the kingship, and he attempted to withhold it from his nephew as his brother had done; but he had neither the strength of character nor the talent which the latter had possessed, and he oppressed the people beyond endurance. The Syracusans had borne the exactions of Hiero, the victorious, the generous, the adorner of the city, the terror of their foes; they soon lost patience with his mean and miserly successor.

Sicily was ripe for a revolution, and the democratic spirit was abroad; the fall of the tyrant of Akragas had prepared the way, and the despots of the minor cities governed in hourly fear of ruin. Syracuse was mistress of the island, and indirectly of Southern Italy; it was certain that if she freed herself from her master, the rest of the country would follow.

But Thrasybulus was strong in mercenary troops and ships, and the numerous relations and adherents of his family stood by him to a man; a memorable struggle began, of which the result was long doubtful and which showed for the first time the extraordinary strength which the older parts of the city possessed, both by natural position and artificial fortification.

Syracuse overlooks an extensive natural harbour, two miles long and a mile across, free from rocks or shoals, and so completely enclosed by the mainland and the island of Ortygia that the entrance is but little over a thousand yards wide, opening due east. The island is divided from the mainland by what is nothing more than a narrow canal; it extends from the entrance northward, and north of it Gelon had walled off from the mainland a strip of land about two and a half miles long, of which the sea-line consists of low cliffs that offer no landing worth the name, and no shelter from any wind all the way round by east, from north to south. This strip of land received the name Achradina, a word for which there seems to be no satisfactory derivation, unless it comes from 'achrades', the wild pear trees, which still abound in this part of Sicily. A modern Sicilian writer suggests that the word might be made to mean 'the height of the cape.' The city of Gelon consisted of Achradina and Ortygia, both strongly fortified. At the time of the revolution against Thrasybulus, the suburb Tyche, 'good Fortune,' was without the walls, on the west, and the larger suburb Neapolis, 'the new city,' extended to the Lysimeleian swamp that open upon the bay. In later years the whole of the great harbour was surrounded by buildings.

Thrasybulus shut himself up within the walls with about fifteen thousand men who bore arms. The population of the city consisted largely of those persons to whom Gelon had given rights of citizenship, whom he had collected about him, and who had remained there under Hiero. In the general revolution these made common cause with the genuine Syracusans of old stock, and, with the latter, occupied the suburbs, making fruitless attempts to drive the tyrant from his position. They soon saw that success was impossible, for by means of his ships he kept his communications open by sea and was able to provision the city at his pleasure. The people then turned to the other Sicilian cities for assistance, renouncing their supremacy over the island by doing so. Those to whom they appealed asked nothing better than to help in destroying the power under which they had fretted so long. Gela, Akragas, Selinus, and Himera joined the Syracusans, sending both men and ships. Thrasybulus attacked the ships first, but lost a part of his own, and the remainder were soon blockaded in the harbour; his attempts to sally out by land were equally unsuccessful, the enemy closed in upon him on every side, he was in danger of famine, and he sued for his life, asking only that he might be allowed to leave the country unmolested. The men who had him in their power had been oppressed by him, robbed by him, and it is more than probable that some of them had been tortured by him; but they magnanimously granted his request, he was allowed to depart unmolested, and he ended his days peacefully in Locri. His fall was the signal for a general rising against the tyrants, and in a few months all the south was in the hands of a jubilant democracy.

The Syracusans set up a gigantic statue to Zeus and instituted the Festival and Games of Freedom, during which four hundred and fifty oxen were to be sacrificed every year to make a feast for the people, and for this purpose they built an altar a tenth of a sea mile long and over sixty feet wide — a Gargantuan expression of gratitude to the gods in the present and the future, which suggests that under Thrasybulus they had never enjoyed a feast, and had rarely had enough. But the revolution was not yet over, for the new democracy took measures to exclude from the higher public offices all those burghers who owed their citizenship to Gelon, Hiero, or Thrasybulus, and a long struggle ensued, during which the offended party held Achradina and Ortygia as the last tyrant had done. With the help of the Sicelians, the old burghers triumphed at last, however, got possession of the walled city, and drove out their adversaries.

One of the first results of the fall of the tyrants throughout Sicily was that the Sicelians reasserted themselves on the ground of having helped the burghers to obtain their freedom, and regained a large part of the lands which had been taken from them by the different Greek cities. When Hiero determined to transplant the population of Catania, to change its name to Aetna, and to fill it with more or less Doric citizens, he settled those whom he had expelled upon broad tracts of country taken from the Sicelians. These possessions now fell back to their original owners. The former inhabitants of Catania besieged it and drove out those who had supplanted them, and the latter established themselves in the new city on the southern slope of the mountain, which Hiero had called Aetna, while Catania resumed its original name. The same thing took place elsewhere, in all places, in fact, where Hiero had endeavoured to change the population in order to create one entirely devoted to his interests. As may well be imagined, the result of this second change was a considerable degree of confusion, to remedy which the various Sicilian commonwealths held a general meeting, at which they agreed that the rights of citizenship should nowhere belong to any but the original inhabitants of the towns and that all other persons, whether natives of other cities in the island, or Greek immigrants, or barbarians, should lose their acquired or usurped rights and depart forthwith. It does not appear, however, that they were driven into any cruel exile, and in the great majority of cases they received sufficient grants of land in other districts.

Girl washing near Reggio, Calabria, formerly Rhegium

When matters were thus settled in a preliminary manner, a period of peace and extraordinary prosperity began, which lasted nearly sixty years and which offers little of interest to the general reader, but which resulted in a vast development of art, literature, and general culture. Of course, men appeared from time to time whose personal influence rendered them dangerous to democracy. For their own safety the Syracusans introduced the law of petalism, corresponding almost exactly to the ostracism of the Athenians. Instead of the fragments of pottery used by the latter to vote the expulsion of a citizen, the Syracusans used the 'petals,' that is the leaves, of the olive tree, and the citizen for whom the greatest number of these were cast into the urns was obliged to exile himself from the city for five years, whereas the time of exile imposed by the Athenian ostracism was ten. As usual, however, the common people promptly made use of this method to get rid of every one with more than average intelligence, and the custom was abolished.

An extraordinary and not altogether unromantic attempt on the part of the Sicelians to regain the principal power in the island produced the only wars fought in this period. Ducetius, who suddenly appears as the Sicelian king, succeeded in raising a considerable force with which he dislodged the inhabitants of the newly founded city of Aetna and seized several other important points; but the Syracusans, though not friendly with the sufferers, looked upon their defeat as a slight upon Greeks in general, and gathering their allies, soon drove Ducetius to desperate straits. Seeing himself lost, he conceived the strange idea of throwing himself upon the mercy of his enemies. Under cover of a dark night he rode alone across the intervening country, entered the city at dawn and took sanctuary upon the altar in the market-place; the people assembled in multitude from all parts of the city, and in the presence of a vast throng the vanquished king declared that he gave up his leadership and all his possessions to the Syracusans. Immediately a great discussion arose. Some were for making an end of him at once, but more generous counsels prevailed, and as in the great revolution the tyrant Thrasybulus had been allowed to go his way in peace and security, so also now the Syracusans voted that Ducetius should go free, on condition, however, that he would exile himself to Corinth and promise faithfully to remain there during the rest of his life. He swore the required oath and departed, but he found means to elude the obligation; for it was in the interest of Greece to weaken the Greek power in Sicily if possible, and an opportune oracle, doubtless inspired by Corinthian gold, bade Ducetius return to Sicily and found a peaceful colony upon the shore known as 'the beautiful.' With the full consent of the Corinthians, the Sicelian king, who was in their eyes no better than a barbarian, sailed away with many ships and a great body of armed Greeks, and actually became the founder and father of a flourishing Hellenic colony on the north coast, where he was practically beyond the reach of his former enemies. The strange result of this move was that the people of Akragas regarded it as a stratagem of the Syracusans, gathered an army, attacked the latter, and were badly beaten, while neither party molested Ducetius in his new city. He lived about eight years more and died a natural death. After the defeat of the forces of Akragas, Syracuse became once more the leading power in the island, not without exciting jealousy among the other cities and stirring up the envy of the Athenians by her extraordinary prosperity and magnificence.

The chief fault of the Greeks was a direct result of that gift of individuality, which has never belonged in the same degree to any other nation. They loved freedom as few people have loved it, but at no time in their history were they ever reconciled in any sort of unity or harmony. The wonderful talents displayed by men born in every part of the Greek world produced both a variety and an opposition of initiatives which were easily fostered into violent dissension by the competitive spirit that was so strong in the Hellenic race. All opponents, not Greeks, seemed unworthy to men who had vanquished the Carthaginians in the west, and made a laughing stock of Persia's gigantic attack from the east. If after the battles of Himera and Salamis the whole Greek nation, from Asia Minor to Western Sicily, and from Italian Naples to the shores of Africa, had united to effect the conquest of the known world, Europe, Asia, and Africa would have been theirs, and the Hellenes would have filled the part afterwards played by Rome. But their instinct threw them into competition with each other, rivalry led to strife, and strife to destruction; their patriotism was local pride, their loyalty was incapable of any broad interpretation, and they squandered in petty wars with each other the strength, the courage, and the military genius that should have made them the masters of mankind. If the famous line of Nathaniel Lee, 'When Greeks joined Greeks, then was the tug of war,' has passed into a proverb, the reason is that the saying is profoundly true. To them it seemed hardly worthwhile to fight except against each other. The long period of peaceful prosperity, during which the free democracies of Sicily rose to supremacy in culture as well as in wealth, was brought to an end by the jealousy of the Athenians, who seized the opportunity of a quarrel between Syracuse and Leontini to interfere in favour of the latter, which represented the party disaffected under the Syracusan leadership of the island; and this interference had its origin in the long struggle between the Dorian and Ionian Greeks which we call the Peloponnesian War, and which was practically fought to a finish in the harbour of Syracuse. It was the outbreak in Greece of the old enmity between the two great branches of the Hellenic race which revived the same almost forgotten hatred between the Sicilian cities.

At that time, taking free men and slaves together, the population of Sicily seems to have been about three millions and a half, all of whom, both the original Sicelians and Elymians, and the Phoenician colonists and traders, were so far Hellenized that they used the Greek language and practised Greek art, even in cities such as Panormus, which were not at all under Greek political domination. Sicily was already the granary of the Mediterranean, and just then was a commercial rather than a military power, possessing but few ships and a limited number of trained soldiers. On the whole, Syracuse and the principal Sicilian cities were more closely allied with the Peloponnesian confederation than with the Athenian state, and it was natural that a city like Leontini, hard pressed by the Syracusans, should turn to Athens for help, and that Athens should promptly grant the request, by sending a small expedition of twenty ships. The force was absurdly inadequate, the generalship of the leaders was lamentably insufficient, the result was a miserable defeat before Inessa, and the Athenians barely made good an ignominious retreat. A year later, when they had succeeded in seizing Messina, which was distracted by factions, the Syracusans made interest with the stronger party and in alliance with the men of Italian Locri drove the Athenians out again without difficulty, but lost the day in a sea-fight soon afterwards; and so the small warfare went on from year to year with very little result except to stir up old enmities between the Sicilian cities, some of which feared Syracuse, while some feared the possible domination of Athens; but their own general interests soon got the upper hand, and holding a peace conference in Gela, they were easily persuaded by the Syracusan Hermocrates that it was necessary to face Athens as a common foe. Therefore the Athenians retired altogether and left the island to itself for a time.

The great expedition under Alcibiades was made against Syracuse, and against Sicily generally, at the instigation and on the representations of Segesta. The latter city was at war with it neighbouring enemy Selinus, and being worsted, began, as most of the states did in those days, to appeal to its powerful friends for help, and first of all to Carthage. The Selinuntians, on their side, asked assistance from Syracuse, which was granted in a small measure. But Carthage would do nothing for Segesta, and the latter, allying itself with Leontini, always oppressed by Syracuse, sent an embassy to Athens, ever ready to interfere, making great promises of payment for the alliance. The Athenians took the precaution of sending representatives by sea to Segesta to find out whether there was any probability of obtaining the promised payment in case the required assistance were given. It was on this occasion that the Athenians became the victims of one of the most extraordinary and amusing frauds in history. Their ambassadors were received with unsurpassed splendour, and the Segestans, who were in reality very poor, succeeded in producing upon their guests the impression that they possessed vast wealth. Leading them up to the ancient temple of Aphrodite on Mount Eryx, above Drepanon, which is Trapani, they showed them what they called their war treasure, an immense collection of sacred vessels of fine workmanship and seemingly of precious metals, but of which a great number were in reality worthless imitations, apparently made for the occasion. The ambassadors were dazzled by the display and were doubtless told that the treasures were too sacred to be touched or examined. It appears certain that such objects as were really of any value had been borrowed from Sicelian cities that hoped to profit by the coming of the Athenians. The ambassadors were then entertained for some time in Segesta with the most profuse hospitality, and the sailors from their ships were feasted by the inhabitants. For these occasions every available dish and vessel of gold or silver was collected together, and as much plate as possible was borrowed from the Sicelians, all of which was sent secretly from house to house to make a fresh appearance at every feast. On a less magnificent scale the same was done for the entertainment of the soldiers and sailors, who drank the rich wines of Western Sicily from vessels of wrought silver for the first time in their lives, and formed a correspondingly high opinion of their hosts. The whole fraud was perfectly successful, and the ambassadors sailed away to tell the citizens of Athens that Segesta was one of the richest cities in the world and well able to pay for any assistance in war. To confirm the impression they had thus created the Segestans soon afterwards sent ambassadors to Athens bearing sixty talents of silver in bullion, borrowed from their friends, and asking for sixty ships; the silver was offered as payment in advance for the first month's service. What would have happened to Segesta if the Athenians had ever been in a position to enforce their demand for more, when they discovered how they had been imposed upon, may be left to the imagination of the reader; as it turned out, matters took another direction.

The "Gran Sasso d' Italia," from Aquila

At that time Alcibiades was the representative in Athens of all that meant change, movement, and popular excitement. He had long dreamt of a conquest of Sicily, in which he saw magnificent opportunities for satisfying his boundless vanity; he was at that time thirty-five years of age, the handsomest, the bravest, the wittiest, and the most worthless of mankind. He advocated the Sicilian expedition with irresistible eloquence and claimed the right to command it, in a speech of which the brazen impudence is historical.

"It belongs to me," he said, "above all others, to be in command, and to tell the truth I consider myself worthy thereof. The very things for which I am so noisily attacked are not only an honour to my family and to myself, but also a benefit to my country. If the Greeks admit that Athens is greater than she ever was, this is in a measure due to the display I made as your representative at the Olympic Games, where I entered seven chariots, which no private citizen had ever done before, and won the first prize, and had the second and fourth places, and did everything in a manner suitable to such a victory. And if I give choruses and dances at home, my fellow-citizens of course envy me, but the strangers who come here see the outward appearance of greatness. The unfortunate do not share their misfortunes with others; why should a man who glories in his own prosperity set himself down to the level of common mankind?"

It seems strange that a man should carry his point by talking in such a strain, but of all men living Alcibiades knew his fellow-citizens best, and Nicias, the leader of the conservative party, made no attempt to oppose him on his own ground, but contented himself with making a fair statement of the possible advantages and evident risks which would attend the expedition, giving at the same time an opinion as to the manner in which it should be conducted.a He concluded by modestly offering to withdraw his claim to any command it any one understood the matter better than he. The result was that he and Alcibiades were appointed joint leaders with Lamachus, and preparations were at once made on a very great scale. Meetings succeeded meetings, speeches were made without end, and Athens went mad over the anticipated conquest and possession of one of the richest spots in the world. Nothing else was talked of for many weeks strolling lecturers held forth upon the subject to delighted crowds at the corners of the streets, and drew imaginary maps of Sicily in the dust. It was clearly demonstrated and proved in the mind of every patriotic Athenian that as soon as Sicily was taken, Athens would take Italy, Carthage, and the western islands of the Mediterranean, and lord it over all the coasts of the sea to the very Pillars of Hercules.

In the final discussion from which I have quoted fragments of Alcibiades's speech, the latter, in order to persuade the people, spoke disparagingly of the Sicilian power and declared the conquest of the island an easy matter. Nicias, who disapproved of the expedition at heart and understood its real difficulty, did not hesitate to say that the force must consist of at least a hundred triremes, sixty being full war-ships and the rest transports, and five thousand heavy-armed troops, with all the light-armed men and followers which such an armament implied. He perhaps thought it probable that the Athenians would be discouraged from the enterprise by his demands; but if so, he has miscalculated their tempers. They granted without hesitation all that he asked, and would have given more also. For, as Thucydides tells us, the city had recovered from the effects of the plague and from the long war, and a new generation of young men had grown up, and there was abundance of money in the public treasury.

But Alcibiades had many enemies, who hated and envied him. They hit upon an unexpected way of injuring him, and he might have been ruined and even executed before the departure of the expedition, if only they had all agreed. There were in Athens a great many images, called Hermae, which were heads of different gods set on pillars of stone squared and tapering to the foot. In earlier times the head had always been that of Hermes, whence the name. These were set up in doorways both of private houses and of temples, in honour of the tutelary divinities, and were regarded with a certain degree of reverence. Some enemies of Alcibiades took advantage of a dark night to mutilate almost all these images throughout Athens, hacking the features of them to pieces, and in the midst of the excitement that followed they accused Alcibiades and his friends of having perpetrated the outrage in a drunken frolic, as a direct and wilful insult to the gods. Athens was in an uproar, the gods had been offended on the eve of the greatest expedition ever sent out, the mutilation of their images was an omen of shipwreck and defeat, and the Athenians trembled for their reputation, their lives, and their money. Great rewards were offered to any one who would give information against the impious evil-doers. In a moment Alcibiades was accused of a hundred crimes of sacrilege, the greatest of which was that of holding mock celebrations of the mysteries, and as for the Hermae, it was clear that he had broken them, because the great statue of Hermes near his own house was almost the only one that was untouched. Informers also swore that they had seen him and his friends doing the deed and had recognized them by the bright light of the moon, forgetting in broad daylight that the moon was new on that very night. Alcibiades demanded immediate trial, but his enemies feared the army, for he was beloved by the soldiers, and insisted that he should set sail with his command, yet hold himself ready to stand his trial when called upon to do so. He was obliged to submit to this iniquitous decision, and it being now midsummer, the great fleet set sail with solemn pomp and ceremony.

Before they got under way the sixty men-of-war and the forty transports were drawn up in line at the Piraeus, with all their flags and their standards in the morning sun; and a trumpet call rang out upon the air, high and clear, calling the host of warriors and seamen to offer the last libation and the final prayer. So the gold and silver goblets were filled with purple wine, and the dark red libations stained the dark blue sea, while the orisons of those who were departing and of all those who were gathered on the shore went up to the gods together. This being done, they weighed anchor at once, and the great array went forth upon the calm waters; and the ships raced with each other from the Piraeus to Aegina and then steered for Corcyra, where the allies were to muster with transports and provisions. Then, with all the allies, there were a hundred and thirty-four triremes besides two fifty-oared Rhodian galleys, with more than seven thousand fighting men, a noble army and fleet if one considers the size of the Athenian state, but an inadequate force for the conquest of a civilized country having three and a half million of inhabitants. Holm, however, whose authority is generally indisputable, reckons that with the crew of the fighting ships and the necessary number of squires for the heavy-armed soldiers, the whole company must have numbered about thirty-six thousand souls; and before the war was over Athens had sent more than sixty thousand men and two hundred warships to Sicily. Not a single vessel ever returned, and few indeed were the wretched stragglers who found their way back to Greece at last.

Eucalyptus trees near the site of Sybaris

One of the decisive struggles of the world was at hand, and there was to be no compromise from first to last; it was to be fought to the end, and the end was to be destruction. The greatest sea-power in existence was determined to get possession of the richest island in the sea, and the greatest Greek power, the power of the south, was united in self-defence. The news of the coming fight went out and rang along the shores of the Mediterranean and was carried inland by traders and merchants, and the whole civilized ancient world watched the contest with anxiety.

The Athenian command was divided between three men of entirely different natures, — the slow and obstinate Nicias, the boastful and ill-advised Alcibiades, and Lamachus, who was the best soldier of the three but the least influential by his political position. As matters developed, each proposed a different plan, according to his character.

The Athenian fleet, having met the allies at Corcyra, crossed the narrow part of the Adriatic to the Iapygian headland, and bringing to before one city after another endeavoured to induce the inhabitants to join in a general movement against Syracuse. But these efforts were vain, and the cities declared that they would afford no help, but would ultimately act in accordance with the decision of the other Greek cities of Italy. Reaching Rhegium, the Athenians were for the first time treated with some friendliness; for though the city would not admit them within its walls, it gave them permission to encamp on the shore without, and to establish a market whither the country people might bring them provisions for sale; and there the whole Athenian force established itself for a time. In the first place three ships were detached from the fleet and sent to Segesta in order to obtain some part of the great sum of money the latter city had promised. To the dismay and disappointment of the Athenians, the messengers soon returned bringing word that the Segestans could only raise the absurdly small sum of thirty talents. A discussion then arose between the three generals as to the conduct of the war. Nicias, who had been opposed to it from the beginning, advocated a naval demonstration against Selinus, during which efforts should be made to extract money from Segesta, failing which the city should at least be forced to provide a large quantity of provisions. These being obtained, he advised that the whole expedition should return to Athens.

Lamachus, who was the practical soldier, said that Syracuse was wholly unprepared for resistance, and that it would be an easy matter to fall upon it unexpectedly, gain a brilliant victory, and return home with vast spoil and sufficient honour.

Alcibiades, who was always the evil genius of his country when he did not appear as her deliverer, was bent upon permanent and extensive conquest. With his usual eloquence and more than accustomed insistence, he addressed the council of war, and proposed that before attacking Syracuse, the Sicilian cities should be systematically canvassed in order to secure an overwhelming body of allies for the great undertaking. He proceeded to exhibit the advantages of this course in the most brilliant and attractive light; his momentary great popularity with the troops gave him an unfair advantage over his colleagues, and the discussion ended in their reluctantly approving his design.

Had the situation been anything like what he supposed it to be, the plan might have succeeded; but he was in reality altogether ignorant of the state of Sicilian feeling. Many Sicilian cities were indeed envious of Syracuse, and the great body of the original Sicelians resented its supremacy; but none desired to fall under the rapacious rule of Athens, and the vast majority would have considered such subjection as calamitous to their country as a Carthaginian conquest.

The plan of campaign having been decided, a number of ships sailed southward along the Sicilian coast to Naxos and Catania, the only cities which were known to be unchangeably hostile to Syracuse; and Naxos indeed promised the Athenians such assistance as she could give, but in Catania there was a party that favoured the cause of the Syracusans and was strong enough to keep the Athenians out. Thereupon a squadron of ten ships was detached to make a sort of declaration of war in the very harbour of Syracuse, at a time when the appearance of the whole of the Athenian force there might have terminated the war in a week. Instead of this, however, the whole expedition returned to Catania and succeeded in seizing that city by a stratagem which caused the Syracusan party to depart secretly and in haste. But nothing of any importance was accomplished, and the hour of victory was squandered in puerile negotiations with Camarina and other small places.

At this juncture the Athenian senate, having agreed upon a plan for sentencing Alcibiades to death, sent a ship for him with orders to bring him back to stand his trial. Being fully aware of the danger to which he was exposed, he embarked upon his own vessel, under convoy of the Athenian man-of-war, but cleverly slipped away from the latter under cover of the night and escaped to Sparta, after which he was in due course sentenced to death, in contumacy; and therewith he disappears from the history of the south, leaving behind him the evil he had done to the Athenian cause.

Nicias and Lamachus being now left together in command, the counsels of the former prevailed, and the whole fleet began to sail round Sicily by the north, striking a blow here and there, taking a few prisoners who were afterwards sold as slaves to raise money, and receiving at last the thirty talents which Segesta was able to give. They sailed on by the west and south, but a large body of the soldiers appear to have crossed the island by land to Catania. So more time was wasted which was of immense advantage to the Syracusans for making preparations.

Two years had passed since the first arrival of the Segestan ambassadors in Athens when the Athenians at last laid formal siege to Syracuse, nearly one-half of which time had been shamefully wasted on the one hand by the assailants and had been used with great profit by the assailed on the other. Some reference has already been made in these pages to the position of the city and the nature of the land adjoining it, but a more complete description is now necessary in order to understand the nature of the great struggle which took place there.

Old well at Cotrone

Let the name of Syracuse mean for us not only the city as it is, and the five cities that once composed it, or the two, with their suburbs, of which it consisted at the time of the Athenian invasion, but the whole, with the neighbouring land and including both the great and the small harbours; let it take in what the traveller can see below him and around him when he stands on the rampart of Epipolae, facing northwards first and then turning by his right till he faces south — one of the most wonderful sites in the whole world, consisting of two small peninsulas of gentle outline and of even height, extending outwards and towards each other like the claws of a crab and enclosing the great harbour between them, with the island of Ortygia across the entrance. The island was the beginning of the city, which was first founded there and afterwards bridged the narrow channel and grew out to Achradina, thence westwards to Tyche and Neapolis, then down through the Lysimeleian swamp and across the Anapus, the swift and silent stream where grows in rich profusion the papyrus, extinct in Egypt now and everywhere but here — and up to the Olympieum, due west of the harbour — spreading at last all round Plemmyrium to the sea again, to face its starting-point across the water; and in its great days the whole was •fourteen miles round about. But by great catastrophes and again by small degrees, in the alternating haste or slow delay of ruin, it has all shrunk back to the island, saving only a few newer buildings just on the mainland below Achradina; and now it may have come to life once more, to overgrow its long-buried destruction with all the profitable dulness of a modern commercial city. For the history of the south is not ended, and he who gazes at the most magnificent natural harbour in the Mediterranean, and then turns his eyes to the most fertile lands of Italy behind him, and upwards to the mountains stored with rich minerals, and who is able to forget his prejudice and see that though the Sicilians are a hot-blooded tribe, prone to use the knife and not averse to bloodshed, they are nevertheless a manly and a hard-handed race, fearing neither danger nor toil — he who judges these things at their value, understands that the future holds some good thing for such a country and for such men. Moreover, guessing at what Syracuse was in the past, he can understand also why the Athenians so much coveted it for themselves that they fought for it on the spot for a whole year, to their utter ruin and destruction.

Syracusan coin with the head of Arethusa

Of all Sicilian cities, Syracuse was the richest in pure water, and even now, though the old aqueducts are in part destroyed, there is such abundance in this respect as few cities would not envy. Arethusa first, the matchless and mysterious spring, rises almost from the sea under Ortygia, within the harbour. It is certain that the water passes in some way under the sea, but whence it comes will perhaps be never known. The Greeks said that it was Alpheius, the river of Arcadia, which plunged into a mountain chasm and disappears from sight. The lonely nymph of the Acroceraunian mountains, chased by the strong river god, sent up a piteous prayer to Artemis and sank beneath the stream; and the goddess brought her back to the sun by the Syracusan bay, and Shelley's magic voice has sung her song. Science conjectures that the mysterious water rises in the neighbouring hills, in a spur of Thymbris, and, flowing under Achradina, passes below the small harbour and beneath Ortygia to its rising place. We do not surely know, for it is a mystery still, and a wonder. At this spring Nelson watered his fleet when he anchored in the harbour on his way to fight the battle of the Nile. It is well cared for now, and the Syracusans have planted the lovely papyrus in the central pool. Then beside Arethusa there were three great aqueducts, and a fourth, the greatest of all, which draws its water from the higher part of the river Anapus, eighteen miles away. Southward, too, in the Plemmyrian peninsula, I myself have explored a part of a great subterranean channel which I do not find mentioned in books, cemented for the flow of abundant water and having openings at intervals for the air; but in some later age this was used as a catacomb, and rough cells were hewn here and there in the walls. It is quite certain that the united waters that supplied the old city in Greek days would fill a river.

It would have been strange if the Syracusans had felt much apprehension, after their enemies had wasted so much time in futile excursions along the coast and in objectless waiting in their camp at Catania. Bands of Syracusan riders traversed the country in all directions, and cantering up to the Athenian lines, inquired sarcastically whether their inactive foes had come to restore the rights of the Leontini or to settle as colonists. At last Nicias decided to act. He began by sending a treacherous message to inform the Syracusans that if they would attack the camp at Catania before sunrise on a certain day, a large number of the Athenians would then be within the city, that the party which favoured Syracuse would shut and hold the gates, and that it would thus be an easy matter to destroy the Athenians who were left in the camp. The Syracusans believed the message and appeared at the appointed time, only to find the camp deserted and the Athenians gone, for they had sailed away on the preceding evening and were entering the harbour of Syracuse at the very time when the Syracusan cavalry reached the empty camp.

At the last minute the city was therefore unprepared for the arrival of the armament. The Greeks had already carefully observed the harbour when their ten ships had entered it to make the declaration of war, and they now took advantage of the knowledge gained on that occasion to establish themselves in a position which was all but impregnable. Without approaching the inner side of Ortygia, they sailed directly across the harbour, landed to the southward of the mouth of the Anapus, and immediately occupied the heights of Olympieum. They then proceeded to beach their vessels upon the sand, and according to the custom of those times erected a strong palisade to protect the ship-yard from a land attack. Finally they destroyed the bridge over the Anapus by which the so-called Helorine road crossed from the swamp to the Olympieum. They thus commanded the principal height in the bay, were at liberty to launch or beach their ships as they pleased, and were protected from the city by the narrow but very deep and rapid stream. They could accept or refuse battle as they pleased.

The Syracusans were bitterly disappointed to find that the enemy had left Catania, and fearing the worst they rode furiously back to the city. The Athenians were already encamped and intrenched and the bridge was destroyed. Crossing the stream at a highest point, probably on the road to Floridia, the Syracusans rode round the great spring of Kyane, and skirted the hill of the Olympieum on the west side till they reached the camp. They then endeavoured to lure the Athenians out to fight, but without success, and having failed in this first attempt they withdrew, crossed the road that led to Helorus, and bivouacked for the night.

The battle took place on the following day, and Thucydides describes it with graphic clearness. The Athenians drew up their forces before their camp, taking the centre themselves, with the Argives on the right and the rest of the allies on the left. They divided their forces into two portions, half of which were drawn up in advance, eight deep, while the rest were formed in a hollow square behind them close to the tents. Opposite them, and therefore facing the sea, the Syracusans placed their heavy infantry in a line sixteen deep, having their twelve hundred horse on their right towards the Olympieum, and the road, which they had again crossed, being behind them.

Before the Athenians began the attack, Nicias made a short speech to the soldiers, in which he did not rise above the level of his usual dulness on such occasions. It appears that even at the last moment the Syracusans did not really believe that there was to be a battle, and that some of them even rode away to the city to their homes. Nevertheless, when the time came, they took up their arms and advanced to meet the Athenians. The stone-throwers, slingers, and archers skirmished on each side, driving each other backwards and forwards. Under cover of the heavy infantry the priests in their robes and fillets brought up victims to sacrifice on the field of battle, and at last the trumpets sounded the general charge of the heavy-armed men on each side. So they rushed upon each other, the Syracusans to fight for their lives, their country, and their freedom, the Athenians for the hope of conquest and wholesale robbery.

The forces met with the shock of heavy arms and fought savagely hand to hand, the Athenians with the coolness and steady fence of veteran soldiers, the Syracusans with fitfully furious energy; and when the combat was at its height all along the line the sky grew suddenly dark and a great storm burst upon the field with thunder and lightning and much rain. The experienced Athenians laughed at the tempest, but the Syracusans were suddenly chilled and disheartened; the Argives drove in their left wing, the Athenian centre forced back the other, and in a few moments their lines were broken. Yet the Athenians could not pursue them far, for the Syracusan cavalry, which had not suffered, charged again and again and held them in check. So they returned to their camp, and collecting the richest armour from the slain, set up a trophy after their manner; but the Syracusans, though they had been defeated, retired in good order, and sent a garrison up to the temple of Zeus on the Olympieum to protect the treasure there before they returned to the city. The Athenians, however, made no attack upon the sacred building, and immediately proceeded to burn their dead upon a funeral pile. On the following day, under a truce, they restored to the Syracusans their dead to the number of about two hundred and sixty and collected the ashes and bones of their own, who numbered not more than fifty; and thereupon they launched their ships again and sailed back to Catania. They spent the rest of the winter there and in Naxos, after ascertaining that Messina was too cold. Nicias seemed incapable of following up an advantage, and moreover it was winter, and the Greeks seemed to have considered it impossible to fight successfully, even in such a climate as that of Sicily, except in the summer months. The consequence was that the Syracusans had ample time to remedy the defects in their organization which had been evident in the first engagement; they elected three competent generals, despatched envoys to Corinth and Sparta, and built a great wall of defence on the mainland between the city and Epipolae. They also erected palisades along the beach wherever it was easy to land and built forts at Megara on the north, and on the Olympieum.

Meanwhile Alcibiades had established himself in Sparta, and was exciting his old enemies the Lacedaemonians to make a general attack upon Athens, by way of revenging himself for having been unjustly sentenced to death.

"And now," he said, addressing the Lacedaemonians at the conclusion of a long speech, "I entreat that you may not think the worse of me because I am now strenuously attacking my own country on the side of its bitterest enemies, though I once was called a patriot; for though I am an exile from Athens by the villainy of those who banished me, I am not one here, if you will hearken to my words; and the party that was really hostile to me was not you, who only hurt your enemies, but rather they who compelled their friends to become their foes. I was a patriot while I safely enjoyed my civil rights; I am none now, since I am wronged, for I am turning against the land that is still my country, and I am recovering that country which is mine no more."

The speech was well timed, the man's reputation in Greece was enormous, and the advice he gave the Spartans was diabolically wise. He planted a thorn in the side of Athens which weakened her resources and hastened her defeat in Sicily, if it did not directly cause it, and he taught his former fellow-citizens and present enemies to believe that he alone could save them from destruction; and besides following his advice in other respects the Spartans deliberated with Corinth about sending help to the Sicilians. Meanwhile, the Athenians had sent a trireme to Athens, asking for money and for cavalry, without which they felt unable to meet the Syracusans on equal terms; and when the spring was come, the Athenian force did some damage to the Sicilian crops near Syracuse, but gained no signal advantage. Athens sent them money, but only sent two hundred and fifty horsemen, without horses, supposing that they could be mounted in Sicily. They afterwards got about four hundred more cavalry from Segesta and Naxos, and from the Sicelians.

The Syracusans had in the meantime finished their wall, completely enclosing the city with its suburbs towards Epipolae, from the harbour to the sea on the north, and taking in the theatre, the ridge above it, and the quarter called Temenites, from a portion of it sacred to Apollo, as well as the extensive inhabited suburb called Tyche, the whole being a gigantic piece of work, but extremely necessary for defence. It must have followed very nearly the modern road by which one drives from the esplanade northwards, and out of which, to the right, the narrower road leads, at right angles, to the Latomia dei Cappuccini. The Syracusans knew that when they were at last besieged the Athenians would attempt a systematic circumvallation, and try to blockade them by land and sea and starve them out; for in those days of small armies, the besiegers rarely ran the risk of losing a number of men in an assault. The Carthaginians alone, who did not fight themselves, but employed mercenaries altogether, sacrificed men with the recklessness familiar in modern warfare. From the great wall they had built, the Syracusans hoped to throw out counter-walls at right angles to westward, so as to hinder the Athenian works. Before the siege was over the Syracusans alone had built seven and a half miles of fortified stone wall, a fact which gives some insight into ancient methods of attack and defence. But even after building the first great wall, the Syracusans saw that it was more or less commanded by the still higher ground of Epipolae, which means the upper town, and they selected for the defence of that place a band of six hundred chosen heavy-armed men, who p130afterwards distinguished themselves in many feats of courage.

AA.   Wall of Ortygia.

BBB.   Wall of outer city.

BCD.   Wall enclosing all the suburbs.

EF.   First section of intrenchments.

FG.   Upper section of intrenchments.

H.   First counter-wall.

I. Second counter-wall.

J. Third counter-wall.

Map of Syracuse B.C. 414−413.

The siege now began in earnest. The Athenians did not bring their fleet into Syracuse at first, but anchored in the small but safe natural harbour of Thapsus, just north of the Syracusan promontory, and surprised Epipolae while the Syracusans were reviewing their troops in the meadow below. After some desperate fighting, in which the leader of the six hundred was killed, the Athenians remained in possession of the high ground, whence they descended after the usual truce for burying the dead, and offered battle before the new wall. But the Syracusans would not face them, and the Athenians then proceeded to fortify the heights, constructing a storehouse there for their baggage and money. They had previously provided themselves with an immense supply of bricks and building tools, which they brought up from Thapsus, and the road they built, some of which is hewn in the rock, is still distinctly traceable. They hastened to begin the tedious work of circumvallation by constructing a circular fort of which the nearest point was about half a mile from the Syracusan wall. Not a trace remains of those works. The fort was intended as starting-point from which to build a fortification north and south. Such was the extraordinary rapidity with which they worked that the Syracusans hastily determined upon a sally that ended in a cavalry engagement on the broken ground, in which the Athenians ultimately succeeded in bringing up a detachment of infantry and got the better of the fight.

It was but a small affair, however, and the Athenians had no sooner begun to build their wall northwards from the central point, at the same time collecting stones, lumber, and other material along the projected line, than the Syracusans set to work to build a counter-work due west in order to intersect that of the Athenians. The Athenian fleet being still at Thapsus, the Athenians were obliged to bring up their provisions and materials from that place to Epipolae by land. The Athenians next succeeded in cutting off at least one of the aqueducts which supplied the city with water. Then, one day, when the Syracusans had completed their first counter-wall and had retired within their tents during the noonday heat, some having even returned to the city, the Athenians suddenly sent a strong picked force at full speed to seize the counter-wall, moving up the rest of their army in two divisions at the same time. The counter-wall appears to have been at first lightly constructed as a sort of stockade with stones heaped up against it, and the Athenian advance guard had no difficulty in taking possession of it and in tearing it down. The Athenians then carried off the material to their own lines and erected a trophy, which they did on every occasion when they had obtained the smallest advantage. Works and counter-works were now carried on with the greatest energy for some days, and when the Athenians considered that their works were sufficient they ordered their fleet to sail round from Thapsus into the great harbour, whither they themselves descended, crossing the swamp in the firmest part by laying planks upon the mud. And here again a short and bloody engagement was fought near the river Anapus, and the Syracusans succeeded in driving in the picked three hundred of the Athenian van, which produced something like a panic among the heavy-armed troops upon whom they fell back. Lamachus, seeing the danger, came up at full speed with a few archers and a body of Argives, crossed a ditch, and being followed only by a few men, was surrounded and killed, the Syracusans carrying off his body in triumph just as the main Athenian force came up.

Seeing from a distance that the Athenians had lost the bravest and most energetic of their officers, those of the Syracusans who had at first been driven back to the city took heart and came back to charge the Athenians once more, and destroyed a thousand feet of a new outwork built by the enemy upon the heights of Epipolae. But within the lines Nicias himself lay ill, and he at once ordered his attendants to set fire to all the timber collected at that point so as to defend himself by a wall of flame, for he had no soldiers with him. So the Syracusans withdrew as the Athenians were bringing up reënforcements. At that moment the fleet from Thapsus entered the great harbour, and the whole Syracusan army immediately retired into the city.

Matters now looked very badly for the besieged. The Athenians continued their works unhindered, and built a double wall down to the harbour not far from the city gate. From all parts of Italy provisions began to arrive in great quantities, and the Sicelians, seeing that the invaders were getting the advantage, offered themselves as allies. The Syracusans had received no answer from Sparta, and supposing themselves deserted by their friends lost hope altogether, for they were completely cut off from the mainland by the circumvallation, and the Athenian fleet had destroyed their communications by sea. They began to discuss terms of capitulation, and to treat with Nicias, who held the sole command after the death of Lamachus. There was confusion within the city, they had lost confidence in their generals and chose others, they were entirely dependent upon Arethusa for their water, which therefore had to be carried •nearly three miles to supply the furthest extremity of Achradina, and it's clear that before long there would be a scarcity of provisions.

But at the very moment when despair was settling upon the Syracusans help was at hand. The Spartans had dispatched Gylippus to the aid of the beleaguered city, and he was already off the Italian coast. He was a man of brilliant resources and untiring energy, a most complete contrast in mind and character to the hesitating but obstinate Nicias who was soon to be his opponent. The latter had heard of his expedition and looked upon him with scorn, considering him to be rather than a pirate than a general, for he had only about fifteen ships and no great number of soldiers. But he possessed in abundance the military genius which was wholly lacking in Nicias, and nothing else was necessary to turn the fortunes of war.

After experiencing violent storms and being obliged to refit in Tarentum, instead of making directly for Syracuse, by which course he would probably have been obliged to fight the Athenians at sea, he sailed round by the north and picked up considerable auxiliary forces in Himera, Selinus, and Gela. Meanwhile Corinth had sent more ships, and the one which put to sea last of all, but was the fastest sailor, reached Syracuse first, just in time to prevent the Syracusans from capitulating. Gylippus appears to have left his ships either at Himera or at Gela. By forced marches and with less than three thousand men he arrived suddenly under the heights of Epipolae. The Syracusans meanwhile came out in force and effected a junction with the army of rescue. A better general than Nicias would have prevented the enemy from obtaining such an advantage, and it proved his ruin. The united forces now seized the heights, and the Athenians formed to give them battle. Gylippus sent forward a herald with a daring message to the Athenians. They might choose, he said, whether they would depart from Sicily within five days or remain where they were and fight to an issue. The Athenians returned no answer and sent the herald back with contempt. Nicias had chosen, and his choice had fallen upon his own destruction. Gylippus boldly seized the Athenian fort on the height and slew the garrison, and on the same day the Syracusan a captured one of the Athenian triremes. The Syracusans then set to work upon building an enormous wall, over two miles in length, from the city right across Epipolae, thus effectually shutting off the Athenians from the sea on the north side.

Nicias now made that mistake which has been considered to be his greatest by military men. He wasted time and labour in fortifying the Plemmyrium, south of the great harbour, and he transferred thither the greater part of his stores, regardless of the scanty water supply in the newly occupied region. By this time also the other Corinthian vessels were known to be rapidly approaching, so that Nicias was obliged to send out twenty armed vessels to cruise in search of his assailants.

Gylippus experienced a slight reverse, for he attacked the Athenians in the narrow space between their works and his, where the Syracusan cavalry had no room to manoeuvre and was consequently useless. Once more the Syracusans were driven back with slaughter, and the Athenians erected another trophy. Undaunted by this check, however, Gylippus rallied his men with an energetic speech, continued the works actively, and waited for a more favourable opportunity. It was not long in coming. Gylippus succeeded in giving battle with both walls ended; the Syracusan cavalry charged the Athenian flank at furious speed, while the heavy infantry engaged the centre. The Athenians were completely routed, and during the night that followed the whole Syracusan force worked at the wall. In the morning it had reached the Athenian works and crossed them, and all hope of completely investing the city was lost.

Fortune now favoured the Syracusans in every way. The Corinthian vessels eluded the flying squadron which Nicias had sent out to cruise for them, and entered the harbour unexpectedly, before the Athenians could get ships under way to oppose them. Reenforced by the arrival of these allies, the Syracusans completed their works, and began to get their own ships ready for sea and to exercise their crews. Gylippus then made a journey through Sicily to raise more troops and money from the friendly cities, and sent messages to Sparta and Corinth asking for further help, for the Athenians were sending to Athens to make a similar request.

Indeed, the letter written by Nicias and read aloud in Athens by the secretary of state is a confession of powerlessness, if not of defeat, and is, moreover, a singularly honest statement of the situation; for he frankly says therein that from being the besieger he was become the besieged, that his ships were leaky and could neither be beached nor hove down for caulking, in the face of the enemy's fleet; that it was becoming extremely difficult and dangerous to get supplies of food, either from Italy or the island, and that he himself was almost helpless from nephritis.

Both parties, Corinth and Sparta on the one hand, and Athens on the other, responded in the most liberal way to these appeals. The Athenians sent ten ships at once, and sixty later on under Demosthenes, with several thousand men; and Gylippus having raised large reënforcements in Sicily, the armies on both sides began to assume formidable proportions. At this time, Demosthenes not having yet arrived, Gylippus planned an engagement which, though only in part successful, ultimately decided the fortunes of the war. A part of the Syracusan fleet lay in the small harbour outside of Ortygia and north of it; the rest were anchored in the great harbour within a sort of defence made by driving huge piles into the bottom, leaving •about twenty feet projecting above water, with a narrow entrance. The leader determined upon a general battle, by land and sea; the two divisions of the Syracusan fleet were to sail round the opposite sides of Ortygia and effect a junction at the mouth of the harbour, where the Athenian ships would of course meet them, and, as Gylippus hoped, would be caught between them and easily destroyed. Meanwhile, he himself intended to march his army round the bay and storm the forts on Plemmyrium. It was clear that if both movements succeeded, the Athenians would be caught in the harbour like mice, with no possibility of escape.

The operation began under cover of the night, of course, and the engagement opened at daybreak. The Athenians, warned, perhaps, of their danger, succeeded in getting thirty-five ships out of the harbour in time to engage the outer Syracusan division in open water, while, with twenty-five more, the inner squadron of the Syracusans was kept at bay. The outer squadron forced its way through the Athenian ships, instead of driving them in, or sinking them, and was caught, as they should have been. The fighting continued in the harbour, and eleven of the Syracusans' vessels were sunk and most of their crews killed. The remainder of the fleet withdrew inside the stockade of piles, badly damaged. The Athenians only lost three vessels. Nevertheless, the result of the day was a victory for Syracuse. Gylippus had carried out his plan on land without a check. He had seized Plemmyrium, with its three forts, its vast stores of grain and lumber, and the considerable treasure which was deposited there. He razed one of the forts to the ground and placed strong garrisons in the other two. The Syracusans now held every point, all round the bay, from the city to Plemmyrium, the Athenians were driven back to their old camp below the Olympieum, opposite the entrance of the harbour, and, being completely hemmed in by land, were obliged to fight their way in and out of the harbour in order to maintain communications and receive supplies. Their destruction was now clearly a question of time.

They exerted every energy to prevent the safe arrival of the Corinthian reënforcements, and made desperate attempts to destroy the ships anchored within the stockade. To this end they moved up to it one of their largest ships, a vessel of ten thousand talents' burden, equal to about two hundred and fifty tons by our measurement, fitted with cranes and windlasses that were protected by armoured screens; and making fast ropes to the piles as far below water as possible, they hove them out and towed them away. There were divers among the Athenians who, for a reward, went down with saws and sawed some of the piles off at such a depth that the stumps could not injure the vessels; and the Syracusans had also purposely driven in stakes at certain places, below the surface, that the Athenian ships might run upon them, but these also the divers succeeded in sawing away. Now no man can work at sawing below water for more than thirty or forty seconds at a time without coming up for breath, so that the divers must have worked many hours, and perhaps a whole day, at cutting through a single pile. The Syracusans, however, were not slow to replace those which the Athenians removed or destroyed, and the latter gained no advantage in that way, while the difficulty of obtaining provisions increased daily, and the malarious fever caused by the Lysimeleian swamp in the summer months made ravages in the Athenian camp.

At this juncture the fleet commanded by Demosthenes appeared off Syracuse in magnificent array. Seventy-three galleys sailed down in even order, their signals streaming on the wind, their richly adorned and painted bows rising high above the blue water. From the decks gleamed the shields and helmets of five thousand heavy-armed men, and as they neared Ortygia, soldiers and seamen raised the song of war and the loud Grecian trumpets blared out triumphant notes.

Street of ancient tombs, Syracuse

Demosthenes intended to terrify the Syracusans by making all the display of military and naval power of which he could dispose, and the Syracusans almost lost heart again at the approach of a new host of enemies. As soon as Demosthenes had landed he proposed to Nicias to make a general attack by sea and land, and if his advice had been taken, a signal success might have been gained. But Nicias had grown timid and was broken down by illness, and Plutarch even says that he had an understanding with certain traitors in Syracuse, who advised him to wait patiently, as the inhabitants were weary of the war and of the exacting energy of Gylippus, and would soon begin to dispute among themselves. But Demosthenes inspired the Athenians with courage and at last succeeded in carrying his point. He determined to make a night attack upon Epipolae, and taking the guards by surprise he slew a great number and was hastening on, supposing that he had carried the position, when he suddenly came upon the Boeotian detachment, which was already under arms. Uttering their tremendous war-cry, they closed up with levelled spears and charged the Athenians with the force of a solid mass. The young moon was hastening to her setting, and shed an uncertain light. The wildest confusion fell upon the Athenians as they fled in disorder, or attacked each other, unable to distinguish their friends from their foes. The faint moonlight, reflected upon the gleaming shields of the Syracusans and upon their glittering arms, made them appear ten times more numerous, and as the victorious force preserved its compact order, shoulder to shoulder, every soldier knew that he had only foes before him and friends behind, every thrust went home and every blade was dyed in Athenian blood. Many, in their flight, fell from the low cliffs and were killed, a few lost themselves in the fields beyond Epipolae while attempting to escape, and as the dawn lightened, the Syracusan horse scoured the country and cut down every straggler. Between midnight and morning two thousand Athenians had perished.

Nicias had expected nothing better, but yet he would not hear of a general retreat, and Demosthenes, having failed in his first enterprise, attempted no further action for some time. At last, as fresh reënforcements strengthened the Syracusan army, Nicias reluctantly consented to withdraw and gave the order to embark the troops. But on that very night, the moon, being full, was totally eclipsed,b and not only Nicias himself, but all the Greeks with him, were paralyzed with fear by what they considered a terrific portent. After consulting a diviner, Nicias declared that the army could not embark until the moon had completed another revolution. He was approaching his destruction, and even nature seemed to conspire with ill fortune to ruin him. In total inactivity he passed his time in sacrificing to the gods, while his diviner consulted the auguries presented by the victims. His ships lay idly at anchor, their seams opening under the blazing sun; his disheartened soldiers made no attempt to prevent the Syracusans from hemming them in; hundreds died of the malarial sickness spread by the pestilential swamp. The Syracusan fishermen and boatmen pulled out to the men-of-war and jeered at them, offering them fight. A boy, Heraclides, the son of a great Syracusan house, ventured in a skiff close under an Athenian vessel that was unmoored, and reviled the captain amid the laughter of the other boys. Furious at being insulted by a child, the officer manned the oars and gave chase. Instantly ten Sicilian galleys, now always ready for fight, put out to save the lad, others followed, and a sharp engagement ensued in which the Syracusans did considerable damage to the Athenian vessels and slew a general and a number of men.

The Syracusans lost no time in completely blocking the entrance of the harbour, after this success, and Nicias was reluctantly driven to fight where starvation and death by fever were the only alternatives. He embarked the best of his heavy infantry, and chosen detachments of archers and spearmen, manning a hundred and ten vessels, and he marshalled the rest of his army on the shore to await the event.

It was the end. The swift Syracusan ships pulled out in wide order, provided with their catapults, and with vast numbers of stones which could be discharged terrible effect at short range, and against which the Athenians had no missiles but darts and arrows. The Athenian fleet was so crowded together that the ships could barely advance, and were unable to execute any manoeuvre; the Syracusans, on the contrary, could charge, turn, and retire as they pleased; from the shore and from the city a hundred thousand spectators watched the struggle for life or death. Driven together upon each other, rammed and battered by their assailants, the Athenian ships sank one by one with the living and the dead together, and as the sun declined to the west what had been a battle became but a universal massacre; at evening the Athenian fleet was totally destroyed, and no alternative remained for the survivors ashore but to cut their way through the Syracusan lines in a hopeless attempt to escape by land. Gylippus would have fallen upon them in their camp without delay, but the Syracusans, in wild rejoicing at their great victory, could not be induced to postpone a universal feast. Hermocrates, however, whose counsels and ready wit had helped his countrymen throughout the war, sent a treacherous message to Nicias, warning him that every pass was held and every point of the works completely manned, and he was deceived and waited for the morning. Then indeed the Syracusans, having feasted and rested, went out and held the whole line during all that day and the following night. At last the Athenians, still forty thousand strong, began to move, going up from their camp with tears and loud lamentations, and leaving their sick and wounded behind them. They broke a passage through the lines indeed, but the whole Syracusan force was upon them, flanking them continually, following them, and slaying them like sheep as they struggled hopelessly and almost without food through the valley towards Floridia. Eight days the massacre lasted, until there was no hope, and the remnant of the greatest army of that age surrendered unconditionally to Spartan Gylippus. Some say that Demosthenes and Nicias killed themselves, and this is more likely, but others say that the Syracusans stoned them to death. Then the Syracusans dressed those tall trees that still grow by the river for miles, with the arms of their fallen foes, making blood-stained trophies all the way; and they plucked leaves and autumn flowers and made themselves garlands for their helmets and adorned their horses too; and thus marched back in a glorious triumph, driving their prisoners before them; for the war was over, and of all the vast armament that had come against Syracuse not one vessel was ever to return to Greece, and not one man had escaped to bear arms or to lift a hand against the victorious city, but all were dead or slaves. There was not even one to bring the frightful news to Athens, and it was late in the autumn when a travelling merchant carelessly told the story to a barber in the Piraeus, supposing that all Greece knew it. Thus ended the great Athenian expedition, and thus was Alcibiades revenged.

Forty thousand men had left the Athenian camp to begin the retreat. After the battle about seven thousand prisoners remained alive. They suffered a hideous condemnation; let anyone who wishes to understand their fortunes go down into the great quarries of Syracuse and see for himself; for, saving that the quarries are larger now than they were then and full of trees and flowers, they are the same in their shape and in their appalling isolation. They are still called the Latomie, the 'places of stone cutting,' and the tale of what once happened in them is told still, handed down perhaps without a break, through the changing generations of many races of inhabitants, Greeks, Romans, Saracens, Normans, Spaniards, and Italians. They are situated on an irregular line which leads eastward from the one nearest to the theatre, across Achradina to the last and most extensive of all, called the Latomia dei Cappuccini, which is very near the sea. In all that region the soil is thin but very rich, and below it the yellowish white stone lies in a solid mass, perhaps hundreds of feet deep. Straight down from the surface the stone has been quarried to depth of from eighty to a hundred feet, making sheer walls of rock on every side, so that the only means of descent is by wooden ladders, and neither man nor beast can scale the height without help from above.

Latomia dei Cappuccini, Syracuse

Below, it is all an enchanted garden now; two thousand and three hundred years ago it was a bare quarry of white stone, strewed with stone chips and stone dust. By day the sun beat down into it, with the glare of the unpitying sky, and was reflected from its sides, and the rock radiated an intolerable heat; at evening the upper air, suddenly chilled at sunset, rushed down and filled it with an icy dampness. A furnace in summer, bitterly cold in winter, a fever hole in the autumn rains, a hell at all times save in the spring, the Syracusans found it ready to their hand to be a place of torture and death for their beaten enemies. Therefore they let them down into by the cranes that served to lift the stone, being seven thousand men in all; and lest it should be said that they had starved prisoners to death, they sent to them rations, for every man half a pint of water every day, or very little pmore, and twice as much of raw barley or other grain; and this was only half the measure of food that was given to common slaves in those days, and the slaves had water in abundance.

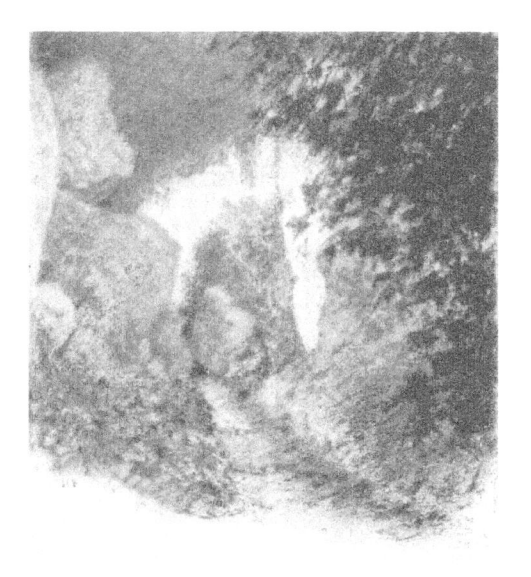

Path under rocks, Latomia dei Cappuccini, Syracuse

Now among the miserable captives there were many who had been wounded in the last fight and had been taken alive, and these suffered less, for they died first, of their injuries and of fever. But the strong and the well lived on in torment, and the bodies of the dead lay in the quarry among the living, and the poison of death made the air horrible to breathe, so that mortal sickness fell upon the strongest, and they died daily, while each dead man became a new source of pestilence. Ten weeks long they died, and yet they were not all dead; and when the sun was declining, and the people of Syracuse went out to taste the sea breeze, many came and stood at the edge of the quarry, on the windward side, lest their nostrils be offended, and looked down at men who were rotting alive, all that remained of the great Athenian army, men who were not men, but half-clad skeletons, scarce moving or breathing between the heaps of shapeless corpses that had been their friends. And the fine ladies of Syracuse held little vials of scent to their noses and leaned upon their slaves' arms, and looked down curiously; for the Athenians had been handsome men.

When seventy days had gone by, the Syracusans took out those of the living who were not Athenians, and sold them for slaves, many being not worth a day's purchase; but they left the Athenians to suffer a little longer, and when at last they brought them up, they heated branding-irons red hot, and branded them all in the forehead with the mark of the Syracusan horse, and sold them as slaves for the public benefit. Yet amid so much shadow of cruelty there is one redeeming light. The Syracusans loved the verses of the tragic poet Euripides above all other poetry, and in the great theatre, carved with its high ranks of seats from the solid rock in the hollow side of the mountain, they had been used to sit enthralled and listen to the 'Medea' and the

'Alcestis' and the other great plays, through long summer afternoons, when the sun was behind them, and behind the mountains. Among the Athenian captives there were many who could repeat and sing long passages from Euripides' plays; and these men were favoured far above the others when they were sold as slaves, so that some of them were even freed for the poet's sake, and long afterwards went back and found him and thanked him, branded though they were, for life and liberty. Nothing we know of to tell, and no story that a man might build up with the material of imagination, could show as this does the difference between that age and ours. There was divinity in the poet then, and his inspiration was from a god, deserving to be worshipped and revered as a heavenly gift; and those who had skill to sing his words, as he would have them sung, were sharers in his genius and blessed with a talent half divine, which others recognized and loved.

Old well in the Latomia dei Cappuccini, Syracuse

There is a sort of taste in nations which belongs to their young days, when they have not done their best, a living and creative taste that is closely akin to hope and aspiration; and there is another sort that comes with decadence and is satisfied more with the past than with the present or the future, that knows neither the elation of hope nor the satisfaction that lies in creation, but which is easily cast down, sad, self-tormenting, and as often a source of pain as of pleasure. So the degenerate Sybarite writhed upon a ruffled rose leaf and ached at the sight of a man digging hard ground, and the modern exquisite utters poor little cries of distress at the sound of a false note or the glare of a false colour.

In those days Sicily was in the stronger, brighter, earlier stage of life, and it would have asserted itself in a vast artistic productiveness after the failure of the Athenian invasion, if that event had been followed by a period of peace. The first impulse of the Syracusans and of the other free Greek cities of Sicily was to build temples and to raise up statues to the gods, in gratitude for the greatest victory ever won by Greeks over Greeks; and as peace followed war, and plenty grew up where famine had followed the destruction of crops, the hearts of the people were lightened and the song of rejoicing filled the land. While the law-givers they chose at home were occupied in framing a code that would not disgrace a modern civilization, Sicilian fleets and Sicilian soldiers sailed eastward to the islands and even to the shores of Asia Minor, paying back war with war, allied with the Peloponnesians for the final destruction of Athens, the common enemy, and bringing home shiploads of treasure and booty. Could this condition of things have lasted, there is no telling to what heights the prosperity of Sicily might have risen in a few years. But the old causes were at work to produce new disasters; the Athenians had invaded the island ostensibly to right the wrongs inflicted upon Segesta by Selinus and on Leontini by Syracuse; in the terrific struggle with Syracuse, Selinus had been more than half forgotten, and one year's crop had not been sown and reaped before those very circumstances renewed themselves which had led to the destruction of a great fleet and of sixty thousand men. The Selinuntians fancied that since Athens had fallen they could harass their enemies at their pleasure, and boldly crossing the border they made havoc of the Segestan country. Now the land subject to Segesta lay in a broad tract between the Phoenician colonies of Panormus and of Lilybaeum, and a free and safe passage across was essential to the commerce of both, the distance by sea being far greater and the voyage not always free from danger. It was therefore to the interest of Carthage that Segesta, which had always been friendly to her, should not be overrun by the Selinuntians who had always been her enemies, and when Segesta appealed to her for help as it had appealed to Athens some six years earlier, a ready assistance was granted on interested grounds. The despatching of a few thousand men to help the oppressed state had the natural result of sending Selinus of Syracuse for assistance in its turn, and Syracuse promised it readily, not dreaming of the magnitude of the undertaking. Carthage, mindful of the ignominious defeat suffered at the hands of the Syracusans in Himera seventy years earlier, and dreading lest, since Athens was fallen, Syracuse should obtain the empire of the Mediterranean, put forth all her strength and began to raise an enormous army.

In the spring of the year 409 B.C. sixty Carthaginian men-of-war convoyed no less than fifteen hundred small vessels from Carthage to Lilybaeum, carrying an army of something like two hundred thousand foot-soldiers and four thousand cavalry, together with an immense supply of war material and siege engines. At the head of this formidable force was the grandson of Hamilcar, who had perished in his own sacrifice at Himera. This was Hannibal, the second of the name who appears in history, and who is said to have sworn a solemn oath to avenge his grandsire. Landing on the headland of Lilybaeum, he at once began to lay waste the country, and moving rapidly forwards, attacked Selinus itself with all the energy which Nicias had lacked. He fell upon the city from the north; six iron-headed battering rams were brought to make a breach in the walls, six lofty towers, which overtopped the fortifications, slung masses of stone into the city, while slingers and archers picked off the defenders one by one. Nevertheless, the people defended themselves courageously, trusting to the speedy arrival of help from Syracuse. The young men fought, the old provided them with fresh weapons and missiles, and the women brought food and drink to the combatants. But Hannibal promised the soldiers the whole plunder of the city, and the siege was prosecuted with surprising energy. The men fought in watches and by turns, marching up to relieve each other with trumpet call and war-cry. Day and night the battering rams, hanging in their frames by iron chains, pounded the walls with the sound of unceasing thunder. A breach was broken, and Hannibal's Campanian mercenaries charged in; but as their need grew greater the defenders fought more desperately, and the first attack was repulsed with frightful slaughter. Messengers rode for life and death to Akragas and Gela and Syracuse, bearing the news of their city's supreme need. But it was too late. The battering rams still pounded at the wall, and still the catapults hurled large stones from the towers; the breach was widened and held by the enemy, while still the defenders fought like madmen and looked eastward for help through nine long days. Driven back from the breach at last, as a great cry of woe went up from their women, they defended themselves to the end. They threw up barricades of stones, fighting from street to street; the old men, the wounded, the women and the children, climbed to the roofs and dashed down stones and tiles upon the Carthaginians. But at last it was over and the city was won. Then fire and the sword did the rest, for Hannibal knew his men and kept his word and gave them their hearts' desire. Slaying every living thing they met, they broke into every house, flung the booty into the streets, and set each dwelling on fire before they left the door. The soldiers paraded the streets, bearing on their spears the heads of the vanquished, and hideous festoons of hands cut off and strung together. Only those women and children were spared who had taken refuge in the temples, not from any reverence for the gods, but in fear lest they should fire the temples in self-defence and destroy the rich treasures preserved there. On that day sixteen thousand lives fell to the Carthaginian swords; less than three thousand persons escaped alive to Akragas, and, weary of slaughter, the victors carried off five thousand prisoners.

Then at last the first three thousand of the Syracusan troops appeared and sent heralds demanding that Hannibal should at least respect the temples and give up their prisoners for a ransom; but Hannibal answered roughly that since the Selinuntians had not been able to defend their freedom they must learn to be slaves, and so far as the temples were concerned the gods appeared to have abandoned both them and their city. From this destruction Selinus never recovered.

Hannibal crossed unhindered to Himera next, and proceeded at once to a formal siege, undermining the walls and soon producing a wide breach. A Syracusan fleet of five and thirty sail came in sight, and the hopes of the city rose to enthusiasm; but by treacherous messages Hannibal made the admiral of the fleet believe that he was about to raise the siege because the whole Syracusan army was advancing by land, and that Syracuse being therefore undefended he intended to attack it without delay. The admiral made ready to go to the rescue, and seeing themselves about to be deserted, a great part of the population abandoned the city to the enemy, crowding the ships until there was no more room, and the remainder marching out by land. On the following day the Carthaginians entered Himera; the women and children were carried out to the camp to be sold as slaves in Africa, and on the spot where his grandsire had perished, Hannibal appeased his unquiet spirit by the mutilation and slaughter of three thousand Himeran warriors. Last of all he burned the whole city and razed the ruins to the ground.

Here in the story appears for the last time Hermocrates, in a short and brilliant campaign that ended in his violent death at the gates of Syracuse. From the beginning of the Athenian invasion his counsels had helped Syracuse, his labours had been unceasing, his submission to the generalship of Gylippus exemplary; he had seemed a man above passion, inspired only by the purest love of country. But his country feared the return of a tyranny like that of Thrasybulus, and accusing him of plotting to get the despotism, Syracuse exiled her best and bravest. In exile he had not turned against the state, as Alcibiades had turned against Athens; he remained faithful and devoted, waiting and longing for an opportunity to return. He saw his chance when the Carthaginians withdrew after the final slaughter at Himera. Provided with large sums of money, he came to Messina, built five warships of his own and raised a thousand men. He collected the fugitives from Himera, sailed round to Selinus, and rapidly fortified the ruins left by the Carthaginians. Without losing time, but gathering an army of six thousand men, he dashed across the island, surprised Motye and Panormus, and laid waste the country. Even then Syracuse would not recall him from banishment. He marched down to Himera and collected from the field of battle the unburied bones of the Syracusans who had perished there, and sent them reverently to Syracuse; but yet his native city would not receive him back. Mad with longing to see his home, and believing that if he appeared in person, the false accusations would be forgotten, he rode with a few followers to the very gate of the city. His friends received him, but could not save his life, for his enemies spread the report that he had returned with an army, and they fell upon him and cruelly slew him on the threshold of his home. But some of his followers saved themselves, and though they were all banished, there was one among them who, being desperately wounded, was given out to be dead, and escaped the ban; he was Dionysius, who was to save Syracuse from the Carthaginians, and was to be her lord and despot before many years should pass.

Garden of the church of S. Nicola, Girgenti, formerly Agrigentum

For soon the Carthaginians bethought themselves how they should avenge the raid made by Hermocrates upon the Phoenician west, and they fortified beforehand a strong place on the coast, which is now Termini, near Himera, and equipped another great army, under Hannibal the victorious; and they brought over between two and three hundred thousand fighting men, to attack Akragas, rich in corn° and wine and oil, as Girgenti is to-day. For the Akragantines were a peace-loving people who kept out of war and enriched themselves with agriculture and trade; and their city was beautiful with many temples, and with many monuments, some of which were even erected to the memory of horses that had won some famous race, and the maidens of Akragas sometimes built tombs for their favourite song-birds. There were also marvellous paintings there, and there was vast wealth. Once, before this war, a certain Exainetos of Akragas won the two hundred yard race at Olympia, and when he came home, there went out to welcome him three hundred chariots drawn by as many pairs of milk-white horses. In their gymnasium the people used golden strigils and gold vessels for oil. At the door of the house of Gellias, a rich man of the city, slaves stood in waiting all day long, inviting every passing stranger to enter for rest and entertainment, and once, when five hundred riders came from Gela, Gellias took them all in, and presented each one with new garments, for it was winter. In his cellars, instead of casks and hogsheads, three hundred reservoirs for wine were hewn in the solid rock, and each one held one hundred amphorae, which is equal to nearly nine hundred gallons. And of the Akragantines Empedocles said that they built as if they were to live forever, but that they feasted as if they were to die on the morrow; and it is recorded that at a certain marriage eight hundred carriages and innumerable riders brought the bride home at night, while the whole city was illuminated. Moreover, during the war which now began, a decree was issued which forbade a soldier on the watch to be provided with more than two mattresses, two pillows, and a blanket.

Ruined rampart of Girgenti

Nevertheless their allies defended them manfully for some time, and the strong position of their city helped them at need, as it had doubtless contributed to create that feeling of absolute security which is the most favourable condition for the development of idleness and luxury. It is easy to understand that even a slack defence of such a place might suffice to hold it. Standing on the ruined rampart of Girgenti, at the southeastern point, near the temple of Hera, the traveller can take in the extent of the city at a glance, from the modern town, where stood the ancient acropolis, cresting the hill, round by a wide descending sweep to the right, then westward along the south side, protected by the abrupt falling away of the ground, and from beyond the temples of Zeus and the Dioscuri up the steep hill to the acropolis again. Only on this last stretch could Hannibal see any chance of success, where the old burial ground came up to the walls; and there he intrenched himself and set up his engines of attack, but the citizens sallied out and burned his wooden towers; in digging his trenches, he exposed a great number of dead bodies, from which a plague arose among his soldiers, and he himself died of the sickness. Then his father, Himilcon, lost six thousand men in an engagement with the Syracusans who were advancing to relieve the city. The Greeks were elated and contemplated making a destructive attack upon the Carthaginian camp. The besiegers, as the winter came on, were short of provisions; some even died of hunger; matters looked ill for the rest, and the mercenaries threatened to depart.

But Himilcon learned that an immense supply of corn was on the way to Akragas from Syracuse. He bribed his soldiers to wait a few days, sent out warships, overcame the Greek triremes that formed the convoy, and seized the whole provision. Among the defenders were Spartans and other allies, who began to sell themselves to the Carthaginian general, and presently all the allies deserted almost in a body. The luxurious Akragantines were paralyzed with fear, for they remembered the horrid fate of Selinus and Himera. Incredible as it must seem though there was not so much as a breach in the walls, the whole population abandoned the city, leaving the old and the sick to their fate. Himilcon entered at daybreak and slew all these. The rich Gellias had collected such of his treasures as he could gather quickly into a temple, to which he set fire, and he perished in the flames. A few patriots who would not fly destroyed themselves. The vast booty fell into the hands of the Carthaginians without a blow, and Akragas ceased to play a part in Sicily. There is hardly a parallel in all history to such an ignominious evacuation.

Pessant near Reggio, Calabria

Dionysius the scribe, who by the accident of his desperate wound had escaped being banished with the friends of the murdered Hermocrates, was a man who possessed those gifts of courage, eloquence, and cunning by which obscure individuals have from time to time raised themselves suddenly to empire. Yet even such gifts as these could have produced no result without the opportunity for exercising them. After the fall of Akragas, which had been largely due to the defection of the more important allies for the sake of Himilcon's rich bribes, a profound disgust for the existing government, under which such things were possible, manifested itself among the Sicilian people; the conviction grew in the minds of the masses that although a democracy might be the best form of government in times of peace and prosperity, yet, in a moment of public danger, it was absolutely necessary that all military power should be in the hands of a single individual. The Sicilians had not the cool sense of fitness which made the Romans name a dictator during war, and return to republican forms as soon as it was ended. The Greek cities, and Syracuse first of all, felt the want of a strong hand; the days of the democracy were over, and it fell to the lot of the most talented man of his day to restore the tyranny. He began by ingratiating himself with the remains of Hermocrates' party, and being sure of their support, he took the earliest opportunity of exhibiting his eloquence at a general meeting of the people. Himera, Selinus, and Akragas had fallen a prey to the Carthaginians, their vast army was fattening on the spoil got from their latest conquest, from Akragas they would march to Gela, and once there, the fate of Syracuse would be a foregone conclusion. The leaders hesitated, the people murmured, no one dared to speak out. Then Dionysius suddenly arose and impeached the Greek generals, the government, the rich and powerful throughout the land, taking, as every great adventurer has done at first, the side of the oppressed many against the overbearing few; nor did any ambitious man ever take that side in vain. Dionysius proposed that the generals responsible for the fall of Akragas should be punished summarily and without trial. This was against the law of Syracuse. A few of the aristocrats, with loud protests, cried out that the speaker was liable at once to the fine imposed by law; but a friend of his rose instantly and bade him go on, saying that he would pay not only the fine imposed upon Dionysius, but all other fines exacted from any who should speak in the same spirit. With fiery energy Dionysius proceeded to the end; the generals were then and there degraded from their office, others were chosen in their stead, and among them Dionysius himself. From this to the sole command was a difficult step. He began by refusing to associated with his fellow generals, hinting that they were in secret understanding with the Carthaginians. The people trusted him, and when he proposed that they should vote the immediate return of all political exiles, they acceded to his request without hesitation. By this means he gained a vast number of enthusiastic friends.

Another opportunity for gaining fresh power soon presented itself. It was clear that Gela would be the next city to fall, and its garrison was under the orders of one of the captains who had sold himself to Carthage at Akragas. Dionysius hastened thither, to find the city in a frenzy of excitement. He presented himself as the protector and liberator of the people, he paid the troops the stipend which had long been owing to them, and he brought the suspected traitors, chiefly the richest in the city, to prompt trial and execution, their property being seized for the public good. Having thus settled matters for a time, he returned with speed to Syracuse. Entering the city at sunset, just as a great audience was leaving the theatre, and being asked what news he brought from Gela, he delivered a magnificent speech in which he told the people that their worst enemies were not the Carthaginians, but their own corrupt and grasping generals. They were selling their country inch by inch for Carthaginian gold, and he would no longer be one of them. His words were received with unbounded applause and wild acclamation; on the following day a public meeting of the people was called, he addressed them again, his friends rose up in force to support all he said, and amid the universal enthusiasm a measure was carried which removed the other generals from office, and conferred upon him the sole military command.

The tyranny was now restored in fact, and all but acknowledged in name. Dionysius needed only a devoted body-guard to protect him from the assassin's knife, in order to assume the position of absolute lord. He obtained this also, and by the same stratagem which had served Pisitratus for the same end. He called upon the whole available force of armed men which Syracuse could furnish, bidding them meet him in Leontini as if for a great review. That night a great tumult arose in the camp, Dionysius rushed from his tent, declaring that an attempt had been made upon his life, and fled to the acropolis, calling upon all who trusted him to follow him up thither. Then and there the soldiers, to whom he was already a hero and almost a demigod, voted him a life-guard of six hundred men. He was to choose them himself, and he took advantage of the privilege to select a thousand. Armed to perfection and receiving twice the pay of other soldiers, their fate was now bound up with his, and he could count upon every man to the death. The blow was struck, the tyranny was restored, and Dionysius was the despot of Syracuse.

In Syracuse he established himself in the arsenal, which became at once his palace and his stronghold; he strengthened his position by marrying the daughter of the ill-fated Hermocrates, giving his own sister in marriage to the latter's brother-in-law. He caused the people to execute the two men who had principally opposed his advancement, and he issued orders for gathering together into one army, besides the Syracusans, every soldier of fortune in Sicily who would serve for pay.

What he had foreseen was not long in coming. Himilcon had spent the winter with his army in Akragas; when the spring came, and he no longer needed shelter, he ordered the city to be destroyed and marched upon Gela. The inhabitants determined to send their wives and children to Syracuse, but the devoted women clung to the statues of the gods and to the altars in the market-place, crying out that they would share the fate of their men. As usual Himilcon moved up his battering rams and towers to the walls; but though he broke down great breaches in the fortifications, the besieged men fought with fury by day, and by night even the women and children helped to build up the broken ramparts. In spite of Himilcon's ceaseless exertions the city was held against him until Dionysius came up with fifty thousand men. He formed a plan to surround the enemy and the whole city and to make three simultaneous attacks. The well-conceived scheme failed in execution; Dionysius lost many men, and was at once accused of betrayal, since he had done no better than his predecessors. Yet he kept his command, being most likely preserved from instant death by his life-guard, and by a clever stratagem he so far retrieved himself as to effect the safe evacuation of the city with the women and children, and the sick and wounded. Two thousand light-armed troops, men of heroic courage, remained behind in the city, and completely deceived the Carthaginians by making bonfires and simulating a tumult in the streets. In the end they also escaped unhurt.

Little by little the Greeks were being driven from city to city towards Syracuse, where the final struggle was to take place. The enemy came upon them as the Huns fell upon Europe many centuries later. The Carthaginians spared neither man nor beast, nor woman nor child, and prisoners were horribly tortured, torn to pieces, and crucified by hundreds. Before such an enemy the people fled to their last refuge like sheep to the fold when the wolves are upon them. That Dionysius should have been able to direct the storm of such a panic and regain all his power and influence proves his genius; that he afterwards attacked Carthage with success demonstrates his masterly military talent; but that he utterly vanquished and blotted out his foes in the end is little short of miraculous.

The spectacle of a whole population hurrying in desperate confusion to their last shelter, women and children and old and sick and dying of exhaustion by the way amid the tears and lamentations of the survivors, roused the Syracusan soldiers to exasperation against the leader to whom alone they attributed such disaster; the well-born youths who composed the cavalry watched for an opportunity to slay him, but finding him too well protected by his mercenaries, they rode on before and reached Syracuse in time to stir up a revolution against him; they seized his house and treasure, and in their blind rage so frightfully treated his wife that she died of her injuries. But they had to deal with a man of genius and action who knew no fear. Dionysius had no sooner learned of their desertion than he hastened to follow them with a chosen band of seven hundred men. At midnight he was before the closed gate of Achradina, where brave Hermocrates had been murdered; in an hour the doors were burned down; when the day dawned his enemies lay dead in the market-place, and as the sun rose he was once more master of the city.

And now the Carthaginian advance was checked by the plague, which ever wrought havoc among the Phoenician mercenaries, and Himilcon made a treaty of peace, with an exchange of prisoners and of ships taken in the war, and an extension of the Phoenician territory. More than half of the Carthaginian army perished in the pestilence, Himilcon withdrew to Carthage, and the first part of the conflict came to an unexpected termination. The strong man set about consolidating his power.

He occupied the arsenal, and the island of Ortygia, allowing none but his most faithful adherents to set foot upon the island; using the methods of Gelon and Hiero, he conferred citizenship upon his mercenaries and even upon freed slaves, and created a new body of devoted friends. He matured his plan for dominating all Sicily in order to make war upon Carthage, but at his first attempt at extending his power a mutiny broke out, his chief lieutenant was murdered, and he saw himself obliged to fall back upon his fortified home in Ortygia, while the mutineers encamped upon Epipolae and besieged the city, setting a price on the tyrant's head. The situation was perilous in the extreme, and for once the iron man seems almost to have lost hope. Yet he held his stronghold grimly, and secretly communicated with certain Campanian soldiers of fortune, while proposing terms of capitulation for himself to the besiegers. In their simplicity they believed him, many of their force dispersed. Twelve hundred Campanian soldiers swept down like a whirlwind upon the Syracusans, slew all they met, broke through their siege works, and joined Dionysius in the fort. The besiegers now disagreed among themselves and, choosing his time, Dionysius sallied out and defeated them in one of the suburbs, but checked all useless slaughter, that the vanquished mutineers might owe him their lives; and he honourably buried their dead.

Master of Syracuse once more, he entered into close alliance with Sparta. Tyranny was growing popular in theory, if not yet in practice, and the Lacedaemonians, while still in name recommending a democracy, privately gave their whole support to Dionysius, although their conduct brought them into opposition with Corinth, which faithfully advocated the freedom of Syracuse. Thus strengthened, he began the conquest of Sicily. Henna, which is Castrogiovanni now, and Catania and Naxos fell successively under his dominion, and Leontini surrendered on condition that the inhabitants should receive the citizenship of Syracuse. His plan was to destroy the Greek commonwealths, to spare the Sicelian ones, and to found Italian cities, in order to equalize the various elements and produce a homogeneous Sicilian nation; and as the Syracusans began to understand that he was not cruel but ambitious, and as much for them as for himself, their confidence in him rose and his influence became unbounded. Remembering what Syracuse had suffered during the Athenian invasion, and mindful of his own experience during the mutiny, he determined to extend the fortifications so as to take in Epipolae. The huge ramparts that still crown the height are his work. Knowing that there was still some danger of revolution in the city, he exerted his whole energy to accomplish this quickly, and the great wall, more than three miles in length and made of large hewn stones, was completed in twenty days. It was built by sixty thousand free men, who received double wages for their labour; thirty-six thousand, in one hundred and eighty detachments of two hundred each, worked upon sections •one hundred feet long, each section being under a master-mason, and every six sections under an architect. Four and twenty thousand men, with six thousand carts, quarried the stone and hauled it up the heights. Most of the stone was quarried in the Latomie, in Syracuse. Dionysius himself hardly left the works till all was finished.

The main wall being built, he soon afterwards prepared to attack Carthage, and set to work upon the vast equipment which he knew to be necessary for such an undertaking, for the success of the Carthaginians had generally been due to their superior numbers and excellent munitions of war. Dionysius worked on a great scale; he built two hundred new ships of war and refitted a hundred and ten old ones; one hundred and forty thousand shields with an equal number of swords and helmets were made, and fourteen thousand cuirasses with their fittings. Great engines were constructed for hurling stones; and it is known that in the year 399 he called together a general meeting of engineers, who planned the first ships ever built with five banks of oars, and the first long-range catapults, though what the range of the latter may really have been we do not know: those in use earlier could hurl a stone six hundred feet.

The first five-banked ship, splendid with gold and silver, brought home from Locri one of two brides whom the despot married on the same day, — a wedding unexampled, I believe, in Greek history. A few days later he addressed the people and exposed his plans with the fervid eloquence that had seldom failed him, stirring up the hatred that was not yet old, and firing every hearer with the spirit of revenge. The news of the unequalled preparations at Syracuse had already gone forth; the tidings of the master's speech spread like flame through straw.

All Sicily rose, and wheresoever, in cities that once had been all Greek, there were Punic masters, or merchants, or landowners, or travellers, they were put to death; and wheresoever the Carthaginians had torn to pieces or burnt or crucified a Greek, there the Greeks tortured and impaled a Carthaginian.

At last, in 397, when all the African coasts were exhausted by a pestilence that had raged for two whole years, Dionysius declared war, and his ambassadors gave proud warning to the high council of Carthage that she must set free and evacuate every Greek city in Sicily or fight to an issue. As soon as the ambassadors returned, and without giving Carthage time to collect the mercenary troops on which she always most depended, Dionysius struck the first blow, and attacked Eryx, now Monte San Giuliano above Trapani, and Motye, a dozen miles to southward. Eryx surrendered without a blow; Motye had received a small reënforcement from Carthage, and made a brave defence.

In those times the two small islands with lie north of Marsala, or Lilybaeum, formed a part of the mainland and enclosed a wide harbour; in the midst of this sheet of shallow water Motye was built upon the little island which now bears the name of San Pantaleo and was connected with the land by a narrow causeway on the northeast side. The town itself was strongly fortified and was one of the most valuable points held by the Carthaginians. Before the arrival of Dionysius the inhabitants destroyed the causeway. Dionysius determined to rebuild it, entered the harbour, and beached his war-vessels north of the little island. He left his admiral Leptines to see to the reconstruction of the dam and withdrew his land forces for a time in order to make a raid upon the Phoenician country. Meanwhile Himilcon reached Syracuse with a small fleet of ten vessels, hoping to draw Dionysius away from Motye; but failing in this intention and having done such damage as he could with so small a force, he sailed back again and appeared before Motye at daybreak, with one hundred of his best ships. Having easily destroyed the few Greek vessels that were lying outside, he at once blockaded the entrance to the harbour, within which the whole of the Greek war fleet was drawn up high and dry. It seemed as if the Greeks were caught in a trap from which they could not escape, but the courage and decision of Dionysius were not at fault, and he turned the tables upon his adversary in a day. The north side of the harbour was separated from the open sea by a low neck of sand about four thousand yards wide. Across this space Dionysius actually hauled eighty ships of war on chocks, in a single day, and at the same time he moved his newly invented long-range catapults down to the entrance of the harbour. The warships he had now launched sailed down in a body and attacked the Carthaginian fleet from seaward, driving it in, and at the same time the astonished Carthaginians, who believed themselves well out of range from the shore, received a terrific volley of stones from the catapults. Himilcon himself would have been driven into the harbour and caught, if he had not at once made good his escape; but he lost no time, left Motye to its fate, and breaking through the line of Syracusan vessels, got out to sea.

During the siege of Motye which followed, the inhabitants made a memorable defence, opposing the engines of the Greeks with every conceivable device, and sometimes setting them on fire; and when at last a breach was made in the walls, and Dionysius believed that the city was in his hands, he still had to carry on the siege from street to street and from house to house through many days and nights. When the last defence was broken down, the Greeks wreaked their vengeance in a wholesale slaughter, in which neither women nor children were spared, until Dionysius himself bade them take refuge in their temples. The Carthaginians who were taken alive were sold as slaves, but every Greek who was found on their side was crucified at once.

Intending to follow up his victory, Dionysius at once moved upon Segesta, the city of all others in Sicily the most hateful to the Syracusans; but here, as if misfortune were attached to the mere name of the place, he suffered a considerable reverse almost before the siege had begun. Meanwhile the Carthaginians had set on foot for the third time a vast army of mercenaries, and we now hear for the first time that war chariots accompanied the host. Those that had left Carthage at the beginning of the first invasion had been lost at sea.

Dionysius awaited him near Panormus, but only succeeded in destroying some fifty ships and about five thousand of his soldiers, the rest entering the harbour in safety. In a few days Himilcon had undone all that the Syracusans had accomplished; Eryx was won back, Motye was retaken, and the other Phoenician cities of the west found themselves free. In face of such an enemy Dionysius was reluctantly obliged to withdraw to Syracuse. Himilcon now marched eastward and seized Messina, whence the greater part of the population had already escaped. Out of two hundred who sprang into the sea and attempted to swim the straits fifty reached the Italian shore in safety. Himilcon saw the great difficulty of holding Messina and, lest it should be of use to his enemies, determined to destroy the city. The allies of Dionysius now began to desert him, but he did not lose heart; he fortified and provisioned the Syracusan towns and completed the fortifications of Syracuse, while Himilcon was marching down upon Naxos. At Catania he attacked the Carthaginian fleet in the hope of preventing it from effecting a junction with the land force, but suffered an overwhelming defeat in which he lost one hundred ships and twenty thousand men. Retreating upon Syracuse again, he prepared to make a final stand, while Himilcon advanced upon the city by land and encamped a little more than a mile north of Epipolae.

Seeing the enormous strength of the fortifications raised by Dionysius before the war began, Himilcon determined to starve the city to a surrender, and built three forts which commanded the southern side of the harbour. Meanwhile, however, reënforcements of ships arrived from Sparta, and the Syracusans, gathering courage, fell upon a detachment of vessels which were bringing corn to the Carthaginians; a naval engagement followed in which the Carthaginians were badly beaten and lost twenty-four ships.

The position of Dionysius was dangerous, but not desperate, and before long the plague, which seems to have accompanied the Carthaginians wherever they went, came to his assistance. The men died at such a rate that it was impossible to bury the bodies, and the condition of Himilcon's camp was too hideous to be described. Quick to take advantage of everything that could weaken his enemy, Dionysius now executed a general movement which terminated the war. On a night when there was no moon the Syracusan fleet got under way in the harbour, and Dionysius himself marched a large force round Epipolae to surprise the Carthaginian camp and one of Himilcon's forts. He sent a thousand mercenaries against the camp, and a body of cavalry, instructing the latter to pretend flight as soon as the enemy came out. These mercenaries were men whom he distrusted, and he coolly sacrificed them for the sake of occupying the enemy on that side. He himself seized the fort on the Olympieum, and sent the cavalry down to take the next, which was near the shore. At daybreak the Greek ships surprised the Carthaginian fleet, and gained a complete victory over the vessels which were afloat. Dionysius himself set fire to forty ships that were on the beach, and a strong wind drove the flames out to the transports. In an indescribable confusion the whole sea force of the Carthaginians was destroyed before their eyes, while every kind of small craft, manned even by old men and boys, put out from the city to plunder the half-burned wrecks, and thousands of women and little children climbed the roofs of the city to watch the tragedy of fire and sword. By land the fighting lasted all the day, and at night Dionysius encamped by the Olympieum. All but forty of Himilcon's ships were destroyed or crippled, and more than half his army of three hundred thousand men lay dead in the camp or on the field. He humbly treated for his life and safety, and at last for the sum of three hundred talents, which was perhaps all he had left to give, Dionysius suffered him to depart and to take with him, upon his forty ships, those of his soldiers who were Carthaginian citizens. When the Greeks entered the Carthaginian camp at last, it is told that they found within it the unburied bodies of a hundred and fifty thousand men. Thus ended the great Carthaginian expedition for the conquest of Sicily.

At first sight one may wonder why Dionysius did not completely destroy the remains of Himilcon's host, execute their general himself, and drive out the Phoenicians from the western part of the island; but a little reflection will show how much wiser that course was which he actually pursued. The strength of Carthage lay, not in a warlike population, but in the great wealth by which she commanded the service of numerous mercenaries, and although she had now suffered an extraordinary defeat, which was followed by something like a revolution, her losses were chiefly financial, while her resources were practically inexhaustible. By not driving her to extremities, Dionysius both practised wisdom and displayed magnanimity. Moreover, his real ambition was to be the ruler of the western Greeks rather than a mere conqueror of barbarous nations. By treachery or arms, indeed, he soon got the lordship of the Sicelian cities of the interior, but these were already so completely hellenized as to be practically Greek, and were so situated as to be necessary to him. His fortune, however, did not follow him everywhere, and in attempting to seize Tauromenium he once more suffered defeat, in spite of the most tremendous exertions. Climbing the steep ascent behind the modern town, on a dark winter's night when it was bitter cold, he seized the castle, the 'Castello' of to-day, and thence tried to storm the city; but the Sicelians drove him back into the darkness, slaying six hundred of his men; he himself fell, and barely escaping with his life rolled down the hill, bruised and bleeding, with no arms left but the cuirass on his body. But his defeats were always followed by victories. He crossed the straits and attacked Rhegium on the mainland; failing to take the strong place at once, he laid waste the country. When he took it at last it was by starving the garrison to a surrender. In their agony of hunger the people crept out from the beleaguered city and devoured the grass under the walls, but Dionysius turned cattle and sheep upon it, that cropped it close while his soldiers guarded them. When at last he had possession of a city half full of dead men, he allowed the rest to buy their freedom, and sold the poor for slaves, but he took evil vengeance upon their brave general Phyton, for he drowned his son, and told the unhappy father what he had done, then scourged him through the city, and drowned him also at last, with all the rest of his family.

Straits of Messina abeam of Rhegium, now Reggio, Calabria

Thenceforward Dionysius ruled the south for twenty years, for Rhegium had been the last strong place that had held out against him. It was at this time, in the year 387, that the Greeks of Greece had practically abandoned the Greeks of Asia Minor to Persia, and Rome had not yet recovered from the invasion of the Gauls; the Greeks of Sicily alone, by the genius of a tyrant, held in check their strong enemies the Carthaginians, and were themselves united under Dionysius; and he, on his side, maintained a sort of friendly alliance with the Gauls, and had done his best to contribute to the humiliation of Greece. Yet, as the acute Holm truly says, he was the chief stay of Hellenism in the Mediterranean, and without him the Persian from the east might have met the Carthaginian from the west to bring about the total extinction of the Greek power. Little by little, by ceaseless war and untiring activity, he extended his dominion into Italy, and joined the Gauls in the destruction of the Etruscan power, even plundering Caere, not thirty miles from Rome. On the Adriatic coast he was supreme, and if Tarentum still was independent in name it was his tributary in fact, and was forced to receive his colonists into its lands.

So strong a despot might well have been free from little vanities; yet he wrote verses for public competition, and after proving himself a soldier of genius showed the whole world that he was a poet without talent. Fortunate in great undertakings and at the most critical moments of his life, he could not win a prize at Olympia, his horses ran away on the track, and the ship that brought home his representatives went to pieces on the Italian coast. His small undertakings failed, and his small talents betrayed him into fits of inordinate vanity, followed by disappointment out of all proportion with their cause. In this respect the man whom Publius Scipio called the bravest and keenest of his time was not superior to many other sovereigns and men of genius; for the man of genius looks upon his favourite minor talent as a prodigal son to whom all sins are forgiven, and it is perhaps only he whose chief gift is not beyond question, who dares not trust himself to play with a small accomplishment. Dionysius was great enough to have written even worse poetry than he probably produced.

What he did for Syracuse was so great that after two thousand and three hundred years, the remains of his work belong to the greatest monuments of antiquity, and it is impossible to follow the wall of Epipolae, or to wander through the enchanted gardens of the vast quarries, without marvelling at the man who deepened the one and built the other.

Cavern called the "Ear of Dionysius" Latomia del Paradiso, Syracuse

As is the case with many romantic characters in history, who lived in distracted times and appeared upon the stage of the world, like the gods in the plays of Aeschylus, to make order out of chaos by the mere miracle of their presence, a vast mass of fable and fantastic legend clings about the name of the elder Dionysius. He made prisons of the quarries, in which captives were kept so long that they married and had children and brought up a second generation of prisoners; and in order that he might know how they spoke of him he constructed the astounding acoustic cavern still called the Ear of Dionysius. He visited without mercy even the passing thought that an attempt upon his life might be possible; one of his favourite guards was executed for having dreamt that he murdered his master, on the singularly insufficient ground that before dreaming of such a deed he must have often thought of doing it. His own brother one day, when explaining to him the position of a fortress, borrowed a javelin from a guardsman in order to draw upon the sand with its point; the soldier was instantly executed having given up his weapon. Again, when playing ball, he laid aside his upper garment with his sword, giving them into the care of a favourite youth. One standing by said in jest that the sovereign seemed willing to trust his life to the lad, and the latter smiled at the words. Both were instantly put to death. It is said that he would never trust himself to the services of a barber, but that he used to make his own daughters clip his beard, or singe it with burning walnuts. In meetings of the people he would not speak from a platform, but built himself a stone tribune which was nothing less than a small tower. The legends say that he had his bed surrounded by a broad channel of deep water, crossing it on a plank which he drew after him; that he wore night and day an iron cuirass, and seldom was without weapons; that he employed an organized band of spies, both men and women, as the first Hiero had done; that neither his sons nor his brothers were allowed to approach him till his guards had changed every one of their garments, lest they should have some weapon concealed about them; and finally that he brought up his eldest son, who became Dionysius the second, in ignorance and solitude within the palace, allowing him no amusement nor occupation except carpentering. To him belongs the legend of the sword of Damocles, which has passed to proverbial use in successive ages, and the fable of Damon and Pythias belongs to his reign.

Of his cruelties, so far as concerns those of which there is historical evidence, it seems certain they were perpetrated from no bloodthirsty motive, but were necessary to his system of self-defence at a time when the murder of tyrants was so common as to seem natural and logical. Of temperate life and untiring industry, ambition was the only passion that could hold him. Long afterwards, during a drinking bout, Philip of Macedon asked the younger Dionysius how his father had found time to write poetry. "He used the time," answered the son, "which happier men like you and me spend in drinking together." Holm considers it a sign of his firm character that he lived in harmony with two wives at a time, dining daily with them both together, and indeed he seems to have lived peacefully with them and with his seven children. The great man's only weakness seems to have been for his own verses, and when at last, doubtless for political reasons, the prize was awarded in Athens to his tragedy, the 'Ransom of Hector,' he only outlived that great and final satisfaction to his vanity by a few days. It is even told that in his delight, he, the most moderate of men, drank so deeply as to cause his death. Yet he encouraged joyous excesses among his subjects, as many another despot has done since, and there is evidence that while himself leading what may almost be called a moral life, he preferred for his amusement the society of rakes, gamesters, and spendthrifts. Though it is said that he rarely laughed, he made jests of the kind that seemed witty to historians, but which have either lost their savour by two thousand years of repetition, or offend our sense of fitness by vulgar blasphemy of the gods, to whom, though false in our view, he owed the respect which good taste concedes to all objects of devotion and civilized belief.

Under him the Sicilian power reached its height, and we may make the sad reflection that in the past history of all great nations the acme of strength and culture has been attained under a despot, often under the first who has appeared after a long period of freedom. Dionysius ruled alone during thirty-eight years, one of the most extraordinary men of any age; he saved Hellenism from destruction in the central Mediterranean and he reduced chaos to order in founding a new and powerful state; but he destroyed freedom and the very meaning of it, root and branch.

He was succeeded by the younger Dionysius, his eldest son, who began life at twenty-eight years of age as one of the most powerful sovereigns in the west, and ended it as a schoolmaster in Corinth. Few dynasties have been enduring, of which the founder was a conqueror, and Dionysius the Second exhibited all the faults and weaknesses which were to be expected in a youth who had been brought up without experience of the world, still less of government, whose chief occupation had been a manual art, and whose only amusements had consisted in unbridled excess. It was no wonder that he could not wield the power which had fallen to him as an inheritance, or that he should have been completely dominated by a man who, although himself not strong of purpose, was a tower of strength compared with such a weakling.

This man was Dion, sometimes said to have been the father-in-law of the young prince, but who was really his brother-in-law; a Platonist, a mystic, and a dreamer, wise in his beginnings, devoted in his pursuit of an ideal, honourable, as some weak and good men are, with sudden lapses from the right that shock us the more because their right was so high; a man of sad and thoughtful disposition, who gradually degenerated from a noble beginning to a miserable end.

He conceived the plan of inducing Plato himself to make a second visit to Syracuse, that his influence might save the young Dionysius from destruction, and teach him to make a fact of the Ideal State, and the great philosopher fancied that his own opportunity was come at last and yielded to the tyrant's request. The aspect of the Syracusan court was changed, the sounds of revelry died away, the halls were strewn with sand that the master might draw geometrical figures upon them, and the scapegrace despot became as gentle and forgiving as an ideal Platonist should be. But he became as weak to the influence of his courtiers as he was docile to the new teachings of philosophy, and before long Dion was banished to the Peloponnesus and afterwards to Athens, under the thin pretence of an embassy. For a time Plato remained with the tyrant, against his will perhaps, for Dionysius made him live in the castle on Ortygia and had him closely watched. But a small war in which Syracuse became engaged soon required the attention of the sovereign, and the philosopher was suffered to depart to Greece. Yet he was induced to return a third time, and chiefly through his friendship for the banished Dion; but though he was received magnificently and pressed with splendid gifts which he refused to accept, he was not able to obtain anything for his friend, whose great possessions were presently confiscated, while Plato soon found himself treated almost like a prisoner, if not worse; for he had been constantly advising Dionysius to give up his life-guard, and the soldiers who now watched him, being of that body, hated him and would gladly have murdered him. But a ship having been sent from Greece by Archytas, Plato's friend, with orders to bring the philosopher home, he was allowed to sail without opposition. "I fear," said the tyrant when they parted, "that you and your friends will speak ill of me when you get home." "I trust," answered Plato, smiling, "that we shall never be so much at a loss for a subject of conversation as to speak of you at all."

Then Dionysius married his sister Arete, who was Dion's wife, to a courtier, against her will, and Dion's gentle nature was roused at last. He raised a small force of mercenary soldiers, in Zacynthus, that is now called Zante, and led them up to make a solemn sacrifice in the temple of Apollo; and though the moon was eclipsed on that very night, to the consternation of his men, his soothsayer Miltas persuaded them that the portent foretold the overshadowing of Dionysius' power, and they were satisfied. A storm drove the five small ships far to southward, and they made Sicily at last at Minoa, a Phoenician town west of Akragas. Dion landed by force but without bloodshed, and marching eastward gathered an army of twenty thousand men. The tyrant was known to be absent from Syracuse, and the letter that warned him of his enemies' approach was lost by the messenger, who had a piece of meat in the same wallet with it, and fell asleep under a tree: a wolf carried off the bag with all its contents. Dion passed on, and came within sight of Syracuse at dawn; in the level rays of the morning sun he sacrificed to Apollo for the freedom of the city and of Sicily, and his devoted followers crowned themselves with garlands. At the first news that Dion was at hand, the whole city rose, the tyrant's governor, Timocrates, fled in headlong haste, and the citizens came forth by thousands, in festal garments, to bring Dion through the gates in triumph. Entering the city, he caused it to be proclaimed that he was come to free Syracuse and all Sicily from the despot's hands, and to restore the democracy of earlier days. The wildest enthusiasm took possession of the people. Only a small body of loyal troops held Epipolae and the castle of Ortygia. The first place Dion seized at once, and he set free all the prisoners who were kept there. The castle withstood him for a time, and the result was an irregular war, in the course of which Dion lost his hold upon the people, was removed from his generalship by them to make way for his secret enemy Heraclides, and was obliged to retire to Leontini. In his absence the people were badly beaten by the tyrant's soldiers, who made a vigorous sally, slew many hundreds, and plundered the houses as if they had been in an enemy's city. Humiliated by this defeat and even more terrified than humiliated, the Syracusans sent messengers entreating Dion to return and save them. They found him in his house at sunset and appealed to him with all the eloquence of terror. His gentle nature, incapable of Achillean wrath, yielded to their entreaties, and calling his soldiers together he set forth at once to the rescue. At the news of his approach the besieged force withdrew into the castle, and once more the people hesitated as to whether they should admit Dion or not. But before morning the garrison of the castle sallied out again, and by way of hastening a solution of the situation set fire to the city. Dion reached the gates in time to witness the spectacle, but too late to save more than half the city. Heraclides surrendered to his old leader unconditionally, and many entreated Dion to give him up to the soldiery to be dealt with as they chose. But the kind-hearted man gently quoted the maxim of Plato and asked whether, because Heraclides had been envious and faithless, Dion should therefore be wrathful and cruel.

A formal siege of the castle was now undertaken, while the friends of Dionysius were gathering forces elsewhere to rescue it. But Dion's military operations were systematic and complete, the promised assistance did not reach the besieged, and they finally capitulated, on condition that the members of the tyrant's family should be allowed to depart with such treasure as they could take with them.

It will be remembered that Dion's expedition to liberate Syracuse from the tyrant had not been undertaken until his wife had been forcibly married to another. During the whole time and up to the capitulation of Ortygia, both she and Dion's son, and her mother Aristomache, had been within the castle, helpless to render him any assistance or to communicate with him. As he entered the stronghold, they came forward to meet him. First came Aristomache leading his son, while his wife Arete followed at a little distance with streaming eyes, for she knew not how Dion would look upon her after she had so long been the wife of another. But when he had embraced his son and Aristomache, the latter led forward his wife and spoke these words: "Your banishment has made us all miserable alike, and your victorious return has filled us all with joy, excepting her whom it was my ill fortune to see married by force to another. How shall she salute you now? Are you only her mother's brother, or will you be still her husband?" Then Dion clasped Arete in his arms very tenderly, and they took their son and went to his own house, where he intended live thenceforward. He was too conscientious to make himself despot in Dionysius' place, yet too aristocratic by nature to found a true democracy. He had freed Syracuse and liberated all Sicily, but he was unable to follow up his advantage. He dreamed of something between a monarchy and a commonwealth, and between those two forms of government there could only be an aristocracy. He attempted to control the people, refused to allow them to demolish the castle, and prevented them from tearing the ashes of the elder Dionysius from the tomb; he kept himself aloof from the masses and chose Corinthians for his counsellors; his intention, as Plutarch says, was to restrain the government of the people, which, according to Plato, is a warehouse of governments, and to set up a Lacedaemonian constitution. Meanwhile, Heraclides, whose life he had spared, opposed him at every turn and accused him of every crime against liberty, until the gentle Platonist fell into the state of exasperation which is peculiar to weak characters, and, out of sheer weariness and annoyance, consented to the suggestion of his friends that Heraclides should be murdered. It was his own death warrant. The deed being done, in a sudden revulsion of feeling he decreed that the murdered man should have a magnificent funeral at the public expense, and he addressed the people in a speech which was at once a political harangue, an impeachment, a panegyric of the dead man, and an apology for having slain him. After this his character and his intelligence rapidly degenerated; his only son, scarcely more than a boy, committed suicide in a fit of disappointment over a trifle; the furies of Heraclides pursued him even in his own house, and the gigantic spectre of a woman swept the hall of his home at nightfall with a phantom broom; a settled melancholy that was fraught with terror possessed him, and he saw a conspirator and a murderer in every man who approached him. Like the elder Dionysius, he employed spies throughout the city, but unlike him, he lacked the cynical courage to execute unhesitatingly every one whom he suspected. On pretence of creating an imaginary conspiracy for the sake of detecting it, and increasing Dion's popularity by a general pardon of those concerned, — a trick which could hardly deceive a schoolboy, — his former friends conspired in good earnest to take his life. They came to him at last in his own house, all unarmed, lest they should be searched by his guards and their weapons taken from them, and they trusted to slay him with their hands; but when they could not, because he was very strong, none dared to out to fetch a sword wherewith to kill him, and so they held him fast for the greater part of an hour; but at last one of their number who had remained outside, came to the window and passed in a knife to them. And so they slew him. That was the miserable end of the attempt to restore liberty in Sicily.

The leader of the murderers was one Callippus, an Athenian, who had long been Dion's friend. He instantly seized the power, and reigned thirteen months, a military despot hated by all alike, till he was driven out on his first attempt to extend his dominions. Two or three years later he was slain near Rhegium, and with the very knife by Dion had died, by two of his fellow-murderers.

Syracuse became the sport of any adventurer who could gain the momentary support of the soldiery, and at last it was the turn of the younger Dionysius, who had succeeded in holding Rhegium and Locri throughout the confusion of those years. Returning to Syracuse, he showed himself at his worst, and ruled by a system of terror which has rarely been equalled and never surpassed. Not Syracuse only but all Sicily had fallen into a miserable condition; the mercenaries employed by the tyrants at the height of their power overran the country far and wide, supporting themselves by plunder and revelling in every species of licentious excess. Anarchy reigned supreme; Carthage had concluded a treaty with Rome and again stretched out her grasping hand in an attempt to get possession of the coveted island; in utmost fear the Syracusans turned to Corinth for help, imploring the assistance of a general if not of an armed force. Their request was granted, and Corinth sent them a man whose name stands almost alone in history, the patriot soldier Timoleon, he who saved his brother's life in battle by a miracle of reckless courage, but gave him over to a just death when he seized the power and attempted to make himself the tyrant of Corinth.

We contemplate Timoleon's almost unattainable moral greatness with a sort of despair, and with realize that an example may be so perfect as to discourage all attempt at imitation. He risks his life with magnificent recklessness to save his brother from the enemies' spears, and then, with antique virtue, after using every means of affectionate persuasion in vain, he orders the same brother to be executed before his eyes, that his country may be saved from tyranny; yet being very human at heart, he withdraws from public life, and almost from the society of mankind, to mourn in solitude for nearly twenty years the deed which he would have done again. Emerging at last from his retirement in the hope of setting free an enslaved country, he exhibits, with the most exiguous resources, the most magnificent gifts of generalship, carries all before him in a series of brilliant actions, liberates Sicily, restores democratic freedom, vanquishes the Carthaginians, and establishes just laws. The idol of his adopted people, the arbiter of their destinies, and almost their predestined master, not a thought of holding the rulership assails him, nor is the lustre of his patriotism dimmed by the least breath of ambition; after teaching a nation to govern itself wisely, he retires to the peaceful privacy of an ordinary citizen's condition, and he lives out the calm remainder of his days in the enjoyment of the liberty he has created, and under the rare protection of the laws he has called into existence. It is indeed hard to see how human nature could approach nearer to perfection from the beginning to the end of a career fraught with danger, difficulties, and perplexing problems.

Timoleon's departure from Corinth was accompanied by the most propitious signs and auguries. Demeter and Persephone appeared to their priestesses in dreams, clad in the garb of travellers and promising to accompany and protect the expedition. When Timoleon sacrificed to Apollo in Delphi, a wreath embroidered with crowns and images of victory fell from its place and encircled his head; and when at last his ships put to sea, mysterious fires came down from heaven and floated through the darkness before them, night after night, until the ships made the Italian coast. Nor is the last occurrence perhaps altogether a fable, for in fair weather, and in certain conditions of the air, seafaring men are familiar with the lights of Saint Elmo, the electric glow that sometimes settles on the mastheads and hangs at the yardarms in balls of fire for whole nights together, and which must naturally have seemed to the ancients but nothing less than a heavenly portent.

The story of Timoleon's war of liberation must be briefly told. In Rhegium he found a Carthaginian fleet, of which the commanders were disposed to prevent his movement upon Syracuse; but in concert with the people of the city he called the Carthaginian generals to a council within the walls, and while long arguments were made to cause delay, Timoleon's fleet slipped out of the harbour and got to sea; then, when he received news that they were under way, he himself disappeared in the crowd, reached his own vessel, which had waited for him, and was beyond pursuit before the council broke up and the Carthaginians discovered that they had been tricked. Sailing down the east coast, he was received with open arms in Tauromenium, and he looked about for a second ally. At last the people of Hadranum, now Adernò, being divided into two parties, the one asked help of Timoleon, the other of Icetes or Hicetas, who held all of Syracuse except Ortygia and was in good understanding with the Carthaginians; Timoleon surprised and put to flight his force, and Hadranum opened its gates.

Dionysius was meanwhile driven to last extremities in his castle on the little island; he was hemmed in on all sides, and he saw that whether Icetes or Timoleon won the day, his own lordship was at an end. He sent messengers to Timoleon secretly, and treated with him for the surrender of the island, on the condition of being allowed to escape with one ship and all the treasure he could carry. This was granted; four hundred of Timoleon's men entered the fortress in spite of the vigilance of Icetes, and the Dionysian dynasty was at an end. Timoleon held Catania and supplied Ortygia with provisions by means of a number of small vessels which regularly ran the blockade. Icetes went out to attack Catania in order to destroy the base of supplies. He was not in sight of the latter place when news came that in his absence the Corinthians in Ortygia had succeeded in seizing Achradina, and had connected it with the island by hasty works, and he hurriedly returned to Syracuse. And now a long siege followed, with little fighting, and it came to pass that in the idle days Timoleon's Corinthian soldiers came out to catch fish in the ponds near the marsh, and the Greeks who were with Icetes came likewise, so that they made friendly acquaintance; for they had no reason for quarrelling except that they were mercenaries on opposite sides, and had to fight when they were led out to battle. They told each other that Icetes ought to side with Timoleon, and that both should drive out the Carthaginians, and presently it was rumoured that Icetes would do so. Thereupon, without striking another blow, the

Carthaginian general suddenly withdrew his whole army and fleet, and sailed away to Africa. They were hardly out of sight when Timoleon led up his force, and in a triple attack drove Icetes out of Syracuse altogether. He had accomplished the first part of his task, and he set to work to reorganize the liberated people.

He now showed his vast intellectual and moral superiority over Dion. The latter's first move was to establish himself in the castle on Ortygia, as if expecting to be attacked by the people he had freed; Timoleon called upon the inhabitants to raze the tyrant's fortress to the ground, and to build the people's tribunal upon the spot, and he began to make them frame laws which should be administered there, while he himself lived simply, openly, and unattended.

Sicily had been reduced to a desperate condition by civil war, and Syracuse, like many other Sicilian cities, was half depopulated. The grass grew high in the market-places, the deer and wild boar from the forests grazed under the very walls of the towns, and sometimes made their way into the deserted streets. The few rich survivors had retired to strong castles of their own in the mountain fastnesses, as men did in the desolation of the dark ages, and the poor had been enslaved or exterminated. The need of a new population was evident, and Timoleon called upon Corinth for colonists. The mother city sent ten thousand; the rest of Sicily together with Southern Italy sent fifty thousand; the new colonists consented to pay for the land and houses they occupied, and the old inhabitants actually paid for what was already theirs, in order that a public fund might be created. To increase the resources of the state, Timoleon took several cities from the Phoenicians, the most important of which was Entella, and sold them to Greek colonists, a proceeding which is justified when one considers the extent of the injuries done to the Greeks by the Carthaginians, but which doubtless contributed to bring on a new struggle with Carthage. The shameful retreat of the latter's general from Syracuse, almost without having struck a blow, led to his speedy disgrace, and though he died by his own hand, even suicide could not save him from infamy, and his dead body was nailed to the cross.

Carthage now prepared for another great expedition, Hasdrubal and Hamilcar were chosen as generals, the usual vast army of mercenaries landed at Lilybaeum, and another reign of terror began in Sicily. Timoleon's force was insignificant, and his war material was scanty; as he was marching to Akragas, a mutiny broke out in his little army, and a thousand of his mercenary Greeks deserted him and returned to Syracuse. The Carthaginians marched upon Entella, which Timoleon had taken from their people; he had determined to intercept the enemy, when he was checked by meeting with a number of mules laden with parsley; for parsley was used for funeral crowns, and the omen was therefore evil. But Timoleon took some of the leaves, and made a chaplet, and crowned himself, saying that parsley was used also for the victors in the Isthmian Games, and encouraged his men, saying that crowns were given them even before victory. So they took courage and marched, and a heavy mist hid the enemy from them, while they heard the inarticulate hum of the camp at no great distance; and when the mist began to lift the

Carthaginians were already crossing the river, with their chariots and a thousand men who carried white shields. So Timoleon sent down his cavalry, but the chariots drove furiously up and down in front of the enemy's ranks and the horses would not charge them.

Then Timoleon cried aloud to his foot-soldiers to follow him, and his voice was clearer and louder than the voice of a man, so that it was as if a god spoke to them; he took his sword and shield in his hands, and the trumpets screamed, and he rushed forward, and a great tempest with thunder and much rain had gathered behind him on the hill and came down with him and beat into the faces of his enemies, and the thunder roared, and the hail rattled on their iron breast-plates and brass helmets with a deafening noise, so that they could not hear the orders their officers gave; and the Greeks put them to sudden rout and wild confusion, and ten thousand of them were slain or drowned in the river, for they were weighed down by their heavy armour. This is the first time that as many as three thousand natives of Carthage were slain in a battle. After that the Greeks took the camp and all it held, with many prisoners; and so that expedition ended.

Now the Carthaginians, seeing that the Greeks were the bravest and most invincible of men, hired Greek soldiers to fight for them, and a new expedition was sent out with seventy ships, and sailed to Messina, where a dim war was fought of which not much is known; but three tyrants, Icetes of Leontini, Mamercus of Catania, and Hippo of Messina, were allied with the Carthaginians against Timoleon, and he beat them one by one; yet when peace was made he was obliged to leave Carthage the lordship of the western cities. Of the three despots, Hippo fell into the hands of his own people, and they scourged him and put him to death in the theatre of Messina, gathering thither all the children of the city to see the tyrant's end, that they might always remember it. Icetes was executed by the Corinthians as a traitor to the Greeks, and because he had drowned the wife and the sister of the son of Dion, the Syracusans also slew his wife and daughters after a mock trial. As for Mamercus, when Timoleon had beaten him in battle, he surrendered; but Timoleon gave him up to the Syracusans to judge him, which they did in the theatre. When they would not hear his defence, he, being unarmed, broke from his keepers, and running at great speed across the open orchestra, he threw himself forward upon his head, against the wall, hoping to die; but he lived to perish on the cross, like a common robber. And with his death the most strenuous part of Timoleon's task was accomplished. He had freed all Sicily from the tyrants, and he had reduced the power of Carthage. He repopulated the deserted cities of Sicily and taught them how to enrich and strengthen themselves, and unlike Dionysus the elder he did not aim at the aggrandizement of Syracuse to the detriment of all the rest: it was under his guidance that Akragas, which had never recovered from the Carthaginian conquest, became once more a strong and independent city.

He spent his old age, afflicted with total blindness, in encouraging the work he had begun; on important occasions, when his counsels could not be spared, he was carried to the theatre where the people went to deliberate, and every appearance was a triumph, followed by his immediate return to the privacy of his house given him by the city, in which he dwelt with his wife and his children, and in which at last he died, one of the most splendid types of human honour, courage, and wisdom that ever freed a nation from slavery.

Chosen youths bore his body over the ground where the tyrant's castle had stood, and the whole population of Syracuse followed it to the market-place, where the funeral pile was erected. His ashes were buried on the spot, and about his tomb a great gymnasium was built. Games were then and there instituted in his memory, and the proclamation which decreed them called him 'the destroyer of tyrants, the subduer of barbarians, the man who had peopled again great cities that lay desolate, and who had restored to all Sicilians their laws and ancient rights.'

A Sicilian courtyard

The immediate result of Timoleon's labours was not lasting, but it was long before the spirit he had instilled into the life of Syracuse altogether disappeared, and even under the worst tyranny of Agathocles some of the forms of freedom were preserved. During some twenty years after Timoleon's death, the city remained free, and as is often the case in prosperous times the records of that period are few and confused. Agriculture prospered, commerce throve, architects built, sculptors modelled, and poets made verses; but history is silent and only resumes her labour to tell of new disasters. The story of the extraordinary man to whom the tyranny of Syracuse next fell is so fantastic that it deserves telling for its own sake, as well as for some resemblance that it bears to the fable of Oedipus.

In Rhegium, in the days of Timoleon, there lived a Greek called Carcinus, of noble birth and great possessions, and he was exiled by his fellow-citizens, and went and dwelt in Sicily, in the city of Thermae, which is now Termini, on the north side of the island. He married a woman of that city, and when a son was about to be born to him, he was visited by evil dreams. At that time certain Carthaginians were going to the oracle of Delphi, and he besought them to ask for him the interpretations of his visions. They brought him word that his son should be the cause of great misfortunes to the Carthaginians and to all Sicily; therefore, when the child was born, he caused it to be exposed in a desert place, and set a watch lest anyone should come and save it or by any means keep it alive. Yet the child did not die, and the mother watched her opportunity until the guard grew careless, and she took up her child and fled with it to the house of her brother and named it Agathocles, after her own father. The child grew up and was very beautiful, and stronger than other children, and when he was seven years old, his father, not knowing him, praised his beauty and strength, his mother answered, feigning sadness, "So would our boy have been, if you had let him live." Then Carcinus repented suddenly of what he had done and turned away weeping bitterly; but his wife comforted him and told him the truth, and he acknowledged his son and brought him home. By and by Carcinus left Thermae with all his family and went and lived in Syracuse, where he died soon after, and Agathocles grew up with his mother. She, believing in great things for him, caused a little statue of him to be made and set it up as an offering before one of the temples, and at once a swarm of bees settled upon it and built their hive; the soothsayers interpreted the sign to mean that the boy should win high fame.

He grew up of great stature and marvellous strength, and a rich man of Syracuse, named Damas, took him under his protection and caused him to be appointed one of the leaders of a thousand in the army. Damas died childless, and Agathocles immediately married the rich man's widow, and became thenceforward one of the most important persons in Syracuse. He kept his military position in spite of his wealth and showed extraordinary military talent; but when he did not receive the advancement he expected, after a brilliant engagement in Italy, and when no attention was paid to his claims, he left the city and seems to have lived for some time as a sort of free lance, while cherishing the most adventurous designs. He even besieged Crotona on his own account, and failing to take it, sought employment as a general of Tarentine mercenaries. Meanwhile, the party that had opposed him in Syracuse fell from power, and he returned to his home, to find himself before long in his old command of a thousand men, opposed to the Carthaginians, with whom the fallen party had allied itself. In spite of his courage and brilliant actions the Syracusans would not confer upon him the generalship, since it was clear to them from the first that he aimed at making himself despot. Turning upon him as suddenly as they had turned upon the opposite party, they bade him quit the city at once, and sent out men to kill him as he should ride by; but he, being warned, dressed a slave in his own armour and clad himself in rags. He escaped, and the slave was murdered in his stead.

Being now banished, he immediately came to an understanding with his country's enemies, the Carthaginians, and by their influence upon the oligarchy of six hundred which now ruled Syracuse he obtained his recall, and took solemn oath before the people to do nothing contrary to their freedom or their rights. He had now reached the stage at which aspirants to despotism appear as the friends of the oppressed populace, and he did not hesitate to use his power for the destruction of the oligarchy. On pretence of reducing a small revolution in the interior, he was allowed to get together a chosen force, and on the day appointed for his departure he gathered his soldiers in the buildings about the tomb of Timoleon in the market-place. In an address of stirring eloquence he accused the six hundred of setting him aside from public offices on account of his attachment to the people; and as his impeachment turned to a fiery arraignment and at last to a tremendous invective, the soldiers cried out for the blood of the accused. Then, as if only yielding to pressure, he ordered that the trumpets should give the signal to fall upon the six hundred and upon all who should help or harbour them. The gates were shut against any who should escape death, and the infuriated soldiers stormed every house which might give shelter to their prey. The streets ran blood. Four thousand of the richest citizens were put to the sword, and many perished in attempting to leap from the walls in flight. Some were brought bound before Agathocles to be executed or banished at his will. About six thousand escaped to Akragas.

On the following day Agathocles called a general meeting of the people, and, acting out the favourite comedy of the despot, he declared that he had freed the city from the tyranny of the oligarchy, that he was worn out by the struggle for a righteous cause, and that he refused to keep even the semblance of a power to which he had never aspired. Thereupon, he laid down his military cloak and turned away, well knowing what was to follow. The thousands who were before him were the men who yesterday had plundered the houses of the nobles at his word; they would not lose a leader who might bid them plunder again; they unanimously declared him their general and dictator, and he made a pretence of refusing the dignity only that he might be the more certain of holding it for his life.

From the first he showed that he had profited by the example of Dion the unsuccessful, and of the half-deified Timoleon. Strong, brave, and no longer young, he scorned to surround himself with a body-guard, and took that surer means of safety which lay in binding the populace to him by the joint bonds of gratification and greed; for he gave them what was not his, and promised to give them whatsoever was not theirs already. What the nature of his patriotism was, is clear from the fact that he did not hesitate to ally himself with the Carthaginians, the hereditary enemies of his country.

Tyranny is as often remembered by the people for the immediate advantages it brings them, as for the evils it sooner or later inflicts. The order which Agathocles introduced by force was more advantageous to Sicily than the chaos that had followed when the quarrelsome nature of the Greek people had rendered futile the noble institutions of Timoleon; and though it is true that under Agathocles Sicily produced no famous artist or poet, there can be no doubt but that her wealth and power increased suddenly and prodigiously. It would be impossible to explain otherwise how the tyrant could have so far got the advantage of Carthage, after the old quarrel was renewed, as to carry war into Africa, winning many battles and failing only at the last when he had been on the point of decisive victory.

Friendly relations were broken by the discontent of the Carthaginians when their general interfered to make peace between Agathocles and the Greek cities, and so arranged matters as to give Syracuse the lordship of the island, with the exception of the old Phoenician towns; for the tyrant's treaty had really been rather a personal agreement with Hamilcar than a national affair, and Carthage did not hesitate to set it aside. Then began the usual gathering of mercenaries, and the preparations for a great invasion, while Agathocles, on his side, collected a great force of mercenaries, though not without difficulty; for whereas Dionysius the elder had always succeeded in making Sicily feel that he was her true representative and natural leader against foreign influence, Agathocles was distrusted by many and opposed by not a few, and his frightful cruelties may fairly be ascribed to the exceptional danger of his situation. He was not even a native of the city he ruled. He held his position, not by employing spies and paying life-guards whom he could implicitly trust to destroy the few who dared to plot against his life, but by the wholesale massacre of every party that was organized to oppose him; and when he had thus cleared the situation by bloodshed, he went about with careless courage and without ever showing the slightest suspicion of individuals.

Street in Syracuse to-day

Carthage was not ready for war until he had completely established his supremacy in Sicily, and when at last her fleet put to sea, a violent storm destroyed many ships with the troops they carried. Another Hamilcar — the name was frequent — commanded the force, and in spite of all losses succeeded in encamping with an army of forty-five thousand men on Mount Ecnomus, the huge headland that juts out to the eastward of Girgenti; Agathocles encamped over against him, still further east and beyond the salt river. Both armies waited and watched, sending down foraging parties to drive up cattle from the valley. Then Agathocles, having observed how the enemy conducted those small expeditions, laid an ambush for them, fell upon them unawares, drove back the few survivors to the camp, and taking advantage of the momentary confusion, led a general attack. Before the Carthaginians could give battle the Greeks were upon them, filling the ditches that protected their camp and tearing down the stockades. The battle would have been won but for the Balearic slingers, whose slings hurled stones weighing an English pound, and who at last drove the Greeks out; and then defeat followed upon repulse, as an unexpected reënforcement landed from Africa, and defeat became disaster in a general rout, in which no less than seven thousand of the Greeks were slaughtered. Yet strange to say the survivors remained faithful to their leader, who burned his camp and fell back first upon Gela, now Terranova, and at last upon Syracuse, while Hamilcar made a triumphal progress through the island, the cities opening their gates to him as to a liberator. Agathocles seemed lost. He saved himself by a stroke of astonishing boldness. He determined to leave a small garrison in Syracuse and to invade Carthage without delay, while all her forces were abroad. It was the conception of a man of genius, and though he did not accomplish the conquest of Carthage, which was reserved for the vast power of Rome, he succeeded in freeing Sicily and in reestablishing his despotic position. Hamilcar had pursued him to Syracuse, had besieged the city, and was actually blockading the harbour with his fleet, when Agathocles set forth on his expedition. He waited until the Carthaginian ships put out to capture a convoy of vessels with provisions for the city, and sailed out with sixty men-of-war. The Carthaginians saw him, supposed he meant to give battle, and drew up to await his attack, and by the time they understood that he was heading to southward he had gained enough distance to greatly reduce the chances of being overtaken. Nevertheless, the Carthaginian fleet gave chase, while the corn° ships quietly entered the harbour, and Syracuse was provisioned for a long siege. The whole affair was one of those brilliant manoeuvres that prove the born general.

The Greeks believed that they were beyond pursuit, heading for the African coast, when, on the morning of the day, the Carthaginian ships hove in sight, still in full chase, and gaining visibly. A race for life and death began, in the dead calm, and the oars pulled desperately, hour after hour. If the Greeks could reach the land and intrench themselves, they would have the advantage, for their enemies would have to attack them from the water's edge; but if they were overtaken on the high sea, they could expect nothing but destruction in a battle with a force so far superior to their own; and Syracuse would be lost also. Still the Carthaginians crept up astern, hour after hour, while Agathocles counted the miles that lay between him and the land, and knew that his fate hung by a hair. His men knew it too, and they reached the shore in time, southwest of what is now Cape Bon, in a strong place at the entrance to an ancient stone quarry of vast extent, and they threw up fortifications and beached their vessels. But the leader knew that the ships were a weakness and a temptation to flight, where men were to win or die, and with a heroism that has seldom been equalled, and commanding an obedience that has never been surpassed, he burned the fleet as it lay on the shore, firing his own vessel with his own hand, while every captain followed his example.

During the fire, the Carthaginians, at some distance from the shore, were filled with joy; but their mood changed when they saw that Agathocles was leading his army to the interior, without waiting to give battle. It was too late to overtake him now; he was entering the richest part of their country with a large army of the bravest men in the world, and men whose only hope lay in victory; the Carthaginians fell to weeping and mourning and draped the bows of their ships with black.

Agathocles marched on without hindrance, seized the rich city of Megalopolis, plundered it, and took Tunes next, only ten miles from Carthage. The great city, even in such sudden and utter need, when her main force was either in Sicily or at sea, was able to send out forty-one thousand men and two thousand chariots to meet the invaders. Agathocles had less than fifteen thousand soldiers, all told; he helped himself by strange stratagems that savour of Homeric times, spreading out the shield-covers of his heavy-armed infantry on staves, to represent a reserve of soldiers that did not exist, and losing a number of owls among his men, who suddenly took great courage as the birds sacred to Pallas settled blinking upon their helmets and shields. One thinks of the young Louis Napoleon and the trained eagle that was allowed to fly at his first landing — a trick which Ulysses might have invented and Homer described.

The Greeks fought like madmen, the drivers of the enemy's chariots were shot down and the cavalry pelted to death, the famous heavy-armed infantry charged, the chief general of the Carthaginians was slain, and their ranks wavered, — the next in command turned traitor, it is said, and commanded a hasty retreat, which presently became a rout and massacre, and Agathocles was master of the field. In the Carthaginian camp he found twenty thousand pairs of manacles, brought out to shackle the Greeks who were to have been taken prisoners.

With the small force at his disposal he could not hope to take the strong city, fortified as it was at every point and more than amply provisioned. But it was the policy of Carthage to allow no other town to protect itself by fortifications, lest any should turn against her, and Agathocles seized one place after another, with vast booty. Meanwhile the Carthaginians sent to Hamilcar in Sicily for help, and made horrible burnt sacrifices of many little children to their cruel gods.

Hamilcar received the news of the Carthaginian defeat before Syracuse and, at the same time, the bronze beaks of the ships burned by Agathocles were brought to him. Hoping to prevent the beleaguered were trophies, and proclaimed to them the defeat and destruction of Agathocles, calling upon them to surrender at once; but they held firm, and before long they were informed of the truth in an unexpected manner. For Agathocles had sent a vessel with the news of his victory; it appeared off Syracuse in the morning, and after an exciting race, in which it escaped the enemy's blockade, it entered the harbour with flying streamers, the whole ship's company drawn up on deck, and intoning a victorious chaunt. Hamilcar tried to take advantage of the excitement that reigned in the city in order to storm a weak point, but he was repulsed, and soon afterwards despatched five thousand men to the help of Carthage. Agathocles performed marvels of quick marching, as he darted from one point to another, subduing the cities in succession, but unable to hold them for any length of time, for lack of men. He created a sort of floating domination of fear that centred round him in a movable kingdom wherever he appeared, but which could not under any circumstances become a permanent conquest; he plotted and conspired with native princes and Carthaginian traitors to obtain some influence more lasting than that of the sword, and more than once it seemed as if he might succeed. For instance, there was a certain Ophellas, who had been a general with Alexander the Great and had made himself prince of Cyrene on the African coast; Agathocles induced him by great promises to join in the conquest of Carthage, and the old soldier, after overcoming the difficulties of a three months' march through a desert country, reached Tunes with over ten thousand fighting men and as many camp-followers, besides women and children. Agathocles did not hesitate to do one of the most atrociously treacherous deeds in history; he wanted the troops without their leader, whose influence might rival his own; he spent a few days in friendly intercourse with him in his camp, and then returning to his own soldiers, accused Ophellas to them of attempting his life. Wrought up to fury by his words, they rushed upon the camp of his new ally, a great number of whose men were absent to collect provisions, and after a short and desperate struggle, Ophellas was slain. Agathocles then took the army into his own pay and shipped the camp-followers with all the women and children to Syracuse. A storm dispersed the miserable convoy, most of the ships sank, one or two were driven as far north as Ischia in the bay of Naples, and but a very few reached Syracuse alive.

Meanwhile, the conspiracy of the Carthaginian traitors broke out in open revolution in the capital, under the leadership of Bomilcar; but they had miscalculated their strength, the movement was crushed, and he himself was executed. This was in reality the end of Agathocles' hopes in Africa; had the revolution succeeded, he would without doubt have destroyed Bomilcar as cynically as he had murdered Ophellas, and Carthage might have been his; but, as it turned out, the Carthaginians learned their own strength by the failure of the attempt, and from that time forward the power of the Greeks diminished. Not realizing the situation, Agathocles left his son in command and crossed over to Sicily with a small force; for while the Carthaginians had all this time maintained the blockade of Syracuse, Akragas, once more an independent and powerful city, was making an attempt to dominate Sicily, and to that end had taken into its friendship all those whom Agathocles had exiled. In a short time, however, Agathocles put a stop to these schemes, and, having effectually checked the Akragantines, had only to contend with the exiled Syracusan aristocracy under Dinocrates. Meanwhile, in his absence, his son suffered a succession of defeats in Africa, and found himself driven down to Tunes, and so hemmed in that he sent an urgent appeal to his father to return and help him. It was some time before Agathocles was able to leave Sicily, and when he reached Africa, he found himself with a small force opposed to one of those enormous armies which the Carthaginians again and again collected in the course of their wars. They, on their side, did not desire battle unless Agathocles attacked them, and when he did so, they had no difficulty in driving him back to his position with fearful loss, and the end of the war was hastened by a hideous fire which broke out in the Carthaginian camp on the following night. As usual after a victory, the handsomest of the captives were burnt alive as a sacrifice to the gods; a sudden squall drove the flames from the altar upon the sacred tent, which caught fire and set the neighbouring tents of the generals in a blaze. In an instant the whole Carthaginian camp, consisting chiefly of huts of reeds and of straw, became a sea of fire, and the entire army fled in the direction of Carthage, in the wildest confusion. A large body of Libyans deserted from the Greek army, believing that the flames proceeded from bonfires lighted to celebrate the Carthaginian victory. When they attempted to join the Carthaginians, however, they were taken for a hostile force, in the confusion, and thousands of them were slain. The rest returned to the Greeks, and, being again taken for enemies, were most of them slaughtered. Had Agathocles known the condition of the Carthaginians on that night, he might have struck a decisive blow; but the truth was only known in the morning, when the remainder of the Libyans deserted in a body.

The situation was now desperate, and Agathocles attempted to escape to Sicily, intending to leave the rest of his army to its fate. His son, who was to have been left also, discovered his father's treachery, and disclosed it to the soldiers, who seized Agathocles and loaded him with chains. It was not until a false alarm of the enemy's approach was raised in the camp that the tyrant was released from his bonds, in order that he might lead the Greeks in a final attempt to save themselves. But Agathocles had more regard for his own safety. He was brave to recklessness, but not devoted; when a cause was lost, he abandoned it. With a few faithful followers, he got on board a small ship and slipped away in the night. The next day the soldiers murdered both his sons, and treated with the Carthaginians for peace, which was granted. Those of the Greeks who refused the terms were either crucified or forced to work in chains upon the lands they had laid waste but a few months earlier. It is said that the sons of Agathocles were slain on the anniversary of that day on which their father had murdered Ophellas.

But the career of the great adventurer was not yet over, nor was his influence in Sicily by any means gone. Landing in Selinus, he gathered a small force, which he led at once, with the unerring instinct of the born tyrant, against Segesta, the ancient rival and enemy of the Selinuntines. After laying a heavy tribute upon the city, he suddenly accused the citizens of attempting to murder him, and turned his soldiers upon them with orders to spare no living thing. He caused the rich men to be tortured before him, till they revealed the hiding-place of their treasures, and they had them put to death. Only the most beautiful boys and girls were spared to be sold as slaves in Italy. The city was levelled to the ground, and the very name of the place was changed when he gave the site to be inhabited by those of his adherents who would take it. That was the end of Segesta, and of the great city that in its day had brought so much evil upon Sicily; nothing survived the destroying wrath of Agathocles but the little lonely theatre high on the overhanging hill, and the great temple that still stands in its dark beauty up the deserted mountain side.

Greek Theatre at Segesta

But this was not all. The army of Africa which he had abandoned in its last need had murdered his two sons, and they also must be avenged. He sent word to his brother Antandros to take vengeance upon all the relatives of the soldiers he had left behind him in Africa, and Antandros executed the order to the letter. Thousands of old men, women, and children were driven down to the seashore and slaughtered on the beach like sheep. The sea was red with their blood and none dared to bury their bodies.

Gathering strength, as it were, from each new deed of terror, and imposing himself upon the Sicilians by fear rather than by strength, he turned against the party of the exiles, whose army counted nearly thirty thousand men, and with a force of scarcely six thousand defeated them totally in a single battle. It is needless to say that he massacred in cold blood several thousands of the prisoners he took, but it is a strange fact that he spared Dinocrates himself, treated him with the greatest kindness, and employed him as a general of his troops during the rest of his life.

From that time forward the power of the hoary tyrant was unchecked, and he extended his dominions far up the mainland and through the islands, laying Lipari under tribute and seizing Corcyra, which is Corfu, after completely vanquishing a Macedonian fleet; and when the people of that island complained that he laid waste their land, he laughed and said it was the vengeance of the Sicilians because Ulysses, an island man, had blinded the Sicilian shepherd Polyphemus long ago; and again, on his return from that expedition, he massacred two thousand of his soldiers who dared to demand their pay that was overdue. He plundered Crotona, too, by a piece of outrageous treachery, and the gradual decay of the great southern city began from that day, and continued through the wars that followed; and he who stands by the solitary column which is all that remains of Hera's temple, may remember that Agathocles must have sacrificed there in gratitude to the gods for the abomination they had permitted him to work in the beautiful city.

He made himself also a friend of Ptolemy Soter and married that king's daughter by Berenice; and he gave his own daughter to Pyrrhus the Epirote conqueror; he also allied himself with Demetrius, king of Macedonia, who was called Besieger of Cities, and he perhaps dreamt of conquests in the east. But most of all he desired to humble the Carthaginians and to be revenged upon them for the defeats he had suffered at their hands, and he was seventy-two years of age when he began to fit out a great expedition against them.

But his destiny overtook him before his ships were ready to sail out from Syracuse. He had a favourite slave, named Mainon, whom he had brought from Segesta and trusted, whose eyes had looked upon the slaughter of his people and had seen his home levelled to the earth; and though this slave smiled, and did his service, and was promoted to high office, he would not forgive, and he waited for his opportunity more than sixteen years. Then he took a tooth-pick which the tyrant used, and he rubbed upon it a very subtle poison, which bred a dreadful corruption, with unspeakable pain, first in the mouth and by and by through the whole body. So when Agathocles had lost even his power of speech, Mainon and those who hated him took him and laid him still alive upon his pyre; and so he perished, in the year 289 B.C., as strange a compound of genius, cruelty, reckless courage, and shameful faithlessness as ever ruled by alternate terror and popularity.

It is said that during the awful and protracted sufferings caused by the poison, he formally presented the Syracusans with their freedom, hoping, perhaps, by a piece of theatrical magnanimity to obtain the privilege of dying in his bed. We do not know the truth, but he was no sooner dead in the flames of his own funeral pile than the people seized upon his possessions, destroyed his statues, and banished all his mercenaries, attendants, and creatures. Even Mainon, who had delivered them of the tyrant, fled from the city. He afterwards raised a force among Agathocles' veterans and attempted to seize Syracuse, but was successfully opposed by the people, who chose a certain Icetes for their general. As Holm says, with his usual keenness, it is clear that Syracuse remained a free city for a time, as the citizens immediately made war upon each other.

The days of Sicilian unity, such as it had been under Dionysius and Agathocles, were over, and were never to return. Icetes seized the tyranny of Syracuse, and tyrants sprang up in other cities, while Carthage still held her possessions in the west, and the Italian mercenaries of Agathocles founded a state of some power in the north, calling themselves Mamertines from Mamers, the Oscan god Mars, familiar in Roman mythology. It was to be foreseen that during the internal struggles which decimated the population of Syracuse, and surely destroyed its power, the Carthaginians would make another attempt at conquest. They appeared with a hundred ships and fifty thousand men and laid siege to the city as of old. Then Syracuse appealed to Pyrrhus, once the friend of Agathocles, who was called the Eagle and the Alexander of his day, and whose alliance had already been sought by Tarentum against the Romans. He dreamed of conquering all Sicily, all Italy, all the world, and he equipped himself for a great struggle, and carried war into the heart of the Roman country. He beat the Romans in battle, but he knew, and said frankly, that a few more such victories would ruin him. He was in winter quarters in Tarentum when the Syracusan ambassadors came to him and implored his help. Hoping for easier conquests, he set out for Tauromenium with his army and his famous elephants. The Carthaginians did not await his coming, but withdrew with their fleet and their forces, and he entered Syracuse in triumph; the rival factions united to deliver up their city, their fleet, their army, and their treasure to his care. But he was determined to drive the Carthaginians out of Sicily altogether, and he now advanced westward with more than thirty thousand men, accompanied by two hundred ships that sailed round the coast.

Before Eryx, the lofty stronghold above Drepanon, a position which even now looks almost impregnable, he went forward alone and fully armed, and made his vow of games and sacrifices to Hercules; the trumpets sounded, the scaling-ladders were set against the walls, and he himself was the first to reach the rampart. Hand to hand he grappled with the foe, stabbing, thrusting, wrestling with superhuman strength, unhurt in the thick of the perilous fray, till men shrank away from him in awe, as if he had been a god, and the fortress was taken with great slaughter. A half-ruined mediaeval castle, partly a town gaol, is built round all that remains of Aphrodite's temple — a bit of marble, a tank hollowed in the rock, and the marvel of Sicily lying far below in a haze of colour. As he stood there, the Molossian king must have felt that he could take the island in the hollow of his hand; and so he did. But he used his conquest ill, and he tried to press the people to serve under him against Carthage, until they rebelled; and he murdered some of the great in Syracuse, as the tyrants had always done; but before his expedition was ready he found himself so hemmed in by treachery, smouldering revolution, and sedition, that he took an excuse to go back to Italy and left the island to itself. It is told that as he sailed away he looked back, and said to those about him that they were leaving behind a great field, in which the Romans and the Carthaginians might exercise their arms. And so it came to pass, for he was beaten by the Romans at the river by Beneventum, on the same ground where Charles of Anjou destroyed Manfred and his army fifteen hundred years later, and where many other famous fights were fought in after times.

With the reign of Hiero the second the story of the Greeks in the south hastens to its close, while the vast shadow of Rome spreads wide over the mainland and the islands. With the departure of Pyrrhus and the consequent freedom from all restraint, the old troubles broke out in Syracuse, the usual consequences followed, and while the citizens took one side, the soldiers took the other. The troops chose two generals, Hiero and another; they entered the city by treachery, got possession of the power, and from that time Hiero appears alone in command. He was a man of no great birth, but as soon as he had made himself ruler, the usual fables and legends were told of his childhood and early years; how he had been exposed to die of hunger as an infant, and afterwards recognized by his father; how, when he was a boy in school, a wolf rushed in and tore his tablets from his hand, and how, when he ran out to follow the wild beast and get them back, the schoolhouse fell in, and he alone was saved of all the children; owls perched upon his lance, and eagles on his shield, in short, of him was told the whole cycle of fairy tales, which, for the people, distinguished the great man from the command crowd. Yet in one respect he was unlike the rest of those strong men who had grasped the power with rude hands and held it with an iron grip before him; he was young, kind, and gentle, and after the first bold stroke he seems to have held his own, or what he had taken for his own, more by the love of his subjects than any rougher means. To strengthen his position he married the lovely Philistis, through whom he allied himself, by the female line, with the great house of Dionysius. Of all the beautiful heads which we find upon the gold and silver coins of Sicily, and there are many, none can compare with that of Hiero's queen. One may fancy that Helen of Troy had such a face, or Semiramis, or divine Athene herself, but it is hard to believe that so fair a woman ever lived; and if such little history of her as has come down to us be true, she was as good and wise as she was beautiful.

Coin with the head of Queen Philistis

Hiero could no longer hope to face Carthage in war as Agathocles had done, still less to stem the tide of Rome's advancing might; he could not even hope to rule all Sicily, and he contented himself with opposing the nearer and more dangerous enemies of Syracuse. Foremost of these were the Mamertines, who had already given Pyrrhus trouble and whose compact strength was penetrating into the interior of Sicily like a wedge. Hiero did not ally himself with the Romans, but succeeded in keeping on good terms with them by occasionally doing them a service, and while they were engaged in conquering the people of Rhegium, he endeavoured to make himself master of Messina on the other side of the straits. After taking a number of small towns belonging to the Mamertines, he fought a pitched battle with them near Messina itself and so completely defeated them that they were about to abandon the city, when a Carthaginian fleet appeared, not with the open intention of helping the Mamertines, but with such a considerable force as left no doubt of their ultimate intentions, in Hiero's mind. Contenting himself with the victory he had won, he withdrew to Syracuse, where the people crowned him king with great festivities and rejoicing. From this time forward, Messina was coveted by three powers, — by Hiero himself, by the Carthaginians, and by Rome; and as the population divided itself into two parties, the one for Carthage, the other for the Romans, it was almost a foregone conclusion that the latter should gain the upper hand. And so it happened. The Mamertines sent an embassy to

Rome from Messina, asking for help, in the year 265 B.C., and the favourable answer returned by the Romans became the cause of the first Punic war.

But this was not the end of Hiero's reign, for the events which followed occupied a considerable time and it was not until he had governed more than fifty years, and was nearly ninety years of age, that he at last left his kingdom to his grandson, who, after a series of mistakes chiefly attributable to his advisers, lost his life by the hands of conspirators and left his kingdom a prey to the Romans.

It must not be forgotten that during Hiero's long reign, Sicily became the battlefield of Rome and Carthage, as Pyrrhus had seen that it must, and that the first part of the struggle for empire occupied no less than three and twenty years, during which the war was waged without ceasing from one end of Sicily to the other, through more than half of Italy and over many hundred miles of sea. It must be remembered, however, that the first Punic war was called the Sicilian war in Rome, and that the first move of importance made by the Romans was the capture of Messina, or perhaps, as we should say, the occupation of that city, since Caius Claudius got possession of it without striking a blow. As the Carthaginians had frequently done on former occasions, they now landed their forces at Lilybaeum and marched along the southern coast towards Akragas, which now becomes Agrigentum in history. But the situation was not the same as in former times, since the adversary of Carthage was no longer Syracuse but Rome; and it was the object of Hanno, the Carthaginian general, to make alliance with the Sicilian cities against a common enemy instead of destroying everything he found in his way, as his predecessors had done. Hiero and the Syracusans joined him, as Agrigentum had already agreed to do, and the Sicilian armies moved up to the neighbourhood of Messina, where it was expected that the fighting should begin. Before attempting to bring over his troops the Roman general, who was the consul Appius Claudius, attempted to persuade both the Carthaginians and Hiero to retire. As soon as he had received their refusal, he brought a large force over by night, in all manner of little craft, of the roughest and poorest description, whereupon he got the nickname 'Caudex,' which may be interpreted to mean the trunk of a tree hollowed to form a boat, in fact what we familiarly call a 'dug-out.' When one considers the difficulty of navigating the straits of Messina at the present day, when steam vessels under way sometimes become unmanageable in the currents and are driven into collision, it must be admitted that what Appius Claudius accomplished was no light undertaking, even with the help of fishermen and boatmen who knew the waters; yet the immediate result of the daring move was of less importance than might have been expected. Hiero and his troops were nearer to Messina than the Carthaginians, and sustained the first attack, the result of which was so much to their disadvantage that Hiero withdrew towards Syracuse on the following night with all his force, and evidently with the intention of withdrawing from his alliance with Carthage as soon as possible. Left to deal with the Carthaginians only, the Romans found them strongly intrenched between the little lagoons, which are still to be seen near the Faro, and the sea, and after a fruitless attempt to carry the works Appius Claudius left a garrison in Messina and made a move against Syracuse. He accomplished nothing, however, though he exposed himself to great personal risk, and he soon afterwards retired to Italy.

In a book of the present dimensions it is impossible to narrate in detail the stirring events of the first Punic war, even so far as they concern Sicily. The reader to whom German or Italian is familiar should read the masterly work of Holm, whom I have followed very closely in the main, and of whom Professor Freeman says that he appears to have collected everything of value in Sicilian history, and from the most varied sources. The principal matter with which we are concerned is the general condition of affairs in the south, when the first war with Carthage began, and the general result upon the country when the war ended, after a duration of twenty-two years.

When Pyrrhus had been decisively beaten, Rome ruled the south of Italy to the Straits, having gradually got possession of all those rich Greek cities, and their dependencies, which had still refused to acknowledge her supremacy after she had finally defeated the Samnites and Gauls at Sentinum in 295 B.C. Her occupation of Messina gave her a hold upon Sicily, which was before long greatly strengthened by the more or less voluntary submission of a great number of other cities that foresaw the result of the struggle and wished to be on the winning side, even though the Romans were exacting allies. As for Hiero, he waited and temporized, with a skill at which we can only guess, but which proves him to have possessed that true historical sense that alone can give a keen intuition of future history, and which has been possessed by every really great statesman in all times; and after manoeuvring to avoid anything like a battle with the Romans, so long as he was still nominally on the Carthaginian side, he became convinced that the Romans were to be the winners, and he openly allied himself with them. A Carthaginian fleet which arrived near Syracuse soon afterwards, ostensibly to help him, but of course in the hope of getting control of the city as a base of operations, sailed away again. The conditions of the alliance acknowledged Hiero as king of a small territory in the southeast corner of the island, but required of him the payment of a proportionate tribute to Rome, and it is no wonder if Hiero, remembering the deeds of his predecessors, who had never really consolidated their power, should have supposed that Rome could conquer Carthage with comparative ease. From the outbreak of the first Punic war to the destruction of Carthage, the fight lasted a hundred and eighteen years; but though Hiero was deceived as to the magnitude of the memorable struggle, his judgment of the result was correct, and his instinct was not at fault in regard to the immediate advantages of the alliance he made. If he had remained the friend of Carthage, there can be no doubt but that Syracuse would have become their chief stronghold, instead of Agrigentum, and would have suffered the final disaster which overtook their city. Instead, and without at any time performing any brilliant action, or winning any great battle, he shielded Syracuse from danger throughout his reign, and at last made himself so indispensable to Rome that she was forced to accept from him a present of money, which the Senate would have given much to refuse, for the sake of Rome's dignity; yet, as soon as the first long war was over, he helped the Carthaginians to put down the great mutiny that broke out in their own army.

His character was upright and honourable in the extreme, and while protecting his small kingdom from the consequences of the war which was being waged between the two great nations, he devoted himself to its welfare in every other way, improved its agriculture and made it one of the most important trading states in the world, at a time when the commerce of Carthage was necessarily greatly reduced. The position occupied by Syracuse under Hiero may aptly be compared with that of Belgium from the date of its independence to the present day, though under a totally different form of government, and in widely different conditions; but a solid modern representative government possesses over the very best form of the ancient absolute monarchy the inestimable advantage that its stability at no time depends upon the genius of an individual, and therefore, to use a comparison from commerce, it bears the same relation to absolutism that a long-established corporation bears to an individual banker who has no partners.

While the Romans were besieging Agrigentum, losing a fleet at Lipari, winning battles in the west of the island, slowly driving their enemies back and establishing their power with that astonishing comprehension of military supply which they early displayed in warfare, Hiero was enriching Syracuse, extending his trade and multiplying those resources of wealth and provisions which made him indispensable to the Romans themselves. His success in this respect proves what Sicily could do in peace after a century and a half of bloodshed, or much more, if one choose to go farther back, beyond the first Carthaginian invasion — a century and a half of foreign wars, internal dissensions, race struggles, and cruel tyrannies. The same boundless recuperative power is in the island to-day, and the time is not far distant when the commerce and manufactures of Sicily will equal that of all Italy, from the straits to Florence, and will compare favourably with that of the whole Italian peninsula.

Hiero's government has been described as a wise combination of magnificence and economy, of strength and gentleness; he dealt with foreign powers in the name of the Syracusan people, not in his own; he refused the outward insignia of royalty, and seems to have lived simply in the vast city he had restored and beautified, surrounding himself with such men of talent as he could attract to Syracuse. He made presents of great value not only to Rome but to Egypt, and even to Rhodes, most often in the form of corn and probably in times of scarcity; but we hear no tales of his own extravagance, still less of any excessive exactions, whether to satisfy his own caprices or for any purpose of aggrandizement or conquest. His was a model government for times of peace; it lacked every element, except wealth, which could have made it successful in war, and would have been obliged, like Carthage, to employ mercenaries altogether, for lack of a standing army. Two great nations, the one warlike, the other commercial, tried the two methods on a vast scale, and Carthage, the commercial nation, lost in the end, and the poor Roman annihilated the rich Phoenician.

The greatest man at Hiero's court was without doubt Archimedes, and the most extraordinary of Hiero's works, though by far the least useful, was the ship of four thousand and two hundred tons which he sent to Alexandria as a present to Ptolemy.

Archimedes was born in 287 B.C., being according to some authorities a relative of Hiero's family. He must certainly be ranked with the greatest mathematicians and mechanics that ever lived, and his natural gifts developed to the proportions of genius in the congenial atmosphere of Syracuse. It will be remembered that the Syracusans at all times showed considerable inventive talent, especially in the arts of war, and that the elder Dionysius held a sort of congress of engineers and shipbuilders, who designed the first ships that were built with five banks of oars, as well as the long-range catapults which did such execution upon the Carthaginian fleet, when planted at the entrance of the harbour. The magnitude of the works which remain in Syracuse, the astonishing ease with which the builders handled the great masses of stone, the marvellous beauty of the theatre hewn out of the live rock, by sheer quarrying and without any builder's work, the graceful curves and the harmonious proportions of the amphitheatre,a which far surpasses the Roman colosseum, and which almost rivals it in size, all these show to what a height the art of architecture, the science of mathematics, and the skill of the stone-cutter were carried in the only city of that day which rivalled Athens and Alexandria. From his earliest youth Archimedes must have watched the builders at work and studied the plans and sketches and working drawings that were used on the spot, and his intensely practical genius must have begun to grapple with the greatest problems in mathematics and the most difficult theorems of geometry, long before he dreamed that he possessed the power to solve the one or demonstrate the other. The results his studies have left to the world are enormous, and can hardly be completely understood without some mathematical learning. His method of squaring the parabola was the first step towards all accurate measurement of curved figures. His discovery of the relation between a cylinder, of which the height equals the diameter, to the greatest sphere it can contain, has remained for all time one of the greatest mathematical feats accomplished by the human mind. His theory of the centre of gravity justified Lagrange in calling him the father of mechanics. He was the discoverer of specific gravity, which is one of the chief foundations of modern chemistry, and it was when he found, in testing a gold crown for the king, that the difference between the weight of any body when weighed in the air and when weighed under water is equal to the weight of the volume of water which the object displaces, that he uttered his memorable exclamation, 'Eureka!' 'I have found it!' That he should have invented the lever as a mechanical engine is impossible, but he undoubtedly invented some of its applications, and he must have discovered its laws when he said, 'Give me a place to stand and I will move the world.' Holm doubts whether he actually set fire to the Roman fleet with a burning-glass, when, after Hiero's death, the city was besieged by Marcellus; but the historian cites two interesting parallel instances to prove that such a feat was possible. In 514 A.D. Proculus is said to have fired Vitalian's fleet before Constantinople by the same means. Further, in 1747 Buffon succeeded in setting fire to wood at a distance of a hundred and fifty feet, and in melting lead at a hundred and forty feet, by means of a system of one hundred and sixty movable mirrors, by which, in the month of April, and when the sunlight was not strong, he concentrated the sun's rays upon a point. Archimedes invented countless machines of less importance, such as the hydraulic serpent, which was probably the instrument worked by a single man in pumping out Hiero's ship. His whole life was spent in the application of mathematics and mechanics to useful needs in peace and war. His end was characteristic of his life, for when Marcellus, on taking Syracuse, gave orders that no one should harm him, it is said that a soldier came upon unawares and stepped upon the figure he was drawing in sand. The man of genius protested sharply against the disturbance. The soldier drew his sword and killed the greatest man in the world with a foolish laugh.

Peasant woman of Monteleone

We have in Athenaeus a very elaborate description of the great ship which Hiero built and launched inside the harbour of Syracuse. Judging from the nature of the ground, and with some knowledge of shipbuilding, I think that it would have been impossible to build a vessel of four thousand tons and more in the arsenal near Ortygia. The work must have been done in the low land by the shore, outside the gate, and between it and the swamp.

Athenaeus says that Hiero brought enough timber from Mount Etna to build sixty triremes and that he got planks and lumber for various purposes from other parts of Sicily and from Italy. Archias the Corinthian was the chief builder, and three hundred workmen were employed only to trim the timber. As soon as the planking was finished it was covered with sheet lead, as we use sheet copper. The hull was built in six months, and Archimedes launched it by a system of screws worked by a few persons. The vessel was bolted with brass, and brass nails were used, the holes being plugged with lead, driven in upon tarred canvas. The ship was constructed with twenty banks of oars, and here it is as well to say at once that nothing whatever is known as to the arrangement of the banks, even in the ordinary trireme; the late Professor Breusing, who was not only for many years the director of the celebrated naval school in Bremerhaven, but also a very eminent philologian, has completely destroyed the old-fashioned belief of scholars that three banks of oars situated one above the other could under any circumstances have been pulled at the same time. Those who are interested in the subject may consult his invaluable work, 'Die Nautik der Alten.' That Hiero's ship had at least three decks is certain from the otherwise confusing description of Athenaeus. He says that it had three entrances, the lowest leading to the hold, which was reached by two long ladders; the second gave access to the eating-rooms, and the third was for the soldiers. A great number of rooms are described, of which the floors were made of mosaic and depicted very beautifully the whole story of the Iliad. On the upper deck was a gymnasium, and also a garden filled with all sorts of plants, set in casks full of earth, and there were walks shaded with awnings, and a temple to Venus paved with Sicilian agate, the walls and roof being made of cypress wood and the doors of ivory and citron. There was a state cabin, containing five couches, a bookcase, and a clock set into the ceiling, and there was a complete bath having a tank lined with marble from Tauromenium. There were also stalls for ten horses on each side. In the fore part of the vessel there was a large fresh-water tank made of wood and tarred canvas, and holding two thousand measures; there was also a fish tank filled with salt water. Figures of Atlas at well-proportioned intervals, and apparently carved in wood, carried the rail or were placed outside the bulwarks to support the great weight of the wooden turrets. There was a catapult on deck which hurled a stone weighing three talents, or an arrow twelve cubits long, equivalent to eighteen feet. The vessel had three masts, each carrying two yards, which latter were fitted with a curious device for dropping heavy weights upon an attacking vessel. Finally, the bulwark was protected with iron throughout, and there were a number of very long grappling hooks.

This vast construction appears to have been launched and sent to sea as a present to Ptolemy during a time of dearth in Egypt, with an enormous cargo, consisting of sixty thousand measures of corn, ten thousand jars of Sicilian salt fish, five hundred tons' weight of wool, and five hundred tons of other freight.

The reign of Hiero the Second connects the story of the Greeks with that of the Romans, and his alliance with the latter helped to determine the future position of Sicily; the destinies of the southern mainland were already decided, and Italy was altogether Roman. One of the most important turning points in Roman history was the subjugation of the great island, which became Rome's first province, because it was too thoroughly Hellenic to be incorporated in the Republic. The influence and domination of the Greeks in the south had lasted, at the beginning of the first Punic war, from about 700 B.C. to 264 B.C., that is to say, more than four hundred years, during which the original elements of the population, as well as the greater part of the Phoenician colonies in Sicily, had become completely hellenized in speech, manners, and culture, and to a great extent also in blood, by constant intermarriages in time of peace. The reason why greater Greece never became a consolidated empire lay in the Greek character, and not in the lack of enterprise, of military ability, or of a common interest. Had the whole south at any time remained united for a century, it would have easily grown to be a match for Carthage. The astonishing success of Gelon, of the elder Dionysius, and of Agathocles, are sufficient proof that this is true. But the Greek had neither the Roman's conception of political unity, nor the Carthaginian's commercial talent. He was as incapable of sinking his highly original personality in the ranks of an organization as he was of devoting his whole energies to money making; he was a free lance rather than a trained soldier; an artist, not a middle-class citizen; a man of genius, not a banker. In the heat of enthusiasm there were few feats which he could not accomplish, but his restless blood could not brook the daily round of a humdrum existence. In war he loved the brilliant pageant, the high paean song, the splendid arms, the woven garlands, the air of triumph before the battle, and the trophy and the sacrifice after the fight. When peace followed war, he craved the excitement of the great Greek games, the emotions of the almost impossibly beautiful in art, the heart-beating of the reckless player throwing for high stakes, the physical intoxication of wine, and the intellectual intoxication of the theatre; and when these palled he lost patience with peace and became the most gratuitously quarrelsome of human beings, taking offence at the hue of his neighbour's cloak, attacking a friend for an imaginary slight upon the least of his innumerable vanities, and making war about nothing, with the fine conviction of a thoroughly ill-tempered child that smashes its new doll to atoms rather than be good for five minutes. There is often something rudimentary and childlike in very gifted men; a lack of patience that makes the long way of thought intolerably irksome and drives the man of genius to the accomplishment of the apparently impossible by the shortest road.

As the Greek was individually, so were the Greeks in a body, wherever they established themselves, in the fertile plains and undulating hills of Asia Minor, in the wild mountains and isolated valleys of their own Greece, and in that greater Hellas with which this story has been concerned. They were always at odds with each other, and they rarely fought a foreign foe without seeing the faces of their born countrymen in the ranks that opposed them; they were alike incapable of submitting without a murmur to the rule of a single master, and of governing themselves as one whole by the orderly judgment of the many. Wherever they appeared they excited admiration and they often inspired terror; wherever they dwelt, even for a brief term of years, they left behind them works of lasting beauty; but whereas, as artists, as poets, and as philosophers, they created a standard that has made rivalry impossible and imitation ridiculous, their government has left no trace in the lands they once inhabited, and their laws have had less influence upon the subsequent law-givers of mankind than those of the Chinese or the Aztecs. In their arts and in their literature they worked for all time; in their government they were opportunists and intriguers, when they were not visionaries, and the type of their race having disappeared from the world, the conditions under which it lived are beyond the comprehension of other civilized peoples. 'These Greeks,' said the Roman, 'can do everything to perfection, yet they are the barbers and we are the praetors.' The slight foundation of truth contained in the paradox explains the failure of the Greek race to reach that height of domination to which many other races have attained. When we see what they did for themselves we cannot but wish that they might have obtained the power to do as much for others, that they might have outnumbered and outfought the Romans, spreading over Italy, over Europe, over Asia, and Africa as the Romans did. The vast monuments of Rome would have been as perfect in beauty as they are stupendous in dimensions; four-fifths or nine-tenths of the best Greek literature would not have perished utterly, or have been preserved in miserable fragments; and the enlightenment of an Augustan age might not, perhaps, have been closely followed by the brutal horrors of a Nero's reign.

But these are idle dreams. The Greeks filled the south with their monuments and overspread it with their civilization during more than four centuries, and when the end of their story came they were no nearer to extinction as a people than the Poles were when their kingdom was divided among the nations of Europe. They simply ceased to have any political existence and became, with all they had, with their resources undiminished, their wealth unspent, their energies still all alive with them, the possession, body and soul, of a race that had mastered the only art they could ever learn, the art of governing men; and thereafter, recognizing once and for always their position as a part of their conquerors' property, they worked for him and for Roman money as they had once laboured for glory and for themselves; and in the slow decadence of genius in captivity, their supreme gifts were weakened by degrees, then scattered, and then lost. Henceforth the history of the south becomes for more than half a thousand years the story of the Romans, from the days of Appius Claudius who took Messina till after the times of Christian Constantine.

Volume II

Watch tower of Charles the Fifth at San Nicola, Calabria

The Goths and the Byzantines

A cliff at Sorrento

The short domination of the Goths in the south is parenthetic rather than vital, and came to an end as soon as the Eastern Roman Empire, which had created it, stretched out its still powerful hand to undo it. The collapse of the Western Empire had been very sudden. In the chaos produced by the arbitrary acts of Ricimer, the Suevian general of the Roman army, the last rivets were loosened and the whole construction tottered to its fall. Ricimer being dead, Orestes, who had been secretary to Attila the Hun, seized the power and created his son emperor, being a child of six years old. This was Romulus Augustulus. The mercenary troops, under Odoacer, at once demanded a third of Italy for themselves, and when Orestes attempted to oppose their demands, he was killed in fight and the child emperor was shut up in a villa in the country. Odoacer then sent the imperial insignia to Zeno, Emperor of the East, and asked for the right to administer Italy, with the title of 'patrician.' Half acknowledged, and yet never quite authorized, he governed the country for some time, till in a war with the barbarians he took prisoner one of their princes, who escaped and appealed to Theodoric, king of the Ostrogoths. Theodoric invaded Italy and overcame Odoacer in a great battle at Verona in 489. He was supported by the Italian bishops against Odoacer, who was an Arian like Genseric; and before long, in 493, Odoacer made negotiations for peace and a division of the kingdom of Italy. A feast was held to celebrate the conclusion of hostilities, and Theodoric rendered a renewal of them impossible by murdering Odoacer at the table.

In the fewest possible words, this is the history of the transition from the last days of the Western Empire to the Gothic kingdom that followed it, and which endured for a time in conditions so unfavourable that even its short existence seems almost inexplicable. The only explanation that presents itself lies in the fact that the Goths were physically stronger than the Italians. They were supposed to own but one-third of the soil of Italy, but on the other hand they were the only soldiers in the country, and they were commanded by a man of high military talent who was not at all inclined to enter into small quarrels. Both Odoacer and Theodoric had understood, in fact, from the first, that their best policy would be to maintain the Roman administration, to which the people submitted by force of habit; but to control it themselves and to except all their Goths and other mercenaries from its jurisdiction. There was, therefore, a Gothic law for the conquerors and a Roman law for the conquered, and the iron hand of Theodoric was able to enforce both.

The consequence of this state of things was that the administration of the south scarcely changed at all, and that it peaceably submitted to the government to which it was accustomed, indifferent to the fact that the sovereign was a Gothic king instead of a Roman emperor. There are few records of Gothic actions in Sicily. When Theodoric married his sister Amalafrida to the king of the Vandals, he presented her with the district of Lilybaeum, which became Marsala, 'the harbour of God,' under the Saracens. It appears that there was a Gothic garrison there, as well as in Syracuse, Palermo, and Messina; and it is certain that in the division of lands some estates in Sicily and on the southern mainland fell to the lot of the Gothic captives; but there is excellent historical evidence to show that there were practically no Goths at all in the south when Belisarius landed, in 535. The fact that there were none is adduced to explain why the south surrendered to the imperial general without a struggle.

The Gothic law, for Goths, was administered by counts created by the king for the purpose; in differences between Goths and Romans, that is to say, free Italians, the Gothic count was associated with a Roman judge well acquainted with Roman law. This fact implies that there were counts in Sicily, at least where there were Gothic garrisons, and a few letters are extant in which some of them are mentioned by name, and which deal with matters of administration. They are largely of the time of Athalaric, and it is remarkable that a number of them were written to censure the Gothic officials for having collected taxes beyond the amounts due. There is ample evidence that it was the intention of the kings to treat the south well, and that they did so; and the vast amount of corn which Sicily was able to send to Rome in the final struggle that resulted in the victory of the Byzantines, shows clearly enough that under Gothic domination the island recovered from the ravages of Genseric with its usual vitality and became extremely prosperous. The instructions given to the Count of Syracuse with regard to his journeys when 'on circuit,' as we should say, exhibit a care for the people's interests which contrasts strongly with the rapacious methods tolerated in the days of Verres. His functions are to be exercised for one year, during which he is to be escorted by a detachment of Gothic soldiers; the latter are to be quartered on the citizens, but the count is warned that he is not to allow any rudeness or rough treatment on the part of his men, who are everywhere to take what is given them without complaint and with a modest behaviour.

Nevertheless this Gildilas, Gothic Count of Syracuse under Athalaric, seems to have had an eye to his own advantage, for we find him severely taken to task for oppressing the provincials. He is told that he has received money for repairing the walls of the city, but has used it for other purposes, and must now either refund it or execute the work; that he has appropriated to the treasury the property of natives who have died without heirs, a proceeding only authorized in the case of foreigners; that he has made the costs of judicial proceedings excessive; that he has presumed to judge cases of difference arising between Roman parties, whereas his jurisdiction only extends over Goths; that he has forced merchants to sell him the cargoes of incoming vessels at a derisory price; and on the whole that he had behaved very badly, in a manner unbecoming to a Gothic count, that he is to remember that it is the glory of the Goths to protect all citizens, and that he must immediately mend his ways.

In order to understand what there is to tell about the situation in Sicily at the end of the Gothic domination, during the wars in which Belisarius, and Narses after him, commanded the Byzantine armies, we must glance at the causes of those wars, which were fought by the Emperor Justinian, against the successors of Theodoric, for the possession of Rome. Their result may be described as a preservation of Rome's identity as a Latin capital; for if the Goths had beaten Justinian, as it at one time seemed probable that they might, Rome would soon have ceased to be a true Latin centre, though it might not have become more really Gothic than Vienna is German in our own times.

We have seen that the powers delegated by the Emperor of the East to Odoacer and Theodoric were undefined, if they were unlimited. They had in fact been granted purposely in such a manner as to make them revocable at the emperor's pleasure, and in this respect the kingdom of Italy resembled a feudal holding of the Middle Ages. Odoacer was a mere adventurer and a general of mercenary troops; Theodoric was indeed by right a king, but was not King of Italy in any correct acceptation of the title. He was, in the imperial theory, the governor of the country as long as the emperor chose that he should remain in office. In real fact, he was the chieftain of an army of giants who, to use an expression proverbial among seamen, would rather drink than eat, and would rather fight than drink; huge men, of huge appetites, gifted with a sort of honourable judgment which would have been common sense if it had not been strongly imbued with a spirit half poetic, half theatrical, and altogether barbaric; guileless as children, and yet dangerous as madmen when thwarted in their immediate desires or when roused to anger, especially by any piece of deception or treachery; spendthrifts who squandered their possessions, their strength, and themselves, and who, speaking figuratively, would swing a sledge-hammer to crush a fly; they were, in a word, a tribe of big, handsome, headstrong, quick-tempered boys, among whom a man like Theodoric appeared now and then, who knew how to manage them, and had something of that cool and unerring spirit which, at a later period, distinguished the Normans from other northern people.

It is doubtful whether the struggle for the possession of Rome was brought on by circumstances into which questions of religion entered, but it is certain that the Catholic Church in Italy stirred up the people against Theodoric in his old age. He was an Arian, but he did not behave like one; on the contrary, he favoured the attack made by the emperor on the Arian Genseric, and had himself assumed the government with the approval and support of the bishops, who already played so important a part in the state. But towards the end of his reign there was something like a religious revival throughout Italy; there was at all events a sudden and great increase of religious fervour all over the country, and it is not unreasonable to suppose that such a movement, proceeding as it did from a Latin and Catholic source, should have produced some manifestation of Latin patriotism as opposed to foreign and Arian domination, by drawing the Latin people more closely together.

Now Latin patriotism had come to mean adherence to the Eastern Empire. The patriotic sentiment of Italians was not for Italy, but for the Empire under which they had lived five hundred years, and the fact that its seat had long been transferred to Constantinople did not affect that sentiment in any great degree. The Emperor Justin was as wise as he was enterprising, and he was quick to take advantage of a change of feeling in Italy at a time when that country had practically been long separated from his dominion and seemed forever lost to the Empire. He was assured that to reconquer it he had only to drive out the Goths, who, though very warlike, were by no means a military nation, who could therefore be beaten by a scientific general commanding trained troops, and who, moreover, would have to fight in the enemy's country, since the whole south and a great part of central Italy were decidedly in favour of what was certainly a reoccupation. Justin began to seek occasion against Theodoric, and maintained continued relations with the Catholic party in Italy.

It has been said that Theodoric was at no time an independent sovereign, that he understood what he was made to do by his great prime minister, and approved, so to say, of his own actions, but that he was nothing more than a lay figure of royalty, wholly directed by Cassiodorus. There is much evidence in favour of this theory. The only objection to it which suggests itself to me is that Cassiodorus was a Roman by birth, by character, and by education, and one would therefore suppose that if he had possessed the directing power attributed to him by some historians he would not have used it to widen the breach between himself and all that distinctively belonged to Rome. Yet he had served Odoacer before serving Theodoric, and it was undoubtedly owing to his efforts that the south submitted peaceably to the Gothic rule. He retired from political life in the last years of Theodoric's reign, but he returned to serve the latter's daughter and grandson in his former capacity; he outlived the fall of the Gothic kingdom and still had nearly thirty years of life to spend in the retirement of the cloister he had founded in his native place, Squillace, not far from Catanzaro, in southern Calabria, near the sea. There he composed a great part of his many books, most of which have been preserved.

The struggle for the possession of Rome, which Felix Dahn has told in one of the most remarkable historical novels ever composed, did not begin until Theodoric was dead. In his old age the king had done unworthy deeds, yielding to the counsels of courtiers who played upon him at his will; he had caused the great Boethius to be put to death with horrible tortures and had beheaded the equally innocent Symmachus, and it is said that Boethius died because he protected the provincials against the extortions of the public officials, a fact which shows how much Theodoric's government had degenerated in his later days. Before his death Justin had issued an edict requiring that the Arian churches in Constantinople should accept the Catholic rite; Theodoric forced Pope John the First to act as his ambassador to the emperor to request a revocation of the order. Justin received the Pope with every honour, but refused the request, and Theodoric retorted by imprisoning the unfortunate pontiff, who died in prison, if he was not actually murdered. In the same year, 526, and only three months later, Theodoric himself passed away, and while the Gothic nation mourned him and buried him magnificently in Ravenna, a hermit of the south gravely assured the Catholic world that he had seen the shades of Pope John and of Symmachus casting the soul of the dead king bound into the crater of Volcano, the island that lies close to Lipari, off the Sicilian coast. Theodoric was succeeded by his daughter Amalasuntha, for he left no son, and his grandson Athalaric was but a boy. In 527, the next year, Justin died and was succeeded by the great Justinian, his nephew and adopted son. Amalasuntha, brought up in the Roman civilization and culture, effected a reconciliation with the new emperor, but the Arian Goths hated her, and her own cousin murdered her nine years after her father's death. She had allowed the imperial troops to land and collect provisions in Sicily during the Vandal war, and Justinian found it convenient to avenge so useful an ally since vengeance was an excuse for seizing Rome. Sardinia and Corsica had already declared their allegiance to the Empire, and Belisarius appeared before Catania with a force of which the cavalry comprised Huns, Moors, and several thousand nondescript allies, while the infantry was composed of a few thousand Isaurians. Palermo alone was defended by its Gothic garrison, but Belisarius sent his ships into the old harbour, which was in the midst of what is now the city, and actually hoisted his archers in boats to the mastheads of the vessels, whence they were enabled to shoot over the low ramparts. Palermo having been thus easily reduced, Sicily received Belisarius and the imperial power with open arms, Naples fell into his hands by the discovery of a disused aqueduct that led into the city, and the victorious general advanced upon Rome itself. The unapproachable Gibbon has told the story of what followed, and the genius of Dahn has adorned it; to those who come after such writers nothing remains but to quote or to condense the result of their labours. The Goths chose the brave Vitiges to be their leader, but he was unable to prevent Belisarius from entering Rome. Such armies as the Goths possessed were scattered throughout their dominions, whereas the imperial force was concentrated, well trained, and commanded by a general of genius. During the winter, however, the Gothic warriors assembled at Ravenna to the number of one hundred and fifty thousand men and marched thence through the open country upon Rome. With a thousand cavalry Belisarius rode out to reconnoitre the enemy's position. Almost before he realized his danger, the general was surrounded, and a desperate fight ensued in which the leader's life was only saved by his own extraordinary strength and skill. Instead of retiring at once he pursued the Goths to their camp, and it was not until a thousand of them lay dead upon the field that Belisarius was forced to retreat. The vast army of the Goths immediately besieged the city, but Rome was strong, and the walls of Aurelian made an almost impregnable defence, the mausoleum of Hadrian was for the first time converted into a fortress, chains were thrown across the river, and the engines of war were immediately got ready and planted in position. Before the arrival of Vitiges and the Goths, the city had received from Sicily such a quantity of grain as enabled it to defy the terrors of famine, and during the fruitless siege, which lasted a whole year, it does not appear that the inhabitants suffered any great hardship. The Goths brought fascines, scaling-ladders, and battering-rams against the walls, and wooden towers on wheels; and the Romans opposed these with all the military devices of antiquity, among which were enormous catapults, to provide missiles for which the priceless statues on Hadrian's tomb were broken into fragments. Belisarius himself fought from the walls with a bow and arrows, and so completely was the first assault repulsed that the Goths determined to blockade the city, though it was now defended by scarcely four thousand men-at-arms. Reënforcements arrived at last, which the Goths believed to be only the vanguard of a great army, and they treated for peace. Their forces were greatly diminished; for a vast number of their soldiers had succumbed to the malarious fever of the Campagna, while it is certain that the besiegers suffered more from lack of provisions than the besieged. The Goths at last gave up the siege in despair, burned their tents, and retired. Within a few months all that remained of the Gothic monarchy in Italy had taken shelter in Ravenna, and it seemed as if the Gothic cause were lost beyond all hope. But the Gothic kingdom in Italy was not the Gothic nation, and the handful of warlike foreigners who remained in the country had friends beyond the Alps both able and willing to help them. Ten thousand Burgundians took Milan and destroyed it, and the king of the Austrasians descended upon Italy at the head of a hundred thousand men, who, if they did not appear out of disinterested friendship for the Goths, were certainly not inspired by any friendly feeling for the emperor. They retired, however, after committing every species of cruelty, and Belisarius was again left to deal with Italy as he could. He forced or tricked Ravenna to a surrender, and the flower of the Goths took service in the imperial army. Belisarius now departed to Constantinople with a vast amount of spoil, and taking with him as a captive the brave but unfortunate Vitiges.

Nevertheless the end of the Goths had not yet come. Belisarius left behind him, as governors of the reconquered country and as chiefs of the imperial forces, a number of officers to whom he gave equal authority, and most of whom proceeded to abuse it. The mistake, or it would be more just to say the crime, of all governments seated in the East has been, and still is, excessive financial oppression. For Italy, Justinian appointed a number of officers who were called 'logothetes,' who acted as tax-gatherers and some of whom soon accumulated vast fortunes by a regular system of embezzlement. They did not confine their operations to the citizens and provincials, but extended them to thefts from the pay of the army, for they acted also as controllers. One of their favourite methods for making money in this way was to keep down a great number of veterans, who would be entitled to an increase of pay, by pretending that the deceased soldiers who had held the higher rank were still alive, and keeping their names on the rolls as if this were the case. Moreover, the provincials were called upon to render an account of all money which had passed through their hands under the Gothic administration, and in this way a great number of Italians who had been in sympathy with Belisarius were again turned against the emperor. At the time of Belisarius's departure in 540 only about a thousand Gothic soldiers were left in Italy. Within a year their numbers had so increased that they defeated one of the governors near Venice; and though a quarrel for what was no longer anything more than the chieftainship of the Goths soon led to the murder of the chief himself, and though his immediate successor had no hold upon his people, they continued to regain their strength at such a rate that when they at last chose Totila to be their king, they immediately became once more a match for the imperial oppressor. They seized Verona, and Totila pursued the Roman generals with a force of five thousand men. Before long Totila was able to cross the Apennines, and in a battle which ensued at a place once called Mugello, but of which the site is now forgotten, the Goths completely routed the Roman troops. Avoiding Rome, Totila crossed the Tiber and marched southwards upon Beneventum, which he destroyed lest it should harbour an imperial force; a little later he besieged Naples, which was defended only by a thousand men. Justinian now appointed a praetorian prefect of Italy, to whom he intrusted the supreme power over all his forces; but this officer lingered in Syracuse while another general failed to relieve Naples, and the squadron with which he arrived there was seized by the Goths. It was winter when the prefect sailed from Syracuse, and his fleet perished in a storm within sight of Naples, amid the cries and lamentations of the people who were assembled on the walls. The city now surrendered, and Totila dismantled the fortifications, though he treated the inhabitants with great kindness. All sense of discipline was lost in the imperial armies; the generals gave themselves up to a licentious existence in the cities which they still held, the soldiers of Justinian plundered the country, and the emperor was soon informed that it was no longer possible to hold Italy. Totila wrote a sort of open letter to the Roman Senate, boldly stating that it was his purpose to rescue Italy from her tyrants, and copies of the writing were posted in the Forum and in the chief streets for the people to read. Yet the Romans did not see fit to open their gates to him, and he therefore advanced with the greater part of his army to take it by siege. This happened in the year 544.

Garden of the Capuchin Convent at Amalfi

Meanwhile, by an extraordinary concatenation of intrigue and misfortune, Belisarius had been utterly disgraced and the command of the Eastern armies had been taken from him. But in the moment of danger it suited the ends of the Empress Theodora to restore him to favour; he was created Count of the Sacred Stable and was informed that he would be permitted to fight Totila and the Goths in Italy on condition that he would ask for no funds from the imperial treasury. It was with the greatest difficulty that he succeeded in raising a force of volunteers in Thrace, with whom he crossed over to Ravenna, intending to march at once towards Rome. But everywhere he found the Goths opposed to him, the imperial troops were defeated on the shores of the Adriatic, and after fortifying the little city of Pesaro, Belisarius took refuge in Ravenna, whence he sent a desperate appeal to Justinian. After a long time help came, indeed, but the relieving armies were commanded by generals who secretly hated Belisarius. Meanwhile, in 545, Totila had begun the siege of Rome, which was commanded by Bessas, the most corrupt of the governors under whom Italy had suffered. His defence is a record of inactivity, and Belisarius, checked at every turn, was unable to relieve him. The city had not been previously provisioned, as it had been for the former siege, and was driven to the last extremity of famine. Dogs and mice were eaten and were regarded as luxuries, and the dead bodies of horses and mules were sought for with avidity. The people plucked the nettles which grew about the walls, as they still do, and boiled them for food, and when all else failed they began to devour each other.

The citizens sent an embassy to the Gothic king and chose as their representative the deacon, Pelagius, who was made Pope nine years later. Totila treated him with profound respect, but before he had spoken refused to grant three requests which he expected the churchman to make. He declined beforehand to pardon Sicily for having gone over to the emperor and having supplied Rome with corn, to leave the walls of Rome standing, and lastly, to surrender the slaves who had fled to him from their Roman owners. Pelagius, disappointed by Totila's tone, refused to ask anything else; he returned into the city and the frightful state of siege continued. The inhuman Bessas at last sold to the non-combatants a permission to escape if they could, and most of those who attempted it perished by famine or the sword.

Meanwhile, after much hesitation, Belisarius and the Byzantine leaders sailed from Durazzo, and Belisarius reached the mouth of the Tiber, while one of the leaders inflicted a defeat upon the Goths near Reggio. With consummate skill Belisarius made his preparations, seized Portus, and would perhaps have relieved Rome but for the foolish blunder of a colleague, who attacked Ostia at the wrong moment, failed, and was taken prisoner. Belisarius lost his presence of mind, retreated immediately, and soon fell ill of a fever. Thereupon certain Isaurian soldiers in Rome betrayed the Asinarian Gate to the Goths, and the whole Gothic army marched in without striking a blow, while the evil Bessas fled with his army, and in such haste that he left his ill-gotten treasure behind him. The Goths were again masters, but in spite of his previous threat Totila did not destroy Rome, being moved to moderation by a letter from Belisarius, who asked the barbarian king whether he would not rather be remembered in future ages as the preserver of the greatest city in the world, than as its destroyer. He had already torn down one-third of the walls, but he now desisted from further destruction, evacuated the defenceless city, and withdrew his army to the Alban hills. These things happened at the end of the year 546. Six weeks later Belisarius reoccupied Rome, and repaired the walls in a fortnight with such materials as he could collect from the ruins. Totila, enraged at learning that the city was again a stronghold, returned to attack it and was thrice repulsed. He fell back upon Tivoli, with his discontented army, and rebuilt the citadel he had before destroyed.

The stupendous conflict for the possession of Rome was not even now at an end, and though Totila longed to be revenged upon the south for its adherence to the imperial cause, he only succeeded in taking the little fortress of Rossano, near the site of ancient Sybaris, in spite of the efforts made by Belisarius to relieve it. The Byzantine general was rendered almost powerless by Justinian's refusal to supply him with funds and men, and in the following year, 549, he returned to Constantinople. He had not arrived there before Perugia, which had been besieged for three years by a detachment of Totila's troops, surrendered at last, and the king at once proceeded to besiege Rome again. Garrisoned now by picked troops, it might have resisted long; but the soldiers had already mutinied, in the previous year, because their pay was in arrears, and the promises made to win back their loyalty had probably not been fulfilled: from the walls the men could see the rich dress and accoutrements of those whom Totila had rewarded for betraying the city the first time; they hesitated, discussed among themselves, and decided the fate of Rome to their advantage. The gate of Saint Paul was opened to Totila in the night, and once more he entered without striking a blow. In the short fight that followed most of the loyal garrison were slain, but a few hundreds took refuge in the Mausoleum of Hadrian and were starved at last to an honourable surrender. Instead of destroying the city, Totila now set about rebuilding it, repopulating it, and stocking it with provisions; and he sent an embassy to Justinian to propose a peace. Justinian would not even receive the ambassadors; though the north of Italy was now practically in the hands of the Goths, Rome was theirs, and Totila was able to turn southwards at last, to satisfy his desire for vengeance upon Sicily.

In the beginning of 550 Reggio was forced to surrender. Totila had already crossed the straits, and for nearly two years he ravaged Sicily without mercy, and collected together a vast amount of plunder. Procopius dismisses Totila's deeds during this time with a single short sentence, saying that the Goths then devastated almost all Sicily without opposition; but it is not hard to imagine the horrors that attended his long stay in the country. Dahn, Holm, and Hodgkin have extolled the character of the Gothic king, praising his generosity towards his enemies when he was the victor, his steadfast purpose and courage in adversity, his dignified bearing, his gentleness to the women of the vanquished, and the admirable control which he exercised over his savage soldiers even in moments when they could hardly have been blamed for some excess. But neither these historians nor those from whom they have derived their information have concealed the fact that Totila, like Theodoric, was subject to fits of anger, under the influence of which he sometimes exhibited barbarous cruelty; that he more than once caused a prisoner to be horribly mutilated, cutting off his hands, his nose, his ears, and even tearing out his tongue. It is true that these occasions were rare, and the provocation was often great; but he was a hot-tempered man who felt he had a right to act barbarously when his anger was just, and who remembered injuries long and resentfully. He had never forgiven Sicily for the help it had rendered Rome against him, he had expressly refused to pardon the Sicilians when Pelagius came to him as ambassador, and, now that Rome was his once more, now that he had regained possession of all Italy, and that Belisarius had been recalled, he gave the rein to his fury and turned his wild soldiers loose upon the peaceable islanders. It is clear that he had no intention of holding Sicily; he understood too well that with the small army at his command it would have been absolutely impossible to extend his power permanently so far. Had he intended to annex the island, he would certainly not have passed by Messina without reducing it to submission. His object was to exact compensation for an injury, and at the same time to make it impossible for the Sicilians to help the emperor as they had helped him before. So far as we are able to judge, he set to work with the deliberate purpose of so crippling the island's resources as to make its recovery within a few years almost an impossibility. We read of no redeeming acts of mercy on his part during this time; we do not hear that he offered the islanders the alternative of serving under his standard; it is not stated, as it is so often in the accounts of his other campaigns, that he spared women and children and abstained from useless bloodshed: Procopius briefly says that Totila laid waste the island, and we know that his raid upon it lasted nearly two years. He had ships at his command which he must have loaded again and again during that period with the rich spoils of the south, transferring the movable wealth of the island to the strong points he held in Italy; he took not only the corn, the gold, and the silver, but he carried off the herds, the flocks, and the horses in a wholesale spoliation, the like of which Sicily had probably never suffered before. It must have been a reign of terror. He garrisoned the stronger towns, such as Syracuse, Palermo, and Lilybaeum. Some of the cities in which there were imperial troops had indeed resisted him, and there can be no doubt that the Sicilians did what they could to defend themselves in the hope of speedy assistance from Constantinople; but all resistance was useless. That he maintained some kind of method in his mode of plundering is evident from the fact that he had created a quaestor or treasurer in the person of Spinus, a Roman, who was destined to liberate the island at last from the presence of the insatiable Goths. It appears that a Roman force was still in the neighbourhood of Catania, of which the walls had been destroyed, and that this Spinus, who chanced to be within the city, fell into the hands of the imperialists. Totila, being most anxious to set him free, offered to give in exchange for him a noble Roman lady whom he held captive, but the Romans objected that a woman was not an equivalent for so distinguished a personage as a quaestor. In fear of his life Spinus promised the Romans that he would persuade Totila to evacuate Sicily with the whole Gothic army. The Romans required him to bind himself by an oath, and they sent him to the Goths, keeping his wife as a hostage. As soon as he came into Totila's presence, Spinus began to assure him that the Goths were making a great mistake in remaining in the island after having completely plundering it, merely in the hope of taking a few small places that held out against them; and he said that he had just heard that a large imperial force was already in Dalmatia, that it would proceed thence immediately to Liguria, and that it would be an easy matter for the enemy to make a descent upon the Goths there, and to carry off their wives and children and all their possessions. It would be better, he said, to oppose this plan by wintering in that region, and, moreover, if Totila conquered the imperialists there, it would not be hard for him to invade Sicily again.

Whether the Gothic king was only weary of plunder and irregular warfare, or whether, as Procopius says, he was really moved by the argument, which was sound enough, it is hard to determine; he did, however, leave Sicily almost immediately, after placing garrisons in four of the strongest points. Having loaded a number of vessels with booty, he embarked his troops, apparently from Catania, and crossed the straits again to Italy, leaving destruction and famine behind him. This was in 551.

He never returned. The man who was destined to drive the whole Gothic army to final ruin was already on his way to the Italian shore, well provided with all that he could need, with men and abundant money. He was the old Narses, once the favourite groom of the bedchamber, who had become grand chamberlain, and whose beardless, wrinkled face and sexless looks masked the mind of a great statesman and the heart of a fearless soldier. The young and great-limbed Goth horseman smiled at the thought of being opposed to an aged eunuch, a small wizened creature of seventy-five years; but Totila's own days were numbered, and in less than two years the terrible remnant of humanity destroyed him and his successor and all their armies, and drove the handful of survivors out of Italy forever.

The end of the long struggle was short and quick. On hearing that Narses was appointed, Totila pressed the siege of Ancona, which had lasted long, and in Rome he made frantic efforts to increase his popularity by recalling the Roman senators and hastening the rebuilding of the city. At the moment when Ancona was about to fall an imperial fleet appeared a few miles to the northward, engaged the Gothic ships, destroyed most of them, and forced the Goths to burn the rest. Masters of the sea, the imperialists seized Sicily again under Artabanes the Armenian. In the north the Franks took advantage of Totila's defeat to lay their hands on all they could think, but were as ready as the Goths to oppose the imperial army. Meanwhile the main body of Narses' army arrived, a host made up of all the varied elements controlled by the Eastern Empire, comprising many Lombards and many Huns and thousands of warriors from minor tribes, but all perfectly controlled by the genius of the general, and all thirsting for Gothic blood and Italian spoil. They outflanked and outfought their opponents, and marched southwards through the Apennines by the Flaminian Way.

There Totila met them and came to his end. Many have described the great battle, telling how the imperial army spread out to the right and left, and caught and crushed the Gothic cavalry when it made its great charge upon the centre. The incidents of that day, the duels of chiefs, the wild advances, the furious fighting round the little hill that was the key of the field, the splendid riding of Totila and his obscure death, all these things are more like the tale of a Homeric battle fought in an earlier world than the romantic encounters of chivalry to which some writers have compared them. Indeed, the battle of the Apennines was almost the last of those that belong to ancient days.

One more such contest was to be fought, and was to be the very end of the Gothic episode; but before it came Narses had accomplished the greater part of his work in Italy. He took Rome with ease, after what could not be called a siege; many of the Gothic fortresses surrendered, and, though the Goths had elected their bravest warrior, Teias, to be king, he soon saw that nothing was left to him but to die for the cause that was already reduced to the last extremity. In the reign of Justinian Rome had been five times taken, and the keys of the city were now sent to him again, while Narses drove the remnant of the Goths steadily southwards.

The hunted army encamped at last by the bay of Naples, at the foot of the volcano and on the side towards Castellamare,° set out the little stream of the Sarno, and the remains of their fleet brought them provisions. Narses encamped on the bank of the river and waited, for the Goths had fortified the bridge and he had no ships. He knew also what despairing men could do, and he would not attack them until he was sure that the struggle would be short and final, or until they attacked him; and meanwhile he corrupted the commander of their ships. When these had been betrayed into his hands, the Goths retired a little way further inland, to an eminence now called Monte Lettere.

All authors who have described this final battle have, as is usual in accounts of the Gothic war, taken their material from Procopius. It may interest the reader, therefore, to read a literal translation of his own account, remembering that he was a contemporary and a soldier, as well as an historian, and that although he was not present at this fight, he knew the ground well, and received his information from an eye-witness, probably from Narses himself.

"At last," he says, "a Goth betrayed to the Romans all the enemy's fleet, and innumerable ships arrived from Sicily and from other parts of the Empire. At the same time Narses disheartened the barbarians by placing wooden towers on the river bank. Fearing these engines, and suffering from lack of provisions, they took refuge on a hill nearby, which the Romans call, in Latin, 'Milk Hill.' The Roman army could not follow them to that point, as the inequality of the ground was against them. But the barbarians did not cease to regret that they had ascended thither, when their want had so greatly increased that they no longer had food for themselves or their horses. Thinking, therefore, that it was better to die in battle than to perish by hunger, they attacked the Romans, when the latter anticipated nothing of the sort, and suddenly made an unexpected charge. The Romans repelled the assault as well as they could, considering the time and circumstances, their line not being marshalled according to their generals, nor in classes, nor by numbers, and they being neither separated from each other in ordered ranks, nor able to hear the commands given in the battle; but as chance decided, so they opposed the enemy with all their might. And first the Goths dismounted, left their horses, and stood on foot, turning their faces to the enemy, so that their line was in a high position. Then, when the Romans saw this, they also sent away their horses, and ranged themselves in a similar order of battle.

"I shall here," continues Procopius, "describe this memorable battle, in which Teias, by his splendid behaviour, proved himself equal, in warlike bravery, to any of the heroes, while the despair of their present situation imparted courage to the Goths; and the Romans, seeing them to be desperate, fought with all their strength, ashamed to yield to inferior numbers; and each fell upon those nearest, most furiously, while those on the one side sought death, and those on the other desired praise for their constancy. The fight began in the morning; Teias, protected by a shield, and brandishing his spear, stood out with a few others before the line. When the Romans recognized him, they thought that if he fell the combat would thereupon be broken off, and all who dared united against him, of whom there was a great number. All thrust at him with their spears, and some hurled them, while he, receiving their darts upon the shield with which he covered himself, in a sudden rush slew many in their midst. Seeing his shield full of the shafts that stuck in it, he passed it to one of the men armed with shields, and seized another. When he had spent a third part of the day thus fighting, it happened that he was hardly able to move the shield, in which twelve darts were planted, nor to repel the assailants with it. Then he earnestly called to one of the shield-armed men, not moving even one finger's breadth from the spot, not drawing back his foot, nor suffering the enemy to advance. On the contrary, he neither turned round, nor set his back against his shield, nor bent to one side, but as if he were cleaving to the soil, he stood fast in his tracks, dealing death to the enemy with his right hand, parrying the attack with his left, and loudly asking for the armour-bearer by name. The latter, having brought a fresh shield, quickly exchanged it for the other, that was heavy with darts. In that instant of time the king's breast was exposed; as fortune would have it, he was pierced through by a javelin, and immediately breathed his last. The Romans set his head upon a spear, and raising it on high, carried it about, exhibiting it to both armies, that the Romans might go forward more boldly, but that the Goths should give up all hope and lay down their arms. Yet even then the Goths would not give over fighting, but persisted until night, though they knew that their king was already dead. When darkness separated the combatants, both armies spent the night in arms, where they were. On the morrow they rose together at dawn, and having drawn up their ranks in the same way, fought on until night, each determined not to yield to the other, nor to turn their backs, nor to break ground, though many had been slain on both sides; and they persisted in action, wild with bitter hatred for each other. The Goths saw that they must united for the end; the Romans would not give way to them. At last, the barbarians, sending some of their nobles, made it known to Narses that they understood that they were fighting against God; that they felt His adverse power, and perceived the real nature of the matter, deducing their conjectures from the things which had happened; that they were willing to desist from fighting, not, however, on condition of serving the emperor, but that they might go and live according to their own laws, with other barbarians. They asked that the Romans should neither molest their departure, nor trouble themselves to show kindness, but that each should receive, by way of provision for the journey, the money which he had previously deposited in the Italian military stations. As Narses was deliberating about the matter, John, the grandson of Vitalian, induced him to accede to the request, and to desist from fighting with men who wished to die, and not to make trial of a daring born of the despair of life, fatal alike to those whom it animated and to their opposers. 'For,' said he, 'men possessed of prudence and moderation think that victory is enough; but a vainglorious eagerness leads surely to ruin.' Embracing this opinion, Narses consented to an agreement by which the surviving barbarians were immediately to evacuate all Italy, taking their possessions with them, and were on no account to wage war further against the Romans. Meanwhile, a thousand Goths had left their camp, and they reached the city of Ticinum and the region beyond the Po, some following Indulph, who has been mentioned already, and some under other leaders; the rest ratified the compact by taking oath. And so the Romans took Cumae and all the other strong places, and this was the end of the eighteenth year of this Gothic war, of which Procopius wrote the history."

And here ends the invaluable chronicle of the soldier historian, without whose book it would have been quite impossible to understand the nature of the struggle for Rome, and the transition from the fall of the Western Empire to the temporary supremacy of Pope Gregory the Great, and thence to the story of the Saracen domination. There can be no doubt but that Narses stemmed the stream of history in the battle of the Apennines and turned it at Monte Lettere, and he deserves to be numbered among the world's great generals. The chronicler, Agathias, has given us the best brief description of his character. "He was, above all, a man of sound mind, keen and clever in adapting himself to the times; and though he was not versed in literature nor practised in oratory, he made up for these deficiencies by the fertility of his wit, and did not lack words with which to express his opinions, which was an extraordinary thing for a eunuch brought up among the follies of the royal palace. In stature he was small and of a lean habit, but stronger and more high-spirited than would have been believed." Such was the general who, in his old age, reduced the story of the Gothic kingdom to the limits of a page in the history of mankind, and against whom such heroes of arms as Totila and Teias fought and gave up their lives in vain. Again the difference between warlike spirit and military genius presents itself, and while distinguishing between the two, and according our admiration to the great general, we need not withhold our sympathy from the fair-haired warriors who fought so bravely and died so manfully under the southern sky.

Grotto church at Praia d' Aieta, Calabria

So far as the south is concerned, the story of the Gothic domination divides itself into two periods, of which the first comprises Theodoric's long reign, a time of peace and plenty and agricultural activity, while the second includes about two years of robbery and violence, that left the land a wilderness and reduced the cities to desolation. The Goths avenged themselves, and Narses took vengeance upon them in turn; but after him, in the changing fortunes of the miserable Empire, there came Franks and Lombards, and all Northern Italy was laid waste with fire and sword. One of their kings, Autharis the Lombard, rode southward far, and reached the straits. For the Deacon Paul says that he went down by Spoleto to Benevento, and took it, and that he went through the country to Reggio, the Italian city nearest to Sicily, and it is said that there a column stood out alone, washed by the waves of the sea. Then Autharis spurred his horse through the salt foam, and he smote the pillar with the point of his spear, saying, 'Here shall be the boundary of the Lombards.' Which column, says the good deacon, is said to be standing to-day, and is called the Pillar of Autharis. But a little further on he tells us that this Autharis died of poison at Ticinum, which is Pavia, in the north; and he died in 590, in which same year a greater man than he arose, who was Pope Gregory the Great. But by that time the Lombards had taken all that part of Italy from the empire, and they held it, and made a kingdom.

As for the rest of Italy, the great struggle had meant only that the East was trying to get possession of the heritage of the West, in spite of the barbarians who wanted it for themselves, since it no longer had any emperor. The result of it was that the East got all Italy, then lost a part of it and kept the rest, that is, the centre, the south, and Sicily, governing the provinces by an exarch residing in Ravenna, leaving Rome to a prefect much under the influence of the Pope, when the latter was a strong man, and appointing a praetor and a quaestor, according to the ancient Roman custom, to govern Sicily, to keep the peace, and levy war taxes, while the regular revenues of the country were under the management of officials controlled by the so-called 'Count of the Patrimony of Italy.'

At this time our notice is first attracted by the existence of vast estates, in Sicily, Italy, Corsica, Africa, and elsewhere, which were the property of the Catholic Church, and constituted what were called the Patrimonies; that is, as we should say, the Patrimony of Saint Peter. It appears that these lands had been left by will to the Church of Rome, before the final disappearance of the Western Empire, it was even then customary for individuals to leave property in that way, and also to the churches of other cities. These estates were controlled by the Pope, who appointed a rector to manage them, paid taxes and titles in kind to the imperial government, and enjoyed the income or decided what use should be made of it.

The lands thus held by the Church of Rome in Sicily were so extensive as to enable the popes to supply Rome with Sicilian corn, and it is not surprising to find Sicily again the granary of the Italian capital. It was the possession of these lands that laid a first foundation for the temporal power of the popes, which became a fact when actual possession of a territory on the mainland was necessary, in order to compensate for the financial disaster suffered by the Church through the loss of Sicily to the Empire. Pope Gregory was a man whose intellectual superiority would in any case have led him to distinction, and whose charitable disposition could hardly fail to procure him a well-deserved popularity; but the real power which he wielded with such wholesome energy was based upon the Church's already vast possessions in the south, and was perhaps supplemented by the great private wealth he is generally believed to have inherited from his mother. This fortune likewise came to him in the shape of Sicilian lands, on which he was able to found rich monasteries before he became Pope; and though Gibbon observes with some sarcasm that his devotion pursued the path which would have been chosen by a crafty and ambitious statesman, it is the general opinion of mankind that he deserved the title of Saint and the veneration of Christians, at least as truly as any man since the Apostles and the early martyrs.

Positano, between Sorrento and Amalfi

The fall of the Gothic kingdom was followed within a few years by the rise of the Papacy. The Eastern Empire was never able to hold and govern Italy directly, owing, perhaps, to that radical defect in all Eastern governments to which I have already alluded. On the other hand, the emperors could not and would not relinquish such a possession, and where the authority of their exarchs and their praetors was insufficient, they supplemented it by increasing that of the popes, which was sure to be exercised in a more or less conservative spirit. A right understanding of these simple facts is all that is necessary in order to trace the evolution of the Papacy, with its organized temporal power, from the chaos that followed the extinction of the Western Empire. In other words, and to recapitulate briefly, chaos was followed by a tremendous effort on the part of the barbarians to get possession of Italy; this having failed, and Justinian having reoccupied the country, he found himself unable to govern it without the support of the popes, who gradually turned their assistance into a domination. The connexion of all this with the story of the south lies in the fact that the popes relied upon their possessions in Sicily for the greater part of their worldly wealth and power, before the union and consolidation of these produced their temporal sovereignty.

The Synod of Constantinople, held in the year 381, had acknowledged the supremacy of the Bishop of Rome by giving him precedence over all others, and this action was confirmed by the Synod of Chalcedon in 451. Justinian had further acknowledged this precedence of the popes by the manner in which he had received Pope John when the latter came to Constantinople as Theodoric's ambassador, and it was not unnatural, therefore, that the emperor should suffer the popes to exercise such very great influence upon Italian affairs; and since Sicily is spoken of at that time as the 'Asylum and Paradise of the Church,' it is quite certain that the papal influence must have been especially strong in the island, and may have amounted to a positive domination under such a Pope as Gregory the Great.

This extraordinary man was born in Rome about the year 540, and was therefore thirteen years old at the time when the Goths were finally overcome. He was the son of a Roman senator, Gordianus, and of his wife Sylvia, who is believed to have been a Sicilian lady of great wealth. Gordianus himself afterwards entered the Church, and died one of the seven cardinal deacons who administered the seven ecclesiastical districts of Rome. Gregory received an education befitting his birth and fortune, and it is a sign of the decay of Greek influence in Central Italy that he never learned the Greek language. At the age of thirty-four, as most writers think, he was appointed Prefect of Rome by Justin the Second, which means that he presided in the Senate, was the chief magistrate of the city, and was largely responsible for providing t with food. How long he remained in this high office is not known, but it was probably not more than a year, and on the death of his father he inherited a palace on the Coelian. His mother, who was still alive, appears to have abandoned to him her Sicilian possessions, for he founded there six monasteries on lands of his own, and he converted the Coelian palace to monastic uses in 575, and dedicated it to Saint Andrew. It probably occupied the site of the hospital which now stands opposite the Lateran basilica, and within which there is still a church of Saint Andrew. He had always loved the society of monks and ecclesiastics; he now gave himself up entirely to devotion, and injured his health by the severity of his fasting. After this, having seen certain fair Anglian children exposed for sale as slaves, he desired to convert Britain, saying that it was 'a lamentable consideration that the prince of darkness should be master of so much beauty and have such comely persons in his possession; and that so fine an outside should have nothing of God's grace to furnish it within'; and he played also upon the words 'Anglians' and 'Angels,' for playing upon words in this manner was a sort of weakness with him, and many of his jests are recorded. At first the Pope permitted him to undertake the conversion of those heathen; but when he had journeyed three days towards Britain, the Pope sent a messenger after him, because his fame was already so great that the people murmured and cried out, saying that without Gregory Rome was lost. So he returned, and soon afterwards he was made a cardinal deacon, and was then sent as nuncio, or ambassador, to Constantinople, where the Emperor Tiberius the second was reigning, to whose grandson Gregory stood godfather; and there he remained long enough to write his work of Morals upon Job, 'in such a manner as to reduce into one body the most excellent principles of morality.' In the year 584 he was recalled, and resumed his tranquil monastic life, of which many anecdotes are told. The Pope died in 590, in the great pestilence, and the clergy, the Senate, and the Roman people chose Gregory to be his successor; but in those days it was the custom to consult the emperor about the election of a Pope, and Gregory wrote many letters to Constantinople, imploring that his own election might not be approved. The prefect of Rome intercepted them all, and wrote very strongly requesting the imperial approval. During the pestilence Gregory publicly prayed with the people, walking in procession and singing a solemn Kyrie, and while he walked through the streets four score of those who went with him fell dead of the plague. When he learned that his letters had not been delivered, he tried to escape from Rome, lest he should be made Pope, and in order to elude the guards at the gates he had himself carried out in a wicker basket, and lay three days hidden in the woods. But he was found and brought back with great joy and acclamation, and he was consecrated, and made profession of faith at the tomb of Saint Peter, which is called the Confession to this day.

Then, says the best of his biographers, he became the common father of the poor, relieving their necessities with such gentleness as to spare them the shame of receiving alms. He made them sit at his own table, and he made exact lists of them. As each month began he made distribution to all of corn, wine, lentils, cheese, fish, meat, and oil, and he appointed officers over districts and streets, whose duty it was to see that poor sick persons were fed and cared for. He redeemed captives taken by the Lombards, and for this purpose he even ordered the Bishop of Messina to break up and sell certain sacred vessels. He ordered the Bishop of Terracina to restore to the Jews their synagogue, which had been taken from them, saying that if they were to be converted, it should be done by meekness and charity.

He issued the same orders for the Jews of Sicily, as well as of Sardinia, and in his letters to his stewards he constantly inculcates the duty of dealing liberally with the farmers, and even of advancing money to them in bad times, to be repaid in small sums. Yet he was a man of undaunted courage, who could be hot in anger, and he said of himself that he tolerated long, but that when he had once determined to bear no longer, he would face any danger with delight.

With regard to Sicily and its administration, we find that Syracuse was still regarded as the natural and traditional capital of the island, and Gregory's vicar, the Subdeacon Peter, was established there. The first of the Pope's letters which has been preserved enjoins upon the Sicilian bishops to meet the vicar once a year, either in Syracuse or in Catania, for the discussion of important matters. The monasteries founded by him are believed to have been the following: Saint Herma, now San Giovanni degli Eremiti, in Palermo; San Martino, at the head of a valley not very far from the same city; Saint Maxim and Saint Agatha, called 'Mons Lucusianum'; Saint Theodore; Saint Hadrian; and the Praetorianum or Praecoritanum. With the exception of the first two, their sites are not positively known, and it will probably never be possible to determine them. The influence of these religious institutions, founded as they were by Gregory himself, may have been considerable, and they were most probably not subject to the papal vicar, but were under the control of the superior of the order, who resided in Rome, and occasionally conferred with the Pope himself.

Saracen-Norman Church of San Giovanni degli Eremiti, Palermo

As for the Vicar Peter, he began by being Gregory's most trusted friend and servant in Sicily, but he was guilty of all manner of neglect, he tried his master's patience beyond the limit of endurance, and was ultimately removed from office. As a specimen of the Pope's manner of rebuke, it would be impossible to give anything better than the fragments which Mr. Hodgkin has selected and translated from the vast mass of Saint Gregory's letters; and when we remember that it was this Pope who first signed himself in all his letters, 'Servus servorum Dei,' the Servant of the servants of God, thereby inaugurating a custom which still survives, we cannot but be edified and interested by his manner of admonishing those in service under him, both with sarcasm and with earnest exhortations. He addresses his vicar politely as 'Your Experience,' when Peter had shown his signal lack of that quality, and as 'Your Anxiety,' when the slothful vicar had exhibited the most culpable indifference.

A Sicilian courtyard

Professor Grisar, cited as a high authority by Mr. Hodgkin, has estimated that the whole Patrimony of the Church in Saint Gregory's time amounted to eighteen hundred square miles of land, and Mr. Hodgkin speaks of these possessions as, 'wide domains,' the revenue of which is calculated by Professor Grisar at three hundred thousand pounds sterling. I do not know how the estimate and the calculation were made, not being able to obtain a copy of the article from which Mr. Hodgkin quotes them; but there is a manifest discrepancy between the extent of the land and the large income supposed to be derived from it. As I have before said, the modern Brontë estate in Sicily is eighty miles in circumference. If the figure were a square, twenty miles on each side, the area would be four hundred square miles; if a circle, it would be considerably more than five hundred. Four or five such estates would therefore equal the 'vast domains' that composed the Patrimony of Saint Peter, and which were situated in Rome and its environs, in the country of the Sabines, in Picenum, in the neighbourhood of Ravenna, in Campania, Apulia, and Bruttii, in Gaul and Illyricum, in the islands of Sardinia and Corsica — and principally in Sicily. A little further calculation shows that an even distribution would give only one hundred and fifty square miles to each of the regions named, or an estate in each equal to about one-third of the Brontë property. Moreover, the revenue calculated would amount to one hundred and sixty-six pounds sterling per average square mile, or five shillings per acre, roughly, which, at three and a half per cent, a very high estimate, would make the land worth over eight pounds an acre in the year 600; which is impossible, especially as much of the property lay in half-civilized regions. If, on the other hand, we suppose that Professor Grisar, cited by Mr. Hodgkin, meant eighteen hundred miles square, instead of eighteen hundred square miles, we should have an area much larger than the whole of Europe. There is, therefore, some radical mistake in the estimate or in the calculation, or in both, which renders them quite useless as a basis of argument. Of the figures given, that of the income actually enjoyed by the Pope is by far the most probable, from whatever sources the revenue may have been derived; and the conclusions drawn by Mr. Hodgkin are just, namely, that the care of such a property must have been a heavy burden on the shoulders of an ascetic Pope, and that the expenditure, as well as the receipt, of the large income derived from the Papal Patrimony imposed severe labour on so conscientious a steward of his wealth as Pope Gregory.

There was less difference between the position of the agricultural classes in Pope Gregory's day and that which they occupied under the Roman Empire, or even under the Republic, than might be supposed, considering the long time that elapsed; but it was during this first time of papal influence that the population began to be divided into three classes, namely, the clergy, the nobility, and the common people; and the clergy stood between the whole country and the spasmodic government of Constantinople, to protect the one and restrain the other. It was largely because the bishops of that period were truly the shepherds of their flocks, at a time when the officers of the Empire deserved, not unjustly, to be compared to wolves, that the Church acquired that direct influence throughout the country, and won that almost passionate affection of the poor, which she preserved through so many centuries, and has not even yet wholly lost in the south, whatever may be said to the contrary. This position of the bishops is chiefly traceable to the efforts of Pope Gregory, and even Gibbon's sarcasms have not shaken the honourable position he occupies in history. That he succeeded, as he did, in improving the condition of the governed, was in part due to the dominating position he occupied in Rome; but it must not be forgotten that he was supposed to be subject to the emperor, to whom he expressed his wishes in the form of advice in matters of government and of recommendations in affairs that were personal. In a majority of cases the emperor had no choice but to act upon these expressions of the Pope's desires; but a very great amount of arbitrary power was conferred upon the imperial commissioner, who was superior to the governor of Sicily himself, and over whom the Pope could only exercise a moral influence, not supported by any legal force. At all events, the position was such that the Pope could only restrain him indirectly, through the emperor himself; so that in case a good understanding was not maintained, it was possible for the commissioner to do much harm, before the Pope could hinder him, by the circuitous method which consisted in appealing to Constantinople. Yet such difficulties arose rarely, if at all, during the reign of the wise Gregory, and the rich south put out new blossom and fruit under his careful hand. The clergy, the nobility, and people lived peacefully under his paternal guidance, if not under his direct and sovereign rule, and the vast wealth began to accumulate which was erelong to fill the treasury of a new conqueror. When the Arabs destroyed Syracuse in 878 they took, with other booty, more than a million pieces of gold, which is said to have been the largest sum of money ever seized by them in any one city throughout all their conquests.

Balcony at Taormina

Cultivation had become very extensive in Sicily, and individual estates were of enormous extent. One is mentioned which required no less than four hundred overseers, and with the Empire the custom of letting land to small tenants had arisen, as being more practical in some cases than that of cultivating a great estate for the owner's direct benefit, under the supervision of stewards; these small free tenants were called 'coloni,' and the word is used in its original meaning to the present day in Italy. Of the number and condition of the slaves at the time of Pope Gregory we know little, and are not likely to learn more. The free tenants were evidently a substitute for slaves, as a means of getting the greatest possible income from the land, and this fact alone goes to show that the number of slaves had diminished, and that their value had increased, so that it no longer paid the landholder to employ them. That there were still a number of slaves in Sicily, however, we know. We know also that the introduction of the 'Malvasia' grape took place in this period. Malvasia is a corruption of Monembasia, and has been further corrupted in English to 'Malmsey.' Monembasia is a harbour in the Peloponnesus, called in ancient times Epidaurus Limera, and a very close trading connexion existed between it and Sicily in the sixth century. Its sweet white grapes were the original stock whence descended those of which the good white wines of Sicily are made in our day, and there is not a farmer in the south who does not pride himself upon having a demijohn or two of the rich Malvasia wine ripening in a corner of his 'grotta' for some great occasion. Its flavour is like that of Malaga, and it has as much body, and often as fine a colour; but excepting where it has been made with great skill and patience, it is usually a coarser wine. From the same grapes the Marsala is made, and the principal peculiarity of the Malvasia is that in making it a certain quite of grapes are used which have been hung in a dry place till they are half dried, and as sweet as sugar.

While Justinian was discriminating between the relative demerits of a dozen heresies, and while his successors were in vain attempting to imitate what they only half understood; and while the wise and saintly Gregory was ruling the Church for the true advancement and benefit of the Empire, as well as of mankind, a man was growing up whose influence was to change the course of history and modify the lives of many millions. When Gregory was elected Pope in 590, Mohammed was twenty years of age. Two hundred years later the Mohammedan Arabs destroyed Syracuse, and made themselves masters of the south. That period of two centuries, therefore, embraces the first preachings of Mohammed, who began to propagate his doctrines about the year 610, when he gave out that the Archangel Gabriel had appeared to him, declaring those truths which he was to reveal to men. Twelve years later, after converting his family and many other persons to the belief that he was the messenger and prophet of God, he fled before persecution to Yatreb, and thence to Medina, and the date of his escape and flight was the beginning of the Mohammedan era. Seated high upon his swift camel, and wrapped in his Arab blanket, fleeing by night with a few faithful followers, the delicate, red-haired, pale-faced young man was far from dreaming that he too, like his divine predecessor, had brought not peace but a sword into the world; or that the near descendants of those whom his converts were set soon to convert should snatch an empire from the midst of a world which, in his own childhood, had been governed by such men as the Emperor Justinian and the Pontiff Gregory. It may be that the amazing progress of the Mohammedan religion was due to the wretched moral state of man in the East, that the natural force it possessed by the simplicity of the appeal it made to human passions was strengthened by the promises of unbounded satisfaction in a future which the Christian shudders to contemporary; it may be also that Christianity had not fulfilled its mission in those countries where Mohammedanism spread first and most rapidly. Between the death of Saint Gregory and the first descent of the Arabs upon Sicilian shores falls the war of the Images, than which no conflict could give a more precise notion of the condition of Christian worship in the East.

Saint Gregory, who was a practical pastor before he was an enlightened Pope, had declared that the presence in churches of pictures and statues representing not only divine beings, but persons of holy life and death, was conducive to an historical knowledge of Christianity, by affording instruction to the many who could not read. In an age when ignorance of all letters was the rule, and when an overwhelming majority of believers were therefore called upon to accept instruction both in dogma and in history of their faith by word of mouth only, such a point of view as that of the great Pope was not only wise and practical, but seemed to be the only reasonable one. The early Christians had inveighed, with a violence paralleled only by that afterwards displayed by the Arabs, against the heathen idolatry; they had animated the images of Apollo, of Aphrodite, and of Athene with the spirits of devils in order to enjoy, in the destruction of senseless matter, the imaginary delights of vanquishing the Prince of Darkness in his stronghold. The first missionary bishop in Sicily, not yet strong enough to overthrow the oracle in his temple, was believed to have silenced him by secretly fastening a letter round the neck of his image. The fury of the Christians had never been directed against the images themselves, but always against the demons that were supposed to inhabit them. Never, from the earliest times, had the Christians exhibited that horror of a graven image which was an article of faith with the Jews, and was has remained one among strict Mohammedans. From the beginning the Christian slave was impelled to express upon the stone that covered his loved ones, the thought of that peace which is beyond all understanding; and, unlettered as he mostly was, his expression took the form of a rude image, of a symbol, of a mere sign. The simple faith which at first fulfilled its rites in caves, in subterranean quarries, and in the cellars of deserted palaces, rose to the surface and displayed itself in the upper air with a magnificence which was but the outward sign of mankind's approbation; then the mark grew to an inscription, the symbol to a halo, the rude outline of God's image to an exalted image of God himself. Above the dark catacomb wherein had been laid the torn bodies of martyred saints, and where the poor and the outcast had worshipped in hourly fear of death, but in the perpetual certainty of the life to come, — above those places of refuge and suffering rose the splendid cathedrals of a victorious and universal religion. And that religion, like Agag of old, lived in the illusion that the bitterness of death was past; it depicted its past sufferings and present triumphs with all the art which the times could command, it made light of future trials, and it believed that the millennium of the blessed was at hand.

Such was the condition of the Church in Sicily fifty years after Pope Gregory's death; and it came to pass that Mohammedans sailed up to Sicily out of the southeast, and made a furious raid upon the island, and took much spoil. So strong were the adherents of the new faith become in 652, the thirtieth year of their era. But they were not yet strong enough to conquer the south, in spite of Constantinople, and when they had fought with some imperial troops under the exarch himself, they seem to have yielded to the representations of Pope Martin the First, for they sailed away again to Asia, taking their booty with them, and a number of Sicilian prisoners, who settled in Damascus.

At that time, the emperor was that wretched Constans the Second, who sent the Exarch Olympius to Rome to murder Pope Martin, because the latter refused to accept the imperial opinion as an incontrovertible dogma. But Olympius was converted, and went with the Pope into Sicily against the Mohammedans, and died there of the plague. Then Constans accused the Pope of allying himself with the Arabs, and caused him to be brought from Rome to Messina, and thence to Constantinople, where the venerable pontiff was condemned to death, and dragged through the streets by the hangman, before he was sent to die in the Crimea.

Then Constans, having satisfied his thirst for vengeance, attempted to chastise the Mohammedans for their attack on Sicily, but was himself ignominiously beaten at sea, and retired to his own capital, which was distracted by schisms and cankered with seditions. At once restless, foolish, and unscrupulous, he conceived the idea of reëstablishing the Empire in Rome, since he could not reign peacefully in Constantinople; he would attack Benevento, crush the Lombard power in the south, conciliate the Pope, restore what had been, and make himself a reputation out of the rags of failure. He collected troops in Italy and Sicily. The Lombard Duke of Benevento had seized for himself the Lombard kingdom in the north, and reigned in Pavia, but his son defended the Duchy, some say by the miraculous help of Saint Barbatus, and put the unwarlike emperor to flight. Constans paused for breath in Naples, and then hastened on to Rome. In twelve days he had performed his devotions at the tombs of the saints and had stripped the city of its beautiful bronze statues, and of every bit of bronze and copper on which he could lay his hands.

Saracen-Norman court of the Capuchin Convent at Amalfi

A new scheme had formed itself in his weak brain; he would establish the empire in Sicily, and make Syracuse his residence. He returned to Naples, and proceeded thence by land to Reggio. The western side of the south was ruled by Greek dukes, loyal to the Empire, from Gaeta to Naples, Sorrento, and Amalfi, and thence to Taranto; he reached Sicily unmolested by the Lombards, who had no fleet, and he established himself in Syracuse, its last and most despicable tyrant.

Five years he reigned there and ravaged the land that remembered Verres and was soon to be a prey to the Saracens. He seized property by violence, and raised more money by the legal extortion of exorbitant taxes; and when these could not be paid, the miserable debtors were sold into slavery. To fill the measure of his greed, he took the sacred vessels from the churches and convents when there was nothing else left to take.

Then a slave killed him, in the year 668. While he was washing himself in his bath with Gallic soap, the man Andreas — insulted, we know not how, past all bearing — laid hands upon the soap box, which was the only movable thing in the bathroom, and brought it down upon the emperor's head with all his might. Then he fled by an inner way. Either the soap box was very heavy, or the man was very strong, for the work was done, and the last tyrant of Syracuse lay dead on the marble floor. A few courtiers made a puppet-emperor of a certain Armenian, but the soldiers immediately rose and cut off his head, and sent it to Constantinople before the young Constantine the Third reached Sicily with his fleet. Having restored order he retired, and a Saracen fleet suddenly appeared before Syracuse. The Arabs once more plundered the city, carrying off to Alexandria all spoils of copper and bronze which Constans had brought from Rome. Then there was peace for a time, while Constantine reigned in his own city, and Sicily once more felt the beneficial effects of papal administration. Several Sicilians were popes within a few years; there was Agatho of Palermo, and Leo the Second, also a Sicilian, and there was the Thracian Conon, who had been brought up in Sicily, and Sergius the First, of Palermo, who refused to sign certain articles approved by a council in Constantinople. The emperor, who was then Justinian the Second, sent an officer to Rome to arrest Sergius; but the militia of Ravenna came to the rescue, and the poor Byzantine officer, in fright for his life, took refuge under the Pope's own bed, and was allowed to escape unhurt. The Church was strong enough to defy the emperor now.

Then came the conflict about the use of images, of which the result was to establish the supremacy of the popes in Rome. I have already said enough to explain the view held regarding images in Italy. In the year 717 the Emperor Leo the Isaurian ascended the throne of Constantinople. Animated by a spirit of reform, but unable to understand that the Church's real danger lay in the theological dissensions which continually distracted Constantinople and the East, he decreed that all images and pictures should be removed from churches throughout the Empire. A more unwise measure could hardly have been adopted, or one more certain to rouse a storm of opposition in the Eastern and in the West. Had Christianity begun its career, like Mohammedanism, by prohibiting the representation of animate living things, there is no reason to suppose that its followers could ever have fallen into an abuse of symbolism or an excess of images. The Persian Mohammedans have departed from the law of the Prophet in regard to at least two points; they drink wine, and in their arts they depict both human beings and animals; yet they are not a nation of drunkards, and the images they paint and carve have little or no connexion with their faith. With Christians it was otherwise; their history was bound up with countless memories of individuals, and while it cannot rightly be said that the sum of their devotion was divided among many objects, yet, in their worship of those they supremely revered, their doctrine taught them of the constant presence of those who before themselves had died for the faith, of the nameless millions who waited for them on the threshold of heaven, worshipping with them and praying for them in the Communion of Saints, and most of all of those whom they themselves had known on earth and who were gone before to the place of refreshment, light, and peace. The Latin mind was never imaginative; the Greek intelligence had ceased to be; and to unimaginative minds some representation of the thing believed is all but necessary to belief. Half a lifetime spent among the people of the south has convinced me that, in spite of all that northern writers have said to the contrary, the Italian peasant never really confounds the image with the holy person, divine or human, whom it represents. He may call the image miraculous, and to those who do not understand his mode of expressing himself, it may indeed seem that he is attributing supernatural powers to the wood and stone; but a few questions asked in his own language and in terms comprehensible to him, will suffice to convince any fair inquirer that he looks upon the matter very differently. The souls of the departed blessed, he says, are in paradise; they may be moved by prayer to intercede for man, and, as if retaining some of their earthly attributes, they may prefer that men should address them, when possible, in places which their lives and deaths, or their especial choice, may have more particularly indicated. The peasant who makes a pilgrimage to the shrine of Our Lady at Pompeii, or of Saint Michael on Monte Gargano, speaks as if he were going to see the Mother of God, or the Archangel, in their bodily reality; but in real truth he goes to places which he believes they have especially chosen, with the hope of awakening his sluggish imagination by the sight of revered images and objects in the company of many of his fellows. To destroy those images, even when the places wherein they are preserved are not consecrated, would be to attack his right of stimulating his imagination in the manner most natural to him. If such an edict as that issued by Leo the Isaurian were proclaimed in the south to-day, it would produce results that might surprise the world. It is no wonder that in the beginning of the eighth century it should have led to a revolution which established the independence of the temporal power of Rome for many centuries to come. Leo indeed published his edict, but Pope Gregory the Second solemnly declared in a papal bull that the emperor was not concerned in such matters and had no right to decide what belief should be held by the Church; and by way of enforcing theory by practice, he forbade his people in Rome and in Italy to pay taxes to the emperor. The latter retorted boldly by deposing the Pope, so far as a mere written declaration could accomplish such a momentous undertaking. Leo wrote his decree, but the whole militia of Naples and of Venice assembled without delay to protect the Pope. The emperor attempted to enforce his will with a fleet and an army, but the Italians stood by the Pope to a man, and the Lombards of the north took up arms in his defence. The emperor's troops were everywhere repulsed, and their leaders were put to death; the ancient factions and feuds of the Italian cities were forgotten, and the people united to fight side by side for the holy images. At Ravenna, which was the seat of the imperial exarchate, the fighting was long and fierce; the army of Leo was beaten on land and sought a fancied safety in the ships of the imperial fleet; but the people pursued them in small craft and fishing-boats and skiffs, and in a single day the river Po was dyed so deeply red with Byzantine blood that for six years the people would not taste of its fish. Failing in arms, the emperor made more than one attempt to assassinate his stout opponent; but the Pope was secure in the protection of his fellow-countrymen and thundered a general and major excommunication against his defeated adversaries. Gregory the Second could have assumed the reins of independent government had he chosen to do so; or perhaps Liutprand, the Lombard king, might have taken Rome for himself and reëstablished an Italian kingdom. But the skilful diplomacy of Gregory the Second turned his strong ally from the path of conquest on the one hand, and on the other, he did not choose to inflict useless humiliation upon his imperial adversary. The emperor's exarch was suffered to live unmolested in Ravenna, and to enjoy some outward semblance of a departed power. Having been beaten by sea and land, driven to an ignominious flight, and tacitly included under the ban of excommunication, Leo was nevertheless afterwards designated as Piissimus, the Most Pious, and Rome, liberated from imperial oppression, allowed herself to be ruled in the name of the emperors. And so the administration continued to be exercised until another pope crowned Charles the Great as first emperor of a new Western line.

Entrance to Grotto Church at Praia d' Aieta, Calabria

The result of the War of the Images was the final establishment of the temporal power; but in the changing chances of the times it came about that the south, or at least that part of it which was not controlled by the Lombard Duchy of Benevento, began to occupy a new position. The emperor had succeeded in confiscating the Patrimony of the Church in Calabria and in Sicily, which practically meant that the Sicilian Church was thenceforth to be controlled by the Patriarch of Constantinople, instead of by the Pope of Rome. In Sicily, and the south, the edict against images was enforced during more than a century, and Sicilian ecclesiastical writers speak with pride of the persecution suffered by their countrymen. Antiochus, governor of Sicily, and others who refused to submit to what they considered an heretical domination, were martyred in the Hippodrome, at Constantinople, in the year 766, with a cruelty that might have satisfied Nero. In 772, Jacob, Bishop of Catania, died a martyr's death; Methodius, of Syracuse, was scourged, and confined for seven years in a subterranean prison with two thieves, and when one of the latter died, the jailors refused to remove his body. But this same Methodius was freed at last, attained to great dignities, and ended his life as Patriarch of Constantinople. To punish them for their attachment to Rome, the unfortunate Sicilians were forced to pay taxes one-third higher than those levied upon the other subjects of the Empire. As if such misfortunes were not enough, Sicily was exposed to the raids of the Arabs, who as yet had not the power to conquer and hold the island, but who swarmed about it like wasps about a peach tree laden with sweet fruit, and against whom the Byzantine troops seem to have been well-nigh powerless; and it was not until the ninth century that the respectable people of Sicily followed the example of the Italians of Venice and Ravenna, and armed themselves, forming a regular militia for the general protection of the country.

The oppression suffered in consequence of the war of the holy images was not without interruptions. From time to time, when it was known that the Mohammedans were so near Constantinople as to paralyze the forces of the Empire at their centre, or when other circumstances produced a similar state of things, the people of Sicily rose, under the leadership of a discontented Byzantine general, or a disaffected governor. It was the last of those insurrections that led directly to the Mohammedan conquest. Before that took place, however, another event happened which produced results of the greatest importance to history. Gregorius Asbesta, Bishop of Syracuse, quarrelled with Ignatius, Patriarch of Constantinople, and in the course of the conflict won the friendship of the celebrated theologian Photius, who was the emperor's favourite. Ignatius appealed to the Pope, who took his side, and condemned both Photius and Gregorius Asbesta. Thereupon the emperor deposed Ignatius, and made Photius patriarch in spite of the Pope, causing him to be consecrated by Gregorius. The Pope and Photius then disagreed upon the dogmatic point of the Procession of the Holy Ghost, Photius declaring that the Holy Ghost proceeded from the Father alone, while Pope Nicholas the First maintained the Catholic belief embodied in the words of the Creed, 'proceeding from the Father and the Son.' The result of this disagreement, after a prolonged struggle in which Photius was alternately condemned and rehabilitated, was the great schism of the East and West, that divided the so-called Greek Orthodox Church forever from the Roman Catholic. Few persons remember that a Sicilian bishop was the original cause of difference.

It must not be forgotten that there were now two Empires, and that the vast conquests of Charlemagne, which outdid in extent those of Julius Caesar, had not included Sicily. The separation of the island from Rome was finally accomplished, and it remained attached to the tottering Empire of Constantinople, until it pleased the Saracens to take it for themselves. It was included in the same military 'thema,' or circuit, as we may say for lack of a better word, with Calabria and Naples, and the boundary that separated the two Empires was that which for a long time had divided the Duchy of Benevento from the small Greek Duchies that followed the western coast of Italy, from Gaeta to Reggio. The value of this region to Constantinople was twofold; its agricultural wealth made it a most valuable possession, though one not easy to keep, and it served as a basis for attempts at regaining influence in the west. Charlemagne, who never meant to reside in Rome, was not willing to renew his quarrel with the east for the sake of giving back to Rome her ancient granary. Had he chosen to seize Sicily, he could have done so, of course, and if he had taken it, and had unified it with Italy under a good government, the subsequent history of the Holy Roman Empire might have been very different. The popes did not cease to exert their influence to bring about such a result, in the hope of recovering some of their best possessions; but every effort was in vain, and the separation was complete. It was soon to be made still more irrevocable by the Mohammedan conquest of the south. From the very earliest times there seems to have been something fated in the division of Italy into north and south, which more than sufficiently accounts for the hereditary ill-feeling that still exists between the two.

At the close of this period of southern history in the early part of the ninth century, the Byzantine Empire was in possession of the great island and of the western side of the mainland, a great part of which, however, enjoyed more independence than Sicily itself. The east side, from some point north of Benevento to the Gulf of Taranto, was a single Lombard Duchy, comprising the rich lands and pastures of Apulia and Lucania, and the Lombard Dukes threatened to annex Naples. At this time, about two hundred years after the Hejira, the Mohammedan dominions extended from the borders of India, through Persia, Arabia, Egypt, and Northern Africa, to the straits of Gibel-el-Tarik, or Gibraltar, and Spain. The conquest of those countries had continued without interruption since the days of Mohammed, and though the Mohammedans were supposed to live under one sovereign, the Khalif of Bagdad, they had, in fact, founded a number of perfectly independent kingdoms, united only in their hatred of Christianity, but sometimes at war with each other, especially in Africa. Perhaps no one of them would have been a match for Constantinople in a regular naval war at that time, but as the Mohammedans were practically masters of the sea, and collected their pirate vessels from time to time in small but active fleets, they were able to concentrate enough ships and men at any point from Gibraltar to the shores of Asia Minor to bid defiance to the scattered navy and unready soldiers of the Empire. Their conquest of Sicily and of the south was not an isolated action, but formed a part of their national career, and it was to be foreseen that they must succeed in the enterprise with no great loss to themselves, as soon as they should choose to attempt it seriously.

The Saracens

The end of the Byzantine domination in the south was brought about by one of those insurrections against the injustice of the rulers to which reference has already been made. The north of Africa was under the domination of an Arab chief who had succeeded in inducing the Khalif of Bagdad to countenance his independent supremacy. This Ibrahim appears to have had some inkling of civilized government, and in order to promote the commerce of his people with the Sicilians he agreed to a peace which was to last ten years. Unfortunately Ibrahim could not make himself responsible for the peaceful conduct of other Mohammedan princes, who continued their depredations for some time unhindered, and his successor returned to the traditional ways of his race. He prepared an expedition which had no definite object except to plunder Christian countries. On this occasion the Mohammedans fell upon the islands west of Naples, and took what plunder they could gather from Ponza and Ischia; but some part of the fleet having been lost, a new treaty was ratified. It was not observed with good faith, however, and before the time of its expiration another flying attack was made upon Sicily.

The event which was to have such great and lasting results for the south was finally brought about in the following manner. In the year 826, the Emperor Michael Balbus was obliged to exert every energy to preserve his sovereignty and Constantinople against the attacks of a rival. It being known that he was thus occupied, the troops in Sicily seized the opportunity to rise against the governor. They had momentarily underrated the emperor's strength, however, the insurrection was partially repressed, and a new governor named Photinus was sent to reduce the unruly province to order. Among those suspected of favouring the revolution there was a certain rich landholder named Euphemius, who appears to have had a great following. Unable to find satisfactory proof against him, Photinus trumped up an accusation which, if proved, would have ruined him. Euphemius, it is said, had been guilty of no less a crime than that of carrying off a beautiful nun from a Sicilian convent. The accused man gathered his followers about him and defied the governor; a pitched battle ensued, in which he was victorious. He took possession of Syracuse, and not content with the result of the contest, actually declared himself emperor. The idea was novel and daring, and presented so many attractions to adventurous minds that a counter-insurrection almost immediately followed; but in the confusion the Byzantine troops, who seem to have acknowledged some sort of authority, got the better, and Euphemius fled from Syracuse to Africa and to the Mohammedans. He proposed that they should help him to conquer Sicily and establish himself as its sovereign, on condition of paying a yearly tribute forever afterwards. In the execution of this scheme, Euphemius came into contact with a force of which he had not expected the existence. Among the chief persons at the Mohammedan court was the Kadi of the capital, the aged Ased, a man who had the reputation of being a profound jurist, and who was certainly a religious fanatic, willing to go to any length for his convictions. In answer to the representations of Euphemius, he replied that if the war were fought at all, it will be fought in order to carry the Mohammedan faith among the Christians of the south, and he let it be understood that it would matter little what became of Euphemius himself, provided that an unbelieving country could be brought under the rule of the faithful. He himself was appointed the general of the Mohammedan forces, and on the thirteenth of June, 827, he sailed for Sicily with a fleet of a hundred ships, in which he embarked no less than ten thousand foot soldiers, and seven hundred horsemen. According to the Sicilian chronicle, given by Muratori from the Cambridge manuscript, the expedition landed in Sicily in the middle of the month of July, but Amari says that the Mohammedans landed at Mazzara on the sixteenth of June, which allows only three days for the passage. Be that as it may, the Mohammedans overcame the Byzantines in the first engagement, marched with little hindrance along the south coast in the direction of Syracuse, while the imperial troops took refuge in the stronghold of Henna, now Castrogiovanni. Ased made a bold dash at the capital of the island, but he encountered the same difficulties which, long ago, had wrought the ruin of Athenians and Carthaginians alike. The resources of the immediate neighbourhood were exhausted, and the besiegers suffered severely from lack of provisions; with the first autumn rains the fatal miasma of the Lysimeleian swamp spread a deadly pestilence through the Mohammedan army, and the aged general himself fell a victim to the sickness. The Mohammedans now attempted to leave the harbour with their ships as the Athenians had done, but, like them, were beaten by the Syracusan fleet, and like them, also, were driven by sheer necessity to attempt a retreat by land. Where the Athenians had been finally destroyed by the superior activity of Gylippus, however, the Mohammedans succeeded in making good their retreat, and though they had failed to take Syracuse, they were never again driven from the shores of Sicily. Taking refuge in the strong retreat afforded by the citadel of Mineo on the northern slope of the Ereian hills, they soon recovered from the effects of starvation and fever, regained their courage and energy, and prepared to carry on the war with unabated vigour. Descending in force, but no longer in the direction of the capital, they seized Girgenti and boldly attacked Henna itself. Of its name they made Kasr Janna, meaning 'the fortress of John,' and the city has retained the appellation in modern times. So sure were they of reducing the almost impregnable stronghold, that they even coined money which bore its name. But an attempt made by Euphemius himself to induce the defenders to surrender ended in his death, and shortly afterwards a Byzantine army came to the rescue; the Mohammedans were obliged to abandon the siege and to withdraw to Mineo, while the garrison they had left in Girgenti retreated to the little island stronghold of Mazzara, less than twenty miles from Marsala. These were the only two places held by the Saracens in 829, but they succeeded in keeping possession of them until the following year, when they renewed the war with large reënforcements, and they took Palermo in 832 after a siege in which more than nine-tenths of the population perished. They now commanded the western portion of the island, while the Byzantines still held Syracuse and the east. The Cambridge 'Chronicon Sicilum' recapitulates the events of the forty-seven years during which the Saracens completed the conquest, beginning with the statement that they came to Sicily in the middle of July, 827. In 831 they took Messina, and the Patrician Theodotus was slain, and in 832 Palermo fell. Ten years later, in 842, Sicily was plagued by locusts. In 845 the Saracens had advanced so far southward as to capture the fortress of Modica, on the crags above the river Magro, where the wild cactus grows against the ruined castle walls. The next year the Moslems fought the Byzantines before Castrogiovanni, and slew nine thousand of them. In 847 they had moved round Syracuse far enough to take Leontini, and a year later they completed the chain of strong places behind them by seizing Ragusa the first time; and, moreover, there was a great famine. Six years passed after this, during which nothing happened worth recording, and in 854 the Saracens took Butera near the south coast, not far from Licata; but another source informs us that they besieged the strong place five months and departed at last, being bribed to give up the attempt by the surrender of six thousand of the inhabitants as slaves. Four years after this a number of ships, commanded by a certain Ali, were taken by the Byzantines, but in 859 Castrogiovanni was at last taken, and from that lofty height the Saracens overlooked and dominated most of the island. The strong place fell by treachery, every man able to bear arms was slain, and the rest of the people were made slaves. Some of the beautiful women and boys were thought worthy to be sent as a gift to the Khalif of Bagdad.

Bell Tower at Paola in Calabria, the birthplace of San Francesco di Paola

Ibn Khaldoun says that Aghlab, the governor of Sicily, died in Palermo in the year 858, having governed the country for nineteen years, and that the Mussulmans at his death chose Abas for the emir, and that he was officially invested with the governorship. Until he had received this he had only sent out small expeditions to plunder the country in divers directions, but as soon as he had received full authority he went out in person and overran many parts of Sicily, sacking everything in the direction of Catania, Syracuse, Butera, and Ragusa; and that after several engagements he took possession of Castrogiovanni. The fullest account of the events that preceded the taking of the latter place is that of Ibn-el-Athir. According to him Abas was in hopes that by laying waste the surrounding country he might tempt the Byzantine patrician to come out against him, but that he was disappointed in this; that he attempted again to take the place two years later, and that he besieged the place which the Arab historian calls Thira for the space of five months, took it, and 'pardoned the garrison for the price of five thousand heads.' In 865 Abas repulsed the troops which came out against him from Castrogiovanni and besieged a place called Kasr-el-Hadid, of which the population offered him a large sum of money, which he refused, and thereupon, as he continued the siege, they surrendered on condition that he would grant liberty to two hundred of their number. He sold the rest as slaves, and razed the walls. With regard to Castrogiovanni Ibn Khaldoun tells us that Abas was about to put to death certain captives, when one of them, who was a man of importance, offered to betray the place in exchange for his life. Abas consented, and the Mussulmans were led by night to a place that was but weakly defended, and the traitor introduced them by a secret entrance. The Arab adds that the fall of the Greek power in Sicily dates from that day, although the emperor made the most tremendous efforts to regain possession of the island. The mortification of the Byzantines at the loss of their great fortress was boundless, and everywhere the people rose against the conquerors. Noto was taken, indeed, but was lost again; the Byzantines seized a number of Saracen vessels; Ragusa had to be recaptured, and as a basis of operations against Syracuse, the Saracens took Malta in 870. In 872 a Mohammedan army had advanced upon the mainland as far as Salerno, and perished there. At last the fate of Syracuse was at hand; the Mohammedans held the main strongholds throughout the island, reaching hands, as it were, from hill to hill, and constantly narrowing the little territory left to the Byzantines.

We possess a full and graphic account of the last great siege which ended in the destruction of Syracuse. Theodosius, a monk, was in the city and escaped death, though he remained some time a prisoner; the long letter which he wrote on the subject to the Archdeacon Leo has been used by every historian as the only accurate source of information, and has been so often paraphrased that it may interest the reader to know by a literal translation exactly what the good man wrote.

"The Epistle of the monk Theodosius to the Archdeacon Leo concerning the capture of Syracuse.

Most Divine Sir:— To follow out the details of those things what had happened to us, a longer time and a more convenient occasion would be necessary, and a letter is too short to contain the whole series of the things that have been done. On the other hand it seems to me that to be silent about these things, and about the common grief felt by almost the whole world — for I can readily believe that all must pity us who have even heard the name of Syracuse — to keep silence, I say, would seem to be the part of a paralyzed intelligence and of a man overcome by indolence; of which one of the prophets has spoken, as by the mouth of God, saying, 'I have received them with scourges but they have not repented.' But if I undertake the narrative of these events, no matter how, it will be of some use to both of us. For it will bring me some consolation to speak, since by speaking I have some hope of being relieved from the evils by which I am now tormented, because it is a fact in nature that if one explain in words those things by which one is troubled, the bitterness of the soul is tempered; but you on your part shall at least receive the fee of tears if, perchance, you shall bestow them in pity upon the narrative you follow.

"O you, sir, who have enjoyed divine honours, we are fallen into the power of the enemy, and we are taken at last, nor did Jerusalem, when it was taken, experience worse things, neither Samaria which was overcome before Jerusalem; such ruin have we suffered as never the isles of Chetim knew, nor barbarous countries, nor any cities that can be reported. Such was the slaughter that on the same day every weapon with which defence had been made was broken to pieces, bows, quivers, arms, swords, and all weapons; the strong were made weak, and the violence of the foe drove to surrender those defenders, those brave men whom I may well call giants, who laboured with all their might, who hesitated not before that day to suffer hunger and all labours, and to be pierced with numberless wounds for the love of Christ, and who were all put to the sword after the city was taken. At length we are fallen into the hands of the enemy, though for a long time we defended ourselves from the walls, and though many times there was fighting on the sea, which indeed was a horrible sight, filling with consternation the eyes of those that looked, for the vision is indeed dismayed by the atrocity of those things which are often brought before it. We were vanquished after many attacks made upon us by night, and many a hostile ambush, after engines had been brought up against the walls with which these were pounded almost all day, after a grievous storm of stones hurled against our works, when the tortoise-shed that destroys cities had been used against us, and those things which they call subterranean rats; for not one of those things which are of use for taking a city was left untried by those who were in charge of the siege; the intense desire to possess our city had already inflamed their hearts, and they contended to the utmost with one another, excogitating new engines from day to day, the more easily to take and destroy the city. Nevertheless, in the admirable wisdom of His councils,° God protected us in a measure from these. But of what use is it to continue any further in tragic strain, complaining of the chaos of evils which our enemies heaped upon us by their enormous ingenuity? Did they leave anything uninvaded or untried, which seemed to them capable of inspiring terror in the besieged, and of filling their hearts with dismay?

"Time admonishes me to turn to those things which were done within the city, and I shall say a few words at length concerning these matters; without, the sword laid waste our strength, and fear did so within, so that I might well say that in that ancient prophecy Moses spoke of us. For as before we had sinned against God like the people of Israel, we have drunk of the same cup of the divine wrath that Israel drank; we were taken captive after we had suffered hunger long, feeding upon herbs, after having thrust into our mouths in our extreme need even filthy things, after men had even devoured their children — a frightful deed, that should be passed in silence, although we had before abhorred human flesh — oh! hideous spectacle — but who, for his own dignity's sake, could weep such deeds in tragic strain? We did not abstain from eating leather and the skins of oxen, nor any other things soever which seemed capable of relieving men exhausted by hunger, and we spared not even dry bones, but dressed them to make ourselves a cheerful meal — a new sort of food abhorrent to the custom of mortal men. What will not unceasing hunger force men to do? Many of the Syracusans were driven to grind the bones of four-footed beasts in the mill, and these wretched men stilled their hunger with the stuff, after wetting it with a very little water. The fountain of Arethusa supplied us abundantly with water for such uses. A measure of wheat was sold for a hundred and fifty pieces of gold, but the millers sold it for more, even for two hundred pieces, so that, strange as it may seem, a roll weighing two ounces was sold for a piece of gold. Add to this, that a beast of burden was sold for as much more than three hundred gold pieces as it was the more fit for food when put up for sale, and the head of a horse went to fifteen gold pieces and sometimes even to twenty; the flesh of asses was considered something most delicious. No sort of domestic bird or fowl was left, and oil and all sorts of salt provisions had long been eaten up, even such things which, as Gregorius Theologus says, are usually the food of the poor; no cheese, no vegetables, no fish. Already the enemy had forcibly taken possession of the two harbours between which Syracuse lies, having previously levelled to the ground the defences which were called the 'brachiolia,' and which once kept the enemy from entering the harbours. Now this thing came to pass, by far the most terrible thing; a most grievous pestilence, alas, followed upon famine, and some were tormented by the disease called lock-jaw, so named from the contraction of the nerves; apoplexy dried up half of the bodies of some others, it killed others instantly, but many who were attacked by the same disease could only move half their bodies or were altogether deprived of the power of motion; others, their bodies inflated like bladders, presented a horrid spectacle to the beholder, and though death was always hanging over them, it hardly set those wretched creatures free in the end with the severest suffering, for even death was obeying the divine command, and was thereby not a little retarded. Indeed, to those things which I have already mentioned, very many more could be added, which would require a longer narrative than can be sent by a man given up to custody. For what else can I do than condense and crowd such great things into few words, being shut up in prison where I have not one hour of peace and quiet? The thick darkness of my prison, which hangs over my eyes, weakens and dulls my sight, and the noises made by the others who are confined in the same place agitate and disturb my mind.

"The tower, which was built at the greater port, at the right-hand angle of the city, was first struck and then partly fell down under the violence of the catapults with which the enemy hurled enormous stones. Five days after the destruction of this tower, the wall of the rampart, which had before been connected with the tower, was destroyed by the force of the catapults; thereupon great terror entered into the hearts of the besieged, but nevertheless those noble and truly brave men sustained the attack of the enemy under the leadership of his blessedness the Duke and Patrician, and did their best to second his tremendous exertions, beyond all that can be expressed in words, during twenty days and as many nights, when a wall fell down upon those who were bravely and nobly defending the approach on that side, and who thus manifested their inborn nobility of spirit, and held it to be the highest praise to be wounded in every part of their bodies for the defence of the city. And now, indeed, whoever chose to go to that rampart, which was called by the people the Unfortunate, might see there many men mutilated in divers and strange ways; for some had their eyes dug out, and others had their noses cut off, some had lost their ears, others their eyelids; the jaws of others were red with blood from wounds of darts and arrows, and some were wounded in the forehead, and some in the heart, and in many ways; the bodies of some, the breasts of others, lay open from the wounds they had received; they suffered, in a word not here and there, but in every part. For the enemy besieged the city with all their forces, and was so far superior in numbers, that although it is hardly to be believed, a hundred of them fought hand-to-hand with one of us, covering their antagonists with no common glory in dangers which it required the highest courage to face. But I used to call to mind the zeal of the athletes whenever I came to a place where they were fighting fearlessly and splendidly and earning great glory for deeds well done. But when the number of our sins had so greatly increased that the drawn sword of the wrath of God was drunk with them, then, on the twenty and first day of May, and on the fourth day after the wall had fallen, the city was reduced into the power of the enemy; and the mention in which it was taken is well worth describing, for it was full of horror. For when the stern displeasure of God against us had scattered hither and thither the stoutest of those who resisted the enemy, and had called away our famous Patrician with his companions from the walls to their own houses, in order that they might take some food for their bodies' sake, then it was put into the hearts of the barbarians of renew the attack at that fatal tower of which I have spoken; and when they had advanced those engines which they used for throwing stones, the murderous traitors who invaded our city enjoyed the spectacle. Nor had they undertaken a hard matter, since but a few soldiers were guarding the tower, and the citizens did not suppose that it was a time for fighting, so our defenders felt safe and thought of nothing less than of going to the ramparts. Therefore, while the enemy were hurling stones into the city in a fearful manner, and compassed it all round about, a certain wooden ladder, over which the half-ruined tower was usually reached by the garrison, was broken down, and thereupon a great din arose; when the Patrician heard this, he sprang up at once from the table without finishing his meal, full of great anxiety for the ladder. As soon as the barbarians perceived that the ladder was broken down, for they were hurling their stones in its vicinity, they approached the walls with weight greatest alacrity, and seeing but a few men guarding the tower, vigorously drove them back and slew them; and among them was the blessed John Patrinus. After this they ascended without opposition and took possession of the place, and thence they spread through the city like a river in the sight of those who were gathering together to defend it. First they slew to the last man those who were drawn up in line against them at the porch of the Church of the Saviour, and with a great rush they opened the doors and entered the temple with drawn swords, as they panted for breath, to emit fire from their nostrils and eyes. Then indeed people all ages fell in a moment by the edge of the sword, princes and judges of the earth, as we sing in the psalms, young men and maidens, old men and children, both monks and those joined in matrimony, the priests and the people, the slave and the free man, and even sick persons who had lain a long time in bed. Merciful God, the butchers could not even spare these; for the soul that thirsts for human blood is not easily satisfied by the death of those who first face it in anger. And I may use the words of the holy Sophonias to tell of that day of disaster and of woe, that day of fear and ruin, that day of darkness and of gloom. But of what use is it to narrate in many words each separate thing that happened to the chief men, since such an account would strike horror to the ears that heard, and even to the very soul?

"Our great Patrician, who had retired into a certain fort, was taken alive with seventy men on the next day, and on the eighth day after the fall of the city he was executed. He bore his fate with so high and brave a heart as to admit nothing unworthy of his constancy, nor did he show the very smallest sign of fear; nor is that strange, since it had been impossible to induce him by any means to betray the city for his own safety, though there were many about him not only ready to approve the plan, but to help in its execution, had he wished it; but he chose to die without stain, trusting to save those who were with him by sacrificing his own life for many, after the example of our Lord, rather than to let his mind dwell upon anything unworthy of his honour; yet he moved not the hearts of his murderers to any pity whatsoever. His courage was so great, and his readiness to suffer the last extremity, that even Busa, the son of the emir Hajeb, who commanded his death, was filled with great admiration. But he himself had gained this fortitude to die in such good and holy fashion because he had spent the whole time of the war in the contemplation of death, and had excellently exhorted those who were besieged with him, showing them the way that leads to immortality, wherefore, by these deeds of goodness, he had learned to fear the end of life but little; for to those who have prepared themselves by a continual meditation, lest they should find their hearts unready to suffer the end, the journey hence to heaven is not joyless, when it comes at last. But the barbarians took those whom they had made prisoners with the Patrician, all born in Syracuse, and of high station, and some other captives also, and led them out of the city, and made them stand together within a circle; and they fell upon them with a rush, like wild dogs, and slew them, some with stones, some with clubs, some with the spears they had in their hands, and others with such weapons as they found by accident, pressing upon them most cruelly; and furiously raging in their hearts, they consumed their bodies with fire. I cannot pass over with silence the barbarous cruelties they perpetrated upon Nicetas. This man was of Tarsian family, most wise and brave in war, and during the siege he used daily to heap many curses upon Mohammed, who is held by that nation to be the greatest of the prophets. So they separated him from the number of those who were to be slain, and they stretched him upon the ground on his back, and they flayed him alive from his breast downward, and they tore to pieces his protruding vitals with spears; and, moreover, with their hands they tore the heart out of the man while he yet breathed, and lacerated it with their teeth, most monstrously, and dashed it upon the earth and stoned it, and then at last were satiated, and left it; but of these things elsewhere. Now I, who had already returned to favour with the bishop a second time, and was with him in the cathedral assisting him at prayers at the sixth hour, heard with my ears how the tower was taken by the barbarians, as we came to the end of the canticle. At this news no small fear entered into the hearts of those who heard, for what thing not terrible could we expect, being about to fall most certainly into the blood-stained hands of our enemies? Nevertheless, taking courage as we could, and while the enemy were engaged in plunder within sight of the church, we fled with two other clerks to the altar of the cathedral, naked and ashamed, for we had cast off all our garments, excepting what we wore that was of leather. The most blessed father (our bishop) had been accustomed to conciliate the wrath of God at this altar, and to ask help for his children, and his prayers had been answered; and this wonderful thing experience had shown very often, although at this time his prayers were rejected by the mysterious counsels of the heavenly judges. When, therefore, we found ourselves thus in peril, each asked pardon of the other for any sin he had committed, and we forgave one another; and we gave thanks to God that He had allowed us to endure these things. Now, therefore, while the bishop was commending his church to the Guardian Angel, behold the enemy were suddenly there, with drawn swords wet with blood, and they wandered through the whole building, turning hither and thither; and one of them departed out of the throng that moved round and came to the holy altar, and there he found us hiding between the altar and the (bishop's) chair, and he took us; yet did nothing cruel to us, for God had certainly softened his heart a little; he said nothing wrathful nor threatening, feigning timidity in his face, though he was armed with a naked sword which smoked and dripped blood still warm. He looked at the bishop and asked him tolerably clearly who he was. As soon as he knew, he asked, 'Where and are the sacred vessels of the Church?' But when he had learned concerning the place, he led the bishop out of the holy temple apart from all the disturbance and tumult, and us also with him, like lambs following their shepherd. When he had reached, by our guidance, the chapel where the sacred vessels used to kept, he shut us up in it and went about to see that the elders of the barbarians should come together as quickly as possible; and then he began to tell them concerning us. We learned that his name was Semnoës, and that he was of illustrious birth; and moved by his speech, or rather, as I should say, because God brought it all to a good ending, our enemies began to be well disposed towards us. On the same day they plundered the sacred things, and when they had done, the weight of all was five thousand pounds; and they made us go out of the city, overwhelmed with vehement grief, to say nothing of our other ills, and led us to the emir, who had encamped in the old cathedral (San Giovanni).

"He had us shut up in one of those vaulted chambers that are therein, and there it was inevitable that our poor bodies should be afflicted in every way; for the place was naturally filled with evil smells, and with worms that breed and bound in a day, as well as with the mice that were always there, and with swarms of lice and bugs, and literally with armies of fleas; and when it was night, we were overwhelmed by the falling darkness, and the house was filled with smoke which chanced to be made outside, and choked our miserable breath and almost entirely hid us from one another's sight. We were thrown into this chasm with our holy bishop and other clerk of the brethren, for the rest were all butchered when the city was taken; and there we spent thirty days, because the enemy required that time to destroy the defences of Syracuse. Throughout that period the buildings within the circuit of the walls were burned, and the value of all the booty taken was so great that the reckoning when cast up was found to be one thousand thousand° gold pieces.

"Not long after this we began the journey to Palermo which we accomplished in the space of six days, borne on beasts bred to carry burdens, but we were conducted by rough and savage Ethiopians. At length, much vexed by the heat in the daytime and by the nocturnal chills, and not having ceased to travel by day and night, we entered the extremely famous and populous city of Palermo; and as we went into the city, the people came out to meet us. They thronged out in great joy, and they sang songs of triumph, and as they saw the victors carrying the spoils into the city we at length saw the multitude of the citizens and of the strangers who had assembled, and that the number of the citizens, as compared with all accounts, had in our opinion not been overrated; for you would have thought that the whole race of the Saracens had come together there, from the rising up of the sun even to its going down, from the north and from the sea, according to the accustomed speech of the most blessed David. Wherefore the people being crowded together in such a press of inhabitants, began to build and inhabit houses without the walls, to such an extent that they really built many cities round the original one, not unequal to it, if one choose, either for attack or defence. But since, as I began to say, this most evil of all cities possessed a Contarchus — that is the name of the office — he deemed it unworthy of his fame not to make us pass under the yoke. And not only does he promise himself that he will do so, he even threatens to bring under his power peoples that live far away, and even the people of the imperial city (Constantinople). This being then the state of things, we were brought before the chief emir after the fifth day. He was sitting haughtily on a throne, on a terrace, much pleased with himself and his tyrannical power; and, like a towel hanging in the midst, he showed himself to us first from one side and then from the other. The attendants made the bishop stand forth, and through an interpreter the emir asked: 'Hast thou our manner of praying to God?' Our most wise superior would not admit that. 'Why in that manner?' asked the bishop; 'since I am the high priest of Christ and the leader of the mysteries of the servants of Christ, of whom the prophets and the righteous prophesied of old.' 'They are not prophets to you, in truth,' answered the emir, 'but only in name, since by them you would not be led away to your false doctrines, nor turned from the right path. For why do you assail our prophet with blasphemies?' 'We do not blaspheme the prophets at all,' returned the bishop, 'seeing that we have learned not to inveigh against prophets, but to speak in their behalf and to feel proud of them; but we do not know that one who is revered among you.' Amazed by these answers, the emir at once ordered that we should be again thrust into prison, and being led away we walked through the principal open place of the city, in the sight of the people; and many Christians followed us openly mourning our misery, as well as men of the contrary sect (Mohammedan) who were impelled by curiosity and pressed closely about us and kept asking which was the very famous Sicilian archbishop, and in this way we escaped from the people. At length we were thrown into the common prison; and this is a den having its pavement fourteen steps below ground, and it has only a little door instead of a window; here the darkness is complete, and can be felt, the only light being from a lamp, or some reflection by day, and it is impossible ever to see the light of dawn in this dungeon, nor the rays of the moon. Our bodies were distressed by the heat, for it was summer, and we were scorched by the breath of our fellow-prisoners; and besides, the vermin and the lice, and hosts of fleas and other little insects, make a man miserable by their bites; promiscuously with us there were confined in the same prison, to trade (as it were) with these miseries, Ethiopians, Tarsians, Jews, Lombards, and some of our own Christians, from different parts, among whom was also the most holy Bishop of Malta, chained with double shackles. Then the two bishops embraced one another, and kissed one another with the holy kiss, and wept together awhile over the things that had happened to them; but presently the gave thanks to God for it all, and combated their grief with arguments drawn from our philosophy. While we were living in this way, the abominable day of sacrifice appointed among these people recurred; on which day they boast that they hold in memory that sacrifice which Abraham made long ago, when he sacrificed the ram given him to God for a victim, in his share of the covenant; this, out of ignorance, they call the Pasch, but they do not name the day thus from the fact, for they had no passing over from Egypt to the land of promise, according to the ancient naming of the Pasch, nor from that land to the celestial shore, nor from death to life, as the Christian faith teaches us to use this word; but from life unto death and from this corporeal destruction, which falls under sensation, to that everlasting perdition, and to that fire which shall have no end. In the celebration of this day — strange madness — they took council° to burn the archbishop and to offer the most holy Pontiff of Christ as a victim to their evil demons; for a certain man of those who were over the people, having a mouth that breathed like an open sepulchre, said, turning to those who stood round about, 'O fellow citizens, let us keep this feast of the Pasch as joyfully as may be, and make it famous now, if ever, by laying hands upon the bishop of the Christians for our own salvation, for so I am sure that our affairs shall turn out fortunately and shall obtain even a better increase.' So he spoke, but certain old men with wise grey heads, and elders honourably clad in mantles, turned to the people and condemned the thing for the following reason. They said that these things were not true, and that they considered that the record of that day was made sufficiently honourable by the signal privilege of having accomplished the destruction of the city of Syracuse. Thus, God being willing, was the advice of the evil counsellor against the archbishop set at naught. Now from that day to this we have remained captive, in many sorrows, daily awaiting death itself, which perpetually hangs over us prisoners. But thou, O dear and venerable head, remember always thy Theodosius, and mayest thou render our God kind and propitious that He may calm these tempestuous billows, that he may stay them and check them, and that he may turn our captivity, as the flood under the south wind, according to the word of the Prophet King who was of the kindred of Christ. Amen."

Cloister of San Francesco di Paola

Here ends the letter of Theodosius, which was evidently composed in the prison he describes. It is some satisfaction to find it believed among historians that he himself and the good bishop were at last ransomed. The account bears evidence in every sentence of having been written by one who had both seen and suffered the terrible things he describes. It cannot be doubted that the Mohammedans acted elsewhere with a cruelty quite as atrocious; the condition of the unfortunate Christians who now became their slaves is more easy to imagine than to describe, and one might not unnaturally think of the Saracens as utter barbarians, or at least as possessing no higher culture than that of their Semitic predecessors in Sicily, the Carthaginians. We know that this was not the case, and we may well start in wonder at the picture drawn by Theodosius. But we might as reasonably call Oliver Cromwell a barbarian, or the French Huguenot iconoclasts — or, for that matter, Catherine de' Medici. There is only one form of passion which seems able to destroy temporarily every good instinct of humanity, and that is mistaken religious zeal. The conviction that the enemy is predestined to eternal flames easily leads to the instinctive belief that he has deserved every torment in his earthly body; and such a belief, when bound up with such a conviction, and stimulated to madness by the sight of human blood, can make men worse than wild beasts. The barbarians with their dripping swords who terrified poor Theodosius were those same grave Mohammedans to whom we are indebted for so much true science, for the preservation and transmission of so many priceless books, and for so many things of beauty that still remain, from the Taj Mahal to the Alhambra; and they were the men who were about to fill Sicily with a civilization in many ways superior to the older one which they destroyed. They tore Nicetas piecemeal, and trampled upon his Christian heart; but Theodoric the great Goth put the good heathen Boethius to death as cruelly, on an accusation that was palpably false, and Everard Digby, who has been recently proved wholly innocent of any connection with the Gunpowder Plot, was torn to pieces alive by the hangman under James the First. The French are a most civilized people, but in the French Revolution educated men among them behaved with no more show of humanity than the Saracens at Syracuse, and about the year 1900 men who can read and write, and who vote in a free country, have burned negroes alive. No nation has much right to reproach any other for cruelty in times of war or popular excitement; it is only in peace that a fair judgment may be formed of the tendencies of any race, and then only when that race lives under some form of representative government. Countries are too often judged by their capital cities, and nations by the character of their sovereigns, though the rulers of most nations are of foreign descent.

Cloister of San Francesco di Paola, seen from the rear

In connection with the fall of Syracuse I take the following strange story from the annals of Georgius Cedrenus, a monk of the eleventh century, as a specimen of the inventive powers occasionally displayed at that time, even in works that have some historical value.

While the Saracens, whom he calls the Carthaginians, were still besieging Syracuse and pillaging the surrounding country, the Emperor Basil sent a fleet to Sicily under the command of the patrician, Adrianus, although the sailors were at that time engaged in building a temple' — a singular occupation for men-of-war's men, it must be confessed. Adrianus put into a harbour of the Peloponnesus to wait for a fair wind, and while he was wasting time there, Syracuse was taken. He learned the disaster in the following manner. 'There is a place in the Peloponnesus called Helos, on account of the thick woods amongst which it is situated, and the Roman ships were moored near the spot. One night some shepherds heard the voices of the devils that dwell there, talking together, and relating that Syracuse had been taken on the previous day, and this tale, after spreading among the people, reached Adrianus. He called the shepherds before him and examined them, and finding that they confirmed the story he had heard, in order to ascertain the truth of the thing with his own ears he had himself led to the spot by the shepherds, he inquired of the devils by their help, and he heard that Syracuse was already taken. Being overcome by uneasiness at this warning, he sought to reassure and comfort himself with the belief that it would be wrong to put faith in the words of lying Genii, but he noted the day they had mentioned. Ten days later, certain persons who had escaped from Syracuse arrived and announced the calamity.'

This curious tale is found in the first volume of Caruso's valuable work. Another story, taken from the same author and much more worthy of credence, gives a very good idea of the wars that were waged at the same time on the mainland, between the forces of the new Frankish Empire, the Mohammedans, and the Byzantines.

While the Saracens were fighting their way through Sicily, other Mohammedans had extended their incursions far into the interior of Italy and along the eastern coast, and had overrun a great part of the Lombard Duchy in the south, making their headquarters at Bari; whereupon the Emperor Basil appealed to the Pope and to Lewis the Second, called 'King of France' by the monk's chronicle, instead of King of the Franks. Their joint armies overcame the Saracen force in Italy, and they recaptured Bari and took the Mohammedan chief captive. He is called the Soldanus, the Sultan, which is manifestly a mistake, but his story is worth telling for the light it throws on the times.

Chapel in the garden of San Francesco di Paola

This soldanus, then, was carried away a prisoner to Capua by Lewis the Second, and during two years he was never seen to laugh. Therefore the king promised a present of gold to any one who could make the soldanus laugh outright. Now when a certain man came and told the king that he had seen the soldanus laughing, and brought a witness, the king called the soldanus to him and asked him the reason of the change. Then said the soldanus: 'I was looking at a cart and at its wheels, how some parts of them turned downwards and others up; and perceiving that this was an image of man's changing and inconstant fortunes, I laughed; and when I consider how miserable is everything wherein we boast, then also I judge it possible that as I, who was the highest, am become the lowest, so also from this depth I may be lifted again to the summit where I stood.' When the king heard this he considered his own state also, and he thought of the soldanus, and of the command he had held, and of his old age and experience of good and bad fortunes; and judging him to be wise, he allowed the soldanus from that time freely to converse with him and to come and go.

But the soldanus was an astute man and crafty, and he laid a trap for the king, by which he drove him from Capua and prepared his own return to his people. The two Italian cities of Capua and Benevento had not been long subject to the king, and the soldanus knew that they would not remain constantly faithful, but were dreaming of liberty; nor was he ignorant that the king was making every effort to retain possession of them. He therefore addressed the king, and said: 'I see that you are deeply concerned in considering how you may keep these two cities in your power. I will give you advice in this matter. Be sure that you cannot keep a firm hold of these unless you remove their chief men to France. For it is natural that men who are in service against their will should wish for freedom, and that they should seize a favourable opportunity to rise and obtain what they desire.' The king was pleased with this speech; he thought the advice good, and he determined to act upon it. Therefore shackles of bronze and chains were made ready secretly, as if for some other purpose. But the soldanus, having thus deluded the king, went to the princes of the people, for he had acquired familiarity with them in habitual intercourse, and he told them that he had a secret which he would show them, but that he feared lest if they betrayed it they should cause the destruction of their informer, and bring themselves into danger. They promised silence with an oath, and he told them that the king had determined to send them all to France in iron bonds, because he saw that he could not otherwise keep his power over the cities. They were in doubt, and could not quite believe his words, desiring further proof of what he said; so he took one of them with him to the smith's and bade him ask of them why they were working so industriously. Having learned that they were making chains and shackles, he went back to his companions and convinced these that the soldanus had spoken the truth, out of goodwill to them and to the advantage of their country. Thereupon the princes of those cities, being persuaded of the fact, considered how they might be avenged upon the king; and one day, when he went out to hunt, they shut the gates, and when he returned they drove him away. So when he found himself shut out of the cities, and unable to effect anything by his presence, he returned to France. But the soldanus went to the princes, and desired as the price of the information he had given that he might be free and return to his country; and being thus rewarded for the good he had done unto them, he returned to Carthage, regained his former command, undertook a great expedition against Capua and Benevento, and besieged those cities with all his strength, surrounding them with a great encampment.

Then the townspeople, being hard pressed by the siege, sent ambassadors to the king, imploring his help, but he sent them away scornfully, answering that their destruction would be a joy to him. On the return of the ambassadors, after this failure, the people, not knowing whither to turn, and being driven to great straits in their defence, sent an ambassador to Basil, the emperor of the Romans. And he sent back the ambassador at once, to bid his people be of good heart, and to announce the present coming of abundant aid. But the ambassador was taken by the enemy on his return, and the soldanus, before whom he was brought, said to him: 'Thou shalt have a choice; choose therefore the better part. If thou dost wish to be safe, and to receive very splendid gifts, say to those who sent thee, and in the presence of them all, that the Roman emperor has refused to help them; but if thou dost proclaim the truth, thou shalt perish instantly.' The ambassador promised to do what the emir had commanded him, and when they were at an arrow's flight from the walls, he commanded that the chief men of the city should come forth. When they were come, he spoke to them these words: 'Ye fathers, howbeit certain death is hanging over me, and the sword is at my throat, I shall not hide the truth from you, and I beseech you to show kindness to my wife and children. I, my lords, though I am now in the hands of our enemies, have fulfilled my embassy, and presently help will be surely sent you by the Roman emperor. Therefore stand fast. For he cometh who shall deliver you, though not me.' When he had said this, the ministers of the soldanus instantly cut him into very small pieces with their swords. But the soldanus feared the army of the emperor, now that he was sure that it would be sent, and raised the siege and went home. And after that, there was alliance and faith between the cities of Capua and Benevento.

Such is the story of the Lombard Duchy, told by Georgius Cedrenus, and romantic as it is, and closely as it recalls the embassy of Regulus to the Carthaginians, we may safely accept it as authentic in the main. To complete the picture, it must be remembered that Italy and the south were now overrun in all directions by hosts of Moslems, that the sea was at their mercy, and that they had stained the waters of the Mediterranean with Christian blood from Gibraltar to the Bosphorus, and from the Adriatic to the mouth of the Nile. We cannot but see them in our imagination as dark-skinned barbarians, black-browed, turbaned to the eyes, lean and fierce, bringing with them the strength and endurance which the desert breeds, and clothing themselves in the purple and gold of a vanquished civilization. We cannot but think of them as more like Huns than Vandals, as more like devils than Huns. Yet this was the age of Harun al Rashid, whose court in Bagdad delighted in every luxury while exploring the secrets of every science; and if Harun eight times invaded the Byzantine empire, it may be remembered that it had become the plaything of the evil empress Irene whose deeds have left upon her the marks of mankind's execration, while Harun will forever and not undeservedly bear the surname of the Just. Had the Mohammedan Empire been united under such a man, controlled by such a heart, and directed by such an intelligence, and had a worthy successor taken the place of Harun on the throne of the Abbassides, the power of the Moslems might have been consolidated into a despotism of the world, at a time when Christianity was divided against itself. But while the Empire of Constantinople was as yet separated from its final destruction by an interval of six hundred years, the newly risen domination of the Mohammedans was already broken up into small powers, of which the sultans and emirs did not hesitate to make war upon each other almost as readily as upon the Christians. The khalifs ruled indeed in Bagdad, and Harun had destroyed a Byzantine army each time that a Byzantine ruler had refused to pay him tribute; but the khalifate had lost its power in the West, the house of Aghlab and the Fatimites had become independent rulers in Africa, and the Emir of Sicily soon made himself as independent as they. Still farther west the Mohammedans of Spain had founded a kingdom which was to defy the armies of Christianity even longer than Constantinople was destined to withstand the attacks of the Moslems. But the chiefs of these divided kingdoms, though sometimes highly gifted and acquainted with the advantages of civilization, were in reality little more than robbers of tremendous power; depredation and pillage were the business of their lives, and religion was a sufficient excuse for both. Civilization was but an amusement fit for short intervals of unwelcome peace. It was their nature to delight in the discoveries of astronomy, the investigations of medicine, and in the study of the Aristotelian philosophy, and most of the sciences are indebted in some measure to their acuteness and spasmodic industry; but to all such pleasures, to intellectual pastimes of the noblest kind, as well as to the refinements of a sensuous existence which happily is without parallel in modern times — to these things the true Saracen preferred the din of ringing blows exchanged in battle, the hideous carnage of the hard-won field, the heaps of Christian slain, and the confusion of victories that spoiled the world in a day.

Cloister and court of San Francesco di Paola

They had won the East, they had conquered the West, the central basin of the Mediterranean was theirs, and the time came when they aspired to seize Rome itself. Collecting the squadrons of their pirate vessels into a fleet manned by a host of fighters who had survived a hundred deaths, they appeared at the mouth of the Tiber, and ate up land like locusts. Nevertheless, the worn-out and tottering walls of Rome sufficed to discourage an army that was more warlike than military, and was little accustomed to the orderly operations of a siege. They plundered the basilicas of Saint Peter on the one side and of Saint Paul on the other, but they made no attempt to enter Rome, and presently retired to their congenial south, bearing with them the spoils of the most magnificent temples in Christendom. They might have taken Rome with ease, and could have established the Mohammedan dominion amid the ashes of the Roman Empire, but they neglected an opportunity which they had failed to estimate at its true value; and when another Moslem host came against Rome a few years afterwards, in 849, the energy of Pope Leo the Fourth had built up the ruined defences, and not only were the walls standing throughout their entire circuit, but they were also protected at the most important points by fifteen great towers, one of which, still unshaken, was occupied by Leo the Thirteenth as a summer residence one thousand and fifty years later. To complete the defence, the city was provided with new gates made of the most massive timber. Nor was this all. The wise and untiring pontiff had formed valuable alliances with the states of Naples, Gaeta, and Amalfi, and the pirate squadrons of the Moslems were opposed before the port of Ostia by a well-ordered fleet. They had already been repulsed with loss when a storm arose, such as no man of those times could remember, and the ships of the invaders were driven to destruction upon the dangerous lee shore. The rocks and islands with which Gibbon adorned the coast at that point had no existence except in his imagination, or in some source of information other than those he names; but in their stead there exists a real danger quite as terrible to mariners. The long low shore of the Roman Campagna is accompanied from end to end, at a cable's length or less, by a bar, over which there is less than •a fathom of water in calms, and upon which, in southwesterly gales, the surf breaks with enormous force; and therein those 'sons of Satan,' as Anastasius the Librarian calls the Moslems, utterly perished, both themselves and their vessels.

This was the last attempt made by them to extend their power northwards, and when the Saracens at length entered Rome as conquerors, they came as the soldiers of a Norman ruler, to establish the power of a pope.

Though it is true that the Greek power fell in Sicily when the Mohammedans took Castrogiovanni, the most important date which ocrs for a long time is that of the destruction of Syracuse in 878. That city had been the centre and fountain head of Sicilian life during more than fourteen hundred years; the great struggles in which the fate of the island was concerned had almost all been fought for the possession of its chief jewel and treasure. The Moslems took it, crushed it, and threw away its fragments as though it had been a worthless thing to them, which might easily have been of value to their enemies. When the emir marched westwards with his train of captives, his caravan of plunder, and his load of gold, he left behind him a heap of smoking ruins, among which lay the unburied corpses of a murdered population. Never again should the fair walls of a great city mirror themselves in the still waters of the wonderful harbour; never more should Christian maidens come down with their earthen jars to take the cool water from Arethusa's spring; not again should the walls below Achradina reëcho the blows of the shipwright's axe and hammer, or the rasping of the busy saw; nor, on the brink of the deep quarry, wherein handsome Athenians had died of hunger and thirst and sickness, should the holy monks chaunt matins and evensong in the cloisters of Saint John. Men should not go out from the city, so long as history was to last, to cut the great papyrus at the roots and bring it home to make books for the wise man's pen. No living thing was left amid the universal death, and there was to be no possible renewal of life thereafter. The Mohammedan had made his home far to westward in the Golden Shell, and he meant not to leave behind him any good place wherein his enemy might take refuge. He returned indeed not many years afterwards and brought ships into the harbour of Syracuse and built up the walls of Ortygia, and the sea wall of Achradina; but it was not that the city he had built might live again, it was rather because no power he possessed could destroy the safe port which nature had made, and he found himself obliged to prevent others from taking that which he would not use himself. His heart was in the western city, and he loved it and made it his own, and beautified it with all the skill he could command.

Statue of a bishop, outside the cathedral, Palermo

Thenceforward Palermo became what Syracuse had been, the centre of the island's history and the chief goal of each succeeding invader. Syracuse lived again, and lives to-day, a military stronghold, a naval station, a commercial town; but its life as a source of power and as a fountain of individuality was arrested forever on the fatal day. Much of it that was beautiful fell to the base uses of commerce, and the money-changer's booth was set up in the ruined corner of the matchless Greek temple; where Agathocles had feasted in tents of fine linen and purple silk rose the rough defences of a castle that was already mediaeval, that was not a glory but a menace, a thing not of beauty but of fear. On the height the great wall of Dionysius still stood in part, because it would have taken human hands a year to destroy what human hands had built in twenty days; and the indestructible fortress of Euryalus still amazes the traveller with its labyrinth of well-hewn passages, its perfectly designed and marvellously preserved embrasures, and its ramparts of solid rock. But the five cities upon which Marcellus looked down with tearful eyes have sunk out of sight, never to rise again, and a small Italian town, crowded together and irregularly cut by quiet little streets, covers the island, and extends over a few hundred yards of the opposite peninsula. That is all there is left of her that rivalled Athens and Alexandria, and that once far outdid Rome in extent, in wealth, and in beauty.

No such melancholy reflections assail the traveller who ascends the heights of Monreale and pauses, where the road sweeps up the last turn, to look back upon the distant splendour of Palermo. The scene is indeed full of associations that bring back the past, and evoke the grave and terrible memories of an elder time. But that past is not dead beneath a funeral pall of ruin through which the eye guesses only at the outline of the fallen limbs. It is alive still, clothed in royal robes of beauty, and calmly resting in a dignified repose. From the height a keen-eyed man can descry the lofty fortress by the Porta Nuova, wherein Roger the Norman held his court, as the Saracen emirs had held theirs before him; and the vast cathedral that holds the tombs of emperors and kings; the bastions of the great walls are gone, but in their stead there are the graceful outlines of a hundred churches against the broad sea beyond, soft against the softer sky. Between the city and the hill on which the beholder stands, and round by his right and up the valley, the Golden Shell is bright with flower and yellow fruit, and rich with the deep foliage of the lemon and the orange; here and there, among the taller cypresses and spreading pines, the white walls of a half-shaded villa speak of that cool retirement and peace which every Italian loves, and as the glow of evening fades, the sweet and melancholy note of distant bells is borne up on the scented air.

Palermo is not dead, like Syracuse: its ruins do not stretch far and wide beyond its shrunk walls like those of Girgenti, cropping up in vineyards and olive groves and in scattered farmhouses, each a mile from the other; it is there still, as it was there a thousand years ago, in the third century of the Hejira, when Ibn Haukal came thither about a hundred years after the captivity of Theodosius, the monk.

This Ibn Haukal was a merchant of Bagdad, who left that city in the year 943, and travelled through many Mohammedan countries, during more than thirty years. At that time, the first great Mussulman Empire had begun to fall to pieces, from lack of uniform organization, while Mohammedan energy was still as active as ever, and the Saracens in Sicily fought to become independent of the African domination, under which they had got possession of the island; but the turbulent Sicilians had long been fighting with each other, and the rivalry of the principal cities had led to endless bloodshed; and it was not until Palermo and Girgenti made up their differences, and united to make common cause against the African emir, that the latter conceded to the island the freedom it desired, retaining a more or less empty suzerainty over it. Soon after this event Ibn Haukal visited Palermo. He came on the morrow of a great struggle, before all the damage done by the civil war had been repaired, when the people were still suffering from past evils, and when the aristocracy, which had been chiefly responsible for the internal trouble so Sicily, still kept aloof from the people, in scornful isolation; for of all races, the Arabs were always the most aristocratic. He describes a city surrounded by most formidable walls, around which were built four suburbs, each of which had a strongly individual character that distinguished it from the others; and the walled portion occupied what is the middle of Palermo to-day, and was called the Kasr, the fort, and Sicilians still call the main street the 'Cassaro,' though it was named the 'Toledo,' by one of the Spanish viceroys, and has of course been officially christened 'Corso Vittorio Emmanuele,' since the annexation of Sicily. But it is safe to say that its old name will remain in common use, no matter how often the island changes hands.a The Saracen's seal is upon it, and the impression is indelible.

La Piccola Cuba A Moorish Summer-house near Palermo

In the days of the Bagdad merchant there was 'a great Friday mosque' in this quarter 'which was formerly a church of the Christians,' which had been first built by Saint Gregory, and stood on the site of the Norman cathedral: and Ibn Haukal was told that it contained the body of Aristotle, who had been held in the highest veneration by the Christians, and was always ready to answer their prayers for rain, for recovery from sickness, and for every ill that causes man to offer prayers to Allah, whose name be praised. The body, it was said, was in a coffin suspended between heaven and earth, and Ibn Haukal says that he saw a large chest which might perhaps have contained it.

The Kasr was the abode of merchants; the great suburb, called the Khalessah, now the Kalsa, or Gausa, contained the sultan's palace, and the habitations of his courtiers; there were also baths there, a mosque of average dimensions, the sultan's prison — he appears to have kept one for his own purposes — the arsenal, and the government offices. The Khalessah had walls of its own, and it lay between the Kasr and the sea, to the east of the present harbour. It is not easy to define the other ancient quarters, owing to the great changes in the topography of Palermo caused by the gradual filling of the two inlets that once extended far into the city, divided by a tongue of land of which the extremity still projects into the modern harbour. Ibn Haukal tells us, however, that the great markets, and the shops of the oil sellers, were all situated southeast of the Kasr, between the Saracen Norman castle at Porta Nuova and the mosque of Ibn Saklab which stood in the place that was called, until recently, Piazza della Moschitta. Here, also, and outside the walls, were the stalls of the money-changers, and the shops of the drug sellers, tailors, armourers, and braziers. The corn market was also beyond the circuit of the walls. The merchant of Bagdad observed that there were a hundred and fifty butchers' shops in the city, and on visiting the butchers' mosque, — for they had one of their own, — he calculated that more than seven thousand persons connected with the trade were assembled at prayers, for he counted thirty-six ranks, in each of which there were two hundred people. Those who have been present in the mosque of Saint Sophia, in Constantinople, during the great prayer meetings that terminate the month of Ramadhan, will doubtless remember the extraordinarily precise order maintained by the ranks of worshippers, which makes it an easy matter to calculate their numbers. It has been estimated, by those who have commented the merchant's accounts of the city, that the population amounted at that time to three hundred thousand souls. It exceeds that figure at the present time.

Ibn Haukal was much struck by the great number of mosques he saw in all parts of the city, and he observes that the greater part of them were 'standing with their roofs, their walls, and their doors, and were actually in use'; a statement which shows that even a thousand years ago the Mohammedans were accustomed to allow their old mosques to fall to ruins when new ones were built, just as they continue to do in our own times; but he adds that the mosques of Palermo were places of meeting for 'all the wise men and the students of the city, who gather in them to exchange and increase their information.' In vivid contrast with these resorts of the learned, were the so-called 'rabats,' built by the water's edge, outside the city, and which were the quarters of the wild militia that alternately begged and fought for a living, 'a band composed of cutthroats and ruffians, of men who know no law, and have grown old in a disorderly life, and of corrupt youths who have learned to pretend piety in order to extort charity from the faithful, and to insult honest women, — wretches who live in the rabat because they are so vile and universally despised that they could find no refuge elsewhere.' The commentator on this unpleasant picture remarks that the number of these irregular fighters was large at the time of Ibn Haukal's visit, because the new government of the Kalibites was actively pushing the war of extermination against Christians. The passage throws some light on the nature of the atrocities described by the monk, Theodosius, and on the composition of the Mohammedan armies in those times. The ruffians seen in the rabats by Ibn Haukal were, doubtless, the lineal descendants of those who had sacked Syracuse a hundred years earlier.

He dwells at great length on the nine gates by which the city was entered, but of most of which it is now impossible to determine the situation. The most famous, he says, was the sea gate, and of this one we know that it was somewhere in the lower part of the modern Cassaro, or Toledo, that it was destroyed in 1564, in order to widen and straighten that thoroughfare, and that it was ornamented with long Arabic inscriptions in the Cufic character which gave rise to much controversy. For centuries the letters were believed to be Chaldean, and the writing was interpreted to mean that the tower of the gate was built by Sapho, the son of Eliphaz, the son of Esau, the brother of Jacob, the son of Isaac, the son of Abraham. Consequently it was believed even by learned men, that Palermo had been founded by the great-great-grandson of Abraham, a supposition which, for its absurdity, quite equals the story of the veneration of Aristotle's body by the Christians, which was told to Ibn Haukal. He, however, does not even mention the supposed origin of the gate in question, but merely calls it 'the most famous.'

He tells us, further, that in the midst of the city there was a depression almost entirely filled with papyrus plants, then still used for making writing paper, and he adds that he does not know of any papyrus in the world, except that of Sicily, which rivals that of Egypt, and that the greater part of this papyrus is twisted into rope for ships — it would make something like our Manila rope — while the remainder is made into paper for the sultan, and only in quantities just sufficient for his use. In the southwestern part of the city, and within the modern circuit, but outside the ancient walls, there is still a Piazza del Papireto, and a street of the same name leading out of it. The square is only a few steps from the southern end of the cathedral. It is known that until 1591 the place was a swamp, in which the papyrus was there is growing abundantly, and in that year it was drained by subterranean channels and filled up, because it was a cause of fever in the neighbourhood. The few specimens of papyrus now cultivated in Palermo have been brought from Syracuse. Judging from the words of Ibn Haukal, the plant not only flourished in Egypt, where it is now extinct, in the tenth century, but in other parts of the world.

He enumerates many springs of good water, both in the city and in the neighbourhood, but presently contradicts himself flatly, and ends his description of the people with the following comments. 'The greater part of the water consumed in the various quarters of the city is dirty and unwholesome rain water. The people drink this stuff, owing to the lack of sweet, running water, and because of their own folly, and because of their abuse of the onion, and their evil habit of eating raw onions in excess; for there is not a person among them, high or low, who does not eat them in his house daily, both in the morning and at evening. This is what has ruined their intelligence, and affected their brains, and degraded their senses, and distracted their faculties, and crushed their spirits, and spoiled their complexions, and so altogether changed their temperament, that everything, or almost everything, appears to them quite different from what it is.'

The onion has certainly never suffered a more sweeping condemnation, and we are reminded of the exceeding and virulent bad temper with which Horace attacked garlic when it had disagreed with him. What Ibn Haukal says about the degeneracy of the people of Palermo, however, must have been founded on fact, and the fact may have been in part attributable to bad water; but he saw a population only half recovered from the horrors and sufferings of civil war, — men who had been starved, and whose parents had starved, and who were still haunted by dreams of fear, dulled by past pain, half dazed and stupefied by a generation of suffering. Palermo is one of the healthiest towns in the world at the present time, and its people compare favourably, both in looks and intelligence, with the inhabitants of any other city in Europe.

The Normans

About the year 500 a certain rich man named Garganus possessed a great estate in the land where the city of Manfredonia was afterwards built; and a high hill which is there, and which looks out over the sea, was called by his name, Mons Garganus. It chanced one day that one of the steers of his herd went astray and could not be brought back; and when Garganus and his servants found it, the beast was lying before the mouth of a cavern on the summit of the hill. The creature could not be induced to move, and Garganus, wearied by the long pursuit, and in an ill temper, flung his hunting javelin at the steer's head. To the amazement and terror of all who saw it, the weapon left the steer unhurt, and turning backwards, wounded Garganus himself.

The bishop of that region, having been consulted as to the meaning of this prodigy, commanded a rigid fast of three days, and at the end of that time he himself was favoured by a vision of the Archangel Michael, who appeared to him clothed in a scarlet cloak, and in radiant glory. The saint announced that he himself was the author of the miracle, and he ordered that henceforth he should be venerated in the cavern before which the steer had lain down. In obedience to the supernatural command, a basilica, dedicated to Saint Michael, was soon raised upon the spot; the scarlet cloak, which he had left behind him as a proof of his visit, was preserved in the sanctuary, together with treasures of gold and silver; and before long pious pilgrims from all parts of Europe visited the shrine. It has been venerated in like manner ever since, and the silver lamps that burn before the dim altar within the cave have been filled, lighted, worn out, and renewed during fourteen hundred years.

Shrine of Saint Michael, at Monte Sant' Angelo

More than a thousand miles from Monte Gargano, on the borders of Brittany and Neustria, a bold rock juts out into the sea, and is daily cut off from the mainland by the flowing tide. In the beginning of the eighth century, the Bishop Aubert was visited in a dream by the Archangel Michael, who bade him build a sanctuary on the summit of the rock. By a coincidence more familiar in legend than in reality, Aubert found a steer lying in a cavern when he first visited the summit, and regarding this circumstance as a direct instruction from the archangel, he commanded that the church to be built on the spot should be the counterpart of the sanctuary of Monte Gargano, both in shape and size. It stands to-day, and has been a place of pilgrimage ever since its foundation. The existence of these two shrines is the link between Normandy and Italy, and all the early chroniclers laid stress upon the affiliation of the more recently founded one to its predecessor.

The rise and spread of Mohammedanism in the East had not deterred devout persons from visiting the holy places in the eighth and ninth centuries, and as the pilgrims who came from Normandy never failed to visit Monte Gargano on their way to the East, or on their return, taking back with them to their own shrine in the West full accounts of what they had seen, there was a much more lively interchange of news between the two places than might be imagined. Delarc, whom I shall follow in telling the story of the Normans, points out that the two shrines were pillaged, the one by Norman pirates, the other by Saracen corsairs, at about the same period, that is to say, during the greater part of the ninth century. When Charles the Simple had invested Rollo with the sovereignty of Normandy, — for the very good reason that he was quite unable to do otherwise, — the new duke restored tenfold to this shrine of the archangel the treasures which his countrymen had taken from it; for the Normans had adopted Christianity with the readiness they afterwards showed in changing sides when any advantage was to be gained; and having suddenly transformed themselves into a nation of devout Catholics, speaking a Latin tongue, they also imitated their Neustrian predecessors in making pilgrimages to Southern Italy and the East. Being cautious people, they wore coats of mail under their pilgrims' robes, and though they carried the stout staff of the palmer in their hands, they carried at their belts their long Norman swords, merely on the possibility that they might be needed. They regarded the archangel Michael with most especial veneration, on account of his warlike attributes, and accepted his victory over Lucifer as a satisfactory substitute for their Scandinavian hero's destruction of the dragon.

In the year 845, while the Mohammedans were still fighting for the possession of Italy, and were attempting to get possession of the western coast of the mainland, the warning note of their own destruction already sounded in the west of Europe. In that year a party of fair-haired Norman robbers, sailing southward in their long-beaked ships, came upon the mouth of the Seine, and entering the stream, pushed up as far as Paris itself. It was on Holy Saturday, and the chronicler dryly remarks that they had probably not come so far with the object of performing their Easter devotions; and though Charles the Bald came out in time to meet them at the monastery of Saint Denis with a handful of men-at-arms, the inferiority of his force lent to the opposition he made the appearance of an almost peaceful reception, and that which had promised to be a battle degenerated to the ignominy of a bargain and a ransom.

But the Saracens knew not of these things, and pursued their course with occasional checks. In the same year their motley fleet, sailing up to get possession of Ponza and of the other islands which lie in the same waters, was met by the combined forces of Amalfi, Gaeta and Sorrento, under the valiant Duke of Naples, and suffered signal defeat. Sergius drove them southward before the wind, chasing them past Ischia and Capri, and across the wide Gulf of Salerno to the distant islet of Licosa. There the Saracens had gained a foothold, not far from the ancient city of Elea, which was that same Velia where Verres had landed his ill-gotten Sicilian spoils. Thence also the Neapolitans dislodged them and drove them still further down the coast. Soon, however, they repaired their fleet in Palermo, and came back in force; the armament of the Christian allies had already dispersed, and Sergius was unable to prevent the Saracens from taking the strong castle of Misenum, which is Capo Miseno. It was from that point that the young Pliny had watched the stupendous eruption of Vesuvius that destroyed Pompeii, and the harbour and fortifications, of which Romans had made such an important naval station, became a source of strength to the pirate Moslems.

As an instance of the readiness with which the Norman pilgrims could lay down the staff and draw the sword, I shall translate the following passage from the history of Amatus of Monte Cassino, as it is quoted by Abbé Delarc.

"Before the year 1000 of the Incarnation of our Lord, there appeared in the world forty valiant pilgrims; they came from the Holy Sepulchre in Jerusalem, and reached Salerno just at the moment when the city, being vigorously besieged by the Saracens, was about to surrender. Before that time Salerno had been tributary to the Saracens, and when the payment of the tribute was in arrears the Saracens immediately appeared with a numerous fleet, collected the sums due, slew the inhabitants, and ravaged the countryside. On learning this, the Norman pilgrims were angered by the injustice of the said Saracens, and because the Christians were subject to them; they therefore went before the most serene prince Guaimar, who ruled Salerno in the spirit of justice, and they asked arms and horses of him that they might fight against the Saracens. They told him that they did not this thing for the hope of any recompense but because the pride of the Saracens was intolerable to them. When they had attained what they asked, these forty Northmen fell upon the Saracen host and slew a great many of them, so that the rest took to flight both by sea and land; and the Normans had the victory, and the Salernitans were delivered from the bondage of the Pagans. But these Normans, having acted only for love of God, would accept nothing in return. Then the Salernitans gave the Normans lemons, and almonds, and preserves of nuts, and scarlet mantles, and iron instruments adorned with gold, that they might induce their fellow countrymen to come and inhabit a land flowing with milk and honey, and rich in good things. So the victorious pilgrims, when they returned to Normandy, bore witness as they had promised, and invited all Norman nobles to come into Italy, and some took courage to go thither on account of the riches that were there."

From the year 996 Normandy was under the rule of Duke Richard the Second, whose vassals were generally in revolt against him, and at war among themselves. About the year 1015 two Norman gentles, Gilbert Buatère and Guillaume Répostelle, quarrelled about the latter's daughter, and Gilbert, who was the better man of his hands, settled the difficulty by throwing his adversary over a precipice. Fearing duke Richard, however, Gilbert joined himself to certain other Normans, who were also at odds with their sovereign, and with their men-at-arms they departed together to go into Italy. Among these men was Raoul de Toëni, who at once became their leader.

At that time Pope Benedict the Eighth was alarmed by the growing influence of the Eastern Empire in the south of Italy, and was doing his best to reconcile the Lombard princes of Capua, Benevento, and Salerno, in order that they might lay aside their private enmities and join forces with him against the Greeks.

Entrance to church of San Nicola, Bari

Now at this time, also, a certain Meles, a Lombard and a citizen of Bari, which was the capital of the Greek possessions in Italy, made an attempt to free his country from the Byzantine domination, and he had actually got together a force with which he fought a battle against the Byzantines. He was beaten, however, and retired within the walls of Bari, which he held for some time, but was at last obliged to abandon. He then wandered far and wide through Italy seeking allies, but finding none.

It was at this time that Raoul de Toëni and his companions came to Rome, craving the blessing of Pope Benedict the Eighth; and the Pope, on granting it, strongly advised them to join forces with Meles against the Greeks. They did so, and met him at Capua, and became the nucleus of a little army of freebooter patriots who lost no time in devouring whatsoever the Greeks had left untouched throughout the south. The Emperor of Constantinople sent his troops against them, but the wily little Greeks were not a match for the colossal Northmen at hand to hand, and the allies of Meles carried everything before them. More pilgrims and adventurers reached Italy from the north, while Constantinople sent legions upon legions, so that the lances of the Greek army seemed as close and thick as canes in the brake, and its camp was like a hive of bees. At last the Byzantines were so many that they won the day, and on the right bank of the Ofanto, on the very ground which Hannibal had drenched with Roman blood, the little army of Meles was cut to pieces. Out of two hundred and fifty Norman nobles who rode into that fight, ten came back alive; but the dead had sold their lives dearly, and the plain that is called the Field of Blood, for the many battles fought there, was strewn far and wide with the bodies of the Greeks and their mercenaries.

This battle was fought in October, 1019; Meles and Raoul were among the survivors, and were well received by the emperor, Henry the Second, with whom they took refuge, but Meles died in the spring of the following year, and the cause of Apulian freedom seemed lost.

Before this battle of Cannae a few Normans had separated themselves from their countrymen and had taken up their habitation in a small town built by the Greeks in the pass of the Apennines, which was considered the key of Apulia. The stronghold received the name of Troy, Troia, and afterwards played an important part in the struggles which took place. This small party of Northmen seem to have taken service on the Greek side, but they were, of course, not engaged at Cannae, and after that battle they found themselves on the winning side. The survivors of those who had fought against the Greeks, and certain others, were presented by the victors to the Abbot of Monte Cassino, who, with the Lombard princes, had immediately made advances to the Emperor of Constantinople.

At this point, however, the Emperor of the West, Henry the Second, interfered, and sent an army under the Archbishop of Cologne, a famous fighting prelate, with orders to chastise the Lombard princes and the Abbot of Monte Cassino of their defection to the Greek side, to take Troia, and to reduce Apulia to submission. The first part of this military expedition was accomplished without difficulty, but the handful of Normans in Troia defended themselves throughout a long siege against the German troops, and Henry was forced to content himself with a general statement on the part of the non-combatants that they neither had done nor would do anything against the will of the Holy Roman Emperor.

Castle at Monte Sant' Angelo

The only free Normans now left in Italy were those in garrison at Troia, and a few who had been given to the Greek Abbot of Monte Cassino and were set free by Henry the Second and established by him in the imperial domain of Comino, in the neighbourhood of Sora. The first, while pretending loyalty to Constantinople, were really independent in the west, and held a position of the highest strategic importance; the others, with a few more of their countrymen who came down from Normandy, at once set about increasing the domain given them by the emperor. One of the persons most directly injured by their depredations very nearly proved their destruction. With two hundred and fifty men-at-arms he prepared an ambush in the defiles of the mountains, and sent forward a score of his men to decoy the Normans from their camp. The Northmen fell into the trap and rode out at once; but the others turned and fled as they had been instructed, and the Normans, who were but five and twenty in number, dashed after them in pursuit. In a few moments they found themselves face to face with the enemy's full force, and hemmed in so that they could not retreat. Seeing that they were matched against overwhelming odds, they sheathed their swords and threw up their empty hands, but the leader of the enemy would not be cheated of his revenge, and in a loud voice commanded his men to fall upon them and slay them. Then those five and twenty horsemen drew their swords again, and fought for their lives, being one against ten; and they killed of the enemy sixty out of two hundred and fifty, and put the rest to an ignominious flight, and carried back the rich spoil of arms to their camp, having themselves lost but one man.

But now Henry the Second and Pope Benedict the Eighth died in the same year, and the Lombard princes whom the German emperor had deposed at once made a league with the Greeks to regain their possessions. The Normans, having nothing better to do, and always wisely anxious to find themselves on the winning side, promptly joined them. Capua resisted the siege during eighteen months, but was at last taken, and the Lombard Pandolph, surnamed the Wolf of the Abruzzi, got possession of his own again. As soon as he had established himself, he proceeded to distribute the lands belonging to the abbey of Monte Cassino among those who had helped him, and in the following year he even succeeded in getting possession of Naples, which he held for a short time. The Neapolitan duke, however, soon turned the tables upon him by engaging the Normans on his side, and as they had got all they could hope for from Pandolph, they were easily persuaded to take Naples away from him again and restore it to the good Duke Sergius. They now founded the first Norman city in Italy. In 1030, Randolph, or Rainulf, built Aversa, a few miles north of Naples, and surrounded it with a moat and with very strong fortifications; and with the land on which it was built he and his companions received a broad territory in that country which is to this day the garden of Italy.

The year 1030 is therefore a date of high importance in the story of the Normans, for it marks the period at which they ceased to be mere soldiers of fortune, fighting for any prince who would pay them, and began to be rulers in their own right. The way had been prepared for conquest; history paused in expectation of the conqueror.

In the days of Robert the Devil, otherwise called the Magnificent, there lived in a castle that dominated the village of Hauteville-la-Guichard, a few miles northeast of Coutances, a certain Tancred. He was neither great nor rich, but he was a strong man and wise as the Normans were; he was simply a Norman gentle, like many hundreds of others. Within fifty years his sons had taken for themselves Sicily, and all the south of Italy and the islands; they made and unmade popes, bid defiance to the Emperor of Constantinople, and treated the Emperor of the West as best suited their own purposes.

Of this Tancred it is told, that when hunting the wild boar with the old Duke Richard, being then a very young man, he dealt a memorable sword-stroke that helped to make his fortune. It was a law that no man should strike at the game put up by the sovereign, and on that day a boar of vast size and strength had escaped the duke's own spear and was driven by the dogs through a thick wood to the foot of a cliff. Tancred, being swifter and stronger than the rest, came upon the beast there, and saw how he was tearing the poor hounds with his tusks, being at bay where he could not escape. Then Tancred, pitying the hounds greatly, and having lost his spear, pulled out his long Norman sword, and the boar came at him. He stood his ground, and dealt a single thrust at the beast's forehead, and the good blade pierced hide and skull and throat and body, and the cross-hilt struck the bone. But Tancred, fearing for himself because he had slain the duke's game, turned and slipped away through the woods, leaving his sword in the boar, for he trusted that the duke might not find the place, and that he might come back himself and get the blade. Presently, however, the duke and his followers came crashing through the woods, and they found the dead beast lying there; they dragged out the sword, and many of them recognized it. Duke Richard was not angry, though the rule had been broken, and he praised the blow, and made a friend of the man who had dealt it. Tancred, therefore, established himself at the court of Normandy. He was twice married, and had twelve sons — five by his first wife and seven by the second; and it is easy to understand that the estate of a poor Norman gentleman should have seemed an insufficient provision for so many. Tancred, therefore, brought up his sons to know that each must make his own fortune with his own sword. Three of the eldest soon joined one of those parties which now continually left Normandy for the south of Italy, and reaching Naples soon after the foundation of Aversa they took service with Count Rainulf, and soon acquired an extraordinary reputation for courage and quickness of resource. Their names were William, called Bras-de-Fer, or the Iron Arm, Drogo, and Humphrey.

At that time the feudal system of the middle ages had already reached a great development. The idea which was at the foot of it, was that all lordship depended from the sovereign in a regular chain of decreasing links, and that no man could hold large estates, nor small, without owing allegiance to one more powerful than himself, who in turn did homage to a greater, and so on up to the emperor himself, or the Church of Rome. Though Rainulf had a city and a territory of his own, he had nevertheless attached himself in a sort of military service to the powerful Prince of Capua, Pandolph the Fourth, the cruel and unscrupulous Wolf of the Abruzzi. He does not, however, appear to have attached much importance to the idea of fealty towards the feudal lord he had chosen, for soon afterwards, when Pandolph quarrelled with the Duke of Sorrento, who resented the old Wolf's too pressing admiration of his wife, Rainulf did not hesitate to go over, with all his Normans, to Guaimar, Prince of Salerno, who was the lady's uncle; and the consequence was that Pandolph was soon obliged to take refuge in his castle, while the Emperor Conrad himself appeared in Capua, in the year 1038. From his stronghold of Sant' Agata, Pandolph purchased a sort of pardon from the emperor for the sum of three hundred pounds of gold, but the emperor nevertheless deposed him from his principality and presented it to Guaimar, with the standards, or gonfalons, of Salerno and Capua. Guaimar, who knew that he should not be able to take possession of the new principality without a struggle, in which the help of the Normans would be indispensable to him, seized the occasion of recommending them to the emperor, who therefore solemnly confirmed Rainulf in his county of Aversa, and presented him with a lance and a standard blazoned with the imperial arms, thereby creating the chief of the Normans a vassal of the Holy Roman Empire. Guaimar made use of his new position to extend his territory in all directions. In April, 1039, he had got possession of Amalfi, then one of the most prosperous commercial cities in the Mediterranean, and so situated at the mouth of a rugged ravine, protected on both sides by enormous cliffs, that it was altogether impregnable to an attack by land. The Duchess of Sorrento, who had been the indirect cause of so much misfortune to her admiring Wolf, was destined to bring destruction upon her husband; with some show of reason the latter repudiated her, whereupon her uncle of Salerno seized Sorrento, adding it to his wide possessions, and investing his brother Guy with the Duchy. The somewhat hardly treated husband was condemned to a solitary confinement, in which he was permitted to reflect upon his honourable errors of judgment until death relieved him from the contemplation of his misfortunes.

Pandolph, seeing himself at so great a disadvantage, now undertook a journey to Constantinople, in the hope of getting help from the emperor; but the wily Guaimar was before him, and had already sent ambassadors who practically offered, on his behalf, to help the Greeks in driving the Saracens from Sicily, and the emperor accepted his advance without hesitation.

Now in 1034 the Saracens of Sicily, being involved in civil war, had requested the Byzantines to intervene, which they had of course done in hope of reconquering the island; but the other party appealed to the African Mohammedans, who very soon got the better of the struggle. The death of the leader with whom the Greeks had allied themselves relieved them of all obligation, and they immediately resolved to forget that they had been called in as allies and to assume the part of conquerors. Under orders of George Maniaces they sent out one of those extraordinary armies, such as only the Eastern Empire could have raised. Mercenaries were collected from every territory that owed allegiance to the Eastern emperor, — Scandinavians, Russians, Calabrians, Apulians, Greeks, and Asiatics of every race; and the wise Guaimar of Salerno, who was put to much inconvenience by the turbulence of his Norman friends, was glad to lend them to the Greek general, and promised that if they agreed to help the invasion of Sicily, they should be rewarded both by the Greeks and by himself. Three hundred, or perhaps five hundred, Normans volunteered for this service, under the orders of William Bras-de-Fer, Drogo, and Humphrey; and with them went also a certain Lombard of the north, named Ardoin.

In 1038, the Greeks and this little band of Normans crossed the straits, landed at Faro, a little to the west of Messina, and marched upon the town. The news of the Greek invasion had put an end to the civil strife of the Mohammedans, and they met the army of the emperor with fifty thousand men at Rametta. They fought bravely and were beaten, and with the true instinct of the Greek for the old Greek capital, Maniaces at once advanced upon Syracuse. Here the Moslems defended themselves in the fortress they had built among the ruins, and the siege lasted some time. The city was under the command of a Moslem governor, and with him William Bras-de-Fer fought to the death in single combat. Brave as the bravest, and far stronger than other men, the Moslem had long been the terror of the Christians; but his hour was at hand, and the vanguard of a race stronger than his was before him. He fell before the walls of Syracuse, pierced by a Norman spear, and his fall foreran by a few days a surrender of his city. Then the Greeks and the Normans went in together in triumph, and from every nook and hiding place, from the city of tombs, from the catacombs of Saint Martian by the Church of Saint John, from the recesses of those vast quarries whence the Greek tyrants had hewn the stone that built five cities, gathering in such numbers as no man had guessed, the long-oppressed Christians came forth to meet their deliverers, and to show them the treasures of gold and silver vessels, and the relics of the saints and the body of the holy Lucy, which was found whole and fresh as on the day when it had been laid to rest. And the chronicle says that the coffin which held the saint's body was overlaid with silver and was sent to Constantinople. Forthwith Maniaces began to build the castle on the southern point of Ortygia which still bears his name, and to strengthen the other fortifications as a base from which to effect the conquest of the island.

Castello Maniace, Syracuse

The Saracens who had been beaten at Messina had retired to Palermo. The Greek admiral, Stephanos, was not able to hinder their retreat by sea, and Maniaces was so enraged at the failure that when Stephanos arrived in Syracuse he fell upon him and beat him with a stick, in the presence of the troops.

A similar and a worse indignity had been inflicted upon the Lombard captain, Ardoin, most probably after a battle which was fought somewhere between Messina and Syracuse. During the engagement, Ardoin had got possession of a very beautiful horse, after slaying its Saracen rider with his own hand. The battle being over, the grasping Maniaces commanded that the horse should be given to him, which Ardoin refused to do. In a fit of rage Maniaces commanded that the Lombard should be scourged through the camp, and that his horse should be taken from him. The consequence of these two outrageous acts was that the Normans deserted in a body with Ardoin, while Stephanos, the admiral, who had interest at court in Constantinople, caused Maniaces to be recalled. On reaching the capital of the East, he was cruelly mutilated and thrown into prison, where he remained two years. Ardoin and the Normans retired to Aversa and Salerno, vowing vengeance upon the Greeks; and thereafter they kept the oath they took. The Normans were as remarkable for the subtlety with which they could lead their enemies into a trap as they were conspicuously brave when forced to fight against odds in the open field, and in some degree they have transmitted both those qualities to the Englishmen of to-day. Still smarting from the Greek lash, Ardoin hastened to visit the Greek captain of the Byzantine provinces in Italy, gained his confidence and friendship by rich gifts, and persuaded the deluded official to confide to him the government of Melfi, the stronghold which overlooks the plains of Cannae and the river Ofanto, and is the true key to the possession of Apulia from the northwest side. The keen Lombard at once set about secretly stirring up the people against the Greeks, and as soon as he saw that revolution was ripe he made pretext of a pilgrimage to Rome in order to consult Count Rainulf and the Norman chiefs at Aversa. There, in the city they themselves had founded, the daring little band of fighting men distributed the south among themselves. Ardoin was to hand over Melfi, whence it would be easy to expel the Greeks from Italy altogether, and he was to take one-half of the conquered country, while the Normans were to divide the remainder. The Northmen swore a solemn oath, and, as the Abbé Delarc briefly expresses it, three hundred Normans, led by twelve chiefs, followed Ardoin to fight in open warfare against an empire that still held a great part of Europe and Asia, and ruled over many millions of subjects. Among these chiefs were William Bras-de-Fer and Drogo, Tancred's sons, as well as Ardoin himself. With the compactness and energy of those sudden storms which, in the flash of a minute, drive straight clearings through the mighty forests of Suabia, tearing up thousands of ancient trees in their path, the little army fell upon Melfi. The few Greeks that were there fled almost without resistance, and the Normans were masters of the place in a day. With the instinct of true conquerors, they lost no time in fortifying their position; but it was by the habitual methods of highway robbers and pirates that they began to extend their conquest, pillaging Venosa in the south, Ravello in the east, and Ascoli to northward, while none dared stand against them, but all people were amazed and terror-struck under their furious raids.

And now their victims, seeing that the Normans had not come to free them but to devour them, appealed to the Greeks again, and the captain of the south, who had given up Amalfi to Ardoin, came against the Normans with a great army, and met them near Venosa. There a herald of the Greeks rode forward, mounted on a splendid charger, to offer the invaders terms of peace if they would ride away and harry the country no more; and while he was speaking a big Norman, whose name was Hugo Tudextifen, stood by his horse's head. But when he had said all, the giant raised his ungloved fist and smote the horse between the eyes, so that he fell down dead; and this he did that the Greek might know what manner of men Northmen were.

So the next day, which was the seventeenth of March, 1041, the battle was fought, and the Normans had seven hundred mounted men and five hundred men-at-arms who fought on foot, for they had recruited many among the discontented people of Apulia. The Greeks were thirty thousand, and some have said that they were sixty thousand, and they came against the Normans drawn up in a wedge, as was their wont. They were utterly and completely vanquished, and besides the thousands that fell under the Norman sword, many were drowned as they tried to cross the stream in their flight.

But such was the energy of the Greek general that in little more than seven weeks after his humiliating defeat he faced the Normans again, on the fourth of May, in the great plain of Cannae, ever thirsty for blood. Again the same fate met him, again the Normans slew until they could slay no more, again the waters of the river swallowed up thousands of terrified fugitives. On the field of battle were found among the dead two great churchmen, Angelus, Bishop of Troia, and Stephen, Bishop of Acerenza; for in those days bishops rode out to battle like other men, and in the south the Church was bound to Constantinople.

With a tenacity unusual in the Greeks in those days, the Byzantine general collected the remains of his troops, brought over others from Sicily, and prepared to face the Normans a third time; but the Eastern emperor had lost confidence in the unsuccessful leader, and replaced him by another. The Normans on their side made use of the booty they had taken in order to raise fresh troops, and with their usual diplomatic skill they chose as their commander-in-chief a brother of the Lombard Prince of Benevento.

The third battle was fought on the third of September, in the same year, 1041, almost on the ground where the last had been fought. The Normans had suffered great losses, in spite of their victories, the people of Apulia believed that the Eastern Empire was in earnest at last, and the little army of invaders could muster but seven hundred men to face ten thousand. William Bras-de-Fer himself, ill of the quartan fever, sat on his horse at a little distance, looking on. The Greek general harangued his troops in a heroic strain, calling up legends of Achilles and stories of Philip and Alexander. The Greek host came on in even order against an adversary that was despicably inferior in numbers; the Normans faced them like men, and fought like lions, but were driven back by the sheer weight that opposed them. Then William Bras-de-Fer, ill as he was, drew his great sword and rode at the foe for life and death; and the Normans took heart and struck ten times while the Greeks struck only once, and hewed them in pieces upon the plain; and when there was no Greek left to fight them, they bound the Greek general upon his horse, and with great joy rode back to Melfi, bearing of the rich spoil as much as they could carry. The victory was decisive, and its consequences were destined to be enduring.

The history of the following years chiefly concerns two struggles of a very different nature, one of which took place between the Normans of Melfi and the Greeks, for the possession of Apulia, while the other was entered into by the monks of Monte Cassino, in the hope of regaining those territories which at various times had been taken from them. In this war, Normans found themselves engaged on each side, and seldom hesitated to go over from one side to the other when their interests could be served by so doing.

Statues in front of the church of San Domenico, Taranto

It would be impossible within such narrow limits even to recapitulate the events which took place at this time in Constantinople. It is enough to remind the reader that Maniaces had been disgraced and thrown into prison, and otherwise ill treated, and to add that he was now set at liberty after a revolution in which an emperor was deposed, and a former empress brought back to power. The unfortunate general was restored to all his honours, and was immediately sent with a large army to reconquer Apulia. In the spring of 1042 he landed in the safe harbour of Taranto, and rapidly collecting such native troops as would join his standard, he marched northward in the direction of the old fighting ground. The Normans of Melfi had quarrelled with their chief, and had recently chosen for their leader Argyros, the son of the Lombard patriot, Meles. At the approach of the Greek army he made energetic efforts to increase his force, calling upon all Normans in Italy to fight the common foe. In spite of every effort, Maniaces was unable to check the panic which took possession of his army when it was known that the Normans were at hand, and he regretfully followed his men in their precipitate flight to Taranto. When the Normans reached the sea in pursuit, the Greeks had disappeared within the stronghold on the islet, which was connected with the mainland only by a narrow bridge. The chronicler, William of Apulia, quoted by Delarc, compares the manoeuvres of William Bras-de-Fer and the Normans before Taranto to the tricks of the serpent charmer endeavouring to lure a snake from its hole. But nothing availed; the Greeks were thoroughly frightened from the first, and the Normans, who could not hope to take the town, contented themselves with their favourite diversion of pillaging the country wholesale.

They were no sooner out of sight than Maniaces led out his timid troops and marched them along the coast. His progress was marked by a series of the most atrocious cruelties; wherever he suspected the people of having sympathized with the Normans, he ordered wholesale executions; the wretched peasants were hanged and beheaded without mercy, many were buried alive up to the neck and left to die, and the dastardly Greeks hewed little children in pieces in that blind rage of cruelty which only cowards can feel. Meanwhile the Normans, who were now in force, proceeded with their conquest of Apulia, taking one city after another, and they would soon have been in possession of the whole country by force of arms, if a new turn of affairs in Constantinople had not brought about the recall of Maniaces and an attempt on the part of the Byzantine port to bring about an alliance with the Normans. The emperor now offered Argyros the titles and honours of Byzantine catapan and of a patrician of the Empire; the son of the devoted Meles had the weakness to yield to these blandishments, and immediately proclaimed the supremacy of the emperor in Bari. By this step he at once lost the confidence of the Normans, who refused to own him any longer for their chief, and elected the valiant William Bras-de-Fer for their count and leader. Without hesitation he presented himself before Guaimar, Prince of Salerno, as his liege lord, and was acknowledged by him as Count of Apulia; but it appears that in the peculiar scale of suzerainties that made up the feudal system, Rainulf of Aversa became the nominal suzerain of Apulia, a sort of intermediary between Guaimar and William.

Maniaces did not accept his recall with the humility which Constantinople had expected of him; on the contrary, he promptly revolted, proclaimed himself Emperor of the East, and besieged Argyros, the emperor's new ally, in Bari. Failing to take the place, he now appealed to the Normans, who indignantly refused his proposals. He still held Taranto in the south, but before long was driven from that position by another Greek army, crossed the Adriatic, and perished in Bulgaria, while attempting to continue the struggle. His death so far simplified the political situation, that the contest was now continued between two parties only, the Normans under William Bras-de-Fer on the one hand, and the Greeks of Bari under Argyros the Lombard on the other. These events bring us to the year 1043, and during their development the quarrel about the lands of Monte Cassino had begun and continued. I shall try to sum up the question in a few words. The abbots of Monte Cassino had invoked the assistance of certain Normans to defend them, and about this time Pandolph the Wolf had presented other Normans with extensive lands belonging to the same abbey. The Emperor Conrad had contented himself with the promise of the latter party to respect the power of the Abbot Richer, who, on the departure of the emperor, got some help from Guaimar of Salerno, and recovered at least one fortress. Pandolph the Wolf, who had meanwhile gone to Constantinople to ask assistance in recovering Capua, and who had been exiled by a capricious court, now returned to Italy, having been set at liberty by the death of the emperor; and he returned as the open enemy both of Guaimar and of the Abbot Richer. As allies he had on his side the two Norman counts of Aquino, who had married his daughters, as well as the Normans whom he had established on the abbey lands; against him were ranged on the side of the abbot, Guaimar of Salerno and Rainulf of Aversa. Early in the struggle the abbot was defeated at the head of his men and taken prisoner, while one of the counts of Aquino fell into the hands of Guaimar. The two prisoners having been exchanged, Richer began a journey to the north, in order to appeal to the Emperor of the West; he was wrecked near Rome, but was provided with means for continuing on his way by the Roman nobles. In his absence a plague broke out in Aquino and the neighbourhood, and the counts, who were devout men and regarded the epidemic as a visitation from heaven, went up to the abbey as penitents, on foot and with halters round their necks, to implore forgiveness for their evil deeds. Richer now returned, bringing with him five hundred Lombards, but was soon persuaded by Guaimar to travel northwards again in order to recruit a larger force. The plague and the abbot having disappeared simultaneously, the counts of Aquino repented of their repentance, attacked the abbey again, seized it, and installed the former abbot, who had fled with Pandolph the Wolf to Constantinople. This roused Guaimar to action at last, and appearing with a Norman army, he once more set the monks at liberty. Richer now returned from the north with a considerable force, and the Normans who held the abbey lands were brought to reason, and swore fealty to the rightful abbot. There is much confusion of dates in the accounts of these events, but it is certain that after the death of Maniaces the old quarrel broke out again, and matters looked so ill Richer that he thought for a while of returning to his native Bavaria. He appears to have been prevented from so doing by the following incident and its consequences.

Norman doorway at Trapani

A certain young Norman noble named Randolph, son-in-law to Rainulf of Aversa, came one day to the abbey on the mountain with a number of his followers. Before going in they entered the church to say their prayers, and, according to the custom of that time, they left all their arms, excepting their swords, outside the door. Whether the monks had any reason for expecting a hostile intention on their part does not appear, and Randolph's father-in-law had usually taken their side. Possibly it was on general principles that they thought it not good that a party of Norman knights should be within their walls. While the Normans were on their knees in the church the monks and their Lombard men-at-arms fell upon the visitors and slew fifteen of them within the church; Randolph was taken prisoner, and the rest escaped. The immediate result of this treacherous victory was a regular campaign against the Norman holders of abbey lands, who were in a very short time obliged to abandon all their castles and retire to Aversa, where they were well received in consequence of the attacks made upon the monks by the count's son-in-law. These things happened in 1045, and in the same year Count Rainulf died at a good old age. In accordance with the laws of the feudal system, the Normans of Aversa now requested Guaimar to name Rainulf's successor, and his choice fell upon one of the latter's nephews, a youth of great endowments, who unfortunately died almost immediately afterwards. An attempt on the part of the people of Gaeta to make one of the counts of Aquino their chief was crushed by Guaimar, and Pandolph the Wolf, seeing the county of Aversa at odds with Salerno, his most dangerous enemy, immediately persuaded the former to join him in a fresh attack on Monte Cassino. In the meantime Adenulf of Aquino, whom Guaimar had taken prisoner, besought the latter prince to set him free, promising that he would immediately go to the assistance of the abbey. Guaimar agreed, and Adenulf was received with joy by Richer, who named him protector of the monastery, and presented him with a splendid charger, a standard, and a suit of armour. Adenulf, on his side, gave back to the monks a golden chalice and a rich cope which Pandolph the Wolf had stolen from the monastery and presented to him. At first Pandolph refused to believe the news, but on finding that Adenulf was really at Monte Cassino and ready to defend it he retired, leaving his adversary in possession of Gaeta.

Even now the monks were not out of danger, for the young Randolph was at large again, having been liberated at the request of Drogo, Count of Apulia, who paid the monastery a thousand pieces of silver for his ransom, and if an early death had not cut short his career, the young man would probably have taken vengeance for the injuries he had suffered at the monks' hands. The quarrel about the abbey lands, however, was at an end, since the monastery had regained possession of them, and the ground of those differences without which the Normans were still unable to bear the monotony of a prosperous existence, was now removed to another matter. On the premature death of Rainulf's nephew, another of his nephews, also called Rainulf, and surnamed Trincanocte, claimed the county, but fell into the hands of Guaimar of Salerno, who insisted on his right of presenting the county to a man of his own choice. The young Rainulf was imprisoned in that dark fortress which still hangs above Salerno, and to which so many gloomy stories are attached. With him there was another Norman and two men of Amalfi. Before long they gained the sympathies of their jailor, Martin, who allowed the Amalfitans to send to Amalfi for a few measures of drugged wine. The jailor gave the liquor to the soldiers of the guard, who drank it and fell asleep, and he then allowed the four to leave the castle. Swift horses, held in readiness by the men of Amalfi, bore the escaped prisoners by the pass of La Cava to the strong castle of Maddaloni beyond Naples on the highroad to Rome. Of course the irrepressible and indefatigable Pandolph seized the opportunity of allying himself with the young Rainulf; together they drove Guaimar's count from Aversa and planned an attack upon Salerno; but their plans were disconcerted when they learned that Drogo of Apulia was in arms to help his liege lord, Guaimar, and though the two armies came face to face almost at the foot of Vesuvius, the matter was brought to a peaceable conclusion. Drogo had the wisdom to intercede for Rainulf with Guaimar, who at last consented, though much against his wishes, to invest the young man with the gonfalon of Aversa. Rainulf Trincanocte had gained his end, but was now, of course, Pandolph's enemy. All these things seem to have happened in the year 1045. At the same time the struggle in Apulia was continuing, and Argyros of Bari was badly beaten by William Bras-de-Fer at Trani. The combined forces of Guaimar and of Bras-de-Fer had also accomplished the difficult feat of marching down through Calabria, and had built a strong Norman fort at Squillace on the Gulf of Taranto, almost, if not quite, in sight of Sicily.

In 1046, the population of Apulia seems to have revolted against Constantinople, Argyros was replaced by another catapan, who lost Taranto or Trani, or both, in the last battle which William Bras-de-Fer was destined to fight. After a career of little more than ten years, the Norman hero passed away, we know not exactly when, nor where. It is said that he was buried in the Church of the Trinity at Venosa, but I believe that no trace of his tomb is to be found.

It is needless to say that the death of such a man in such times caused new trouble, but the Norman power had already reached the straits, and it was a foregone conclusion that it should before long embrace all the south. Drogo, who seems to have been associated in the leadership with his brother William, succeeded him, and received in marriage the daughter of Guaimar with a great dowry.

At this time the troubles in which the Papacy was involved by the simultaneous existence of three popes, namely, Benedict the Ninth, Sylvester the Third, and Gregory the Sixth, called for the presence and interference of the Emperor Henry the Third, surnamed the Black. With an energy remarkable even in those times, the young sovereign descended into Lombardy at the head of a large army, held a synod at Pavia, deposed the three popes by a stroke of the imperial pen, and proceeded to Rome. Without delay he imposed upon the cardinals the election of the German bishop of Bamberg under the name of Clement the Second, by whom he immediately caused himself and his Empress Agnes to be anointed and crowned. His direct action put a stop to the hideous evils which had begun during the domination in Rome of that extraordinary woman known as Theodora Senatrix, and which had continued under the popes and princes of her evil race; but Henry the Black would have done better had he confirmed Gregory the Sixth in the Papacy.

In 1047, accompanied by the Pope he had made, he marched southwards to Monte Cassino, and was received with the highest honours in the now prosperous abbey. At Capua he convoked the rulers of the south, Guaimar of Salerno, Drogo of Apulia, Rainulf Trincanocte of Aversa, Pandolph the Wolf, and all other lords who were supposed to hold their lands from the Empire. His intention was to pacify and organize the south, but he was no longer dealing with antipopes and clergymen; he was face to face with the strongest and most cunning men of the age, and with men, moreover, who now commanded wealth that could dazzle even an emperor. Pandolph brought such splendid offerings that Henry was persuaded to restore to him the long-lost principality of Capua, to the inexpressible chagrin of Guaimar, who had now held it for nine years. Drogo and Rainulf prevailed upon him by presents to confirm them in their domains as imperial vassals, thus liberating them from the suzerainty of Guaimar, who thereby lost the title of Duke of Apulia and Calabria. This was the beginning of the end of the great Lombard house of Salerno.

Proceeding on his way, and accompanied by his faithful Pope, Henry suddenly found himself opposed at Benevento by the loyalty of its inhabitants to the now almost forgotten Empire of the East. Having already sent back a portion of his army to Germany, Henry contented himself with burning the suburbs of the city, and by way of vengeance, presented the whole country to the Normans on condition that they could take it. His obedient Pope then and there excommunicated the entire population, and the two departed, leaving the Normans to work their will unhindered.

There can be no doubt but that Henry's intentions were good, but his visit to the south was the beginning of many troubles between the Papacy and the Normans; he certainly did wrong in restoring Capua to Pandolph, and his gift of Benevento to men who had no sort of claim to it was most unjust. His departure from Italy and the events just narrated coincided very nearly with the appearance of a new and most extraordinary character upon the scene. It was at this time that Robert, afterwards surnamed Guiscard, the eldest son born of the second marriage of Tancred of Hauteville, followed the example of his elder half-brothers and came to seek his fortune in Italy.

Imitating the example of the Abbé Delarc, my guide through the intricacies of this period of history, I shall quoted here the portrait of Robert, which is found in the 'Alexiad' of Anna Comnena, a princess of Constantinople.

"This Robert was of Norman origin and of an obscure family; he united a marvellous astuteness with immense ambition, and his bodily strength was prodigious. His whole desire was to attain to the wealth and power of the greatest living men; he was extremely tenacious of his designs and most wise in finding means to attain his ends. In stature he was taller than the tallest; of a ruddy hue and fair-haired, he was broad shouldered, and his eyes sparkled with fire; the perfect proportion of all his limbs made him a model of beauty from head to heel, as I have often heard people tell. Homer says of Achilles that those who heard his voice seemed to hear the thundering shout of a great multitude, but it used to be said of this man that his battle-cry would turn back tens of thousands. Such a man, one in such a position, of such a nature, and of such spirit, naturally hated the idea of service, and would not be subject to any man; for such are those natures which are born too great for their surroundings.

"Being, therefore, so constituted and utterly incapable of obeying, Robert set out from Normandy with five horsemen and thirty men on foot, all told, and came and lived in the fastnesses and caverns and mountains of Lombardy (at that time meaning Calabria), supporting himself by robbery and plundering travellers, thus procuring horses, necessaries, and arms. So the beginning of his life was filled with bloodshed and many murders."

It is needless to say that after the Emperor Henry's departure, Guaimar at once made a vigorous effort to regain the principality of Capua; and by the help of the Normans he took the city and received the submission of the old Wolf. The two, however, soon quarrelled again concerning the person of a certain Count of Teano whom Pandolph had long kept a prisoner and had treated very cruelly. Guaimar had caused him to be set at liberty, and Pandolph now attempted to imprison him again. Guaimar again appealed to the Normans, who responded to his call; but Robert, who had received no favours from his brothers since his appearance in Italy, turned against them and fought for Pandolph, who promised him a castle and one of his daughters in marriage. The promises were, of course, not fulfilled, and Robert departed, vowing the destruction of Pandolph's house.

His brother Drogo, wearied by his importunities, now gave him a small castle in lower Calabria, overlooking the valley of the Crati and the site of ancient Sybaris. The place was in a dangerous situation, in the heart of an enemy's country, and Drogo perhaps hoped that his wild young brother would not attempt to hold it, and would leave Italy altogether. But he had misjudged a man far greater than himself. Robert left the place indeed, but only to move up the valley to the famous rock of San Marco, where he established himself and led the life of a desperate marauder. With the true Norman instinct, he made friends also by means of the booty he took from others. In this way, besides his own men, he had a small force consisting of a few score natives, desperate ruffians whose interests were bound up with his own. Once, being almost reduced to starvation, he sent them out by night on a marauding expedition, then secretly dressed himself like one of them and accompanied their march, lest the natives should lead his own men into a trap, and he only showed himself at dawn when the fighting grew hot; and he and they brought home great spoil. The careful chronicler of Monte Cassino, who detested all Normans with good reason, made an extraordinarily accurate list of Robert's thefts, counting up a number of oxen and brood mares, thirty head of horned cattle, ten fat porkers, and so on, and adding that Robert used to capture even peasants, whom he caused to pay ransom in bread and wine.

Furthermore, the chronicler, as if speaking of a great hardship, says that Robert was more than once actually obliged to drink pure water from the spring, and that he visited his brother Drogo again and told him of his great poverty, and that what he said with his lips he showed in his face, for he was very thin.

A trick he played upon a friend about this time describes the man who was to conquer the south. He was on very good terms with a certain knight, the Lord of Bisignano, a man of considerable possessions. One day they met by agreement, and Robert commanded his men to halt at a little distance, while he embraced his friend. He embraced him indeed, for riding up to him, he threw his arms round him, brought him to the ground, and placing his knees upon his chest held him fast, until he promised to pay a ransom of twenty thousand gold pieces. While the money was being collected, he kept him a close prisoner in San Marco, but came to him in his cell and confessed on his knees and in tears that he had committed a great sin, but that his friend's wealth and his own poverty constrained him to do this deed. 'Thou art my father,' he said, 'and it is meet that a father should help his poor son, for this thing is commanded by the law of the king, that a father who is rich in all things should succour the poverty of his son.' When the money was paid, and he was riding sadly homeward, the Lord of Bisignano must have made some curious reflections upon filial piety, and the spontaneous choice of parents.

In spite of such deeds, however, Robert continued to be relatively poor. He suddenly improved his fortunes by matrimony. Being on his way to visit his brother Drogo, probably in the hope of extracting money from him, he was met by a Norman kinsman of his, named Gerard, who appears to have been the first to appreciate qualities that were surprising, if not good, for he first, and on that occasion, addressed Robert as 'Guiscard,' 'the astute.' 'O Guiscard,' said he, 'why do you thus wander hither and thither? Behold, now, marry my aunt, the sister of my father, and I will be your knight, and will go with you to conquer Calabria, and I will bring two hundred riders.'

In spite of Drogo's strong objections, Robert took Gerard's advice and espoused the aunt, of whom we have, unfortunately, no portrait; her name is variously written Adverarda and Alberada, and he afterwards repudiated her. Gerard kept his word, and with his help Robert won castles and towns and devoured the land.

At this time a certain Richard of the Norman house of Aversa appeared upon the scene, having been exiled by the young Rainulf Trincanocte, who feared him on account of his great popularity. Coming to Apulia, he found a friend in Humphrey, but soon quarrelled with Drogo. He must have possessed by great charm, together with the gift of inspiring confidence, for an old Norman noble, the childless Lord of Genzano in Apulia, took him to his heart and home and made him master of all his castles. About this time, also, old Pandolph the Wolf closed his chequered career, dying that last in possession of his principality, and leaving it to his son; and at no great interval the young Rainulf of Aversa also died, leaving an only son, who was a mere child. Richard of Genzano would very naturally have seized Aversa, where he was beloved by the people, but in his quarrel with Drogo the latter had succeeded in imprisoning him, and it was not until the people of Aversa formally requested Guaimar to make him their count that Drogo consented to set him at liberty, and he was invested with the county by Guaimar himself. The south of Italy was now divided between this Norman Richard of Aversa, the sons of Tancred, the two Lombard princes of Salerno and Capua, and the Greeks who held Bari for the emperor. There was, moreover, the city and country of Benevento, which Henry the Third had given over to the Normans, but which before long appealed to the Pope for protection.

We must now briefly return to the troubles in which the Papacy was involved. Henry the Black had returned to Germany, and he had left his German Pope, Clement the Second, in Rome. The latter was alone and without friends, and within seven months the anti-Pope, Benedict the Ninth, succeeded in poisoning him and in taking possession of the Holy See. In the following year the emperor sent a second German Pope to Rome, under the name of Damasus the Second; after a reign of twenty-three days he shared the fate of his predecessor, and was buried also. Henry now held a great assembly at Worms, the result of which was that Bruno, Bishop of Toul, in Lorraine, consented to go to Rome and to be made Pope, on condition that the Roman clergy and people should elect him of their own free will. He arrived, bringing with him as a friend and counsellor that famous Hildebrand who long afterwards brought Henry the Fourth barefooted in the snow to Canossa. Bruno was elected at once and took the name of Leo the Ninth.

At the outset of his pontificate this Pope found himself face to face with something like starvation. The Holy See possessed absolutely no source of income; the Pope had soon expended the little ready money he and his friends had with them, and before long they actually made arrangements to sell their vestments and superfluous clothes in order to raise a little sum with which they might secretly return to Lorraine. At this critical juncture a deputation of nobles arrived from Benevento, bearing rich gifts, and entreating the Pope to revoke the excommunication which the emperor had caused to be pronounced upon their city. It must be remembered that the Papacy had long laid claim to Benevento, rightly or wrongly, and it seems that the people themselves, in spite of their conduct at the time of Henry's visit, preferred to submit to the authority of the Papacy rather than to be left a prey to the Normans. Leo the Ninth at once undertook the journey to the south, where he was well received by the Lombard princes, and a year later he renewed his visit, remaining some time in Benevento. On these occasions he conceived a strong dislike for the Normans, but on meeting the Norman chiefs at Monte Gargano he was completely deceived by their promises. He did not understand that in taking possession of Benevento he had set a limit to the Norman conquest in a northward direction; and when, after a third visit to Benevento, during which he received the most friendly assurances from Guaimar and Drogo, the Normans in the neighbourhood rose and attacked the city, his irritation and disappointment knew no bounds. But the message whom he sent to the Count of Apulia to protest against the outrage was met by the news that Drogo had been assassinated.

The Italians of the south had formed a great conspiracy to rid themselves of the Norman domination by a wholesale massacre. From Benevento Drogo had gone to the castle of Montolio in Apulia, and there, on the tenth of August, being the feast of Saint Lawrence, he went to mass in the castle church. As he entered, the murderer sprang upon him from behind the door and stabbed him, and at the same moment the Italians in the castle fell upon the unsuspecting Normans, and killed many of them before they could defend themselves. In many parts of Apulia the conspiracy broke out at the same time, and many Normans perished, but Humphrey and Robert Guiscard escaped, and swore a great oath to avenge the treachery. So Humphrey became Count of Apulia, and Robert stood by him, and they bound the limbs of him who had slain Drogo, and sawed them off one by one, and because the man still breathed they buried him alive. The rest of the prisoners they hanged, and these executions, says the chronicler, somewhat allayed the grief of Humphrey. And Leo the Ninth, who had believed that Drogo was his friend, sang a mass for his soul that all his sins might be forgiven him.

Drogo had undoubtedly been the man who might have made peace between the Papacy and the Normans, and his death drove Leo the Ninth to make a vain appeal to the emperor for help. He was ready to offer anything in his gift, temporal or spiritual, to Henry the First,° the King of France, and the Duke of Marseilles, if they would only help to deliver the land from the malice of the Normans. But they were not to be moved, and in his great need the Pope turned to the Greeks, who still had a foothold in Bari under the Lombard Argyros. The latter had returned from Constantinople in 1051, bringing immense sums of money, with which the emperor hoped that the Normans might be bribed to leave Italy and serve the Eastern Empire; but the Normans refused all such advances with scorn, and Argyros was obliged to continue the war he had so long waged at a disadvantage. Desiring the expulsion of the Normans quite as much as Pope Leo himself, he turned to him spontaneously and met his advances halfway.

In 1052, the Pope made his first attempt at an attack, and gathered some troops in the neighbourhood of Naples, attempting at the same time to gain the alliance of Guaimar; but the latter remembered that the Normans had helped him in many a difficulty, and sternly refused to have anything to do with such a war; the Pope's troops could no longer be kept together, and the Pope took refuge in Naples. A few weeks afterwards a frightful tragedy changed the course of events in the south.

Guaimar's wife was a daughter of one of the Lombard counts of Teano, and, unknown to Guaimar, her four brothers had long been conspiring to seize his throne. They drew into their conspiracy the people of Amalfi, who had not lost the tradition of their recent independence, and whom Guaimar had been obliged to treat with severity. They, indeed, began something like a regular war by attacking Salernitan vessels on the high seas, and at last they actually appeared with warships before Salerno, and effected a landing. Guaimar seized his arms and rushed down to the shore to repel the attack, but his Salernitan soldiers fled before the determined Amalfitans, and in a moment Guaimar found himself surrounded by his four brothers-in-law and a host of conspirators, who were in reality in league with the men of Amalfi. One of the four pierced the prince with his lance, and the others stabbed him at once. He fell with thirty-six wounds, and his murderers dragged his body along the beach with every indignity.

He was avenged within the week by the Normans, who not only remembered that he had recently refused to join the Greeks and the Pope against them, but were extremely anxious to maintain his dynasty in the principality. In answer to the appeal of his brother Guy, who found some of the Norman chiefs in the neighbourhood of Benevento, they hastily gathered their forces and appeared before Salerno five days after the murder. The city opened its gates to them, but the conspirators took refuge in the strong fortress above. The Normans held the wives and children of the four as hostages and consented to exchange them and liberate them on condition that they would set free Guaimar's son Gisulf, and solemn promises were given that the sons of the Count of Teano and their accomplices should be allowed to depart unhurt. Guy probably meant to keep his word, but his Norman soldiers protested that they had not given theirs, and falling upon the fugitives slaughtered six and thirty of them, one for every wound that had been found in the murdered Guaimar's body. The Duke of Sorrento alone was spared. With splendid good faith, considering the times, Guy set his nephew Gisulf upon the throne of Salerno, and stood by him as a loyal counsellor.

The Pope now took advantage of circumstances which made him a successful mediator between the King of Hungary and Henry the Third, to make a fresh appeal to the latter, but could obtain nothing except the confirmation of the papal Duchy of Benevento; for although the emperor saw the necessity of lending the Pope an army wherewith to hold it against the Normans, he could not make up his mind to do so. Leo the Ninth, with undaunted energy, collected a little force of adventurous Suabians and other Germans, whom he led southwards with considerable strategic skill until he had effected a junction with Argyros of Bari. The hatred of the Normans throughout Italy was only exceeded at that time by the fear they inspired, and during the Pope's progress a motley company of irregular fighters flocked to his standard from all parts of Italy. With the exception of the few Germans who had crossed the Alps with him, his army was chiefly Italian, for the Lombards, who had joined him, had long lost their distinctive nationality. Argyros met them in the low land not far from Monte Gargano and probably within sight of that famous place of Norman pilgrimage. The Normans, on their side, had collected together a little army. Robert Guiscard had brought up his wild marauders from the furthest limits of Calabria, Richard of Aversa was there with his trained men-at-arms, and Humphrey had called out every Norman fighting man in Apulia. Yet the whole army was so small that before giving battle the Normans attempted, with their usual prudence, to effect a compromise, and sent messengers to the Pope suing for peace and declaring that every Norman in Italy was willing to acknowledge his authority.

Leo the Ninth was in the midst of the allied forces, surrounded by his little band of Suabians and Germans; and they, in scorn of men who fought on horseback with pointed sticks, laughed at the Norman messengers and constrained the pontiff to give an overbearing answer. The Normans were to lay down their arms and leave Italy at once; if they refused to do so they should taste of the long German sword. They might choose between instant destruction or immediate departure.

Seeing that they could obtain no terms, the messengers retired, and after a short reconnoissance of the enemy's position, the Normans gave battle on the eighteenth of June, 1053. Count Humphrey held the centre, Richard, with his splendid cavalry, took the right, while Robert Guiscard had the left wing. Richard of Aversa, as commanding the most thoroughly trained troops, made the attack, falling upon the united force of the Italians, says the chronicler, like a vulture upon a flock of doves, and scattering them far and wide in instant panic. The Suabians, on the contrary, stood firm against Humphrey's repeated charges, for the struggle was between Teutons and Northmen. Hand to hand they fought with their swords, and the Germans learned that their own were not the better. Then Robert Guiscard made one of those wild charges that have often turned the fortunes of war and directed the course of history, leading men who, like himself, had little to lose and all to gain. The faithful Gerard was beside him, and together they broke the stout German ranks. Robert's great sword paused not in slaughter, beheading men at a blow to right and left, and inflicting frightful wounds. Three times his horse was killed under him and three times he caught another and mounted again. The huge Germans stood up to him and his followers, and died where they stood, while the less sturdy Lombards fled from the fight, and when the victory seemed won, the wounded and mutilated still fought on. Meanwhile Richard had returned from pursuing his scattered Italians, and came back to strike the final blow, and when the battle was over there was not a Suabian nor a German alive on the field.

The Pope, overcome at the sight of the bloodshed he had caused, rather than disappointed in his hopes, had retired into the neighbouring town of Civitate and watched the last destruction of his army from the ramparts; but the inhabitants of the little town, seeing which way the fight had gone, thrust out the venerable pontiff just as the infuriated Normans had set fire to the houses and sheds that stood outside the gate. With sublime indifference to danger, the Pope and his few attendant clerks marched straight towards the enemy, bearing a cross in their midst. It is said that as they went towards the rising flames, a sudden breeze sprang up and drove the fire back upon the Normans. How this may be we know not, but it is certain that either on that evening or on the next day at dawn, Leo met the Norman chiefs face to face, and he spoke to them with such eloquence, so tenderly and yet so strongly, that they were touched, and kneeled down before him and asked his blessing, and, perhaps in one of their rare moments of sincerity, they promised that they would be faithful to him, and would take the place of his soldiers whom they had slain.

Then he caused the dead to be buried hard by Civitate, and many centuries afterwards men saw the great mound that was raised above their bones; and when he had said a mass for the repose of their souls, he departed towards Benevento. Humphrey of Apulia was himself the first to lead the Pope's escort, and many hundred Normans accompanied him to the end of his journey; and though they might well be glad that they were rid of his army, there was something not unchivalrous, after all, in the reverent courtesy they showed to their vanquished and venerable foe. But at Benevento all the people came out to meet him, and when they saw the sad faces of the bishops and clerks that were with him, and that he was surrounded, not by his own army, but by Norman knights, they all broke out into cries and lamentations, which ceased not while they led him in mournful procession to the church.

During about a year, Leo the Ninth remained in Benevento, still believing that he might accomplish the expulsion of the Normans before his death, for he was only about fifty years of age, and we learn that he at this time began the study of the Greek language. But he had not long to live, and his last months were embittered and disturbed by theological controversies with the East, which ended soon after his death in the final separation of the Eastern and Western Churches. The Eastern emperor and the Pope were both equally anxious to free Southern Italy from the Normans, but the Patriarch of Constantinople, whose influence with the people of that city was paramount, and with whom the emperor was obliged to reckon at every turn, was jealous of Rome and aimed at the absolute independence of his patriarchate. At that time a correspondence which took place between an Eastern and a Western bishop concerning the use of leaven in the consecrated bread, the celibacy of the clergy, and the procession of the Holy Ghost from the Father and the Son, was placed in the hands of Leo the Ninth. He took up the matter and wrote a vigorous letter to the Patriarch Michael, whom the emperor obliged to return a meek answer for the sake of his own political relations with the Pope. The latter then sent three legates to Constantinople bearing an epistle to Michael which condemned the Eastern view of the three mooted points in the strongest possible language. In spite of the letter he had been obliged to write, however, the patriarch successfully avoided a meeting with the ambassadors, stirred up a popular riot against the emperor, and persevered in his errors. An exchange of excommunications and other amenities at once followed, the three legates excommunicated the Patriarch Michael, and the Patriarch Michael excommunicated the three legates, who departed, shaking the dust from their feet. During their absence, Leo the Ninth was taken ill and died in the month of April; in July his bull was burned in Constantinople, and the permanent division of the Eastern and Western Churches, which had begun with the dissension of Photius two centuries earlier, became an accomplished fact.

The Pope died in April. He left Benevento in a dying condition in March, and was accompanied to Capua by Count Humphrey and the Normans. He spent his last days in Rome in visiting the Church of Saint Peter's, and in pious exhortations to his people and the Roman clergy concerning the vanity of human things, and he departed from this world, as he had lived in it, a very upright and just man.

Unsuccessful though he had been at Civitate, his moral influence throughout Italy had been a check on the Norman expansion. When he was gone, the people of Benevento saw that the Roman Church was wholly unable to protect them against the Normans, who set at naught the emperor's donation of their city to the popes. They were able to resist a siege, but restored the Lombard dynasty, and Count Humphrey departed southwards in sullen wrath to wreak vengeance upon the conspirators who had slain Drogo. There being now neither papal nor Greek troops to oppose him, he subjected the south to a reign of terror, and wholesale executions of Italians, by hanging and beheading, avenged the murder of Tancred's son.

Now also came two more of those sons, Geoffrey and a second William; and Humphrey, to establish these two in possessions not unworthy to be compared to his own, took Salerno from the young Gisulf, who indeed had kept little faith with any one, and least of all with his Uncle Guy, to whom he owed his life and estate; and at the same time, Richard of Aversa quarrelled with him and helped Tancred's sons. Gisulf himself was led into an ambush, and only escaped by throwing himself into the sea and swimming for his life.

Meanwhile Argyros of Bari, who was in bad odour in Constantinople since the battle of Civitate, was unable to obtain help from any one, and Humphrey, Geoffrey, and Robert Guiscard inflicted another overwhelming defeat upon him near Brindisi. The Greek cause was now lost beyond all hope.

The Normans quarrelled, indeed, among themselves, and there is an account of a violent scene which took place between Humphrey and Robert at dinner, but of which the cause is not known. In sudden anger at something said by Guiscard, Humphrey commanded him to be thrown into prison, whereupon Robert snatched up a sword and made at his brother to kill him, but was held fast by the bystanders, and was actually kept a prisoner for a short time. But the brothers were soon reconciled, and Humphrey presented his brother with more lands in Calabria, and gave him, moreover, a number of knights. From his grim stronghold of San Marco, whence he ravaged the country continually, Robert was soon after this called to his brother's death-bed, and the dying Humphrey, who foresaw that the terrible young Guiscard would be his successor in Apulia, whether he would or not, wisely made him guardian of his son, a lad. Humphrey was buried with his brothers in the monastery of Venosa, and the Guiscard ruled in his stead.

Ruins of the abbey at Mileto

His first move was upon Reggio in the Straits of Messina; but it was in vain that he attempted to induce the inhabitants to acknowledge his sovereignty without a struggle, and he soon returned to Apulia. At this time the youngest of Tancred's sons joined him. This was Roger, afterwards the Great Count and the father of King Roger of Sicily. He seems to have possessed an abundance of those gifts which distinguished all the brothers. Handsome, strong, and active, his courage was as remarkable as his astuteness, and he was as generous as any of his elders, giving freely to his friends all that he could take from his enemies. By way of trying him, Robert gave him sixty men and sent him to fight the Calabrians in the southern mountains above Monteleone and Mileto. In a short time he had made himself the terror of the surrounding country, and was able to send the Guiscard a large sum of money as the first fruits of his industry. He visited him soon afterwards, traversing the dangerous road with only six companions, and the two now planned a systematic attack upon Reggio; but the place was too strong for them, and they were obliged to give up the siege.

Tower in the castle of Frederick II at Monteleone

Roger had displayed so much courage and talent, however, that the suspicious Guiscard began to fear in him a dangerous rival, and refused to send him money with which to pay his troops. Without hesitation Roger now turned to his brother William of Salerno, who received him with open arms, for he also had some cause of disagreement with the Guiscard; and he gave Roger the town and castle of Scalea for himself, that he might thence make incursions into Robert's territory. The latter lost no time in besieging his brother, but the place proved impregnable. It stands on the cape that bears its name, protected by the precipitous ascent from the dangerous river, by the sea, and by the high cliffs, so that the only approach to it can be easily defended. Robert destroyed the olives and vineyards in the rich valley, but was so harassed by the troops of his brother William that he was obliged to retire.

A reconciliation now followed, by which Robert granted Roger forty men-at-arms, with permission to commit unlimited depredations, and for some time the younger brother consented to follow the life of a marauder, from which Guiscard had risen to such power.

During this time, however, the latter needed his services in some expedition, and when he was rewarded for two months of hard fighting with the present of a single horse, he turned upon his brother indignantly, went back to Scalea, and lost no time in pillaging Robert's lands.

The year 1058 was a memorable one in the south; the Normans harried the land without ceasing, and gave no quarter when their demands were not satisfied; the crops had failed, and the country suffered from severe famine, so that the people were reduced to making bread of chestnuts and acorns, and even out of reeds and aquatic plants, and they ate raw roots, seasoning them with a little salt. Then an abundant harvest followed the lean year, and men died of surfeit as they had lately died of hunger. Meanwhile the quarrel between Roger and Robert continued, and the Calabrians, seeing their opportunity, attempted to shake off the Norman yoke. The oppressors were treacherously murdered, and in one castle sixty Normans were massacred in a single day. Robert saw that he was on the point of losing Calabria altogether, while Apulia was already on the point of revolution, and making a virtue of necessity, he sent ambassadors to the young Roger and made peace, presenting him with a large part of southern Calabria, from Mount Intefoli and Squillace to Reggio.

In the meantime Richard of Aversa had followed the example of Humphrey and Robert, and had done his best to extend his dominions. The old Lombard dynasty had been restored in Capua, and as the opportunity seemed favourable for seizing the principality, Richard marched against the city, but being unable to take it, he systematically destroyed the crops and fruit trees, until the people paid him six thousand gold bezants to quit their territory. He did so at the time, but on the death of the prince, he returned with a greater force than before, and drove out the prince's youthful successor. He now took the title of Prince of Capua, without consulting Pope or emperor, and immediately picked a quarrel with the Count of Aquino, to whose son he had affianced his daughter. The ingenuity of the claim he made was worthy of a Norman and of the times. The young man died before the marriage took place, and thereupon Richard claimed the wedding gift which, according to the Lombard law, the bridegroom was bound to present to his bride on the morning after the marriage. He had the insolence to demand on these grounds a quarter of all the count's possessions, and on the latter's refusal to pay such a preposterous indemnity, he marched against Aquino with his army. It was during the siege that Richard paid a friendly visit to the monks of Monte Cassino; and they, remembering the days of Pandolph the Wolf, received him with honours, committing to him the care and defence of the abbey. He was received in procession as a king, and the church was decked as for Easter Day, the lamps were all lighted, and the cloister resounded with chanting and with praises of the prince. Then he was led into the chapter house, and much against his will was set in the abbot's throne, and the abbot knelt down and washed his feet.

Having obtained the protection of the powerful prince, the monks began to intercede with him to reduce the demands he was making upon the Count of Aquino, and he consented to do so; but the count would not agree to pay even the smaller sum required until Richard had forced him to make payment by bringing ruin upon his possessions. It was about this time that William of Hauteville was engaged in the conquest of Salerno, and the unfortunate Gisulf turned to Richard in his need. Richard helped him at least to hold the city, in consideration of great promises, and for a short time the Lombard seems to have recovered something more than a semblance of power; but he worked his own destruction by his refusal to keep his word to his ally.

We now reach that important period at which the Papacy, from having been determinately opposed to the Normans of the south, was driven to seek their alliance. The death of Leo the Ninth was followed by an interregnum that lasted about a year, at the end of which time Henry the Black created a Pope in the person of the Chancellor of the Empire, who was also a bishop, and who reigned under the name of Victor the Second. This wise pontiff began his career by making a sort of truce with the Normans. A little before this time the Duke of Lorraine, who had been despoiled of his possessions by Henry the Third, married Beatrice, the mother of the afterwards celebrated Countess Matilda, and the widow of the Marquis of Tuscany, the greatest prince in the north of Italy. Fearing lest the duke should ally himself with the Normans, the emperor descended into Italy, in the hope of falling upon him unawares; but he fled, and the emperor only succeeded in capturing his wife and step-daughter, whom he carried away prisoners to Germany. Pope Victor now found himself in a most difficult situation. His political judgment would have led him to seek the Norman alliance, and at the same time he received the most bitter complaints from the Italians whom the Normans oppressed in the south. In this dilemma Victor appealed to his friend the emperor, judging that for the good of the people, and in spite of his own judgment, it would be better to make a final effort to get rid of the Normans altogether, and it was not impossible that the emperor might have been persuaded to undertake a war of extermination against them had he lived. But he died in 1056, after a very short illness, leaving for his successor Henry the Fourth, then a child only five years old. Victor, who had for many years been the great chancellor of the Empire, and was familiar with all the matters of state, now took the reins of government, and the world beheld with surprise a condition of affairs in which the Pope of Rome ruled the Holy Roman Empire as the infant emperor's guardian. A churchman of such experience and of such gifts might have succeeded in inaugurating an era of peace in Europe; but he too was overtaken by an early death soon after his return to Italy. He was immediately succeeded by Frederick of Lorraine, who took the name of Stephen the Ninth, who was the brother of that Duke of Lorraine who had now returned to his great possessions in Italy through the intervention of the late Pope, and who, as a friend of Leo the Ninth, had been one of those who most strongly urged that pontiff to make war upon the Normans.

If the pontifical treasury had not been in its almost chronic state of depletion, the Normans might now have found themselves opposed to a really dangerous adversary, whose brother was the reigning sovereign over a great part of Northern Italy. But Pope Stephen was without funds, and being obliged to seek assistance, he meditated a truly gigantic scheme. His plan was undoubtedly to ally himself with the Empire of the East as well as with his brother, in order to drive the Normans from Italy; then to set his own brother upon the throne of the Holy Roman Empire, in place of the infant Henry the Fourth, and, finally, to crush the Eastern Empire out of existence, and to reëstablish the universal dominion of Rome. His ambassadors were already on their way to Constantinople, and in conference with Argyros at Bari, when death overtook the scheming pontiff, and the ambassadors returned to Rome.

A handful of turbulent Roman nobles, in the midst of a frightful tumult, and in spite of the protestations of many cardinals, elected a certain John of Velletri Pope, or rather, antipope. He ascended the papal throne under the strong protection of the Roman barons themselves and of a party throughout the country which demanded an Italian pontiff. Hildebrand, that extraordinary man of strength and genius who had been the tried and trusted friend of many successive popes, now appeared upon the scene and directed affairs. Without hesitation he went directly to Rome, reassured the trembling cardinals, declared the election of Benedict the Tenth null and void, and immediately sent an embassy to Germany, perhaps accompanying it in person. After a short consultation, Gerard, the Bishop of Florence, was chosen to be Pope, and the powerful Duke of Lorraine and Tuscany conducted him to Rome, where he was duly elected and crowned under the name of Nicholas the Second. In a short time Hildebrand had driven out the antipope, Benedict, and had established Nicholas in comparative security; but he now recognized the great fact that the Normans were the invincible rulers of the south, and that without them no authority could long hold its own in Rome. Accordingly, and by the intervention of Desiderius, Abbot of Monte Cassino, he obtained the help of Richard of Capua, who appeared in the neighbourhood of Rome with a Norman army, and drove the antipope and his friends to take refuge in the castle of Galera, while, as usual, he looted the surrounding country.

This Desiderius, Abbot of Monte Cassino, whom the Pope soon afterwards created a cardinal, was a Lombard prince by birth, whose father had been killed by the Normans, but he, nevertheless, became the intermediate between them and the Holy See, and his first friendly relations with them began when, being at Bari, Robert Guiscard lent him three horses in order that he might get back safely to his abbey. Soon after the raid which drove out Benedict the Tenth, Pope Nicholas held a synod or council in the Lateran, during which it was determined that in future all popes should be elected by the cardinals only, without consulting the nobles and the people, by agreement with the Emperor Henry the Fourth, who was at that time a child, and of whose successors no mention was made in the decree. The independence of the Holy See was thus greatly strengthened, and although the dignity of the living emperor was respected, it was made clear that the cardinals did not intend to subject their choice to the approval of the emperors thereafter succeeding him; it became, therefore, more and more necessary to strengthen the papal alliance with the Normans. Two months after the date of this decree, the Pope visited the Norman capital of Apulia, and there held a council, at which a hundred bishops from all parts of Italy were present, and at which a number of Norman nobles assisted; and in order to be present the Guiscard was obliged to leave to his lieutenants the conduct of the siege of Cariati. When certain ecclesiastical questions had been settled, the Pope received, in the presence of the council of Melfi, the homage and oath of fealty of Duke Robert. In taking this oath, the Norman styled himself 'Robert, by the grace of God and Saint Peter, Duke of Apulia and of Calabria, and future Duke of Sicily by their aid'; and he promised to pay yearly to Saint Peter, and to Pope Nicholas his lord, and to his successors, to his nuncios, and to the nuncios of his successors, the yearly tribute of twelve deniers of Pavia for each yoke of oxen in his possession. Furthermore, he swore to be faithful to the Roman Church, and to Pope Nicholas his lord; never to take part in any conspiracy 'which could endanger the Pope's life, limbs, or liberty'; never to divulge any secret the Pope might confide to him, and to be everywhere and against all comers the ally of the Holy Roman Church.

It appears probable that Richard of Aversa took the same oath with the same obligations, and by this treaty of Melfi those men whom the predecessors of Nicholas had attempted to treat as a handful of excommunicated adventurers became the authorized allies and representatives of the Roman Church in the south of Italy. This was the work of Hildebrand, and was a formidable move against the arrogance of the Roman barons. It inaugurated a new era of the Papacy, and when the Pope returned to Rome, he appeared at the head of a Norman army. Peaceably, and in good order, the force marched up through Campania; but when they reached the Roman territory the storm broke with disastrous fury. In a few days the country about Rome was reduced to a total desolation, the Roman counts were forced to surrender and make submission to the Church, the host crossed the Tiber and fell upon the castle of Galera, in which Benedict the Tenth had taken refuge. The remains of those war-worn walls are standing still, in the midst of a fever-haunted wilderness, and it was from their ramparts that Benedict the Tenth, looking out towards the city and solemnly raising his hands to heaven, cursed the Roman people aloud because they had made him Pope against his will; and he promised to renounce his claim to the pontificate if his own safety were assured; and so he did, for he laid down the pontifical insignia and came back and lived in the house of his mother in Rome. Then Nicholas departed with his army, and though the Campagna was laid waste, the power of the robber barons, who had lived by plundering every little train of merchants that attempted to reach the city, was broken forever.

Thenceforward the Guiscard's conquest of the south proceeded almost unresisted, but his career was momentarily checked by an insurrection in Melfi itself, which had the courage, or insolence, to close its gates against him. Robert at once began the systematic destruction of crops by which he had reduced so many strong places, Melfi opened its gates again, and the leader of the revolt was hunted from place to place, a lonely and disappointed fugitive.

At this time Robert repudiated his wife, by whom he was the father of an only son, who afterwards became the famous crusader, Bohemund of Antioch. The popes had recently forbidden all marriages within the seventh degree of consanguinity, and Robert suddenly discovered that his friend Gerard's aunt was too near a kinswoman of his own to remain his wife. He presented her with rich gifts, therefore, and put her away; and almost on the morrow he asked the hand of Sigelgaita, elder sister of Gisulf of Salerno. That prince still retained a semblance of sovereignty, in spite of William of Hauteville's conquest, and Robert easily persuaded him to consent to his sister's marriage in return for help against his spoliator. Robert kept his word, and reinstated Gisulf in most of his possessions, and though the latter of course did his best to break his promises, he was obliged to submit, and Robert's position was strengthened by an alliance with the most illustrious Lombard family in Italy.

In 1060, Robert took the strong town of Taranto, and in concert with Roger besieged Reggio, where the Greek captain, upon whom Constantinople had bestowed the proud title of Duke of Italy, had taken up his residence. Here Robert slew in single combat a huge knight who defied all the Normans together, and when the people of the city saw the great engines which the Guiscard was preparing for their destruction, they made terms of peace and capitulated. The Greek troops took refuge in a castle perched upon the tremendous rock of Scylla, but soon lost courage, abandoned the place by night, and sailed away to Constantinople.

Roger occupied the fortress without delay, and gazed from its ramparts upon the great jewel of the south. It lay there like a new world, divided from him by the narrow strait in which the ancients had seen unearthly terrors, but which to the fearless Norman seemed as easy to cross as any river. There were men with him and with his brother who had doubtless fought before Syracuse and at Troina with Bras-de-Fer and Ardoin twenty-one years earlier, and they had told what they had seen, and doubtless, too, their descriptions of the island's wealth had gathered richness in the repetition of long years. And those lordly mountains, ranging hand in hand southward to the dome of snow-capped Etna, were not only the guardians of rich valleys and fertile plains within, but they were also the ramparts of a prison house in which hundreds of thousands of Christian men laboured in captivity under the Moslem rule. There was enough there to stir the adventurous spirits of men who were half Christian knights and still half barbarous marauders.

In the month of August of the year 1060, three Christian merchants of Messina left their city, pretending that they were bound to Trapani, but they put about at nightfall, and came to Roger at Mileto and entreated him to come over and free their city from the Moslems. Roger believed that they were the representatives of the whole Christian population, and he answered that he would come quickly; but the three Christians sailed back to Messina, and when they entered the harbour, the headless bodies of twelve of their friends were hanging from the walls, for the Saracens had suspected their conspiracy.

Messina

To effect the conquest of Sicily, Roger took sixty knights with him, crossed the straits, and landed near the lagoons of Faro. Instead of being received by the whole Christian population in revolt, the Saracens came out horse and foot to destroy the handful of invaders. But Robert pretended fear and flight, and unexpectedly, when the enemy was in hot pursuit, he halted his men and turned short round, and fought for his life; and when the Normans had slain a great number of the foe, and the rest had fled in panic, he took the enemy's riderless horses and stripped the rich armour off the fallen dead, and sailed back that day to Reggio; and surely it was as daring a deed as ever Northman did before or since.

Doorway of the abbey at Mileto

At the very time when Roger was making his reckless raid in Sicily, the Greeks were preparing a final expedition to recover the lost south. A general called Abul Kare, probably a converted Moslem, organized a large army on the eastern shores of the Adriatic, and crossed to Bari. The Norman troops were almost all concentrated at the opposite extremity of Calabria, and when Duke Robert faced his new adversary, with a handful of hastily collected troops, he was obliged to fall back to escape destruction, so that in two months Abul Kare succeeded in retaking Taranto, Brindisi, and Otranto. He even advanced as far as Melfi and laid siege to the Norman capital, a fact which proves that even the Guiscard had been taken altogether unawares. As soon, however, as Robert and Roger were able to unite their forces and make an organized resistance, the Greeks were obliged to give way, Abul Kare was driven back as quickly as he had advanced, and before long his temporary presence in Italy had ceased to cause the Normans any apprehension.

Old well at Mileto

Roger now turned his thoughts to Sicily again, and an opportunity for making another expedition presented itself almost immediately. A certain Ibn-at-Timnah, against whom another chief, Ibn-al-Hawwas, had vowed vengeance, came to Roger at Mileto and proposed to him a joint conquest of Sicily. This was the origin of that good understanding which afterwards existed between the Normans and one party of the Sicilian Saracens, for Roger accepted the proposal and soon embarked with a hundred and sixty knights and Ibn-at-Timnah. They landed to the west of Messina, with the intention of passing by the city in order to gain the interior. Riding at night towards Milazzo, Roger suddenly saw before him in the moonlight a Saracen in full armour, and though he was armed only with his sword and shield, he rode at him instantly. The chronicle says that the Saracen fell from his horse, literally cut in two pieces; and when the body was examined, it was found to be that of Ibn-at-Timnah's bitterest enemy, no other than that of the man who had married his much-injured wife.

Roger reached Milazzo without further interruption and collected much valuable booty, which he brought back to Faro in the neighbourhood of the small salt lagoons, and though the Saracens very nearly surrounded him while he was waiting for a favourable wind, he got the advantage by a brilliant movement and put them to flight. Encouraged by this success, he was rash enough to turn again and attack the city of Messina; but he was driven back to his ships by overwhelming numbers, and was obliged to stand at bay during three whole days and nights until the weather moderated. Amari is of opinion that this desperate stand was made on what is now called the

Braccio del Salvatore, which is the extremity of the sickle that forms the natural harbour of Messina; but it appears improbable to me that so small a force should not have been driven bodily into the sea from such a point; it is impossible to lie at anchor with ships outside that point in heavy weather, and lastly, Roger could not have reached it with the booty which he ultimately carried away, unless he had passed through the city which he failed to take. He must, therefore, have made his stand on the narrow strip of land which separates the lagoons from the sea, which could easily be defended, and within the curve of which small vessels such as he had can lie with tolerable safety during most storms. Here, being in the last extremity, Roger vowed to restore a ruined church dedicated to Saint Anthony, near Reggio, and as the weather then moderated, he embarked and succeeded in reaching the opposite shore in safety, in spite of an attack made upon him by Saracen vessels. He lost, besides one of his small ships, eleven men killed by arrows, and the news of this loss was enough to decide Robert Guiscard to join in the great enterprise. He called together a council of knights and announced his intention of delivering all Catholic Christians from the Moslem bondage; and the knights answered that they would do battle with him for that cause, and promised by the help of God to subdue the Saracens, and they received grace and gifts of the lord duke.

Castle at Sant' Alessio, near Messina

In the early days of May in the same year 1061, Robert Guiscard encamped opposite the Faro with an army which the chronicle calls numerous, and which seems to have consisted of about a thousand fighting men. But Ibn-al-Hawwas was before him, and sent from Palermo a fleet of twenty-four vessels with eight hundred soldiers to protect Messina. Robert and Roger solemnly invoked the help of heaven, confessed and received communion, and vowed to live more Christian lives, introducing in their prayers the truly Norman stipulation that the Almighty should crown their expedition with success. Roger took two ships, and in spite of the Saracen fleet, reconnoitred the Sicilian coast, easily outsailing his adversaries; and on his return Robert determined to send a part only of his force in advance. Roger landed two hundred and seventy chosen men at the limekilns, six miles south of Messina, and daringly sent his ships back to Reggio, in order that his men might understand that they were to win or die. Riding fearlessly towards Messina, they came upon a Saracen detachment bringing large sums of money, and having slain the soldiers and taken the booty, they joyously pursued their way. They had not ridden far when they saw their Norman ships sailing back again, and were joined by a hundred and seventy more of their knights. This time the number sufficed; four hundred and forty Normans took Messina almost without striking a blow. Many of the inhabitants followed the Moslem soldiers in their flight, and on the steep hillside that overlooks the straits a tragedy took place which the chronicler thought worth recording. A young Saracen of very noble birth had escaped with his only sister, a girl of the most incomparable beauty. Delicately nurtured, and unused to walking, she was soon exhausted and half fainting with fatigue and terror. Tenderly her brother entreated her to take courage, and he helped her and carried her as far as he could; then, seeing that she could not be saved from rude Christian hands, he drew his sword and killed her, and left her dead upon the hillside. So he went on his way, weeping and vowing vengeance.

Now came the Guiscard himself and landed in Messina with all his force. He held the key of Sicily, but he hesitated to unlock the gate until he had fortified the city itself and got possession of the formidable stronghold of Rametta. He took the latter without striking a blow, for the terror of the Norman name was in the air, and the Saracens either surrendered or fled. Turning inland when he was sure of his retreat, Robert went up the Val-Demone, where there were many Christians who received him as their saviour and liberator. Wherever he found a strong place to take which would cost him some loss, he passed it by and went on, and the Normans ravaged the country like locusts, and the Saracens fled before them.

At last he came to that great plain whence the twin strongholds of Castrogiovanni and Calascibetta rise side by side like brother Titans; and the Normans were seven hundred men, but within Castrogiovanni there were fifteen thousand Saracen riders. So Robert comforted his companions in arms and, looking up at the fearful height, he told them how Christ had said that if a man have faith like a grain of mustard seen he can remove mountains and the Normans confessed their sins and raised the gonfalon and began to accomplish the impossible. The Moslems charged down furiously, but neither numbers, nor weight, nor sword, nor lance availed them, and the Northmen forced them bodily up the frightful steep, slaying them and climbing upon their bodies; and the rocks ran blood in rivulets; and of fifteen thousand Moslems who had ridden out, five thousand beaten men got back alive within the impregnable walls.

Sagely Robert left them within, for he would not waste men and steel upon the huge ramparts; but he destroyed the crops and the fruit trees and drove off the cattle and encamped by the shores of that fair lake by which Persephone had strayed in the days of the gods. But by and by he quietly took possession of Calascibetta, and thither the frightened Saracens came up with presents and prayers for mercy, their heads bowed, and their hands crossed upon their breasts. Thither, too, the Moslem admiral of Palermo sent him rich presents, wearing apparel embroidered in the Spanish fashion and much fine linen, vessels of gold and silver, and mules in royal caparison; and he sent also a purse in which there was gold worth twelve thousand pounds of English money.

Robert now sent an ambassador to Palermo, and he chose for this purpose a certain deacon who spoke Arabic, enjoining upon him to keep his knowledge of the language a secret. So this man spied out the land and brought much precious information, and told Robert that the people of Palermo were but a body without a soul. But Robert, seeing the strength of Castrogiovanni, knew that he could not take it with the few men he had, so he went back to Messina with his vast booty, and three months had passed since Roger had landed with the advanced guard. Messina, Rametta, San Marco, and all the Val-Demone were subject to the Normans now, and Ibn-at-Timnah, their firm ally, was established in Catania.

Robert Guiscard and Sigelgaita returned to Apulia in the autumn of 1061, and Roger, after a short stay at Mileto, crossed into Sicily again with a small force and harried the Moslem lands as far as Girgenti. Returning towards Messina he came to the strong Greek city of Troina, and the inhabitants, who seem to have been almost entirely Christians, opened their gates and received him with enthusiasm. This place was destined to play an important part in the life of the young conqueror. It stands upon the table-like summit of a steep mountain almost three thousand feet high; it is often hidden from the surrounding country by clouds, and is excessively cold in winter, when snow and ice sometimes lie on the ground for weeks. The town its is dominated by a strong citadel, from the towers of which most of the principal cities and fortresses of Sicily are visible in clear weather.

Resting here, Roger learned that the lovely daughter of William of Evreux, with whom he is said to have fallen in love on his way to Italy, had arrived in Calabria and was ready to marry him. Judith of Evreux was the great granddaughter of Richard the First of Normandy, and had just escaped from that country with her sister and half brother, the latter having for some reason incurred the dangerous wrath of William who was soon to be called the Conqueror. Judith is now believed to have been the same person as Eremberga, and to have adopted the latter name when she left the convent in which she was brought up.

Roger lost no time, but returned instantly to Mileto and was married with all the pomp he could afford. A few weeks later he left his young wife behind him and returned to Messina. The chronicler says that she shed many tears, the memory of which perhaps moved Roger to take her with him on his next expedition. On the present occasion he succeeded in getting possession of a fortress on the northern coast near Cefalù, while Ibn-at-Timnah pursued the civil war he was waging on his own account, and much to Roger's advantage. It was now that Roger first placed a Norman garrison in Troina, but the treacherous assassination of Ibn-at-Timnah near Corleone soon rendered the possession of such isolated garrisons very unsafe, and in Roger's absence they hastened back to Messina.

Ruins at Mileto

A deadly quarrel now broke out between Roger and the Guiscard, who had refused to hand over to his brother the lands he had promised him in the treaty the two had made at Scalea. Roger was the more exasperated because he was thus prevented from making a suitable marriage gift to his young wife, and he determined to take by force what was indeed his by right. In one of the first encounters a half brother of Judith was thrown from his horse in the charge and killed, and Roger's anger rose to the pitch of fury. Robert now besieged him in Mileto and built two rude castles, one at each extremity of the city. Roger responded by invariably attacking the one when he was informed that Robert was in the other, and as Robert was obliged to ride round the city, while Roger could traverse it in a straight line, the advantage always fell to the latter.

One night Roger took a hundred men and rode down to the city of Gerace, which owed allegiance to Robert, but promptly opened its gates to the younger brother and provided him with means for carrying on the war. Robert therefore left a part of his troops before Mileto and laid siege to Gerace; but being unable to take it at once, he resorted to a stratagem, entered the city alone, disguised in a cloak and hood, and went to the house of one Basil, a man whom he could trust. While he was talking with Basil's wife Mileta, before dinner, a servant betrayed his presence; instantly the city was in an uproar, and an infuriated multitude beat down the doors of the house; Basil got out and tried to take sanctuary in a church, but was cut to pieces before he could reach the door; the unfortunate woman was dragged out and impaled alive on a stake to die in agony, and Duke Robert, with his hood thrown back, faced the multitude alone and unarmed.

His natural intrepid coolness did not forsake him; he saw that he must win the crowd by gentle words or die, and his eloquence saved his life. With the utmost skill he laid his case before those who thirsted for his blood. He had come to them unarmed and of his own accord, he said, to them who had sworn to be his faithful subjects. It would be a shameful thing for thousands to tear a single unarmed man to pieces, but they might do it if they chose, there he stood in their midst. They would get no glory for such a deed, nor would it free them from the Norman yoke; he had brothers, friends, an army of soldiers at their gates, and did they think the Normans would not avenge the shedding of Norman blood?

He persuaded them to spare his life, but not to give him his liberty, and from the threshold of his dead friend's ruined home the great duke was led away and thrust into prison. Roger soon learned what had happened, and he came into the city with his men and bade the people give him his brother, who was his enemy, bound hand and foot; for he would slay him with his own sword. But when the brothers were alone, they fell into one another's arms, says the chronicler, and embraced one another like Joseph and Benjamin of old — an affectionate effusion which did not prevent them from renewing their quarrel. It ended only when the danger of a general rising in Calabria brought the brothers to their senses. They met at a bridge in the valley of the Crati, which was long afterwards called Ponte Guiscardo in memory of the day, and there they promised to forget their enmity, and agreed to divide Calabria between them.

Roger now crossed to Sicily again, taking Judith with him, and accompanied by three hundred men he reached Troina, where he established himself, strongly fortifying the citadel. The town, as has been said, was almost wholly Greek, and a quarrel having arisen between the Norman soldiers and the inhabitants, the latter attempted to storm the castle when Roger was absent on a raid. The Normans defended the Countess Judith with their usual desperate courage, and Roger returned in time to avert a catastrophe. But the castle gates had barely closed behind him when more than five thousand Saracens swarmed up from the valleys, attracted by the news of a quarrel between the Normans and the Greeks, and uniting with the latter, laid formal siege to the castle. During four months Roger and Judith, as well as their men, suffered incredible hardships. The winter was bitterly cold, and they were so ill provided for facing it that the pair had but one mantle between them, and only one could go out upon the ramparts while the other tried to keep warm within. They were so reduced by hunger at last that the beautiful young Judith could find no remedy against her sufferings excepting sleep. Lean and dangerous as half-starved wolves, the Normans made frequent and desperate sallies against the overwhelming numbers of the enemy; and on a certain day, as Roger was attempting to save one of his men who was surrounded, his horse was killed under him, and Greeks and Saracens were upon him in an instant, attempting to drag him away alive, while he resisted 'like a bull that scents the slaughter house.' But his sword was out, and lifting it up with both hands he mowed down the foe till their bodies lay in a wide circle around him, and the rest dared not lay hands upon him; and while they looked on in fear, he coolly took the saddle and bridle from his dead horse and regained the castle on foot.

But now the besiegers themselves suffered from the great cold, and, having wine in abundance, they drank so much of it that they were often asleep upon their watch, while the hungry Normans waked; and so one night, when they were stupefied with drink, the Normans crept out with muffled feet and made an end. Roger hanged the ringleader of the revolt and most of his accomplices, and then, when the slain were buried and he held the city fast, he left his brave young wife in sole command and went over to Calabria to obtain horses; for in their extreme famine he and his men had eaten most of those they had. While he was gone, Judith herself made the rounds of the ramparts by day and night, and she encouraged the sentinels with good words and many promises, so that when her husband came back he found all well and the city at peace.

At this time the Saracens of Africa sent over a fleet and an army to drive out the Normans, and there was a fight near Castrogiovanni. Roger sent his nephew, Serlo, who afterwards died a gallant death, to draw out the Arabs with a handful of men, and the Arabs rode so swiftly that only two of Serlo's squadron escaped unwounded; but the enemy fell into the ambuscade, and Roger rode back to Troina with much spoil. The Saracens were not checked by so small a loss, however, and before long a great battle was fought by Cerami. There the whole Moslem host was drawn up in order of battle, and the Normans had never faced such odds before; but while Roger and his chiefs spoke words of comfort to their men, says the chronicle, one suddenly rode before them on a milk-white charger, and clothed in steel from head to heel, bearing on his lance a white pennant, whereon there was a blood-red cross, for Saint George himself had come down to fight against the infidels; and all that day the Normans slew and slew, till the bodies of fifteen thousand Saracens were heaped up like great ramparts on the earth, and the Normans slept in their armour on the slippery field, and on the next day they pursued the flying foe far and wide through the valleys and ravines of the mountains.

In gratitude to God and Saint Peter for this great victory over the Africans and Saracens, Roger sent to Pope Alexander the Second four camels, and the Pope thereupon sent his benediction and a general absolution for past sins to Roger and to all those who were fighting, or should fight, to free Sicily from the Moslems; but the Pope added that this pardon could be of no avail unless the Christians felt some real repentance for their sins and made an effort to lead better lives in future.

At this time the merchants of Pisa, whose commerce with Sicily had suffered greatly under the Mohammedan rule, sent out a fleet with a sort of general commission to do as much damage to the Saracens as possible; and finding Roger in Sicily, the admiral sent messengers to him at Troina, proposing a joint attack upon Palermo. But Roger was busy with other matters, and requested a short delay before making the attempt, and the Pisans sailed on without him. The description of their attack is very vague, but it is clear that they made no real attempt to storm the capital, and contented themselves with filing the chain which the Saracens had drawn across the harbour, and carrying it back to Pisa as a trophy.

After this, as it was summer, and the weather in the plains was too hot for fighting, Roger projected another visit to his brother the Guiscard in Apulia. Before setting out he made his usual preparations for a journey, which consisted in sacking a few towns, whence he collected enough booty and ready money to stock Troina with provisions and to provide for his own necessities on the way. He left his countess in command and returned as soon as the great heat was over, bringing with him a hundred men lent him by Duke Robert. An expedition that he made against Girgenti about this time very nearly led to his destruction; for on his return his advance guard fell into an ambush, and in something like a panic dashed up the side of a hill, leaving the train of animals that carried the booty at the mercy of the enemy, who killed the driver. It was with the greatest of difficulty that Roger prevailed upon his men to come back and fight, and though they ultimately did so, and cut their way through with the plunder, they lost one of their best men in the action. Reflecting upon this skirmish, Roger began to see that it would be impossible to maintain the position of a mere marauder forever. The strength of the Saracens in the centre and west of Sicily was unshaken, for it seems that the great majority of those slain in the battle of Cerami were Africans, and the Saracens of Palermo had not yet brought their real forces into the field. Roger therefore now made a serious treaty with his brother Robert, and the time was favourable for a joint attempt, as the Greeks had not caused the Normans much anxiety since the defeat of Abul Kare, and the Greek city of Bari had at last made an agreement with Robert by which he was allowed to enter the walls. The so-called Duke of Italy had been obliged to return to Durazzo, whence he was intriguing with a few discontented Normans to produce a rising in Italy, a danger to which the Guiscard seems to have been indifferent. He therefore turned his attention to Sicily, and in 1064 the two brothers crossed the straits with an army of five hundred Normans, traversed Sicily without opposition, and encamped upon a hill before Palermo. Here the chronicler says that they were tormented by tarantula spiders. This statement has caused some controversy among historians, who were possibly unacquainted with the spider in question. From personal knowledge I am able to say that the bite is extremely painful and irritating, but not fatal in any known case, and that tarantulas really are common enough all over the south. No one has been able to say with certainty which elevation it was that the Normans selected for their first encampment. I am inclined to think that it was Monreale, because that point is the one by which they would naturally have reached Palermo on the march from the interior, and because they afterwards returned to it and built the famous abbey on the site. Be that as it may, they were obliged to give way to the tarantulas and to encamp in lower ground, where they remained during three months, and made futile attacks upon the city, which they were unable to blockade by sea. They retired discomfited, and after a long raid through the country the Guiscard returned to Calabria with the conviction that for the conquest of Sicily a fleet was as necessary as an army. Soon after Guiscard's return a civil war broke out between one of the African chiefs and Ibn-al-Hawwas, who was, however, soon slain, thereby leaving the African Arabs in power. The Sicilian Moslems soon began to revolt against their exactions, and being well informed of the situation, the wily Guiscard resolved to let internal discord do its work.

Meanwhile he proceeded with the final conquest of Calabria, destroyed the city of Policastro in the gulf of that name, reduced the neighbourhood of Cosenza to subjection, failed in the siege of Ajello, but got possession of the place in the end by a treaty with the inhabitants, and then finally turned his attention to Apulia. The conspiracy planned and fostered in Durazzo by Perenos, the Duke of Italy, had reached dangerous proportions. Many Normans were now jealous of Duke Robert's increasing power, and more than one owed him vengeance for some deed of violence and cruelty. The son of Humphrey, who was supposed to be Robert's ward, but to whom the Guiscard paid no more attention than if he never existed, joined the malcontents, and Perenos exacted hostages from them in order to be sure of their good faith, and in return obtained for them large sums of money from Constantinople. Having learned wisdom from the Guiscard himself, his enemies avoided battle, and declined to lay siege to his cities, but ravaged his lands in all directions and when he, on his part, attempted to retaliate by attacking Perenos in Durazzo, on the other side of the Adriatic, a strong Greek fleet under the Admiral Mabrica put his vessels to flight. Mabrica now landed, and Bari, forgetful of its promises, opened its gates. The Greeks possessed the valuable aid of the Scandinavian Varanger guard, and gained more than one advantage in hand-to-hand fight, and it looked as if the fruit of a long and laborious conquest were to be snatched from Robert's hands; but gathering his tremendous energy, as he always could in any extremity, he at last got the upper hand, the Greeks fell back before him, the chief of the Norman conspirators fled in panic to Constantinople, and the duke brought the insurrection to an end when he got possession, by treachery, of Monte Peloso, the fortress on the hill overlooking the often-disputed plains of Cannae. This was in 1068. Robert immediately set about effacing the impression produced in the south by this revolution, and, rather than endanger his returning popularity by vengeance, however just, he consented to be reconciled with those of the conspirators who had not fled.

It was at this time that the Seljuks became the south of serious anxiety to Constantinople, for they had advanced as far as Antioch and threatened the capital itself. The Greek emperor was therefore unable to turn his attention to Italy, and at the same time the Greek cause suffered a serious loss by the death of Argyros, the son of the patriotic Meles. After many vicissitudes, after suffering exile and imprisonment, he had returned to spend the last four years of his life in Bari, and though at the end he entertained friendly relations with the Normans, he nevertheless remained the representative of the Greek-Italians until his death. It is surmised that he left his personal possessions to Robert Guiscard, for soon after his death the duke appeared before Bari with a fleet and demanded that all the houses which had belonged to Argyros should be handed over to him at once; and as they were a group of buildings resembling a castle rather than a palace, and dominating the city, it is not surprising that the Greeks should have refused haughtily to give them up. By way of adding insult to injury, however, they collected together a vast quantity of precious objects of gold and silver, and carried them in procession upon the ramparts under the blazing sun, so that Robert might be dazzled by the sight of the wealth which was refused him. But he, from his ship, answered smilingly that all he saw was his, and that he was much bounden to the people of Bari for taking such good care of his possessions.

Thereupon he began a siege which lasted two years and eight months, and might have lasted longer had not Count Roger lent his assistance at the last. Robert determined to blockade the city by land and sea, in order to starve it to submission, and while his cavalry encamped on the land side, he shut in the harbour by anchoring before it a number of vessels lashed together with chains; and as the shelving shore would not allow the close approach of ships of such draught, he built out two wooden piers from the beach to the two ends of the line. Meanwhile, the patrician of the city, Bizanzio, went to Constantinople and appealed to the emperor, though Robert made an unsuccessful attempt to intercept him. He returned with a number of ships and a quantity of provisions, and though the Normans sank twelve of the vessels, the remainder succeeded in forcing his blockade, to the great joy of the inhabitants. They made a heroic defence, but within the city there was a strong party in favour of the Normans, under the leadership of Argirizzo, who maintained a correspondence with the duke, and served his end in every way. The siege had lasted two years when Argirizzo caused Bizanzio to be assassinated, and his partisans fired a number of houses belonging to the patriotic party. The latter retorted by an attempt to murder the Guiscard, which only failed by the merest accident. For a sum of money a certain soldier, who had a private grudge against the duke, and had formerly served under him, agreed to do the deed. Slipping out of the city unobserved, and armed with his sling and pike, he turned, when he was at a little distance from the rampart, and slung a few stones towards the city, as if he belonged to the besieging army. Then, entering the Norman camp without difficulty, for it was already dusk, he soon found the duke's quarters, a mere hut made of branches so loosely fastened together that the murderer could see through them into the interior. The great Norman was seated at a low table alone, with the remains of his simple supper before him. He was overcome with fatigue, and as he sat there resting, he nodded, half asleep. The man watched some time by the light of the small oil lamp, and then, taking careful aim, he hurled his pike at the duke's head with all his might, and instantly fled through the darkness. But at that instant the tired man had fallen forward upon the table, his face upon his arms, sound asleep, and the dart had passed harmlessly above his bent neck. It was found on the following day, and the Normans at once built their leader a stone house.

During the long siege Robert had made more than one expedition, and had attempted to take Brindisi back, but had lost there a hundred of his men by a piece of frightful treachery. The Greek governor pretended to treat secretly with him for the betrayal of the city, and at the appointed hour and place the Normans were admitted, one by one, by a ladder. As each one then passed through a door, he was silently killed by the Greeks, and so a hundred perished before those behind knew what was happening. But before Bari fell, Robert took final possession of Brindisi.

During all this time Roger was in Sicily, gradually strengthening his position, and now determined to advance upon Palermo by slow and sure steps. It was in 1068, in the first year of the siege of Bari, that he won the decisive battle of Misilmeri. The Moslem, exasperated by his unceasing ravages, had resolved to face him at last, and to stop his advance at the castle called in Arabic Manzil-al-Emir, corrupted into Misilmeri. It is the very spot at which, in 1860, Garibaldi joined the Sicilian revolutionaries before seizing Palermo, and is only nine miles from the city. We know not how many Moslems came out to meet the Normans, but it is told that all were slain. Now the Saracens reared carrier pigeons, feeding them on corn and honey, and took them in baskets when they went out to war to carry back news of victory or defeat; and some of these were found among the booty. Then Roger indeed sent the news to Palermo, for he took slips of white parchment and dipped them in Saracen blood and fastened them to the birds' necks, and let the pigeons fly. And when the people of Palermo saw them, they knew the worst, and the air was full of the lamentations of women and children.

Terrace of Santa Maria di Gesù, Palermo

But Roger did not attempt to take the city itself, for he now fully understood that both an army and a fleet would be necessary for such an undertaking, and the signal defeat he had inflicted upon the Saracens at the very gates of their capital had inspired a wholesome p223terror of the Normans throughout the island, so that he was more free than heretofore to go and come at his pleasure.

Meanwhile, the siege of Bari proceeded. After the murder of Bizanzio, Argirizzo redoubled his efforts in favour of the Normans, and the people cried out for bread before the doors of the Greek general's palace, bidding him capitulate with the duke unless he could feed them. In reply, he made one last desperate appeal to Constantinople; a messenger was found who dared to run the blockade, and who bore to the emperor the tale of suffering. Then the emperor was moved, and commanded that a fleet should be got ready at Durazzo, under the command of a certain Norman who seems to have been one of the conspirators against Robert's life, who had fled to the East after their failure. The messenger got back into the city unhurt, and he bade the citizens light many torches upon the ramparts at night to guide the rescuing fleet.

But at this time, and at his brother's request, Count Roger had sailed up from Sicily with many good ships; and when the Normans understood what was meant by the torches lighted every night on the city walls, Roger set a lookout to watch for the coming enemy. At last, on a certain night, in the mid-watch, many lights hove in sight, like a constellation of stars which men-of-war carried in those days, and the admiral's ship carried two. Then Roger sailed out with his fleet, and a great sea-fight was fought in the dark. Roger himself attacked the admiral, recognizing his ship by its lights, and took him prisoner; the ships of the Greek fleet were almost all destroyed or captured, and the torches that were to have guided a rescuing army to Bari lit up the return of a triumphant foe. The last hope of assistance was gone, and Argirizzo now treated almost openly with Robert for the surrender of the city, sending his own daughter as a hostage of his good faith. He immediately seized one of the principal towers of defence, and the negotiations were carried on without further concealment. Yet even now the patriotic inhabitants would have held out; men and women, children, priests, and monks came in throngs to the foot of the tower where Argirizzo was, and lifting up their hands, implored him with many tears not to betray them to the terrible Normans. But Argirizzo turned a deaf ear to their supplications, and would not even look out and see the people; and on the eve of Palm Sunday, in the year 1071, Robert made his triumphal entry into the city.

With the wisdom born of long experience, the great duke disappointed the expectations of a terror-struck people; he neither took from them the rich treasures which they had tauntingly exposed to his gaze, nor exacted satisfaction for an insult that had brought a smile to his lips; he restored to the citizens the lands occupied by the Normans in the neighbourhood during the siege; he allowed no bloodshed nor violence, and treated the Greek garrison as prisoners of war; the only conditions that he imposed upon the city were that Argirizzo should be governor, and that the tribute formerly paid to Constantinople should now be paid to himself. In order that these conditions should be faithfully executed, he established a Norman garrison in the fortifications. To such a degree had a long career of conquest civilized the wild freebooter of San Marco.

The fall of Bari was the end of all Greek claims in Italy, and it had been brought about by the rapid development of the Norman naval power. Up to the year 1060 no mention is found of any Norman navy; ten years later the Norman fleets were more than a match for those of Constantinople, and from their victory at Bari they sailed almost directly to the final capture of Palermo. Bari was taken on the sixteenth of April, and in the first week of August fifty-eight Norman men-of-war, of which ten were of the largest size, were ready to sail down upon Sicily from the harbour of Otranto, with an army numbering between eight and ten thousand men. Robert had collected not only Normans, but Lombards, Apulians, and Calabrians, and he had taken or forced into his service the soldiers of the Greek garrison taken prisoners. Under his iron hand these men of many nationalities fought with unbroken discipline throughout a campaign that lasted six months. He was not joined by all the Norman princes. Gisulf of Salerno, his own brother-in-law, Richard of Capua, the Count of Trani, and many smaller lords stood sullenly aloof, expecting to witness his destruction, and one, if not more, took advantage of his absence to invade his dominions; but nothing could turn the sons of Tancred from their purpose, and while Robert marched a part of his forces from Otranto to reggio, the rest pursued their way to the same port by sea.

Roger was already in Sicily when Robert crossed the straits, and hearing of his brother's advance he seized and fortified Catania, of which the alliance had been uncertain since the assassination of Ibn-at-Timnah. Roger now took command of the land forces and marched to Palermo through the heart of Sicily, only turning aside to visit his wife Judith in Troina, where he was joined by two nephews. Duke Robert, who seems to have feared the heat in the month of August, sailed with fifty ships to Palermo. With the loss of a few men who were killed while collecting forage, and whose death was amply avenged, Roger reached the entrance to the Golden Shell; and as he gazed down upon the groves of oranges and lemons and carob trees, the villas, and the Moorish palaces, and the gardens of roses that filled the fertile valley then, as now, and as he beheld the walls and minarets and domes of Moslem Palermo beyond, his keen eye may well have descried the white sails of his brother's fleets in the offing, for Duke Robert reached the city almost at the same time. It is certain that the people of Palermo were surprised by the simultaneous appearance of the Normans, both on land and sea, and the invaders took possession of the gardens and orchards and pleasure houses, almost without striking a blow. The few Moslems who fell into their hands were immediately sold as slaves, and what they found they divided among themselves, after choosing for Roger and the princes his nephews 'delectable gardens abounding with fruit and water; and the knights were royally lodged in an earthly paradise.'

The Saracens had built a tower, or castle, at the mouth of the small river Oreto eastwards of the city, by the sea, and as Roger at once saw the necessity of commanding the point, in order that Norman ships might enter the stream, he went up to the walls and defied the Saracens in a loud voice. So they came out and fought, and the Normans killed thirty of them and took fifteen prisoners, and held the tower. Robert Guiscard now landed his army and encamped between the mouth of the Oreto and the quarter still called the Kalsa, which has been already described in the words of Ibn Haukal. Roger took up his position on the south side of the city in the direction of Monreale, and opposite the gate now called Porta Nuova, in the neighbourhood of the papyrus swamp. As the army was not numerous enough to invest Palermo from that point to the sea on the west, the besiegers patrolled the country in order to cut off communication between the inhabitants and the small bay westward of Monte Pellegrino, which the Carthaginians had so successfully utilized in the days of Hamilcar Barca. This fact is to be inferred from our information regarding the famine that soon prevailed in the city. The siege began about the first of September, and was varied by many incidents during the next four months. The people of Palermo invoked the help of the African Arabs, who sent a strong fleet to attack Robert's ships; the Normans protected their own from the stones and darts of their adversaries by means of great pieces of thick red felt, of which they seem to have seized a great quantity in some dyeing establishment in the suburbs; but some writers say that this was an ancient Scandinavian custom. The Arabs ranged their ships in battle order, and came on with a tremendous blare of clarions and trumpets, while the Christians performed their devotions in silence. We do not know how the African ships had succeeded in entering harbour to join those of their allies, though it is clear enough that fifty small vessels could not blockade such a place as Palermo; but we know that the combined fleets of the Moslems sailed out against the Normans and were driven back in a short and furious battle. Some ships were captured and some were sunk, and when the Normans reached the great chain which was drawn against the entrance of the harbour, they broke through it and fired the vessels that lay within.

Now also famine came to the help of the besiegers, and the bodies of the starved dead lay unburied, and poisoned the air. Then the Normans laid loaves of bread upon the ground before the walls to tempt the people out; some came out and took the bread and ate it ravenously and ran back. But on the next day the besiegers placed the bread a little farther away, and farther still on the day after that, and then they caught the miserable people and sold them for slaves.

There were also brave deeds done in single combat. A certain Moslem knight in full armour used to sit upon his horse in one of the gates when it was open and well defended; and one of Roger's nephews rode at him amain, and drove him in and killed him; but when the Norman turned the Moslems had shut the gates, and he was alone within the city. With incomparable courage, seeing that his retreat was cut off, he set spurs to his horse and rode at full speed through the heart of Palermo to another gate, where he slew the guards and let himself out unhurt.

During the long siege Robert received bad news from the continent. The Norman nobles who had refused to join the enterprise, Richard of Capua and many others, after at first making a semblance of neutrality, made incursions into the dukedom, seized the castle of Sant' Angelo in Calabria, and set the whole country in a blaze. A weaker man would have divided his forces and would have sent back a part of them to avenge the outrage and to repel the invaders; but Robert well knew that if he held Palermo and made himself lord of Sicily he could chastise his enemies at his leisure, and he never hesitated in pursuing his purpose. And now the time was come for a general assault, for the Arab fleet had been destroyed, and the garrison was weak from famine and sickness. So Robert prepared fourteen great scaling ladders, seven for Roger's men and seven for his own, and he gave Roger the honour of the first assault.

At dawn on the fifth of January, 1072, Roger made the attempt; the bowmen and slingers went before, bearing the ladders, while the cavalry moved behind them in even order. The Saracens fearlessly opened their gates and rode at Roger's infantry, which gave way under the shock, but the knights soon drove the Moslems back before them in wild confusion, trusting that in the rush they might suddenly enter the city. The defenders within, seeing the great danger, shut the gates and sacrificed their unhappy comrades to save the city. Then the Normans brought up their scaling ladders and set them against the high ramparts, while Duke Robert stood in their midst calling upon them to take that city which was hateful to God and subject to devils, and bidding them know that, though he was their general, Christ Himself was their leader. Then one man, whose name was Archifred, made a great sign of the cross and set his foot upon the ladder, and two others went up with him; but the deed was so fearful that no others would follow. The three reached the rampart and stood upon it, and fought till their shields and swords were broken in their hands; and then, being defenceless, they turned and leaped for their lives, and slipped and rolled and fell down the escarpment, and by a miracle they reached the ground unhurt. Now others, and many, came forward to do as these had done, but the walls were high and the defenders staunch, and Robert saw that he was sacrificing good men for no good end. He therefore ordered Roger to pretend to carry on the assault, while he himself rode round through the gardens to a point of the Kalsa where the enemy expected no attack, and where he had hidden three hundred chosen men with their ladders among certain trees. He was successful at last. Hardly an enemy was upon the walls, and in a few minutes his men were rushing through the streets to open the nearest gate for him. The day had been spent in the long assault, but as the sun went down the Normans were masters of the Kalsa, while the surviving Saracens retired within the Kasr, leaving their heaps of dead where they had fallen in the streets. All night long the Norman soldiers marched up from the encampments and filled the Kalsa, and many of them spent that first night in sacking the rich outer town, slaying the Moslems where they found them, but sparing the children for slaves. Within the fortress the half-vanquished Saracens sat all night in debate, and when the morning came most of them were for surrendering, and they sent out ambassadors to treat with Duke Robert and Count Roger for terms of peace.

The conquerors had learned the worth of mercy and the wisdom of forbearance, and they gave the great city very honourable terms. The Saracens were not to be disturbed in the exercise of their religion; not one of them was to be exiled from Palermo; they were not to° be oppressed by new and unjust laws; and finally, they were to enjoy the right of being judged at law by tribunals of their own.

These points being settled, Roger took a large force, entered the Kasr, and occupied the fortifications, but it was not until the tenth of January that he made his solemn entry. A thousand knights lined the streets through which the army was to pass; Robert Guiscard and his wife Sigelgaita headed the triumphal march, with Count Roger and the others of the house of Tancred, and Guy of Salerno, who had quarrelled with his nephew Gisulf, was also there. So the duke and all the princes and the clergy rode up to Saint Gregory's Church of Our Lady, of which the Saracens had made a mosque, and a solemn mass was said by the Christian Archbishop of Palermo, who had suffered much at the hand of the Saracens. 'Then,' says the devout chronicler, 'a great marvel appeared in this church, for certain good Christians heard in that church the voices of the angels, and very sweet song, which praised God on high, and at divers times this church was lit up with heavenly light, more bright than any light of this world.'

The fall of Palermo did not mean the immediate conquest of all Sicily; lofty Castrogiovanni still held its own, and Marsala, 'the harbour of Allah,' and many strong and good places in the west; but it meant that the Saracen domination was at an end, and then and there the Guiscard and his brother divided Sicily between them. The duke, generous to himself, kept the suzerainty of the whole island with Palermo, the Val-Demone, and Messina, and Roger received the rest of Sicily, conquered already, or still to be subdued, keeping his vast possessions in Calabria as recognized by his brother. From this time he is known in history as Roger the Great Count.

One of the two principal vassals who were to hold the new country under the brothers was their nephew, Serlo, the other was a certain Arisgot of Pozzuoli, a relative of the house of Tancred; but the former's days were numbered, and not long after the taking of Palermo he came to an untimely end by treachery. He was at that time keeping the peace in Cerami against the incursions of the Arabs of Castrogiovanni. But there was a certain Arab with whom he had sworn brotherhood, by touching ear to ear after the manner of the Saracens; and this man betrayed him and told him treacherously that on a certain day he should not ride to a place named, because a small party of seven Arabs had determined then to make a raid in that direction. But Serlo laughed loud, and rode out with a few companions; and his enemy indeed sent the seven Saracens to the place, but he hid seven hundred in an ambuscade hard by. So Serlo and his comrades were suddenly surrounded and they sprang upon a boulder and fought for their lives. When they had slain many, and their weapons were all broken, they still hurled down stones and earth upon their assailants; but at the last they were all killed, save two, who lay wounded and half dead under the piles of slain. The Saracens cut off Serlo's head and sent it as a present to the emir in Africa; but with their knives they cut out the brave man's heart and apportioned it among them and devoured it, trusting that thereby his courage might enter into their own bodies.

Even then, Robert and Roger did not march against Castrogiovanni, for the place was very strong; but they took hostages of the Saracens, lest such evils should befall again, and slowly strengthened themselves in their possessions. In Palermo they built two fortresses, the one on the site of the modern royal palace at Porta Nuova, and comprising the Saracen fortress that already stood there; and still a lordly vaulted room is pointed out, and the traveller is told that after the siege Count Roger chose it for his own. Also the duke saw that the poor little Church of Saint Mary 'was like a baker's oven' amid the splendid Saracen palaces, and he caused it to be torn down, and gave great sums of money to build a better church on the spot; and still in the porch of the later cathedral one may see the pillars of the mosque, with verses from the Koran graven in the cufic character. In the last months of the year 1072 Robert Guiscard, Duke of Apulia, of Calabria, and of Sicily, returned to the mainland laden with spoil.

While Robert and Roger were conquering Sicily, the Normans of the mainland were engaged in ceaseless dissensions and involved in the complicated history of the Papacy. A large part of their story concerns the doings of Richard of Capua and of a certain William of Montreuil, to whom he gave his daughter in marriage, who quarrelled with his father-in-law, repudiated his wife, attempted to marry the widowed Duchess of Gaeta, and failing in his plan was reconciled with Richard and took his wife back; who allied himself with Pope Alexander the Second in his struggle against the antipope Honorius, at one time commanding a force of several thousand men, and who would have continued to cause trouble during many years had he not been providentially removed from history by the malarious fever of the Roman Campagna. In the inextricable confusion of small events two principal figures stand out; that of Richard, determined to extend his principality of Capua, and even marching upon Rome itself, from the gates of which he was driven back by the appearance of the Duke of Tuscany with a large army, and, on the other hand, the gigantic personality of Hildebrand, soon to be Pope Gregory the Seventh, fighting, as only he knew how to fight, for the independence of the Papacy and of the Church itself. It would be fruitless for the purposes of the present work to follow the many entangled threads; the story is one of raids and counter-raids, of ruined crops and blazing towns, and of castles won by assault or betrayed by treachery. It ended in a solemn and peaceful ceremony at Monte Cassino at the very time when the Normans of the south were fighting under the walls of Palermo. The devout and indefatigable Abbot Desiderius had built the great church of the abbey, and at its consecration by Pope Alexander himself there were present with Richard of Capua all the great Norman and Lombard nobles who had refused to take part in the conquest of Sicily, besides a vast multitude of nobles and tenants and countrymen, clerks, laymen, monks and soldiers, Campanians, Apulians and Calabrians who, during more than a week, thronged up the steep mountain side to pray at the tomb of the holy Benedict and to receive the Pope's absolution and blessing. The splendid basilica, with its lofty nave and aisles, its double ranks of columns, and its grand choir, in the midst of which rose the tomb of the saint, eight steps above the floor, was totally destroyed by a great earthquake in the year 1349. Desiderius had spared neither pains nor treasure in the work, and had brought columns from Rome and rich marbles from other parts of Italy, and had called artists together, Latins, Greeks, and even Saracens, from Constantinople and from Alexandria. Moreover, a great noble of Amalfi had ordered the bronze doors to be cast and chiselled in Constantinople, and what remains of these is all that is left of Desiderius' abbey church.

The consecration was, however, a favourable occasion for an interview between Richard and all those who were jealous of the house of Tancred, and it is certain that Richard of Capua profited by it to plan his attack upon Apulia, while Gisulf agreed at the same time to make a raid upon the western coast, from Policastro to Sant' Eufemia. The surprise and disappointment of the malcontents at the news that Palermo was taken may be more easily imagined than described, and when Duke Robert came back in triumph to Melfi and convoked his great vassals, more than one of them must have wished that he had been with the Guiscard and Roger at Palermo. He seems to have satisfied himself by visiting his wrath upon the Count of Trani, who had flatly refused to send any help for the Sicilian expedition, and who at first declined to meet the suzerain at Melfi. Being forced to do so, however, he gave haughty answers to all Robert's questions and commands, and the duke was obliged to make war upon him. It was during this short struggle that, having taken the count prisoner, he made use of him in besieging the castles that remained loyal, for when the defenders began to shoot arrows and hurl stones from the ramparts, Robert set the count himself, loaded with chains, in front of his besieging force, and the prisoner, in terror for his life, besought his own people to abstain from defending themselves, lest they should kill him.

As for Richard of Capua, who had advanced as far as Cannae in Apulia, it is merely recorded that when he perceived himself opposed by Divine Providence, he quietly returned to Capua. Robert pardoned him at the time, promising himself to be avenged at a more convenient season; and when, after entirely reducing the south to submission, he forgave the Count of Trani and gave him back most of his possessions, he prepared to make war against the Capuan prince. But at this juncture he fell dangerously ill, and lay long between life and death in Bari; his wife Sigelgaita herself believed that he was at his last gasp, and hastily calling together the Norman knights, she caused them to choose for her husband's successor her own son, the young Roger, to the exclusion of Bohemund, the duke's eldest born by his first marriage. After this election the news went abroad that Robert was dead, and Gregory the Seventh, who had just ascended the pontifical throne, wrote a characteristic letter of condolence to Sigelgaita. The pontiff spoke of the death of Duke Robert, the most beloved son of Holy Church, as a source of grief irremediable to himself, to the cardinals, and to the Senate of Rome; he expressed his goodwill to the widowed duchess, and requested her to bring her son to Rome, in order that he might receive from the hands of the Church's head those possessions which his father had held from former popes.

At this point, when every one who was with the duke believed that he was about to expire, and when even the Pope himself believed him to be already dead, the Guiscard's iron constitution prevailed against the sickness; he suddenly was better, in a few days he was out of danger, and in an incredibly short time he was completely restored to health, to the great joy of his friends, and to the bitter disappointment of his enemies. As the Abbé Delarc says in the closing lines of his valuable work, the Guiscard was still to live twelve years, astonishing and upheaving Italy and Europe from east to west by his daring deeds and by the surprising energy of his restless life.

Fountain at Taormina

It was in the year 1073 that Duke Robert fell ill and unexpectedly recovered, and in order to carry on the story of the Normans it is necessary to return to Sicilian ground, following for a while Amari's great history of the Moslems in Sicily. In the beginning of the year 1072, immediately after the fall of Palermo, Sicily was divided into three parallel zones from east to west. The most northerly of the three extended from Messina to Palermo, following the north side of the Sicilian range, and in the partition of the island had been taken by Robert himself; the second division followed the south side of the mountains, and was subject to Count Roger; the third and southernmost portion was still entirely in the hands of the Saracens, excepting the cities of Catania and Mazzara, which Roger held, and this domain of the Saracens was equal in extent to the other two. Moreover, Roger's position was weakened by the fact that the Moslems held the fortresses of Taormina and Trapani, situated respectively at the eastern and western extremities of his territory, by the necessity of supporting garrisons in many different castles at the same time, by the unproductiveness of his lands as compared with the rest of the island, and by his obligation to fight on the mainland when required to do so by his brother Robert.

These circumstances made it clear from the first that the Moslems might resist a long time, and if they had been firmly united, the issue might have been doubtful; but they were divided among themselves, they made the mistake of opposing themselves separately to the conqueror, and he took their strong places, one by one. It has often been said that the history of the Arabs in Sicily is yet to be written, and their chief historian, the learned Amari, admits that in the whirlpool of their national and civil wars the distinctions between the successively dominating parties is extremely uncertain. The same writer points out that, if they had been unified, the fall of Palermo would have meant the conquest of the whole island, whereas it produced little or no impression upon the Saracens of the south. Furthermore, the fact that the Moslems of Noto, which comprises all the southeast region, had been in a sort of alliance with Roger, had contributed to increase their strength; and when at last revolutionary leader arose in the person of the Arab Ben Arwet, he found such materials ready as made him at once a most dangerous adversary. The man was the last Moslem patriot in Sicily, and his efforts to restore Mohammedan independence have justly been called heroic. Under his leadership the Saracens were soon in arms throughout the south; from the ramparts of numerous castles they defied the Norman cavalry, and when they sallied from their strongholds they skilfully led Roger's troops into ambush. Almost wholly unprovided with siege engines, or with troops accustomed to such operations, the Normans were forced to fight when it pleased the Moslems to face them. Roger, indeed, strongly fortified the heights of Calascibetta over against Castrogiovanni, and he took one or two other strong places; but in the meantime the African Arabs made a wild raid upon the Italian coast at Nicotera, and returning landed at Mazzara and besieged that castle in that place until Roger arrived in person and drove them off. In those years Ben Arwet commanded the whole province, from Syracuse as a base, and his forces were continually increasing. Being obliged to return to Mileto, Roger appointed Hugh of Jersey his viceregent in Sicily, and placed his son Jourdain in command of the troops in the field, enjoining upon both to avoid a pitched battle with weight Moslems. But neither had the coolness to resist the temptation to an open fight, and when Ben Arwet sent a decoy party to forage under the very walls of Catania, the young Normans rode out and were drawn into an ambush where Hugh of Jersey was killed, and whence Jourdain barely escaped with his life.

At the news of this disaster Roger's anger knew no bounds, and he arrived in Sicily soon afterwards with such an army as Ben Arwet dared not face. He now advanced directly into Noto, and as it was harvest time he so completely destroyed the crops as to produce a famine in the following year. He next assailed Trapani in the West, and the place was taken at a bold stroke by his son Jourdain.

Saracen-Norman window in the Ospedaletti, Trapani

The city of Trapani was, and still is, built upon the landward end of the low sickle-shaped promontory, whence it first took its name; and during the siege the people used to drive out a herd of cattle to pasture in the outer extremity, for, as Roger had no ships with him, the point was completely protected by the sea, and the gate of the city that looked towards it was only closed at night. Saying nothing to his father, Jourdain took a hundred men with him, and under cover of darkness reached the point by means of small boats, and hid his party among the rocks near the city. At dawn the gate was opened for the herd to pass out as usual, and the Normans sprang from their hiding-place and rushed towards it. In a moment the Moslems were in arms, and the odds against the assailants were ten to one; yet in the short and furious struggle the Normans had the better, and without attempting to enter the city they returned by water, taking with them the captured cattle. The assault had shown the inhabitants what might happen if Roger landed a larger force on that side, and rather than risk the consequences of further resistance, they made terms and submitted. Of the two strong places at the opposite ends of his dominions, Roger now held the one, but Taormina still remained to be taken. Roger soon afterwards began the siege and completely surrounded the strong place with works in order to reduce it by starvation. Here he almost lost his life, for in going the rounds with a handful of men he was suddenly caught in a narrow way by a party of the enemy. It was clear that he must retrace his steps or be killed; the path was narrow and could be held for a few moments by one man, and a devoted follower, named Evisand, sacrificed his life to save the count. He fell pierced with innumerable wounds at the very moment when the Normans came up to the rescue, and Roger buried the friend who had saved him with royal honours, and founded a church, or a convent, in memory of his preservation, and for the soul of his preserver.

After a siege of five months, Taormina yielded to starvation and surrendered. But the war was far from ended yet, and nine years after the fall of Palermo, Ben Arwet regained possession of Catania, apparently having bribed the governor of the place to admit him, and it was not till after a battle and a short siege that Ben Arwet fled to Syracuse by night, and the Normans took back the city. And now that same Jourdain, trusting in his own strength and courage, rebelled against his father, and began to occupy certain castles on his own account; and Roger, affecting to attribute his doings to the heat and folly of youth, bade him come with his friends and be reconciled before he had done worse. But when he held them fast he made a strict inquiry, and he put out the eyes of twelve of his sons's chief associates, and sent Jourdain away free, but disgraced.

Stairway in courtyard at Taormina

The war, says Amari, proceeded slowly, because at that time a great part of the Norman forces were with Duke Robert in Greece. For during those years the duke had grown great. Raymond, the Count of Provence, had taken his daughter in marriage, and on the strength of such a great alliance, Robert extended his dominions more and more, and invading Romagna and afterwards Durazzo beyond the Adriatic, of which doings there are elaborate accounts in the monkish chronicles, in the year 1082 he carried war into Bulgaria and won much glory and some spoil, but little else. In the following year, when Henry the Fourth attempted to set up an antipope against Gregory the Seventh, and came to Rome with an army, Duke Robert went up from the south like a whirlwind and burnt half Rome; and the emperor fled before him. After that he returned into Apulia and began to make great preparations for an expedition to the East; and sailing away with a fair wind, and with a vast number of ships, he reached Durazzo, but there he suddenly fell ill, and died in the month of July, in the year 1084. We know little of the manner of his death, for the chronicle merely says that he died, and that his wife Sigelgaita, and his son Roger Bursa, and all the barons, performed the funeral rites with due honours; that his body was brought back to Italy and laid to rest in Venosa; and finally, that in the dispute that arose between Bohemund and Roger Bursa for the succession, Count Roger of Sicily took his namesake's part, in return for which service he received, or appropriated, the other half of Calabria which he had not previously received from his brother.

It was during the dispute about Duke Robert's succession, that Ben Arwet took advantage of the disturbed state of Southern Italy to make a sudden attack upon Calabria. In August or September of the year 1085, he landed by night at Nicotera, •not twenty miles from Roger's favourite city of Mileto, and carried off most of the population captive. Falling upon Reggio next, he sacked the churches of Saint Nicholas and of Saint George, destroying the statues and images; and breaking into the convent of Our Lady at Rocca d' Asino, near by, he took the nuns with him to Syracuse and distributed them among the harems of the chief Moslems. Roger's wrath rose at the outrage, and while he did not fail to propitiate heaven by lavish charity to the poor of Messina, and by walking barefoot from church to church with monks who chanted the litanies, he gathered his forces for a great effort. On the twenty-fifth of May, 1086, he fought Ben Arwet in the harbour of Syracuse; and there, says the monk, the devil entered into the Moslem's heart to drive him to destruction, for when he went against Roger's ship with his own, he was wounded by a dart, and the Great Count attacked him, sword in hand, and he tried to leap to another vessel but fell into the sea, and the weight of his armour bore him down, and he was drowned.

From May to October the Moslems bravely defended their city; then the chief men took Ben Arwet's widow and his son, and fled to Noto, and Syracuse surrendered. After this Roger took Girgenti, and not much later impregnable Castrogiovanni fell into his hands by the treachery, or conversion, of the Governor Hamud. He, being hard pressed, secretly agreed to embrace Christianity, led his best forces into a preconcerted ambush, where they were taken unhurt, and he was received with open arms. He was rewarded with broad lands in Calabria, where he lived out a long and happy life. Butera, on the south coast, was the last city in Sicily that stood a siege, and Noto was the last to capitulate, in the month of February, 1091, the date that marks the final conquest of the island.

Città Vecchia, Malta

After reducing a rebellious baron on the mainland, Roger now set sail for Malta, and in spite of his sixty years, was the first to land, with only thirteen knights. After a skirmish with a few Moslems, he slept upon the beach, awaiting the arrival of his other ships, and on the morrow he attacked the Città Vecchia, which yielded almost at once; and thus, says Amari, he crowned the conquest of Sicily, taking Malta himself, as he had taken Messina in person thirty years earlier.

I cannot but think that the comparative peace in which the Great Count ruled Sicily during the last ten years of his life is to be attributed to the inborn fatalism of the Moslems. It is certain that they never made any serious attempt to regain independence, but that, on the contrary, they served bravely and loyally in Roger's armies. Thousands of Saracens fought under his standard when he helped his nephew, Duke Roger, to reduce Cosenza, and in 1094 when he assisted him in repressing the dangerous rebellion of William of Grantmesnil in Castrovillari. Roger not only protected them, left them full liberty in their religion, and allowed them tribunals of their own, but, according to the biographers of Anselm of Canterbury, he discouraged their conversion, and punished Saracens who embraced Christianity, fearing perhaps that in the great movement of the first Crusade, his Moslem soldiers would imitate the example of the many Christians who followed his nephew Bohemund to the Holy Land. As is well known, the cautious Norman declined to take part in that great movement, preferring to consolidate his power at home, while princes and kings and people went out to fight in Palestine for an ideal so composite that its pursuit promised gain to the greedy, renown to the fighting man, and a martyr's crown to the ecstatic Christian.

Much confusion exists with regard to Roger's marriages; I have adhered to Delarc's view, and those who prefer to suppose that Roger was thrice married may consult the elaborate and conclusive notes written by the learned French historian, as well as a note of Amari's, which goes to prove that Judith took the name of Eremberga on leaving the convent of Saint Evrault. Be that as it may, this Judith-Eremberga, the faithful companion of so much hardship and of so much glory, died in 1089, and the Great Count soon afterwards married Adelasia or Adelaide, the daughter of one of the great nobles of Northern Italy, and became by her the father of King Roger the First of Sicily, and of another son, who was older, but died in infancy. Judith-Eremberga's only son, Godfrey, is rarely spoken of, is supposed to have been of feeble constitution, and either died young or ended his life in a monastery. Jourdain was illegitimate. Roger had a number of daughters, one of whom he married to the king of Hungary, another, Constance, to Conrad, king of Rome, the emperor's son, a third to Raymond of Provence, and a fourth to Count Robert of Clermont, though Philip the First of France had asked her in marriage for the sake of her dowry.

We know nothing of the illness that ended the great fighter's life. He died at nearly seventy years of age in his favourite Mileto, and there he was laid in the cathedral he had built; but centuries later an earthquake overthrew the city and the sanctuary, and the Great Count's sarcophagus is preserved in the national museum in Naples.

It is manifestly impossible to continue a detailed account of the Norman domination after the final success of Roger's enterprise. The feudal system had now taken root in Europe, and the enormous development which it gave to individualities in the persons of the semi-independent imperial and royal vassals, so multiplies the threads of history that every reign is enveloped in a web of crossing and recrossing lines. The Empire contained kingdoms, the kingdoms principalities, the principalities comprised counties, and there was not a count who had not half a dozen or most small barons and knights who held land under him by feudal tenure. It is possible to give a brief and clear idea of a reign, and the historian may sometimes succeed in describing the condition of the people under this sovereign or that; but a work that should contain a full and accurate account of the doings and dissensions of the great vassals, and of the efforts made by king or emperor to control the latter, would fill many volumes, and could only be produced by the industry of a lifetime. In the minds of most readers of ordinary culture, the end of the eleventh century is filled with the romance of the first Crusade, and disturbed chiefly by the quarrels of the Emperor Henry the Fourth with the Papacy. So far as the Crusade is concerned, its story, from a Christian point of view, is too well known to need telling here; but it is interesting to find that Arabic writers of early times, such as Ibn-el-Athir, regarded the general attack upon the Holy Land, not in the light of a religious war, but as the culmination of a great race struggle, retracing its causes to the Norman conquest of Sicily, to the Castilian occupation of Toledo, and to the raids made by Italians upon the African coast. Mohammedans could indeed have understood that they themselves might fight a holy war for the recovery of Mecca and of their own places of pilgrimage; but their contempt for 'men who worship crosses' was then, as it is now, profound and ineradicable, and they found it hard to believe that Christians could be really in earnest, or ready to face danger disinterestedly, for an idea which appeared absurdly unreasonable to the mind of a cultivated Moslem. The worst of it is, that bravely as the Christians fought in the East, they gave their enemies plentiful reason for the supposition that the idea of worldly conquest was intimately connected in the minds of most Crusaders with that of future salvation. Centuries had passed since the Moslems had set out from Arabia to convert the world to Islam, and to keep possession of it when converted, and they did not see the close resemblance that existed between their own religious wars and those which the Christians now began to wage in Asia Minor; but they had not forgotten how they had driven the Western people before them, even to the shores of the Atlantic, and they felt that in the tide of nations the wave of the West was rolling back upon them. In a sense, therefore, it was true that the Crusades resulted more from the opposition of two races than from an antagonism of two religions; and, from an historical point of view, the struggle which began when Peter the Hermit roused Europe with his war-cry, resulted in the victory of the East, and came to its inevitable conclusion when Mohammed the Second stormed Constantinople in 1453.

Saracen-Norman window at San Giuliano

It is characteristic of the times that while the war for the holy places created a certain type of chivalry with which the proudest families in Europe now delight to claim alliance, an amalgamation of Christians and Moslems in Sicily and the south of Italy produced a civilization and an art not only noble in themselves, but unlike anything of which there is record before or since. It may, indeed, be compared to the civilization of the Augustan period, when the victorious Roman suffered himself to laugh and be amused by the conquered Greek, when the Greek language became fashionable in Roman society, and when Greek art, such as it had survived, was the canon of good taste. But that was rather an imitation than an amalgamation; in letters, Horace may stand for the type of those times, and in architecture any temple or monument of the same period represents the condition of art; yet Horace is to the Greek poets as the remains of the temple of Saturn are to the Parthenon or the temples of Paestum, whereas Monreale, the Palatine Chapel, and the Church of the Martorana, built by Mohammedans for Christian masters, are all beautiful in themselves, and in a manner that did not exist before them, and which rapidly changed, or degenerated, in the following centuries. Saracen-Norman art has a place by itself in the history of architecture; and at a later period, when it blended in turn with the dominating art of the Renascence, the result was something still beautiful and never seen elsewhere. In Trapani, for instance, and in San Giuliano, there are remains of doors and windows that exhibit this mixture of styles in which neither the Arab nor his Norman conqueror is forgotten, but in which the artistic spirit of the early sixteenth century finds expression also. The south received strength from the north, and the north was completed and polished by the profound learning and minute civilization of the south; and neither lost its identity in the other, as Greece lost hers in Rome, and both continued to live for centuries in an indissoluble union.

Entrance to the burial-place of the Norman pilgrims, La Cava

But if any one wishes to see the northern element as it developed in Italy, without amalgamation, let him go down into the deep old court of La Cava, in the wild gorge above Salerno; for though the great Benedictine monastery was founded a hundred years before King Roger's day, by a Lombard, the cloistered court is Norman, and of the roughest sort; and far below, in Gothic vaults where a faint glimmer of daylight makes the glare of the wax torches ghostly, there lie the skulls and the bones of many hundred fighting pilgrims of the early days, arranged in a sort of reverent order by the careful monks. One great skull is pierced through the forehead by a thrust of a blade three fingers broad, clean and straight, for the pilgrims did not always die a natural death; and the traveller who pauses to gaze upon the cloven head may think of those forty Normans who put an army to flight, and saved Salerno long ago. The place has not the majesty of Monte Cassino, the mother abbey of the Benedictines; it is wild, rude, and romantic, an abode of warlike ghosts and the war-worn wrecks of dead men, and the peaceful monastery above is the work of a later age. There is nothing in Sicily like La Cava. The cathedrals of the Norman kings are splendid with gold and alive with sunshine, the tender traceries of the south soften the bold spring of arch and vault, but the grim and grotesque mummied figures in the miniature catacombs of the Capuchin Convent, near Palermo, could never have been set in their narrow niches by northern hands. There is something in Palermo that reminds one of Constantinople, a similarity of circumstances, with a renewal of the conditions in which they have taken place. In the East the capital of Christian emperors was turned in a day to the use of Moslem sultans, and the victors used the hands and eyes of the vanquished make mosques of churches, to build a minaret beside every dome, and to adorn the lordly retreats of Asiatic idleness and luxury. And still the Greek is at home in the great city where he has been so long in subjection. In Palermo, it was the African who went down before a Christian conqueror, whose mosques were turned into churches again, whose palaces of delight became the abodes of fighting kings, to whom all idleness was strange, and all luxury new. But still, after eight centuries of change, renewal, and decay, the hawk-eyed, thin-lipped Saracen treads the streets of the royal city with a grace that is not European, and a quiet dignity not bred in the blustering north; while in that beautiful land of contradictions you can visit no village nor hamlet without seeing a score of handsome Norman children, with bright blue eyes and yellow hair, playing little eastern games under the Sicilian sun, and chattering in Italian dialect that is motley with Norman and Arabic and Spanish words. It is not the language of the often conquered, upon which many successive languages have been imposed, but rather the mixed speech of many conquering races, in a country where each has ruled in turn, and where it is hard to say which has left the deeper mark.

Burial-place of the Norman pilgrims, at La Cava

It cannot have been very different in the days when King Roger was a little child, and his mother watched over him and ruled for him, when he alone was left to her, to be the great survivor of Tancred's race. There is not much to tell of those times, save that a woman held easily what the Greek count had spent a lifetime in getting by the sword. Fate worked for the young king until he could go out and fight for himself. The Guiscard's son, Roger Bursa, lived but a short life and left a feeble son, William of Apulia, as duke in his stead, who died prematurely, and without male issue. He was scarcely in his grave when Roger of Sicily, son of the Great Count, sailed up to Salerno with his galleys, convoked the Norman nobles, obtained an investiture from the Holy See, and took Apulia for himself; and three years afterwards, on Christmas Day, 1130, he was crowned King of Sicily at Palermo, in the chapel of Santa Maria l' Incoronata, barbarously destroyed by the bombardment of 1860. It was on this spot that the small church of Saint Gregory once stood, which Count Roger compared to an oven amidst the Saracen palaces that surrounded it, and which he ordered to be pulled down and rebuilt, and here for two centuries and a half each king of Sicily was crowned. The little that remains of it stands by the northwest tower of the cathedral.

Mosaic of Christ crowning King Roger, Church of the Martorana, Palermo

Mummy in the vaults of the Capuchin convent, Palermo

Gibbon accuses King Roger of gratifying his ambition by the vulgar means of violence and artifice, and goes on to say that when he wished to be a king, the pride of Anacletus, the Jewish Pierleone's antipope, was pleased to confer a title which the pride of the Norman had stooped to solicit. The judgment of the great historian is severe, and may well be modified by most readers. Roger was the survivor the house of Tancred in Italy, and he knew that he must keep his dominions free, or lose himself and his subjects. The investiture of the Holy See was necessary, and he was in no position to judge the claims of the ruling pontiff, Pope, or antipope. Innocent the Second was elected, indeed, but was long a fugitive, while Anacletus held the Vatican by the will of the powerful Pierleone; but, when the Emperor Lothair and Innocent joined hands with Pisa to excommunicate and destroy the Sicilian king, Roger fought for his life as well as his crown. Driven back at first into Sicily, he returned in wrath, destroyed the emperor's newly invested Duke of Apulia, and terminated a war that lasted nine years by taking Pope Innocent prisoner at San Germano, near Monte Cassino. With the devotion of fervent Catholics he and his captains humbly knelt down at the feet of their captive; but it was with the cold tenacity of Tancred's race that Roger dictated to the pontiff the terms of a peace which invested himself and his successors forever with the kingdom of Sicily, the Duchy of Apulia, and the principality of Capua. The reconciliation of the king and the Pope, says Gibbon, in sarcastic comment, was celebrated by the eloquence of Bernard of Clairvaux, who now revered the title and virtues of the king of Sicily; but with those who have some acquaintance with Saint Bernard's character, the praise of the saint will outweigh the contempt of the historian, and we can admit without prejudice that King Roger was a brave and honourable man for his times, such as they were. From him, then, dates that kingdom of Sicily which was divided after the Sicilian Vespers, and became the Two Sicilies of later history.

That he did much, if not all that he might have done, for the lands he ruled, there is ample evidence in history and in monument; but the greatest of his doings was that amalgamation of races which took place in his reign. His Moslem subjects were faithful to him and fought for him, even against Moslems, and if it was by their help that he overcame the Pope at San Germano, it was by their arms also that he took Tripoli, the strong Mohammedan city of the African coast; and in the fleet of the Sicilian admiral George of Antioch, which received the submission of Corfù and momentarily wrested all Greece from the enfeebled hold of Constantinople, there were as many free Saracens as there were Christians. That there was an element of fear in the Moslem subjection is true, and the eight-sided tower of King Roger still frowns over Castrogiovanni, the last great stronghold of the Mohammedans, to testify to the strength of his hand; but there was much loyalty also in the Saracens' obedience, and we need not confound submission with servility, nor fear with cowardice.

Tower of King Roger, at Castrogiovanni

So far as King Roger's conduct during the second Crusade is concerned, we know not whether to ascribe it to a certain consideration for his Mohammedan subjects, or to his apprehension of losing them; be that as it may, he imitated Count Roger in quietly refusing to join the armies of the Cross, and while the most glorious armament of the century was divided by the dissension of its leaders, decimated by disease, and at last reduced to a remnant by the swords of the Seljuks, King Roger was extending his dominions, increasing his wealth, and preparing for a war which he knew could not be long avoided. When Lewis the Seventh of France was returning from Jerusalem, disappointed and humiliated by the failure of the holy enterprise, and distracted by domestic troubles, he was almost captured on the high seas by treacherous Greeks, and was rescued from what might have proved an ignominious captivity by the timely appearance of the Norman fleet, which had lately ravaged the coasts of Greece; and being brought to Palermo he was royally entertained and sent forward on his journey by King Roger. With something like old Scandinavian daring, the Admiral George sailed up the Hellespont, dropped anchor with his galleys at the entrance to the Golden Horn, and shot a flight of arrows tipped with silver into the imperial gardens; but the Emperor Manuel's anger soon avenged the taunt, George lost nineteen of his galleys on his homeward voyage, Corfù yielded to the emperor after a brave defence, the Eastern Empire was in arms, and King Roger's last war had begun. While Manuel himself fought the Hungarians and the Turks in the East, he prepared a fleet, an army, and a kingdom's ransom in treasure to win back the Norman's possessions. Before he was ready to invade the West, however, King Roger had breathed his last. He died after a long illness, which some have called consumption, but which others have attributed to excesses: his last years, during which the conduct of his wars was intrusted to lieutenants, were spent in close intercourse with the wise men and learned Arabians he had attracted to his court, chief among whom was the geographer Edrisi, whose greatest work, composed under the direction of the king himself, was called 'the book of Roger, the delight of him that journeys through the world,' and was completed a few months before the king's death. It is said that the composition of this great book occupied no less than fifteen years, during which hardly a day passed on which the king did not discuss some subject connected with it, and during which he explored, in the society of his learned Arabians, every department of known science. The book has remained a vast repository of learning, and a chief authority for the times, reflecting no small glory upon the sovereign who presided over its compilation.

Court in the monastery of La Cava

The great map of the world which Roger caused to be engraved upon a disk of silver weighing between three and four hundred pounds has been fully described, but it is needless to say that it disappeared in the disturbances of later times; upon it were engraved 'the seven climates with their regions and townships, their coasts and their tablelands, their gulfs, seas, springs, and rivers, their inhabited and uninhabited lands, their highroads measured in miles, and the distances by sea from port to port.' It is even said that the particular description of this plate in the Arabic language may have been the work of King Roger himself; it is at least certain that he deserves much of the credit for it. He had founded a sort of academy at Palermo, over which he presided, and of which the perpetual secretary was descended from the khalifs of Cordova. Owing to the king's death the book was not translated into Latin at the time, but the seven centuries that elapsed before a translation made it accessible to ordinary scholars rather increased than diminished the fame which it was to bestow upon its royal compiler. It would be strange if the churchmen of that day had not found fault with the sovereign who surrounded himself with Moslems, and whose most intimate associate was an Arabian, and indeed the priests and monks said loudly that the king was little better than a Moslem himself. But the Moslems praised him as their Maecenas, describing the magnificence of his palaces and gardens, the joyous life men led at his court, and the abundance of golden wine, which seems not to have shocked the pious Mohammedans of Sicily in that day. And true it is that Roger both protected and restored the arts, and that if he filled his coffers by Norman means, he spent his wealth royally in beautifying his favourite cities and in the encouragement of learning.

The fortunes of the house of Tancred really culminated in the reign of King Roger, declined under William the Bad, improved under William the Good, the latter's son, and then vacillated, after the failure of the legitimate succession, until they became involved with the destiny of the Empire under Henry the Sixth and Frederick the Second, of Hohenstaufen. Before going on to give a brief sketch of those changes, I shall endeavour to explain very clearly the connexion between the race of Tancred and King Roger's successors, since it was in virtue of this connexion that they claimed the crown of Sicily for centuries after his death.

Triangular court in the monastery of La Cava

Roger the Great Count was the youngest son of Tancred of Hauteville. Roger's eldest son died an infant, and was succeeded by Roger, the first king.

King Roger's eldest son, Roger, grew to manhood, but died before his father, who was succeeded by his second son, William the First, the Bad.

William the First was succeeded by William the Second, the Good, who left no heir.

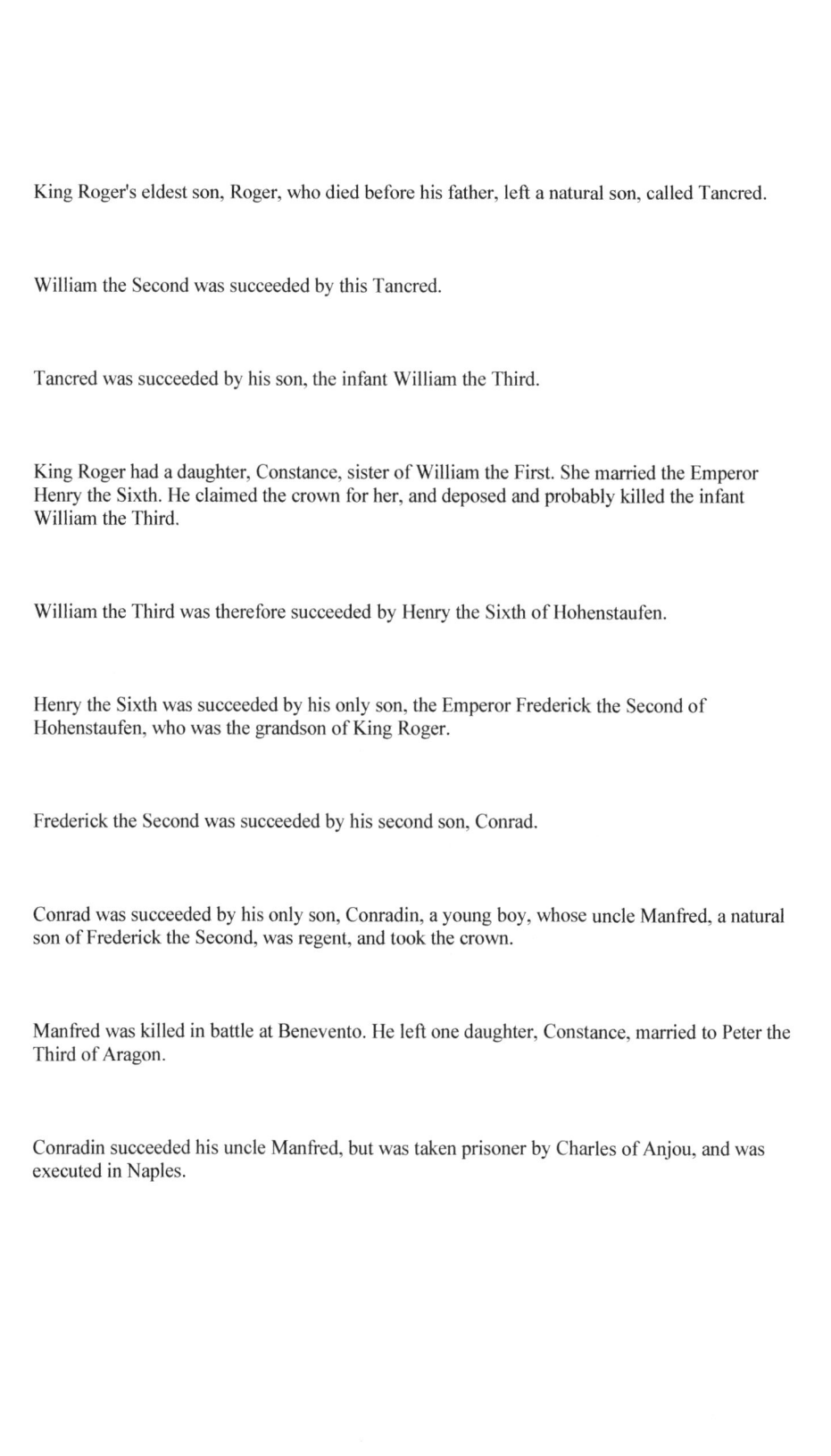

King Roger's eldest son, Roger, who died before his father, left a natural son, called Tancred.

William the Second was succeeded by this Tancred.

Tancred was succeeded by his son, the infant William the Third.

King Roger had a daughter, Constance, sister of William the First. She married the Emperor Henry the Sixth. He claimed the crown for her, and deposed and probably killed the infant William the Third.

William the Third was therefore succeeded by Henry the Sixth of Hohenstaufen.

Henry the Sixth was succeeded by his only son, the Emperor Frederick the Second of Hohenstaufen, who was the grandson of King Roger.

Frederick the Second was succeeded by his second son, Conrad.

Conrad was succeeded by his only son, Conradin, a young boy, whose uncle Manfred, a natural son of Frederick the Second, was regent, and took the crown.

Manfred was killed in battle at Benevento. He left one daughter, Constance, married to Peter the Third of Aragon.

Conradin succeeded his uncle Manfred, but was taken prisoner by Charles of Anjou, and was executed in Naples.

Conradin was succeeded by Charles of Anjou, brother of Lewis the Ninth of France, known as Saint Lewis.

Charles of Anjou lost Sicily in the revolution of the Sicilian Vespers, and the Sicilians elected Peter the Third of Aragon for their king, because he was married to Constance, great-great-granddaughter of King Roger, and also the last heiress of the house of Hohenstaufen.

Peter the Third was succeeded by a long line of Aragonese kings, the second of whom, after him, was his second son, King Frederick the Second of Sicily, often confounded with the Emperor Frederick the Second, his great-grandfather.

Now, as Ferdinand the 'Catholic,' whose queen was Isabella, was of the united houses of Aragon and Castile, he also inherited the Norman blood, which through him was transmitted to his grandson, Charles the Fifth, of the house of Austria, and so on through all the Spanish dynasties to the present day. About nine hundred years have passed since Tancred of Hauteville dealt his famous thrust at the wild boar, and though his house gave Sicily no long and unbroken line of kings, yet the blood of the Norman gentleman is in the veins of almost every royal race in Europe.

My readers will not have lost patience over this page of genealogy, which makes clear a point too often left in obscurity, namely, that with the exception of Charles of Anjou's episodic reign in Sicily, and of Garibaldi's forcible seizure of the island in order to found a republic, which rather unexpectedly turned into a kingdom, and excepting the seven years' reign granted to a Duke of Savoy by the absurd peace of Utrecht in 1713, the succession to the kingdom really continued on the strength of the Norman blood down to 1860, the descent to the Bourbons being traced through Anne of Austria, wife of Lewis the Thirteenth of France and sister of Philip the Fourth of Spain. By its alliance with the house of Hapsburg the house of Savoy may really claim as much Norman blood as the deposed king of Naples.

I shall now return to the task of briefly outlining the reigns of Roger's successors.

It is not surprising that his son and successor, William, afterwards surnamed the Bad, should really have been more a Mohammedan than a Christian in belief, in character, and in manners. He had been brought up chiefly by learned Arabians in the customs and luxuries of what was in reality an Eastern court. Amari describes him as indolent, fierce, proud, and avaricious, and suggests that his admiral, Majo of Bari, personified the Sicilian court with all its sins, while even the Moslems themselves attribute to the evil character of the king and of his general the disturbances which marked the beginning of William's reign. That he lived the life of an Arab emir can hardly be denied; his palace was the abode of an Eastern harem, and both were directed, if not controlled, by Moslem eunuchs hateful to the people. It must be admitted that although he repressed sedition in Sicily itself with wisdom and justice, he dealt cruelly with insurgents in Calabria and Apulia. He was full of contradictions, as men often are who have been educated against their natural tastes. He was slothful, but when roused he was desperately brave; he was capricious, but he could be wise; he was kind, but he could be ruthless. In a community of upright and virtuous men he would have deserved to be called the Bad; but in his own times he earned the appellation by his unpopularity rather than by his surprising wickedness, and he cannot be held responsible for the long struggle between the Emperor Barbarossa and the Emperor Manuel, which had its origin when he was a youth, and ended after his death. King Roger was still alive when Manuel took Bari and Brindisi. King William forced him to conclude an honourable treaty a year after Roger's death, and Sicily enjoyed the benefits of a thirty years' peace, while Europe was convulsed by the quarrels of the Holy Roman Empire and the Holy See. The Vatican received the ambassadors of the East, who almost returned to the ancient allegiance of Constantinople and to the unity of the Eastern and Western churches, but to the indescribable mortification of Manuel, Pope Alexander the Third reconciled himself with Barbarossa, declared that separation of the churches was final, and excommunicated the Emperors of the East.

The excommunication may or may not have affected the spiritual welfare of the warlike Greek; there can be no doubt but that the alliance of the Pope with Barbarossa put a stop to Manuel's reconquest of the West, and that Venice, which had temporarily withdrawn from the strife, took the offensive again as soon as it was evident that in so doing she could find herself on the stronger side. Manuel poured his armies and his gold upon the eastern coast of Italy, and such was the strength of the one and the persuasion of the other that the hosts of the Emperor Frederick were twice driven back from the walls of Ancona; but no sooner had the Pope taken a decided course of action than Ancona returned to the imperial allegiance. Venice descended with a fleet of one hundred galleys, and the Normans of the south completed the destruction of the Greeks with their swords. The thirty years' peace was signed, and it was long before Manuel renewed his quarrel with the emperor. William had already entered into the Pope's good graces, and a series of victories against the African Arabs increased his credit with the Holy See. That he attempted even by bribery to prevent the coronation of Frederick Barbarossa in Rome is more than probable, for in the riot which was stirred up by that ceremony the imperial soldiers fell upon the Roman people with their drawn swords, crying out that they would give German steel for Arabian gold.

William's successes in Africa were short-lived; the garrisons he placed in the conquered towns sorely oppressed the Arabs, and a Moslem patriot of Sfax roused his fellow-citizens to the destruction of their oppressors. William retorted by the cruel execution of a hostage, and the

African towns replied by something like a general rising. William sent twenty galleys to reduce the insurrection, and merciless butchery restored his power for a while; but a general movement of the Arabians which extended as far as Morocco was prepared, the Arabs, or Bedouins, dug wells along the proposed line of march, and during three whole years stored up grain by plastering the sheafs of wheat with clay, and Spain joined Africa in manning a fleet of seventy galleys. Before such a force Tunis soon fell, and the Christian garrison was bidden to choose between death and Mohammed's creed. In other cities the Christians shut themselves up in the forts and prepared for a long resistance, and months passed before the Sicilian fleet, which was engaged in the Balearic Islands, could come to the rescue. But under the walls of Mehdia it was put to flight by a few Arab vessels; the treacherous Majo brought word to King William that the cities of Africa were amply provisioned; and when the unfortunate garrisons had devoured their horses, they only escaped slaughter by the magnanimity of their foes. Majo lost his life in the first outbreak of a revolution in which every member of the house of Tancred took part; King William was taken prisoner in the council chamber, and the insurgents divided among themselves the women of his harem and the accumulated treasure of King Roger; the infuriated Normans, not satisfied with Majo's death, slew all the Moslem eunuchs of the palace and slaughtered the Moslems in the streets; but discord soon broken out in their own ranks, the bishops appealed to the populace to free the king, and presently the people of Palermo were in arms to a man. Quick to take advantage of the situation, the king made terms with the multitude, promised them anything and everything, and with their help took bloody vengeance upon the barons, the murderer of Majo was blinded and hamstrung, and a sort of order was restored. A second conspiracy, which broke out ten years later, ended in the immediate death of all the conspirators, but the religious hatred between Moslems and Christians, which King Roger's wisdom had almost entirely allayed, had now broken out with renewed fury; the massacre of Moslems was followed by a furious reaction under a king who was half a Moslem himself, the reign of the eunuchs was restored, every Moslem had a father, a brother, a wife, or a sister to avenge, and a friend in the palace ready to execute his private vengeance; where Mohammedans had been murdered in the public places their Christian murderers now perished wholesale on the scaffold, until the whole country was tired of slaughter, and sank, with its sovereign, into an apathy of weariness. Then William the Bad, giving over the government of his kingdom to his ministers, amused his slothful hours with the building of a magnificent palace, which was called the Zisa, but before that beautiful retreat was ended, he breathed his last at the age of forty-six years; and when he was borne to the grave, the matrons of Palermo, and more especially the Moslem women, followed in thousands, with dishevelled hair, and robed in sackcloth, striking the funeral cymbal in time with their doleful lamentations. Afterwards it was known by a few that the king had been dead several days before his death was announced, the secret having been kept in order that the chief men might gather in council to assure the succession and coronation of the boy William the Second, then barely fourteen years of age. This was in 1166.

Moorish palace of La Zisa, Palermo

Fountain in the Moorish palace of La Zisa, Palermo

When the days of mourning were passed, the royal lad strode in state through Palermo, and radiantly handsome as he was, says the chronicler Falcandus, his beauty was strangely perfected on that day, and there was such imperial grace in his features, that even they who had most bitterly hated his father, and whom no one had expected to be loyal to his heirs, loved the youth forthwith, and cried out that it would be shameful and unmanly to visit the sins of the sire upon the son. The queen, also, his mother, Margaret of Navarre, who was regent till he should be of age, bestowed great gifts, and many pardons, and all manner of gracious treatment upon those who had been discontented.

DRAWN AFTER A PHOTOGRAPH

Tomb of King Roger in the cathedral of Palermo

So the new reign prospered, and in the days of William the Second the cause of law and justice flourished in the land, every man was satisfied with his lot, peace and security prevailed everywhere, the traveller feared not the ambush of highway robbers, nor did the sailor dread the violence of pirates. William was the flower of kings, the crown of princes, the mirror of the citizens, the glory of his nobles, the hope and trust of his friends, and the terror of his enemies. So at least says Richard of San Germano, with much more to the same purpose. Even the discontented Amari, who outdid Gibbon in sarcasm, rivalled him in learning, but was painfully inferior to him in judgment, admits that the young William was crowned amid hopes which he never wilfully disappointed. It is no wonder that he was surnamed the Good, as compared with his father; they lie side by side in stupendous Monreale, and it may be by an accident that the son, who built that great cathedral, should have been placed in a fair sarcophagus of white marble with traceries of gold, and the father in one of plain dark porphyry, almost black.

William reigned three and twenty years, and so changed the character of the court of Palermo and of the government of Sicily that the Mohammedan element sank into abeyance. According to Richard of San Germano the king's chief counsellors, his 'two most sturdy pillars of support,' were Walter of the Mill, the English Archbishop of Palermo, and the Chancellor Matthew. It was by the advice of the archbishop, says this chronicler, that William the Second gave his aunt Constance in marriage to Henry of Hohenstaufen, afterwards Henry the Sixth, making the counts of the kingdom swear upon the sacraments that if the king died childless they would obey Constance of Hauteville and her husband. Also, this Walter of the Mill first built for William the great cathedral where it stands to-day.

But when William died, and left no heirs, a great dissension arose among the nobles, and they forgot their oaths, many aspiring to the throne; and at last, lest the archbishop should prevail and thrust Constance upon them, they agreed to choose for their king, Tancred, not the great crusader, but the natural son of William the Bad's elder brother, who had died in early manhood. They could not have chosen a braver or a truer man of his race, and he laboured with all his might for the cause of peace; by a liberal expenditure of the royal treasure, which he was the first to touch, and by some brave fighting, he restored the kingdom of the south, and even the Abbot of Monte Cassino swore fealty to him. He was crowned in 1189, the year before Barbarossa died; and Joanna, the widowed queen of the young king, was Joanna of England, own sister of King Richard the Lion-hearted.

It was not to be expected that a man of such temper as Henry the Sixth would tamely relinquish his just claims to the south, but his father was still alive, and the stirring events of the third Crusade intervened; so that it was not until Frederick Barbarossa had perished in the East that Henry came into Italy; and meanwhile Tancred had no small difficulty in prevailing upon Richard the Lion-hearted and Philip Augustus of France to restrain their men from wrangling in his city of Messina and to proceed on their way.

For Richard was a quarrelsome man, and Roger of Hoveden has left a record of his journey through the south, how he left Salerno when he heard that his fleet had reached Messina, and proceeded to Cosenza by way of Amalfi, which is a geographical impossibility that need startle no one accustomed to the chronicles. He came down by Scalea, and saw the island, where, says Roger, 'there is a fine chamber beneath the ground, in which Lucan used to study'; and he slept at

Cetraro and at other places till he came to Mileto, where 'there is a tower of wood close by the abbey, by means of which Robert Guiscard attacked and took the castle and town,' in his quarrel with his brother the Great Count, a hundred years before Roger of Hoveden — but he did not take it, as has been seen. And then, 'the king of England, departing from Mileto with a single knight, passed through a certain small town, and, after he had passed through, turned towards a certain house in which he heard a hawk, and entering the house took hold of it. On his refusing to give it up, numbers of peasants came running from every quarter, and made an attack on him with sticks and stones. One of them then drew his knife against the king, upon which the latter, giving him a blow with the flat of his sword, it snapped asunder, whereupon he pelted the others with stones, and with difficulty making his escape out of their hands, came to a priory called Bagnara.' Thence he hastily crossed the straits and slept in a tent 'near a stone tower which lies at the entrance of the Faro on the Sicilian side.' It must be admitted that the royal progress lacked dignity, but on the following day Richard made up for it by making 'such a noise of trumpets and clarions, that alarm seized those who were in the city,' that is, in Messina; and by way of making himself at home in a friendly country he seized a monastery, ejected the monks, and fortified himself, and presently, 'a disagreement arose between the army of the king of England and the citizens of Messina,' which soon became an open quarrel between the two kings — 'and to such a pitch did the exasperation on both sides increase, that the citizens shut the gates of the city, and, putting on their arms, mounted the walls.'

The end of it was that the kings agreed together, took Messina and forced Tancred to pay over an exorbitant sum of money, supposed to represent the dowry of the childless Joanna. Roger of Hoveden says that before the conclusion of this so-called treaty of peace more than a hundred thousand pagans who were in the kingdom of Sicily indignantly refused to serve under King Tancred, both because Henry of Hohenstaufen had laid claim to the throne of Sicily, and also because Richard of England had taken possession of a great part thereof; and that these Saracens fled to the hills with their families and herds, attacking and plundering Christians. It is interesting to learn that while Richard was making such unjustifiable claims he was profoundly impressed by the prophecies and wise sayings of a certain Abbot of Curazzo,a who interpreted the revelation of Saint John the Evangelist in a modern spirit; and that, the 'divine grace inspiring thereto, Richard, being sensible of the filthiness of his life, after due contrition of heart, having called together all the bishops and archbishops who were with him at Messina, made a general confession of his sins and from that time forwards became a man who feared God, and left what was evil and did what was good.'

So at last the turbulent crusaders departed, and Tancred had leisure to go over into Apulia and insure the fidelity of his vassals by a general exhibition of strength and generosity. And now Henry the Sixth and his wife Constance came to Rome and were crowned emperor and empress in the Church of Saint Peter's, and the Emperor Henry, being pleased with the Romans, made them a present of Tusculum, then the stronghold of the Colonna family, and the Romans promptly destroyed it, as he expected.

Henry immediately entered Tancred's kingdom in spite of the opposition of the Pope who had just crowned him, and the timid monks of Monte Cassino hastened to swear fidelity to him, while many towns, being taken unawares, placed themselves in his hands; and the emperor received the submission of Salerno and left the empress there, while he himself made a futile attack upon Naples. But as usual desertion and disease did their work in the German army; Henry left Constance in Salerno, and retiring with the remains of his forces returned to Germany. In no long time after this the Count of Acerra received back for Tancred most of the towns the emperor had taken, and he went up to Monte Cassino and entered the abbey, no one opposing him; but when neither prayers nor promises could prevail upon the monks to return to their allegiance to Tancred, he departed without doing them any violence. Henry the Sixth, however, had not given up the struggle; he sent a strong army to the south, while Tancred brought up a considerable force from Sicily, after crowning his eldest son Roger as his successor in case of his own death. He fought desperately for his kingdom, and had he lived he might have held his own. As it was, his son Roger came to an untimely end, and Tancred himself, says Richard of San Germano, died of grief. He left his crown to a child, the infant William the Third and the regency to his queen, a woman of no great spirit. The chancellor Matthew, the wise counsellor of William the Good and the friend of Tancred, was also dead, and Sicily was defenceless before the arms of Henry the Sixth. Tancred's widow fled from Palermo with her infant son to a safer place, whence she treated with Henry for her life and safety. She surrendered to him at last, and he handed her over with her royal child to one of his faithful captains, 'to do with them according to his will.' Then Henry, having got possession of the capital, received the keys of the treasury from the eunuchs of the palace and was shown coffers full of gold, gems, and precious objects, part of which he distributed to his followers, while he sent a part back to Germany; and to this day in the museum of Vienna may be seen the cloak of King Roger, the tunic and leggings of William the Good, richly embroidered with gold and pearls and Arabic characters, with many objects of like interest and value. The emperor established himself in the magnificent palace called the Cuba, now used as a barrack, though almost quite uninjured, and on Christmas Day, in the year 1194, presiding over the council of Palermo, he summoned before him Tancred's widow and the infant William, a great many bishops and counts of the kingdom, and indicted them for high treason; and he commanded some to be blinded, some to be burnt alive, some to be hanged, and some to be sent captive to Germany. So perished Tancred's house; and on Saint Stephen's Day, being the very day after that general condemnation, Constance of Hauteville, the empress, being no longer young, brought forth her only son, who was to be the Emperor Frederick the Second. It is said also that because of her years and because Sicily had been so greatly disturbed concerning the succession, she feared lest it should be said thereafter that the child was not her own. Therefore she caused a tent to be pitched before the cathedral, and the curtain was raised that all the women might come and see her at their will; and so the great emperor was born in a public place.

Accusations of frightful cruelty have been brought against the Emperor Henry; the chronicle I have followed gives the mildest account of his vengeance, but the great weight of evidence goes to prove that he commanded innumerable and most atrocious executions, and that after men, women, laymen, and priests had been hacked to pieces, drowned, burned, or boiled in lard, his unsatisfied ferocity required the executioner to nail a kingly crown upon the living head of a descendant of Tancred of Hauteville.

But Henry did not long survive these horrors. Having gone back to Germany, he was recalled to Palermo in 1097 by the news, perhaps not unfounded, that Constance meant to hold Sicily for herself and defy him. He reached Messina, indeed, and thence proceeded to besiege one of the great vassals in Castrogiovanni; but there a deadly disease overtook him, and in a few weeks he breathed his last, and was buried in the cathedral of Palermo, in that stately tomb from which he had cast out the bones of the unhappy King Tancred and his eldest son.

Doorway in the castle of Frederick II at Castrogiovanni

By the death of these princes, a legitimate line was again established on the throne of Sicily, and the daughter of King Roger took up the reins of government in her own right, despite the will of the Emperor Henry, who had named Markwald of Anweiler, the Grand Seneschal of the Empire, to be regent. A few months after Henry's death she had dismissed her husband's German ministers, and crowned her son Frederick king of Sicily, he being then less than four years old. The patriotic Pope Innocent the Third applauded the action of a queen, or empress, whose energies were directed to the expulsion of the Germans from Italy, and approved the coronation of the child Frederick, while asserting for the Holy See certain rights over Apulia and the ecclesiastical revenues in Sicily; but Constance, short-lived, like many of her race, died six months after the coronation, leaving the infant king and future emperor to the guardianship of the Pope himself. Immediately the German vassals of Henry the Sixth, whom Constance had kept down, took courage again and set up a rival to Frederick, in the husband of one of Tancred's daughters, and though the Pope gave him little countenance, he may have debated upon the possibility of bestowing upon him the Sicilian crown. As a matter of fact, the Pope never directly interfered in Sicily during the minority of Frederick.

Meanwhile the Christianizing reign of William the Second had produced lasting results, and the Moslem population had almost quite deserted Palermo; thousands had returned to Africa, and tens of thousands had gone out into the hill country above Mazzara on the southwest coast, and after the year 1200 there are no deeds referring to Moslems in the capital. Those in the provinces were vassals of the churches and monasteries, or of the great nobles, and when Innocent the Third, in his enthusiasm for the fourth Crusade, seized all the ecclesiastical revenues of Sicily for the year 1199, the monasteries ground the Moslems to raise more money; at the same time the Pope issued a proclamation enjoining the greatest severities against those baptized Saracens who had fallen back to Islamism. The oppressed people rose, found a ready leader in their lawful regent by Henry's will, the German Markwald, who had secured the alliance of Pisa, and they besieged Palermo; but their defeat ruined their cause and exposed them to far greater sufferings. The Pope gave the Christians spiritual arms against the Grand Seneschal, promising the privileges and indulgences of true crusaders of the those who fought against Markwald, 'who tempted his Saracens with captive Christian women and draughts of Christian blood'; but he bade them respect the ancient privileges of the Moslems. The regents removed the boy Frederick to Messina, where he was safe, and sent a force of militia to relieve Palermo. The city had suffered a siege of seventeen days and was already reduced to want of bread when the relieving army arrived, cut the enemy to pieces, and drove Markwald to flight. He was again beaten far to eastward, in the wild country about Randazzo, on the slope of Etna, and his career would have been ended had not the Sicilian regents found it convenient to forgive him and make common cause with him against the pretender, Walter of Brienne, the husband of a daughter of King Tancred; and so the fighting went on, with varying fortune, until both Walter and Markwald perished, and the kingdom was left in comparative peace under the regency of the Pope.

The latter soon afterwards declared Frederick to be of age, at fourteen years, and in the same year married him to Constance, the sister of Peter the Second of Aragon and the young widow of a king of Hungary. She was older than he, of course, and she came of a race that lacked neither courage nor astuteness. Frederick, educated in the safe seclusion of a palace, while others disputed his kingdom, now issued from its gates to survey the wreck of the Norman dominions. The mainland was lost, apparently beyond recovery, partly to the Pope and partly to the lawless barons of the south; in Sicily, the royal lands had been either seized by the nobles or given away as bribes by the regents, who had also granted the province of Syracuse to a Genoese colony of traders; and of all King Roger's conquests, Frederick could only count with certainty upon the allegiance of half a dozen Sicilian cities. As for the Empire, it was in dispute between his uncle and his cousin, and the boy, who was to be German emperor, king of Sicily and Apulia, and king of Cyprus and Jerusalem, had difficulty in raising enough money to support five hundred horsemen whom his wife borrowed from her cousin of Provence to defend him. To make matters worse, his cousin of Hohenstaufen, the Emperor Otto the Fourth, occupied Naples and Aversa, by the help of the Pisans, and secretly negotiated with the discontented Moslems of Sicily for the destruction of Frederick, in 1210. The youth seemed lost, but his career was already at its upward turning-point, and from that time he rose rapidly to the height of earthly glory.

Innocent the Third, to whom we may as well give credit for supporting his ward, prepared the way for the latter's elevation to the throne of the Empire. With incredible energy and matchless knowledge of his times, he excommunicated the rival Otto, and formally proclaimed his deposition in Nüremberg, absolved the whole Empire from its oath of allegiance, recalled to the world the election of Henry's infant son, and immediately forced Germany into a civil war, from which the only issue was clearly the coronation of the young Frederick, then eighteen years old. Frederick, as Amari well puts it, was already weary of reigning where he could not rule, and threw himself heart and soul into this German revolution. He left his queen and an infant son in Sicily in 1212, sailed to Gaeta, visited the Pope in Rome, and promised everything that was asked of him, sailed on again to Genoa, and rode by Pavia, Cremona, and Trent to Basle, barely escaping his enemies as he passed. In vain Otto pursued him, in vain allied himself with England; Philip Augustus of France joined Frederick and the Pope, and Otto was beaten in the decisive battle of Bouvines.

Frederick remained eight years in Germany, during which he repressed all opposition and made himself the undisputed master of the situation. His father had come down from the north to claim the southern kingdom as his wife's dowry, and to hold it as his own possession; the son went northwards almost alone to claim an Empire which was his own by rightful inheritance. Henry, with Europe at his back, wreaked his vengeance upon a small and helpless kingdom; his son took that kingdom with him to the heart of the Empire he had claimed and recovered from the hands of usurpers. Henry's body was borne to its stolen resting-place in Palermo, pursued by the curses and imprecations of mankind; Frederick the Second spent much of his life, indeed, in a contest with the popes, was thrice or four times excommunicated, and lies, perhaps unshriven, beside his father in the cathedral; but historians have called him the Philosopher King, and though he attained no saintly honours, his fame is at least unsullied by such dastardly cruelty as his father practised, and by the vile treachery that soon set Charles of Anjou on the throne of Sicily and Naples.

Having been crowned in Rome in the year 1220, he returned to Sicily to find himself face to face with what may be called the made question. The nobles were more or less divided among themselves, and Frederick now had power to control them, but the Moslems, though united, were in a most unhappy position. Those who during more than twenty years had lived like free barons in the castles of the West were, legally speaking, the vassals of churches and monasteries that clamoured to the emperor for satisfaction against them; but Frederick, who found himself at odds with the Church and with his barons, needed these very barons as allies. The emperor did not hesitate to satisfy the most pressing demands of the churchmen by nominally bestowing upon them lands and castles held by the Saracens; but when the former attempted to take possession, they more than once found themselves the prisoners of those they sought to dispossess, and the Mohammedans began to move about the island in strong bands, committing depredations of every description, forming a permanent revolutionary army that fluctuated in strength, but may sometimes have numbered thirty thousand fighting men. Frederick held a sort of parliament at Messina soon after his arrival, and visited many of the principal cities; but he accomplished little until his next visit, when he was obliged to take the field against the great freebooter, Mirabbet, whose predatory enterprises had assumed dangerous proportions, and who had associated himself with two of the most infamous ruffians who ever adorned a gibbet, Hugo Fer of Marseilles and William the Swine of Genoa. These two, though some historians lay the blame entirely upon the first, had collected together, by promises and persuasion, a vast number of young children who were to be transported to the Holy Land under the name of the Children's Crusade, to be cared for and educated by the kings of Jerusalem, and brought up to be defenders of the holy places. The organizers of the enterprise were well provided with money to carry it out, and offered the church's parents such surety of their good faith that thousands of fathers, in those times of general poverty and numerous families, consented, each believing that his child was taken from him only to enter upon an honourable career of arms, and with the Pope's especial benediction. In this way it is said that Hugo Fer and William the Swine gathered a company of fifty thousand boys with whom they embarked on many vessels for the East. The rest is soon told. The traitors sailed eastwards indeed, but not to Palestine, for they were in league with the Saracens, and they sold fifty thousand Christian children into slavery in Africa. Therefore when Frederick took those men alive with Mirabbet in the castle of Giato, he hanged them; and perhaps his father would have found for them worse tortures than boiling in lard or tearing to pieces with red-hot pincers.

Though Frederick now had the upper hand, a desultory war continued for some time, and in the meanwhile the Pope, Honorius the Third, did his best to force the emperor to lead another crusade, not without some crafty intention of seizing Apulia in his absence, and Frederick constantly made use of his troubles in Sicily, real and imaginary, as an excuse for putting off his departure to the Holy Land. He had now given up all idea of employing the Saracens against the nobles, and had accomplished the more difficult task of organizing the nobles against the Saracens. In the year 1225 he so completely defeated the latter in the Sicilian mountains, that during eighteen years afterwards there is no mention of a Moslem rebellion. It was on this occasion that he transplanted six thousand Saracens to the mainland. These colonists perished altogether under Charles of Anjou.

Frederick was driven at last, by the menaces and entreaties of Gregory the Ninth, to sail from Brindisi with an army of crusaders already decimated by the plague. Falling ill himself, he was obliged to put back, and was excommunicated by the ruthless pontiff before he had recovered.

Nevertheless, in the following year he set forth again, founding his claim to the throne of Jerusalem upon his marriage with a princess of Antioch, and he actually succeeded in obtaining possession of the holy city by a treaty with the sultan of Egypt; whereupon the Pope declared the agreement to be sacrilegious, sent an army under Frederick's brother-in-law to take Jerusalem from him, and perhaps from force of habit, excommunicated the emperor again. But the latter returned to Italy with his new title of King of Jerusalem, drove the papal troops from his dominions, and forced the pontiff to a peace. His Mohammedan colonists fought bravely under him in this war, but as many of them afterwards attempted to return secretly to Sicily, he collected them together and established them in Apulia, in the town called from them Lucera de' Saraceni, and they long continued to play an important part in the wars of the continent. The ingenious pontiff, finding it impossible to get rid of his troublesome master in any other way, now exhorted him to lead another crusade to the Holy Land, but Frederick was little inclined to renew his previous experience, and he must have smiled when he received the usual excommunication in return for his refusal. But Pope Gregory had gone too far, and Frederick retorted by occupying the states of the Church, and even by threatening Rome itself. In desperate straits the pontiff called a council, but death overtook him suddenly, and after the two years' reign of his successor, the next Pope, refusing to make peace, fled to France, convened a council in Lyons, and declared the Emperor Frederick deposed.

Fountain of the Ninety-Nine Waterspouts, Aquila

The remainder of the latter's life was consumed in wars in the north of Italy, resulting principally from the attempt made to set up Henry Raspe, Landgrave of Thuringia, as anti-emperor, in which

Frederick found himself opposed to his natural son Heinz, or Enzo, king of Sardinia, while his second son, Conrad, afterwards emperor, fought for the imperial cause in Germany. Frederick's eldest son, Henry, had long ago rebelled against him, and died his father's prisoner in a castle of Apulia. Manfred, his natural son, was with him in his latter days, and upon him has fallen the suspicion of having poisoned his father. Conrad defeated Henry Raspe, who died of grief, but the Pope, not relinquishing the bitter quarrel, caused William of Holland to be elected anti-emperor, he drove Conrad back into Italy. The great defeat of Parma made Frederick's cause almost desperate in the north, and he retired to Apulia, never to return again, and leaving the affairs of the Empire in the most inextricable confusion. His end was mysterious. Some say that he died of an illness, repentant and absolved by the Archbishop of Salerno; others that he went out of the world as he had so long lived in it, the excommunicated enemy of the Church; and there are many who write that Manfred poisoned him, and that when his strong nature bade fair to survive the draught, Manfred smothered him in the night with a feather pillow, in Castel Fiorentino of Apulia, whereby was accomplished a prediction in which he had believed, that he should die 'in the Fiorentino'; but he had thought that the word meant the territory of Florence, had never entered that city. He died •six miles from his Saracen city of Lucera, where his great castle still stands, and where Manfred took refuge from the Pope only four years later. The turbulent emperor was a great builder of castles, from the vast and melancholy stronghold that crowns Castrogiovanni to the fortified city of Aquila in the Abruzzi, founded by him, and populated, it is said, by the inhabitants of ninety-nine townships, in memory of which the great fountain has ninety-nine spouts, and it is said that there were once as many churches within the walls. A great builder, a great fighter, a passionate, headstrong man, held accursed by the ecclesiastical writers of his times, he is gravely censured by Muratori for his ambition, his unbridled passions, and his avarice, which was, indeed, but need of money in a desperate conflict; but he is to be praised also for his great heart and large intelligence, his love of justice, his taste for letters, and his learning in many languages. In him the power of the empire founded by Charlemagne culminated and began to wane, and under him the splendour that rose upon Sicily with King Roger spent its noonday radiance, and declined towards its fall. The south had lived its greatest day, and was soon to sink forever to the level of a province owned by kings who claimed a little Norman blood. It was no longer Greek, it was no longer Saracen, under Frederick the Second it had not even been any longer Norman; he had been born in the public square of Palermo, he had spent his early years in the shadow of Sicilian fortresses, he had used the island as a fulcrum upon which to wield the lever of empire; but Sicily had been to him but an imperial appanage, he had never in any sense been a Sicilian, and he squandered the strength that might have moved the world onwards, in a series of useless quarrels with the Papacy, when he might have better employed his genius, his gifts, and his knowledge of men in civilizing and consolidating the south. The confusion that followed upon his death, the disputes that arose between his sons, and especially between Conrad and Manfred, the quick decay of institutions which should have lasted for centuries, the chaos, in a word, which was the natural result of his reign, could only end as it did, in the disappearance of his heirs, the extinction of his house, and the rise of a new southern monarchy.

Fountain in the Piazza Palazzo, Aquila

There is, perhaps, no greater contrast in history than that between Saint Lewis the Ninth, king of France, the leader of the sixth and seventh Crusades, and his brother Charles, Count of Anjou, the destined destroyer of the house of Hohenstaufen. That extraordinary man, in his struggle with Frederick's heirs, quartered the country as a well-trained dog quarters a field. It was not until Frederick had been dead three years that Charles was definitely called in by Pope Innocent the Fourth, and, to the iniquitous exclusion of all other claims, was named king of Sicily, Duke of Apulia, and Prince of Capua. His principal opponents were Conrad and his half-brother Manfred, then a youth of one and twenty years, and gifted with much of the wisdom of his father, as well as the astuteness of his Norman ancestors. The premature death of another brother, a younger Henry, born of the Emperor Frederick's marriage with Isabel of England, served the next Pope with an excuse for accusing Conrad of murder. He was cited to appear in Rome, but wisely caused himself to be represented by proxies. It is needless to say that he was found guilty and promptly excommunicated. Forty days later, he also died; and it was commonly believed, says Muratori, that he was poisoned by Manfred, with the help of John the Moor, the captain of the Saracens, Conrad's favourite. He left an infant son two years old, who was destined to be known as the last of the Hohenstaufen. Why Manfred did not destroy this child, if he really had poisoned the father, it does not appear. He may have thought that his illegitimacy was an insuperable barrier between him and the Empire, and that the most he could hope for was that he might be the master of a future emperor. Conrad's treasures were, meanwhile, seized by the regent he had designated, and for some short time this regent and Manfred actually exerted themselves to bring about an understanding with the Pope. Failing to do so, the German regent resigned his office, but not his ward's treasure, to Manfred, who, as sole guardian, met the Pope and kissed his foot at Ceprano, on the confines of the papal states; after which the Pope made a sort of triumphal progress to Monte Casino, accompanied by Manfred. The latter, however, had refused to take the oath of fealty to the Church, and the negotiations which doubtless proceeded during the journey were rudely interrupted. Manfred quarrelled with one of the Pope's favourite barons, who was accidentally or intentionally killed by one of Manfred's men; and Manfred himself was soon obliged of take refuge in Lucera. He reached the gates on a dark night early in November, at a moment when John the Moor, who was governor, was absent on a journey. The Saracen sentinels upon the walls, on being told that Manfred was below, were filled with joy, and, fearing that the vice-governor might refuse to give them the keys, which were kept in his house, came down and broke the gates from within to receive Frederick's son. In a moment the news spread through the Saracen town, the whole population came out into the streets, and, though it was night, insisted upon leading Manfred to the palace, where a great treasure, accumulated by Frederick and Conrad and John the Moor, was unconditionally handed over to him.

Church of San Bernardino, Aquila

The death of Innocent the Fourth and the possession of so much wealth materially improved Manfred's position, and for some time he overran the south, losing no time in regaining what he could for his ward Conradin, and followed everywhere by his faithful Saracens. Before long he inflicted a crushing defeat upon the papal army on the shores of the Adriatic, after which the Pope's cardinal legate and general obtained terms with which the Pope should have been satisfied, but the Pope refused to acknowledge the treaty, and proclaimed Manfred an excommunicated member of the Church, to be treated like a Turk or an infidel; yet, strange to say, the Pope admitted the infant Conradin's claim to the nugatory kingdom of Jerusalem. From this time Manfred's position continued to improve. He was a mild and generous prince to those who submitted to him, and from Aversa to Sicily the people volunteered to fight under his standard. We hear nothing of any attempt on the part of Charles of Anjou to take possession of the kingdom presented to him by Innocent the Fourth, and Muratori speaks of Manfred as the master of the kingdom on both sides of the straits in the year 1257. With the treachery that lay under his brilliant gifts he now attempted to crown himself king, spreading the report that his nephew Conradin had died in Germany, and some chroniclers say that he sent emissaries to murder the child. His youth, his courteous manner, and his clemency recommended him alike to the people and the nobles, and when Conradin's mother sent ambassadors to him in 1258, protesting that Conradin was alive and was the rightful king, Manfred answered with a show of reason that the kingdom had been lost, and that, as all men knew, he had reconquered it by force of arms and at great pains, and that it was neither his duty nor for the advantage of the kingdom to give it up to a child who could not hold it against the popes, but that he would defend the kingdom against those implacable enemies of his house during his natural life, after which it should revert to his nephew. By way of impressing the ambassadors with his power, he marched in state from Apulia against the city of Aquila, which had been built by his father but had taken the Pope's side, and having driven out the inhabitants without bloodshed, he burned the town. His power was too great to be humbled by the Church alone, and though Alexander the Fourth did not fail to excommunicate him, the same Pope offered to concede him the formal investiture of the kingdom in 1260, on condition that he would exile all Mohammedans from his dominions. The Pope probably knew that this was impossible, since the strength of Manfred's army now lay chiefly in the Saracen contingent, in whom he could place far more reliance than in his barons of the south. Manfred rejected the proposition, and raised more Saracen troops in Sicily, but made the mistake of accepting the leadership of the Ghibellines in the north, and he sent help to the party, in return for good sums of gold, so that Florence was wrested from the Guelphs, and the famous Guido Novello became Manfred's 'vicar' or viceregent in Tuscany. The Guelphs now made an unsuccessful attempt to bring Conradin down from Germany, in order to oppose him to his uncle; but Conradin's mother refused to consent, and Urban the Fourth threatened to excommunicate all who proposed to make Conradin emperor. The popes hated not Manfred only, but all his race, and Urban bethought him of Charles of Anjou as the only man likely to be a match for the house of Hohenstaufen. It was with difficulty that Urban persuaded the generally docile Saint Lewis to countenance his brother Charles in the enterprise, but his arguments prevailed at last, and he cited Manfred to appear in Rome and answer for his sins against the Church. Manfred appeared by proxy, not trusting his life to Urban's mercy. His case was argued from one side only, with a view to deposing him without delay and with little hearing, and Charles of Anjou was fully authorized to begin the conquest of the south. This was in the year 1263. By way of impressing their intentions upon Apulia and Sicily, the popes had placed the populations of the south under an interdict in a body, and one of the gravest crimes imputed to Frederick the Second and to Manfred was that they had prevented the interdict from being put into execution; yet so many persons were now excommunicated throughout Italy that the terrible spiritual punishment had lost much of its force, and even the relentless Urban began to moderate his fulminatory zeal. At this time it occurred to the always discontented Roman people to choose themselves a chief, called a senator, who should be also a powerful prince, and the choice of some fell upon Manfred, but others were for Charles of Anjou, and others still for James of Aragon. Though opposed to the idea, the Pope was forced to yield, and chose the Count of Anjou in order to exclude the other two. Charles at once sent a representative to Rome to take possession of the senatorial dignity. Destiny was slowly but surely preparing the downfall of Hohenstaufen. On the news of Charles's election as senator, Manfred at once assumed the offensive, and the armies of the Pope that were sent against him bore the outward badge and received the spiritual indulgences of real crusaders. There was some desultory fighting, but Charles did not yet appear in Italy, being engaged in raising an army fit for such an expedition; and the death of Urban the Fourth, closely followed by that of Clement the Fourth, produced a sort of lull in the hostilities. In spite of Manfred's attempt to intercept him, Charles arrived at the mouth of the Tiber in a storm, during which he barely escaped drowning. Soon afterwards he made his solemn entry into Rome and took possession of his new office; but though Manfred advanced far into Roman territory, Charles would not go out to meet him until he found himself at the head of a sufficient army. When all was ready Charles and his wife were crowned king and queen of Sicily and Apulia by five cardinals, in the Church of Saint Peter's, and Charles did homage to the Pope for the kingdom of Sicily on both sides of the straits. Lack of money now obliged new king to take the field before his forces were rested from their long journey; but they took San Germano by storm, and fatigue was forgotten in the sacking of the rich town. One place after another fell into Charles's hands, and Manfred retired upon Benevento, whence he sent ambassadors to treat with the Angevin. Charles's answer has been preserved: 'Tell the Sultan of Lucera,' he said, 'that I will have neither peace nor amnesty with him, but that before long either I will send him to hell, or he shall send me to heaven.' Thereupon Charles marched against Manfred, hoping to terminate the war at a single stroke, and he reached the battlefield before Manfred had determined upon a plan. The position of the famous city has already been described in these pages; the remains of the bridge about which the battle was fought may be seen in the dark recesses of a mill built beneath the modern construction by which the river is crossed. The land by which Charles made his approach narrows to a point between the converging streams, so that as he came forward his ranks gained solidity by the conformation of the ground. Manfred must have recognized at a glance that his fortunes and those of all his house were to be decided on that day; but from the first he was unable to get any advantage over the French. Not trusting his Apulian barons, he sent forward his Saracens and Germans; but they were not the Normans with whom his great grandfather had won kingdom and glory. They fought well, but the French fought better. Seeing that the ranks wavered, Manfred called upon the barons to follow him in one desperate charge. They saw he was lost, they laughed, and they leisurely rode away. Then King Manfred, seeing that he must die, died like a king, and like one of Tancred's house, for he rode alone at the French host where swords were thickest, and he was pierced with many wounds, and was lost among the slain.

Castle of Frederick II at Monteleone, Calabria

The Pope's champion sacked the old papal city of Benevento, and women and children were mown down with the men in the harvest of the sword. The town ran blood and wine, and Charles's threadbare Frenchmen filled their wallets and saddle-bags with gold, and got fine silk and cloth of gold to their backs. Three days they sought Manfred's body among the festering slain; and on the third day a peasant found it, and tied it upon an ass, and hawked it through the French camp, offering to sell it for money; but when it had been recognized by some of the nobles whom Charles had taken prisoners, he commanded that it should be buried in the ditch beside the bridge. Even there the brave man's bones were not allowed to rest in peace, for, though the ground was not consecrated, it was the property of the Church, and the Bishop of Cosenza therefore caused the body to be dug up again and dragged away beyond the river Verde.

Thus died Manfred; and when he was dead the Saracens of Lucera went over to Charles, and Naples sent her keys, and in the castle of Capua Charles found a great treasure, all in pieces of gold. But when he commanded that scales should be brought with which to divide the wealth exactly, a certain knight of Provence pushed the great heap of gold pieces into three equal divisions upon the marble floor with his foot and spurred heel. 'One for my lord the king,' he said, 'and this for the queen, and this other for your knights.' And so it was done. Charles entered Naples in triumph, and it is recorded that he first brought thither the love of show and luxury that have distinguished it ever since, and that the common people cried out in an ecstasy of sheer delight at the procession of splendid gilded cars, and at the richly clad maids of honour, and at the great show of triumph that meant death to Conradin.

Now Charles of Anjou, having disposed of his enemy in one great victory, found himself in peaceful possession of the south, and at once he took the Guelph side, and led armies to Tuscany, and joined in the unending quarrel; wherefore the Ghibellines sent urgent letters to young Conradin, now nearly sixteen years of age, bidding him to come and conquer Sicily, and take possession of his own. He set out with a few thousand men and reached Verona, calling himself King of Sicily, and the Pope lost no time in excommunicating him for this arrogance. Most of his troops deserted him at once, on account of his poverty, but his friends raised his standard in Sicily, and the island rang with his praises; for the French yoke was heavy. But though the patriotic party gained an advantage here and there, the end was not far off. In the beginning of 1268 Conradin ventured to leave Verona, and riding southwards he found more than one of the restless Tuscan cities ready to throw off Charles's authority. Charles prepared to meet him, but was himself at odds with the Saracens of Lucera, who had discovered the character of the master to whom they had readily submitted, and who was obliged to besiege them in their city. Meanwhile Conradin reached Rome, and was received with splendour by his friends, in spite of the papal excommunication. The Pisans sent him twenty-four galleys, with which, sailing southwards, he beat back the vessels sent against him by the Angevin; and Ghibellines flocked to his standard from all parts of Italy. Conradin now marched up by land with a vast host, and there were few who did not predict his complete success. On the twenty-third of August, 1268, the decisive battle was fought in the plain of Tagliacozzo, not many miles from Lake Fucino. Charles, fearing the superior numbers arrayed against him, fought with all the coolness and skill he could command, and while his main force attacked the enemy, he withdrew to a little eminence, where he watched the battle with the chosen reserve of five hundred knights. A wise old captain more than once prevented him from rushing in at the wrong moment, and Charles sat quietly on his horse, though he saw how the ranks of his army were broken by the Ghibellines' furious charge; but when Conradin's army was broken up into small bodies that pursued the French hither and thither, certain of victory, and when, indeed, that victory seemed almost sure, then the crafty old Alardo touched Charles upon the arm, and said that the time was come, and that he should win the field. Then he led his five hundred knights at furious speed, for their horses were fresh, and fell upon the disordered troops of his enemy, hewing them in pieces, and turning the day in a moment. Conradin and the young Duke of Austria and two other friends escaped when they saw that all was lost, and riding desperately reached Astura, on the Maremma shore; there they hired a little boat, hoping to escape into Tuscany; but Frangipane, the lord of that castle, guessed who they were, and seized them, and basely sold them to the Angevin king.

The end of the house of Hohenstaufen was at hand. Of the Emperor Frederick's descendants, six were alive at the time of the battle of Benevento, whose claims might be dangerous to his throne, namely, Conradin and Manfred's five children. Of the latter, Constance, the eldest, was out of danger, being married to Peter of Aragon; of the girl Beatrice we know nothing; the three sons, Henry, Frederick, and Anselm were Charles's prisoners after the decisive battle, and they died in a miserable captivity in Apulia. Ten of Frederick's children and grandchildren died in prison, or by a violent death. One of his granddaughters, a daughter of Enzo of Sardinia, married that famous Ugolino della Gherardesca who was starved to death with his sons and grandsons in Pisa. The shade of King Tancred was perhaps appeased by such an atonement for Henry the Sixth's bloody deeds.

The last act of the great tragedy was played in Naples, on the twenty-sixth or the twenty-ninth of October, for the authorities do not agree, in the year 1268. Determined to destroy every possible claimant, Charles of Anjou ordered Conradin and his fellow-captives to be tried by Robert of Bari, Grand Protonotary of the kingdom, and the infamous judge of an infamous king condemned the imperial boy and his noble companions to death, as 'traitors to the sovereign, contemners of the Pope's commands, and disturbers of the public peace in Italy.' Conradin's claim to the succession was just, and he and his friends were prisoners of war; to put them to death was a solemn and atrocious murder.

On the appointed day the sentence was executed. Charles of Anjou, determined to see the end of his helpless enemy with his own eyes, came in state to the market-place, where the Church of Santa Maria del Carmine now stands, and his throne was placed upon a platform overlooking the scene, and on the stones a great piece of scarlet velvet was spread out, whereon the men were to die. There stood young Conradin, a fair-haired boy of sixteen years, fearless as all his race, and the young Duke of Austria and six others, and the executioner beside them.

Then Robert of Bari, Grand Protonotary, stood up by order of the king and read the sentence in a loud voice; but when he had finished, Robert of Flanders, the king's own son-in-law, gravely drew his sword, and he came and stood before the Grand Protonotary and said, 'It is not lawful that you should condemn to death so great a gentleman.' And when he had said this he pierced the protonotary through and through, so that the sword ran out behind him, and he fell dead, with the written sentence in his hand. Then a great silence fell upon all the multitude, and upon the king, and Robert of Flanders sheathed his sword and went back to his place; for neither then nor afterwards did any one dare to lift a hand against him for what he had done.

So while the judge lay dead before the throne, the execution began; and the young Duke of Austria bent his neck to the stroke, and when his head fell Conradin took it in his hands and kissed it, for they had been as brothers, and he laid it reverently beside the body. Then he drew off his glove and threw it among the people, and cried out that he left his kingdom to Frederick of Aragon, the son of Constance, and his cousin; and when he had asked pardon of God for his sins he knelt down without fear, and his head was struck off, and after him died all his companions. Their bodies lay long upon the scarlet velvet, and Charles commanded that a common ditch should be dug there, in the market-place, to bury them; and afterwards a porphyry column was set up to mark the spot; and now they lie in the Church of the Carmine.

But some who saw that deed took the boy king's glove, and by and by they brought it to Peter, king of Aragon, young Frederick's father, and he swore to avenge the blood of Conradin; and though the atonement was begun by other hands, he kept his word, and Charles of Anjou cursed the day whereon he had gone out to see an innocent boy die by the executioner's hand.

But he had not yet fulfilled the measure of his cruelties. At the news of Conradin's death, Sicily rebelled against him, and he put down the rebellion with such wholesale massacres of the people and such cruel executions of their leaders as even Sicily had seldom seen; and he left a French army there with orders to keep the people down by terror; and neither the protestations of Pope Clement the Fourth nor the entreaties of his brother, Saint Lewis of France, could prevail upon him to stay his wrath, for he was afraid. He also destroyed Lucera, and drove out the Saracens who survived the siege.

Two years after Conradin's death, Saint Lewis set out upon the seventh and last Crusade, and took Tunis by storm, and waited there for Charles of Anjou to join him. But Charles would not set out, and the good French king perished of the plague, with many of his army; and when the remains of the crusaders' fleet were driven upon the rocks and wrecked near Trapani, Charles robbed the survivors of all they could save, alleging that a law of King William authorized the kings of Sicily to seize all wrecks with their cargoes. For a time the body of Saint Lewis lay in Palermo, but afterwards it was taken to France by his son, King Philip, and only his heart is buried in the cathedral.

During fourteen years Charles of Anjou ruled his kingdoms of Sicily and Apulia with every species of violence and exaction; tax followed upon tax, impost upon impost, and tithes both ordinary and extraordinary, the slightest delay in payment being followed by ruthless confiscation. The cities were held by French garrisons under general instructions to inspire fear, to extort money, and to impose instant obedience to the king's decrees. The wives of respectable citizens were nowhere safe from Charles's licentious officers, and the women and maidens of the people were at the mercy of a ribald soldiery. More than once the Sicilians appealed to the popes against Charles, and more than one pontiff exhorted him to a milder conduct; but the Angevin was in a fever of conquest, he dreamed of ruling all Italy, he planned the conquest of the East, and he brought about the election of Pope Martin the Fourth, who was his humble servant and creature.

There lived at that time a certain noble of Salerno, brought up in the school of medicine for which that city remained famous for ages, a man of letters, of singular wisdom, and a very skilled physician. This man was John of Procida; he had been closely attached to the person of the Emperor Frederick the Second, and I find his name among the witnesses to that emperor's will. After the death of Frederick, he had been faithful to Manfred, and after the fall of the house of Hohenstaufen Charles of Anjou confiscated all his goods. He might have lost his life also, had he not retired in good season to the court of Aragon in Barcelona, where he was well received by King Peter and by Queen Constance, Manfred's daughter. He found the king well enough inclined to avenge Conradin and to undertake the conquest of Sicily, but the enterprise was a great one, and he was not provided with means to enter upon it. John of Procida promised to find money. Though he must have been at that time more than sixty years of age, he travelled through all Sicily in disguise, seeking out and ascertaining as nearly as possible what pecuniary help was to be obtained for the impoverished land. It needed no long time to assure him that Sicily was ripe for a revolution, but John was too wise to underestimate Charles's power; from Sicily he went on to Constantinople, and without difficulty persuaded the Emperor Paleologus that, in order to defend himself against the attack which Charles was planning, the best plan was to bring on a civil war in the Angevin's own dominions. The Emperor of the East promised large sums of money to Peter of Aragon for this purpose, and with unwearying energy John made his way at once from Constantinople to Rome; he was received in a secret audience by Pope Nicholas the Third, who was an Orsini, who was believed to be hostile to Charles, and who promised great things, but unfortunately died before the great scheme was ripe for execution.

Peter of Aragon now prepared a fleet and an army on pretence of invading the Saracens in Africa. At the instigation of Charles, the Pope, on receiving news of this armament, sent an embassy to King Peter, inquiring what his intentions might be; but the crafty monarch answered that if one of his hands should reveal his secrets to the other, he would cut it off. On receiving this reply Charles contented himself with reminding the Pope that he had always looked upon Peter of Aragon as a miscreant, and in Muratori's graphic language he fell asleep, forgetful of that old proverb which says, 'If some one tell thee that thou hast lost thy nose, feel for it with thine hand.'

We do not know whether the final outbreak of the revolution, which had been so long and skilfully prepared, took place precisely as John of Procida had intended; but when it came it was sudden and terrible, as few revolutions have been, and the Sicilian Vespers will be remembered so long as men love liberty, and history records their deeds.

Column in the cloister of San Giovanni degli Eremiti, Palermo

From the ancient church and cloister of San Giovanni degli Eremiti, not far beyond the royal palace, a long and dusty road leads out to what is now the chief cemetery of Palermo. It passes through a sort of half eastern, half modern suburb, where the poorer people live out of doors all day, plying their trades and doing their household work before their miserable, but not uncleanly, little houses. In older times there was no suburb there, and the broad road led between trees through the open country to a vast meadow broken here and there by clumps of trees, and surrounding the very ancient Church of the Holy Ghost. In spring, when the cool breezes blow up from the sea, when the trees are already in full leaf, and when the grass is aflame with scarlet and yellow and purple wild flowers, the good people of Palermo used to go out there on great festivals with their wives and children in holiday clothes, and taking some provision with them, wherewith to make little feasts on the grass. So it came to pass that on Easter Monday, in the year 1282, the people went out thus in long procession, in the afternoon; and they sat down in groups, and ate and drank together, and wandered about in little companies, exchanging greetings with their friends. But as they feasted, enjoying the peace and the cool air, and forgetting for a space the tyranny under which they lived, there came out a number of French soldiers of the garrison with their officers; and first they mixed with the people, though they were not welcome, and drank from cups of wine that no man had offered them, and jested grossly with the women and girls, who turned from them in angry silence. The Sicilian men grew silent too, and their eyes gleamed, but they answered nothing, and led their women away. Then suddenly the French captain, a certain Drouet, having drunk much wine, ordered his men to search the people, and to see whether they had not upon them some concealed weapons; and still the men submitted silently. But at last the French officer, seeing a very beautiful Sicilian woman walking near him with her husband, cried out to his soldiers to search the women also, and he himself laid hands upon the fairest, and pretending to look for a knife upon her he thrust his hand out to her bosom. She, being thus outraged, shrank half fainting into her husband's arms. Then he could bear no more, and he cried out, so that his voice rang across the broad meadow, 'Now let these Frenchmen die at last!' And as his words pierced the air, the bells of San Giovanni rang to Vespers, and the bells of the Church of the Holy Ghost answered them, and the French officer lay dead at the feet of the woman he had insulted.

Cloister of San Giovanni degli Eremiti, Palermo

Unarmed as they were, with such small knives as some chanced to have, with sticks, with stones, and with their naked hands, the Sicilian men did their work quickly; but the Frenchmen howled for mercy, and were mostly killed upon their knees. When they were all dead, the men took their weapons and went back in haste towards the city with their women, and the cry that meant death was heard afar off and went before them. No Frenchman who met them lived to turn back, and when they were in doubt as to any man's nation, they held him with the knife at his throat and made him say the one word 'Ciceri,' which no Frenchman could or can pronounce. It was dusk when the killing began in Palermo, and when the dawn stole through the blood-stained streets not one of the French was alive, neither man, nor woman, nor child. The reign of Charles of Anjou was at an end, and from that day to this no man has been king of Sicily who had not some Norman blood.

The Sicilian Vespers took place on the thirtieth of March. The example of Palermo was followed within the month of April by Messina, where the French were almost all massacred, and the fortresses seized by the population. Charles was at Orvieto, instructing his creature, Pope Martin the Fourth, says Muratori, in the art of governing the world; but Villani tells us that when he heard the news from Palermo, he raised his eyes to heaven and prayed that since his good fortune had begun to wane, 'he might be suffered to fall by small degrees.' He reached Naples before he heard of the rising in Messina, and at once ordered that the fleet he had gathered for invading the Eastern Empire should proceed to Messina, while he himself hastened to the straits by land, at the head of the cavalry. A hundred and thirty-three ships weighed anchor; the land forces numbered five thousand horse, and he crossed to Sicily at the end of July and laid siege to Messina. An apostolic legate entered the city, and his eloquence prevailed upon the inhabitants to propose terms of surrender; but Charles rejected them with scorn and attacked the walls, which were defended with the courage of despair by men who feared and execrated their assailants.

Palermo raised the Pope's standard and sent ambassadors to Martin the Fourth, who dismissed them with energy and with threatening words. The defenders of Messina again offered to surrender upon honourable terms, and the legate in vain did his best to persuade King Charles to mercy. He bade Messina deliver up eight hundred hostages, to be dealt with at his pleasure, and submit to all the fiscal impositions and extortions he had practised hitherto. The Messinians answered that they would die, sword in hand, rather than obey. Beside himself with rage, Charles ordered a general assault, which was repulsed with frightful carnage. And so the siege went on for a whole month.

Meanwhile the nobles of Palermo decided upon the final step. They had revolted from Charles, their advances had been rejected by the Pope, they could not hope to resist the Angevin without help; they met in the small church now called the Martorana, and they elected Peter the Third of Aragon, the husband of Manfred's daughter, to be king of Sicily, and his descendants after him. On the thirtieth of August, 1282, exactly five months after the Sicilian Vespers, Peter of Aragon landed at Trapani, with fifty galleys, eight hundred cavalry, and ten thousand men-at-arms, all trained soldiers, for he had been fighting the Moors in Barbary. But when he came to Palermo, after five days, the people thought ill of his knights, from their appearance, for their armour was all tarnished and their accoutrements black with campaigning, and their cloaks were threadbare, and the light infantry men were ill clad, and all were sunburnt and thin; and in their hearts the people did not believe that such men could deliver them from King Charles. Peter held a parliament, however, and promised the nobles that he would maintain all the laws and customs of William the Good.

The two Catalan chronicles of Bernat Desclot and Ramon Muntaner give the most circumstantial accounts of what followed. They have been published in the original Catalan language, in

Barcelona. The Neapolitan historian, Tomacelli, seems to have had access to them in manuscript, but I cannot find that they have been translated.

Peter called out every fighting man in Sicily above fifteen and under sixty years of age to help him against Charles, and sent to him two knights as ambassadors, and they were tolerably well received by a party of skirmishers, who led them to the enemy's camp. They and their squires were roughly lodged, however, in a church, without mattresses or blankets, and they slept on some hay that was there. Charles sent them two bottles of wine, six loaves of very coarse black bread, two roast pigs, and a kettle full of boiled cabbage and fresh pork. In the morning the king sent for them, and they delivered their message. 'My lord Charles,' said the spokesman, 'our king of Aragon sends us to you. That you may believe we are his messengers, behold this credential letter he has given us.' 'It is well,' said Charles. 'Speak what the king of Aragon sends you to say.' The ambassador presented King Peter's letter. Charles was seated on a couch covered with rich silks; he laid the letter beside him unopened. 'My lord Charles,' said the ambassador, 'our lord the king of Aragon sends us, and bids you deliver up to him the land of Sicily which is his, and his son's, and which you have too long most wrongly held. And the people of Sicily, who are grievously oppressed by your rule, have asked help of the king of Aragon. Wherefore the king has determined to help them, they being his people and of his lands.'

The message did not lack distinctness. When King Charles heard it, he was much surprised, and some minutes passed before he answered, and he gnawed with his teeth a little staff he held in his hand. When he had thought a long time he answered: 'Sirs, Sicily belongs neither to the king of Aragon, nor to me, but to the Church of Rome. I desire you to go to Messina, and to bid the men of the city, from the king of Aragon, that they make a truce with me for eight days, until we shall have talked with you, and you with us, of those things concerning which we have to speak.' 'Sir,' said the ambassadors, 'we will do this willingly; and if they will not, it shall not be of our fault.'

With that they left the king and went before the city of Messina, and called to the men on the wall, and the men inquired what they wished. 'Barons,' said the spokesman, 'we are ambassadors from the king of Aragon, and we would speak with your captain, Sir Alaymo.' When the me heard this, they went and told it to Sir Alaymo, their captain; and he came at once and went upon the wall, and asked of the messengers what they required. 'Are you the captain of Messina?' they asked. And he answered: 'Surely, I am indeed the captain of Messina. Why ask you this?' And they told him, and gave their message. 'Surely,' answered the captain, 'I do not believe that you are messengers from the king of Aragon, and for your false words I will not have peace or truce. See that you depart at once and go your way.'

They came and told this to King Charles, and he bade them rest until the next day, promising to take counsel and give them an answer. But on the next morning they learned that he had secretly crossed the straits to Calabria during the night, and three knights came and bade them return to Palermo for King Charles would send his answer at his leisure. They knew, however, that Peter of Aragon was already in Randazzo, only two days' ride from Messina, and they found him there and told him all.

Charles had either fallen into his own trap, or had meant to abandon the siege. When it was known that he had left Sicily a great part of his army became disorganized, many took to the ships and sailed over to Reggio, and the people of Messina sallied out against those that remained and killed many of them, and the rest slew all the horses and burned all the flour and wheat they could not take with them, and escaped. On the very day when the messengers reached Randazzo, a man came spurring towards evening, bringing news that Charles's army had disappeared, and so King Peter rode down and entered Messina without striking a blow. His fleet also arrived from Palermo, and when forty of Charles's galleys sailed out of Reggio, on the fifth day, fourteen Catalan ships attacked them and took twenty-one, and sank others, and put the rest to flight, and brought back many prisoners and a vast spoil; for Charles had met his match, and more, and he had been driven from Italy forever.

King Charles could not have seen the fight in which his galleys were lost, as it took place to the west of Scylla while he was at Reggio; but his rage knew no bounds when he heard the news, and he immediately conceived a treacherous plan for drawing King Peter into an ambush on pretence of single combat. He began by sending messengers to his adversary with instructions to deliver a formal insult, and that their persons might be safe he disguised his messengers as preaching friars. He sent them across the straits by night in a boat, and coming before the king they boldly told him in Charles's name that he had not entered Sicily like a leal and true man, but that he had entered it treacherously, as he should not. But when the king of Aragon heard these words he broke into a laugh, and pretended to attach no importance to the message. 'Sirs,' said he, 'I will send my messengers together with you to King Charles, to know from his own lips whether what you say be true.' He chose out certain honourable knights of high birth and bearing, and bade them go with the messengers, and when he had instructed them he commanded them that, if the king confirmed the message, they should deal with him as with any knight who should attack their faith and honour, for he would do battle with Charles, hand to hand. The knights went over to Reggio and delivered their message. Then Charles remained in thought for a while, and said, 'Whether you say that I have said it or not, I say it now, that he has entered Sicily treacherously and unjustly, and as he should not.' Therefore the messengers of the king of Aragon answered and said: 'Sir we answer you these words by the command of the king of Aragon and Sicily, our lord, and we tell you that any man who says that the king has entered Sicily treacherously and unjustly, speaks falsely and disloyally. And he says that he will fight you, hand to hand, and he gives you the choice of arms, which shall be as you please.'

Charles was enraged at this answer, and his barons besought him not to be angry, nor to answer without taking counsel; and thereupon they led him away thence, and took him into a room, and there he held a council with his barons and returned to his senses; and he answered that he would not fight the king of Aragon in single combat, but that he would fight with a hundred knights against a hundred. And his object in thus answering was that wherever the combat took place he should be allowed to bring with him enough men to get possession of King Peter by some treachery. Immediately after this, further messages were exchanged, and it was decided that the contest should take place at Bordeaux, which belonged to the king of England, who would insure neutrality and safety for all those who came to fight.

The sequel to this celebrated challenge is better known than the details which led to it, and which I have translated literally from the Catalan chronicle. Charles went to Bordeaux, indeed, but with such a force that the English king's governor would have been powerless to save King Peter. The latter was in Catalonia, but was too wise to fall into the snare, and yet too honourable not to appear in the lists. The story of his secret ride through Spain reads like a chapter from the 'Morte d'Arthur,' which, like similar fictions of the age of chivalry, was doubtless imitated from the real chronicles. The story tells how King Peter reached Bordeaux in disguise, with three knights, in the company of a merchant whose servants they all pretended to be, the king himself being fully armed under his disguise. The king passed for the rich merchant's major-domo, and ordered supper at the inns, and the three knights served their supposed master at table. Near Bordeaux they left two of the knights with good horses in case of need. When they reached the gates the king stayed without, and one of the knights went in on foot and sought out King Peter's official representative, who had gone to Bordeaux openly, and bade him tell the seneschal to go out from the city, saying that a messenger from the king of Aragon was there, desiring to speak with him. And the seneschal did so, taking four French knights with him, and the Catalan ambassador, and a notary of the city. Peter did not reveal his identity, but ascertained from the seneschal that Charles had prepared the lists under the walls where a gate led directly into them from the fortress; and also that the king of England had commanded him, the seneschal, to give up the city entirely to King Charles during his stay, and that if Peter appeared in the lists, he would most certainly be taken prisoner. While they were talking they had ridden to the place, and when they were within, Peter set spurs to his horse and rode up and down the enclosed field. Then, riding back together, the king drew the seneschal aside, and asked him whether he should know the king of Aragon if he saw him; and the seneschal; answered that he should know him well, for he had seen him at Toulouse, and that the king had done him great honour, and had made him a present of two horses.

Then King Peter drew back the hood from his face, and said, 'Look at me well, if you know me, for I am here, the king of Aragon; and if the king of England, and you in his name, can insure my safety, I am ready to do battle, with a hundred knights.' When the seneschal knew the king, he wished to kiss his hand, but the king would not; and the seneschal implored him to escape at once, lest he should be deceived and taken by his enemies. Then said the king, 'You shall make me a letter for a testimony that I have been on the appointed day at Bordeaux, in the lists where the battle was to be fought, and that you have told me that you cannot assure my safety, and that whereas the country was to have been neutral, the king of England has delivered it over to King Charles.' The seneschal answered, 'Surely, this is true.' Then the notary who had been brought out of the city drew up the statement, and the French knights were called to witness it, and when they asked where the king of Aragon was, he showed himself to them, and they were much amazed, and bowed low, taking off their caps, and would have kissed his hand, but he would not suffer it. So he rode away towards Bayonne, and its near evening; and when the seneschal and the knights had returned into the city, the sun had set, and King Peter was many miles away.

It would be a pleasant task to tell the history of the war that followed the Sicilian Vespers, from the graphic chronicles of Bernat Desclot and Ramon Muntaner. Their simple accounts of men, things, and battles bear the stamp of truth and the sign manual of the eye-witness. Therein may be found in detail the bold deeds of Roger di Lauria, King Peter's famous admiral, and all that brave Queen Constance did with his help to hold Sicily while Peter himself was fighting against the king of France on his own borders, and against his own brother James of Majorca; and how at last the Admiral Roger defeated the king of France and drove him from the walls of Gerona. And at last, after much brave fighting, and having secured the succession of all his dominions, including Sicily, to his sons, King Peter of Aragon passed away peacefully, after a long illness, on the eve of Saint Martin's Day, in the month of November, in the year 1285. His great enemy, Charles of Anjou, had died in Foggia in January of the same year, while preparing a formidable army with which to invade Sicily, while the French were attacking King Peter in Catalonia. He left his kingdom at war with Sicily and his eldest son Charles a prisoner in the hands of Queen Constance. Nor was the young prince's captivity without danger; Pope Martin the Fourth had sent legates to Messina to negotiate for his liberation, and as they could not obtain it on the terms they demanded, they pronounced the major excommunication against all the Sicilians and the royal house of Aragon. Three years had not passed since the general massacre of the French, and the people of Messina now rose in tumult and attacked the prisons where the French prince and his companions were confined. Crying out for vengeance for the death of Manfred and Conradin, they heaped up wood against the prison doors, and more than sixty French nobles perished miserably in the flames. The young prince, now Charles the Second, was saved, we know not exactly how, but some say that he had been secretly removed from the prison and sent to Catalonia before the attack. Soon after this Pope Martin the Fourth died also, having, as Muratori says, emptied the treasury of his excommunications upon all Ghibellines, and upon whosoever° chanced to be the enemy of his master, Charles of Anjou.

In Later Times

My task is almost ended. I have traced the story of the south from the times of the first Greek settlements to the establishment of the house of Aragon on the Sicilian throne, through a period of about two thousand years, endeavouring to spare the reader all unnecessary names and dates, the accumulation of which has made the history of Italy so difficult a study for persons of ordinary memory. In the few remaining pages I shall briefly explain the succession of events that led directly from the coronation of Peter of Aragon to the sovereignty of Charles the Fifth, requesting the reader to remember that this part of the story of the south is a history in itself, which alone would fill a great space, but that it is also an important part of that history of Italy which exists, indeed, in several hundred volumes written in all languages, but which unfortunately does not exist as a single book in one tongue.

The first result of the war of the Sicilian Vespers was that two sovereigns called themselves kings of Sicily, namely, those of the house of Aragon, who remained in possession, and those of the house of Anjou, who never recovered what Charles had lost. The kingdoms were therefore called the 'Two Sicilies,' the one being the island and the other the mainland, with Naples for its capital, and they continued to be so called even after they were finally united under Ferdinand the Catholic, who was the Second of Sicily, the Second of Aragon, the First of united Naples and Sicily, and the Third of Naples.

The next matter to be understood is that the kingdom of Sicily under the Aragonese kings was often given or left by them to their sons and brothers as a separate and independent monarchy. King Peter left it to his second son, James, who only became king of Aragon when his elder brother died, and he in turn gave Sicily to his younger brother Frederick, whose direct male descent failed, and whose great-granddaughter Mary married the heir of Aragon, who became Martin the First of Sicily, but died childless, leaving Sicily to his father, Martin the Second of Sicily. But the father had no other children, and at his death both Aragon and Sicily went to the son of Martin's sister, who had married King John of Castile, the Norman blood descending three her alone, as it had descended through Constance, Manfred's daughter, to all the house of Aragon and Castile, and to 'Mad Joan,' the elder sister of Katherine of Aragon, Henry the Eighth's unhappy queen; and by 'Mad Joan' it descended to Charles the Fifth and all the house of Austria.

Statue of Saint Urban at La Cava

This fragment of genealogy will serve to show how the kingdoms of the Two Sicilies became involved in the history of Europe, and how the succession to them became disputable, since the whole imperial house of Austria is descended from the same 'Mad Joan.' It is hard to imagine anything more confusing, for after her all the royal claimants were equally Hapsburgs, since they were all descended from her husband, Philip of Hapsburg, Archduke of Austria, the sole progenitor of the Austrian emperors and Spanish kings that came after him, and, by the marriage of Anne of Austria with Lewis the Thirteenth of France, the ancestor of all the Spanish and Neapolitan Bourbons, who are of the house of Austria only by the female side, their male progenitor having been Philip, the younger brother of the 'Second Dauphin,' and a grandson of Lewis the Fourteenth of France. After the conquest of Sicily by Peter of Aragon, and the establishment of the Angevin dynasty in Naples, the principal causes of disturbance lay in questions of succession, so far as Sicily was concerned, and, for Naples, in the relations of that kingdom with the Holy See, which were not by any means always friendly. The great Roman houses of Colonna and Orsini, whose history is so closely connected with that of the popes in the middle ages, fought across the borders of the kingdom of Naples, and more than once the Colonna took refuge in the south, while the Orsini lorded it in Rome; but sometimes also the Orsini got possession of great lands in the southern country, and their ancient arms are conceived over the doors of more than one old castle in the wild mountains of the Basilicata. To name one only, Muro was theirs, — the vast stronghold in which Joan the First at last paid for her many crimes with her life, a place which few have visited, but which gives a far better idea of the existence led by the barons of the fourteenth century than any castle I have examined.

Joan the First of Naples came to the throne in the year 1343, being at that time a beautiful girl sixteen years of age. She was the granddaughter of good King Robert, surnamed the Wise, who was himself the grandson of Charles of Anjou, and whose only son, Joan's father, died before him. She was already married to the young Andrew, brother of the king of Hungary, and it had been understood that when she succeeded to the throne her husband was to take the title of King of Naples; but when the coronation took place, the cardinal legate who performed the ceremony crowned Joan only, to the mortification and disappointment of Andrew and his many Hungarian courtiers. The latter were a cause of dissension between their master and the queen; they brought the manners and bearing of a half barbarous nation to a court that had at first astonished the south by its magnificence, and which had reached a high degree of civilization and outward refinement since the days of its first king. In strong contrast to these rough Hungarians, who were insolent when they were sober, and dangerous when they were drunk, Joan saw around her her numerous cousins of the Durazzo line, who all enjoyed the dignity of princes of the blood, and the chief of whom, Charles of Durazzo, had married Joan's younger sister Mary. It was natural, perhaps, that the queen's antipathy should increase daily; and it was equally natural, on the other hand, that Andrew should feel himself slighted and injured because he had not received the promised crown; and in the meanwhile the princes secretly plotted, each hoping to obtain it for himself. In those times it was almost inevitable that such a condition of things should end in a tragedy, and it was not long in coming.

In the year after Joan's coronation, Andrew's friends at Avignon succeeded in persuading Pope Clement the Sixth to consent to his coronation, and to give his consent a practical shape by ordering the ceremony to take place at once, and by sending a cardinal legate to Naples to perform it. The princes understood well enough that if Andrew were once crowned their own chances would be gone; Joan detested her husband, and let it be understood by Charles of Durazzo that she would be glad to be rid of him. Whether she actually suggested the murder or not, it is not easy to say; it is generally believed that she did, and she suffered for it in the end. It was clear to those who wished Andrew's death that it must take place quickly, and it is quite certain that Joan was well aware of the plot.

The chronicle of Este gives a full list of the conspirators, and describes the murder as follows, saying that in order to plan it they met together beforehand in a certain castle by the sea. They then came and told the queen that the deed could not be done in Naples, where Andrew was too well guarded, and the queen, whom the Latin chronicle rarely mentions without an epithet which I shall leave to the imagination of the reader, persuaded the king to go with her and spend the month of September in Aversa, inviting all the conspirators to accompany them. The conspirators there agreed with the two chamberlains that the latter should open the door to the king's chamber when they desired it; and the queen consented to these things, and on the appointed night they entered. Then Beltram, the son of a natural son of King Robert, and the principal conspirator, seized the king by the hair; but the king dragged himself back and said, 'This is a base jest.' Then Beltram tried to throw the king, but the king seized his hand between his teeth, and did not let go until he had bitten the whole piece out. But Beltram's companion slipped a noose round the king's throat, and the two together drew it and twisted it so that he died. Having done this, they thought of burying him in a stable; but as they were carrying his body down the stairs, they fancied that they heard some of the knights coming, and being afraid, they brought the body back to the hall above and took counsel how they should hide it. At last they threw it out of the window into the pleasure garden, and then each went to his own room. Now the nurse of the dead king, who had come with him from Hungary, and who always suspected that some harm would befall him through the princes who lived at the court, went into the king's room, and there she saw the queen sitting beside the bed, but she did not see the king. She inquired of the queen saying, 'Where is my master?' The queen answered, 'I know not where he is; thy master is far too young!' Then the nurse, perceiving that she was ill-disposed, left the room, taking a light to search for her master, and looking towards the pleasure garden, it seemed to her that she saw a miraculous light there, which was intended to reveal the crime. She saw the king himself lying upon the grass, and thinking him asleep she went back to the queen. 'My lady,' said she, 'the king sleeps in the garden.' The queen answered, 'Let him sleep.' But she knew that he was dead. The nurse, who loved him not a little, went into the garden and saw him dead on the grass, strangled by the noose, and with his boots on, of which one was white and the other red, and one of his leathern hose was embroidered with gold, but the other was black. In the king's mouth she found the piece of Beltram's hand which he had bitten out. Then the nurse began to weep most bitterly, and by the sound of her weeping the crime was known. So the queen and her friends mounted their horses and returned to Naples, and caused the king's body to be brought thither and buried by night.

Castel Nuovo, Naples

The chronicle of Este distinctly states that Charles, Duke of Durazzo, and the princes of Taranto, one of whom Joan afterwards married, were not among the conspirators, and that in the riot which took place on the next day, they led the people to the grave, and exhumed the body in order to be sure of the king's death, and then painted an image of him on a banner, with the noose round his neck, and besieged the queen and the murders, probably in the Castel Nuovo, which still overlooks the arsenal. Although they burned the doors and almost forced an entrance, they were driven back, and at last sent an embassy requesting the queen to give up the traitors. This she flatly refused to do, and the ambassadors remained shut up in the castle. But she, being young and badly frightened by the storm she had raised, at last consented to give up the conspirators with the exception of Beltram and his father; and the sea-gate of the castle was opened, and the conspirators were taken out and put on board of two galleys to be removed to the Castel dell' Uovo; but as the governor of the castle had no orders from the queen he refused to admit them, and they were shut up in Duke Charles's own prisons. Beltram and his father escaped to the castle of Sant' Agata, near the summit of the pass between Garigliano and Sparanisi, but the duke besieged them, took them alive, and brought them back to Naples, where they had the privilege of dying by poison, as being the son and grandson of King Robert. The other conspirators were tortured and hanged, and one of the ladies who had taken part was burned alive. The queen alone escaped, remaining in her castle all the time. The chronicle of Este speaks of Charles of Durazzo as if he had been quite innocent of Andrew's death, but Muratori says that he was believed to be the 'manipulator of this great iniquity.'

It is not to be supposed that any kingdom could hold together under such a sovereign as Joan the First, and her long life was spent in frantic efforts to keep her throne, and in attempting to counteract each crime she committed by one still more enormous. She could not save herself by allowing Charles of Durazzo to execute her husband's murderers, nor by marrying her cousin Luigi of Taranto, nor by obtaining a formal acquittal for herself in Rome. She was obliged to escape by night in a galley before the advance of the Hungarians, who were led to vengeance by their king, the murdered Andrew's brother, and she took refuge in her own Provence, where she was, nevertheless, confined like a captive, because the Pope distrusted her. The king took Aversa, and treated with the princes, and they dined at his table but after dinner, says the chronicle, the king made his men take their arms, as if he meant to ride over to Naples, and then he suddenly asked to see the passage whence his brother's body had been thrown. Standing there, he turned to Charles of Durazzo and accused him of the deed, and the Hungarian soldiers killed the duke where he stood, and threw his body into the garden: and the king sent the other princes to Hungary, where they were imprisoned. During nearly forty years Joan fought, intrigued, murdered, and fought again, adopted Lewis of Anjou for her successor, and perished miserably at last in Muro, by the order of another Charles of Durazzo, who at last got her kingdom and held it, and left it to his children. They died childless, the last being another Joan, called the Second, who adopted first one successor, Alfonso of Aragon, and then another, René of Anjou; and Alfonso took all, whereby the house of Aragon united the Two Sicilies under one crown.

Not long after the first Joan's death at Muro, the throne of Sicily was shaken by the mad attempt of Bernardo Cabrera, the old Count of Modica, to marry the widowed queen by force, and seize the kingship. Martin the First had died childless, and was succeeded by his father, while his widow, the young and beautiful Blanche of Navarre, became vicar and lieutenant of Sicily. Then the elder Martin died also, and for more than two years the throne remained vacant, until

Ferdinand the First, the son of Martin's sister, was crowned as the only legitimate successor. Meanwhile, six other claimants aspired to the crown, and the confusion was indescribable. Cabrera was not one of them, for he could boast of no royal blood; he was Count of Modica, Grand Justiciary of the Kingdom, and one of the greatest nobles in Sicily; but he had conceived a mad passion for Blanche, and he believed that by marrying her he could grasp the crown.

A parliament was held in Taormina, and certain propositions were formulated by the wisest men there; old Bernardo Cabrera opposed them all, claimed the right to ruled Sicily in virtue of his high office, and at once formed a party among the barons, ever anxious for change. He swore loudly that he did not mean to persecute the queen, who would not resign her lieutenantship of the kingdom, and that he meant to hold the country for the crown of Aragon; but he won over the captain of the queen's troops, and before long he besieged her in her castle at Catania. He sought an interview with her under a truce, and she, says the old Jesuit historian, Francesco Aprile, agreed to speak with him from the high poop of the galley, he standing below her on a bridge. In this ridiculous situation the count, 'intoxicated by his insane love and boundless ambition, implored the queen to marry him.' Then with a scornful smile, at once in surprise and complaint contempt, she answered only, 'Oh, you rotten old man!' Thereupon she turned away at once to Torres, to whom the galley belonged, and bade him put to sea; and she sailed away to Syracuse for greater safety. But Cabrera, furious at the insult, and more madly in love than ever, pursued her thither, and besieged her again in the old castle of the Marsetto on Ortygia, between the great and the small harbours. He battered the walls with siege engines, and in vain attempted to get in, and at last, in impotent rage, he pelted the stone walls with mud and garbage. She was at last rescued by John Moncada and Torres, who arrived in the latter's galley at night, and fell upon Cabrera so suddenly that the old man fought for his life in his white nightcap. Queen Blanche was conveyed on board the vessel during the fighting, and the galley set sail for Palermo.

Even there she was not safe. She lodged in the great Chiaramonte palace, now the palazzo dei Tribunali, and once the seat of the Inquisition. Cabrera landed at Trapani, and advanced stealthily through his own possessions by way of Alcamo, enjoining the utmost secrecy upon his vassals, and guarding all the passes and roads, lest any one should warn the queen of his approach. He rode out of Alcamo at midday, and reached Palermo at dead of night, when the whole city was sleeping. But, cautious though he was, the clanking of his men's armour in the street waked the queen. In her nightdress, her hair in wild confusion, she was covered rather by darkness than by any garments, says Aprile. Letting themselves out of the palace by a postern, she and her damsels fled at full speed along the shore, till they reached the old harbour, where Torres's galley was moored. Though it was January, the terrified women waded out as far as they could towards the vessel, and called out with tears, in desperate anxiety, till Torres himself was wakened by their cries, and sent a boat off to bring them on board. He instantly weighed anchor and sailed to the strong castle of Solunto, a few miles to the eastward of Palermo. He had saved the queen a third time with the same galley.

Cabrera entered the Chiaramonte palace a few minutes after the queen had escaped. Her bed was still warm when he entered her room. 'I have lost the partridge, but I have her nest!' he cried, as he threw himself upon the couch and furiously kissed the pillow where the queen's head had lately lain.

A fourth time he besieged her in Solunto, but she was not without friends, and they sent word to Cabrera that he must cease to persecute her, and they appeared in arms to enforce their message. One day, when the count was examining the trenches with which he had surrounded the castle, he was suddenly surrounded and taken by the queen's friends, and before long he found himself a close prisoner in the strong castle of Motta Santa Anastasia, which had been built by Count Roger in old times. He was locked up in a disused rain-water cistern, and he was no sooner installed than the rain, which fell heavily at that season, was turned in upon him. The guards pretended not to hear his cries, the water rose from his ankles to his knees, and from his knees to his waist, till his prison pallet was floating beside him in the dark; then at last the water was turned off, and the wretched Cabrera was dragged out and transferred to a noisome den of vermin in a high part of the castle. There he was constantly attended by a soldier, whom he attempted to win over, and to whom a thousand pieces of gold were actually paid by the count's friends. But the soldier had kept his master well informed, and when the count was allowed to escape, as he thought, by climbing down a strong rope hung from his window, he dropped into a net which had been previously arranged to catch him, and in which he remained exposed to the view and contemptuous jests of the whole garrison. He must have been glad that the beautiful Blanche of Navarre could not see him in such an undignified situation. When his enemies were weary of mocking him, he was taken back to his prison, and kept there until the election of Ferdinand the Just.

This event took place in the year 1412, and put an end at once to the dissensions that distracted Sicily and to the claims of the other six aspirants to the throne. It put an end also to the independence of the Sicilian kingdom, and henceforth the latter was ruled by viceroys until modern times, excepting during the short reign of Victor Amadeus of Savoy.

It was soon to be united with that of Naples, for Ferdinand's son, Alfonso the Magnanimous, claimed and held the inheritance left him by adoption by Queen Joan the Second, the last of the Angevins; and though at his death the kingdoms were divided between his son and his brother, they were before long to be permanently united under Ferdinand the Catholic, Alfonso's nephew.

Old Aprile says that when Sicily was united with Castile she was one of the fairest jewels set in the crown of Spain, and that the union was the special work of Divine Providence. With Ferdinand's conquest of the Moors and of Granada we have nothing to do, but the date of his final victory is that of a serious outbreak against the Jews in Sicily. As usual, the Hebrews were accused of having caught and crucified a Christian child on Good Friday; and the chronicle, to which those who please may lend credence, asserts that the deed was discovered because the body was thrown into a well of which the water was stained with blood, and that, by a miracle, the water rose suddenly and deluged the streets with a red stream. The natural consequence was a massacre of the Jews, and their synagogue was converted into a church. This was neither the first nor last time that such persecution took place in Sicily.

It was at this time that Charles the Eighth conceived the idea of seizing the kingdom of Naples, and his incessant wars in Italy, in which Gonzalvo de Cordova, who led the Spanish armies, earned the surname of the Great Captain, led directly to the treaty of Granada made in 1500 between King Ferdinand and Lewis the Twelfth of France, Charles's successor. By that agreement the two sovereigns allied themselves in order to take the kingdom of Naples from Frederick the Fourth, who was King Ferdinand's first cousin once removed. Ferdinand's chief ground for this act of spoliation was that the unfortunate King Frederick of Naples had invoked the help of the Turks against his enemies. It was agreed, therefore, that Ferdinand, who was already king of Sicily, should have Apulia and Calabria, and that Lewis the Twelfth should take Naples with its royal title, the latter being readily confirmed by Pope Alexander the Sixth, the too famous Borgia Pope. Gonzalvo de Cordova was at that time the vassal of King Frederick, and in order to escape the charge of treason he immediately renounced the territory of Monte Sant' Angelo in the kingdom of Naples. The success of the joint armies of Gonzalvo and the Duke of Nemours was all that either could desire, but it was impossible that their respective sovereigns should long remain in accord, and the captains soon quarrelled about the boundaries of the conquered provinces. The French having occupied Melfi, Gonzalvo de Cordova retorted by seizing places already taken for King Lewis, and he established himself in Barletta, and soon inflicted a defeat upon his enemies, taking prisoner the Duke of Nemours' colleague. It was at this time, in the year 1503, that the famous encounter took place known in history as the Sfida di Barletta, in which, on the thirteenth of February, thirteen Italian knights fought as many Frenchmen in tournament in the sight of both armies, and beat them.

The celebrated fight was brought about in the following manner. The account I give is taken from Zurita's 'Annals of Aragon,' and seems to be as accurate as any. It chanced that in a skirmish near Barletta a number of the French were taken prisoners, and among them was a certain knight, called de la Motte; and while he was captive, he began to boast that the French were better men than the Italians, whereupon a great discussion arose, and the Italian knights went to Gonzalvo de Cordova, begging him that they might have a chance of defending their national honour, which they considered that de la Motte had assailed. The result was that thirteen Italian knights, chief of whom was Ettore Fieramosca of Capua, met an equal number of French champions, on the understanding that each vanquished knight should pay one hundred ducats for his liberty, and lose his horse and arms. The Duke of Nemours could not or would not give surety that the lists should be undisturbed, but Gonzalvo replied that he would protect them, and marched out all his army, horse and foot, to a place five miles from Barletta and encamped there, between Andria and Corato. A monument marks the spot to-day.a For the Italians, Prospero Colonna appeared as second; the French chose for theirs the most honourable knight of any age, the famous Bayard; the judges marked out the ground, and the tournament began. It was a windy day and the gale was in the Italians' favour, as the parties rode at each other, first at a foot pace and then at a trot. Zurita says that they hardly broke into a canter as they met; nevertheless, all the lances were broken on both sides, but most of the French knights dropped the stumps of theirs. Not a horse was killed, not a knight was thrown, and they at once attacked each other with short arms, some using their axes, and some their swords, as they pleased. The French defended themselves stoutly, but the Italians fought so valiantly and with such perfect agreement among themselves, that in the space of one hour — not six, as some have said, — the French were driven across the line and therefore forced to surrender. One of their knights lay dead on the field, and one was severely wounded, but only one of the Italians was slightly hurt. The French champions were led back to Barletta by their victors with huge rejoicings, and the thirteen Italians supped at Gonzalvo de Cordova's own table.

The moral effect of such a victory was great, and the success was followed shortly by a more substantial one in the great battle of Cerignola, where the Duke of Nemours died of his wounds; and in the following year the last of the French were driven to take shelter in Gaeta, which more than once, and even in 1860, was the last refuge of those who had held Naples. The unfortunate King Frederick died of grief, and Ferdinand the Catholic was master of all southern Italy.

The early death of his only son had been regarded as a calamity by almost all civilized nations; but, if the young prince had lived, the greatest of all Spanish monarchs, Charles the Fifth, would never have reigned. He was Ferdinand's grandson by Joan the Mad, whose handsome husband, the heir of the Empire, died at the age of twenty-eight from drinking too much iced water after a game at ball, an excess to which Aprile gives the name of intemperance. The infant Charles, therefore, became the heir of the Empire as well as of Spain, the Low Countries, Southern Italy, and Sicily, besides all that had been discovered of America, and he was by far the greatest sovereign in the world. I may appropriately close this brief sketch of the southern successions by giving some account of the monarch whose strong hand has left its indelible impress upon Sicily and the mainland.

Charles was six years old when his father died, and his mother, it is said, was so distracted by her grief that she never recovered, but buried herself in the convent of Tordesillas, entirely shutting herself off from all human intercourse; and there she lived to old age, and died when the great emperor was in his fifty-sixth year. He was sixteen at the death of his grandfather Ferdinand, and his vast dominions were practically governed and held for him by the inexorable regent, Cardinal Ximenes, during the few months the latter still had to live; before long the young king stood alone and fought his own battles.

Some idea of the unsafe condition of Italy during that time may be formed from the fact that, in 1516, Pope Leo the Tenth was very nearly carried off a prisoner by Barbary pirates while spending a few days at Civita Lavinia, near Albano. The famous pirate Barbarossa, whom the Italian peasants still confound with the Emperor Frederick the First, was master of the seas and made raids upon the southern coast at his pleasure. Deserted villages, still standing in a maze of thorns and creepers, bear witness to his deeds, while the strong beacon towers built all round the coast, each in sight of the next, show what Charles the Fifth did to ward off such attacks. When he came to the throne, Italy was distracted by wars within and threatened by whole fleets of corsairs; the young Francis the First of France, mad with ambition and self-esteem, had inwardly resolved to take the south for himself, and Henry the Eighth of England was ready for any quarrel, with the Holy See, with France, or with the Empire, while his minister Wolsey laboured to keep the peace. There was room for a great king in such times, and Charles the Fifth won the battle of Mühlberg and reached the climax of his career after a reign of thirty-one years, in the very year in which Francis the First and Henry the Eighth breathed their last. He began life with a conception of his duties as emperor and his rights as king which belonged to the middle ages rather than to the Renascence; he considered that, while the seat of the Empire was in Germany, the reason for its existence lay in Italy, and that, as the arbiter and defender of the Christian faith, he must hold the position and wield the sceptre which had been Charlemagne's. The vastness of his possessions was a foundation upon which he had some right to build great hopes of such a universal monarchy. He was but twenty years of age when he was crowned emperor at Aix,° and he chose for his motto the words 'Plus oultre,' which may be interpreted to men that he began life with the intention of extending his dominions, his power, and his influence until the end. The principal adversary whom he found in his way was Francis the First, whose personal courage led him to believe that he could accomplish anything, while his unsuspicious vanity made him fancy that all men were his friends who were not his open enemies. Francis was sure of the support of Pope Leo the Tenth and of Henry the Eighth; the former, says the modern French historian, M. H. Gaillard, joined forces with the imperial army, united Parma and Piacenza with the States of the Church, and died of his joy over the achievement. Henry the Eighth lent Francis nothing but the offer of an arbitration, and in the following year allied himself with the emperor in an attack upon Picardy and Guyenne. To make matters worse, Charles, the Constable of Bourbon, betrayed Francis and treated with Henry the Eighth to divide France with the latter. The plot was betrayed to the king, but his position was already most desperate, and, though he repulsed the English in Picardy, and their vanguard only •eleven leagues from Paris, and although he repelled the attack of the Spaniards in Navarre, he was obliged to retreat on the Italian side of his dominions with the loss of the incomparable Chevalier Bayard, and was unable to check the constable's career. The latter renewed and strengthened his relations with Henry the Eighth, and besieged Marseilles, whence he was driven with difficulty by the emperor's general, the Marquis of Pescara, the husband of the celebrated Vittoria Colonna; but it was impossible to keep the imperial army together in the face of the hostile population, and Francis again penetrated into Italy to renew his efforts at conquest. Charles the Fifth, however, was not so easily beaten; the remnants of his army took possession of Pavia and other strong places, while his captains reorganized their men. In the decisive and famous battle of Pavia the reckless young king was completely defeated and taken prisoner, and was carried away to a memorable captivity in Madrid, where Charles at first refused to see him, and shut him up in a dismal prison, in which there was but one window. The position hitherto occupied by France in European politics was gone, but the emperor had not yet won Italy. The French, in alliance with the Venetians under the command of Andrea Doria, commanded the Mediterranean, and the new pope, Clement the Seventh, taking the side of France, let loose upon Italy the 'Black Bands' of Giovanni de' Medici. But the emperor was always slow in his movements, and after his liberation from Madrid Francis was less ardent for fight. The situation, which might have lasted a long time, was unexpectedly changed by the temerity of the constable. With no hope of a reconciliation with Francis, and well knowing that he could not expect a crown from Charles the Fifth, he resolved to carve out a kingdom for himself, allied himself with the Lutheran captain, Froudsberg, and after seizing Milan marched southwards upon Rome. He was killed in the assault upon the city, but his troops avenged his death in the fearful sack of Rome, of which the whole blame was afterwards laid upon Charles the Fifth. Roused at last, the emperor put forth all his strength. Before long the French were completely driven out of Italy, Charles the Fifth was crowned at Bologna by the Pope who had lately been his enemy, and the latter was rewarded by the reëstablishment of his kindred, the Medici, in Florence. The emperor now turned against the Turks in a war which was dignified by the name of a crusade, a Spanish army landed at Goletta, and Tunis opened its gates after a month's siege. Francis naturally took advantage of this war to renew his attack upon Italy, and easily took possession of Piedmont; furthermore, he announced his intention of conquering Flanders. By the treaty of Cambrai he had lost the suzerainty of the latter province, but he now had the assurance to summon 'Charles of Austria, his vassal,' to appear before him in Parliament, and on the emperor's non-appearance solemnly confiscated his territories for treason.

The conquest of Tunis had produced few results; Barbarossa and his pirate squadrons were still the terror of the Mediterranean, and Francis did not hesitate to ally himself with an infidel corsair in the hope of at last gaining some permanent advantage against the emperor. At the same time Francis had some success in Italy. Henry the Eighth, however, and the Protestant princes of Europe allied themselves with Charles against a fellow-sovereign who had called Moslems to his aid. Henry the Eighth besieged Boulogne and Montreuil, the emperor found himself marched across France, and the end was a treaty which the French king might look upon as a reconciliation, but which finally established the supremacy of Charles. Henry had taken Boulogne, for which he demanded a large ransom; Francis was forced to sign a treaty, or reconciliation, with him also, and died soon afterwards, worn out by the fatigues, emotions, and disappointments of his unhappy career.

This, in a few words and so far as the possession of Italy is concerned, is the history of the memorable struggle between Charles the Fifth and Francis the First which contributed so large an element to the general disturbance of Europe at that time. Throughout it all, we see the great emperor, always calm and self-reliant, delaying rather than hesitating, and always examining his own policy beforehand with cool judgment, never surprised, never at a loss, never swerving from his original conception of the Holy Roman Empire, moderate in victory, patient under defeat, and in almost every way the model that a strong sovereign should imitate. He found the south distracted by parties, riddled by conspiracies, and disturbed by popular revolutions. When he came to the throne Naples and Sicily were looked upon by more than one sovereign of Europe as a possible prey, to be fought for on the mere chance of a conquest. When he died they were the possessions of the house of Austria, and they remained so even when the succession to the crown of Spain became an object of contention on the failure of the direct line in 1700, and when thirty years later the Bourbons of Spain drove out their Austrian cousins. It is as impossible to imagine Sicily without Charles the Fifth, as it is to think of it without King Roger, and in the present condition of the country the monuments of the Austrian far outnumber those left by the Norman. From thousands of churches, castles, and palaces all over the country the huge stone shield that bears the quartered arms of Spain and Austria, with the imperial eagle, proclaims the lordship of Charles's successors; and there is perhaps not in all Sicily one church that is not the last resting-place of some great Spanish noble. From Charles's time the architecture of the south lost all its independence and originality, and the art of the Renascence, after overspreading the nobler works of the Norman and the Saracen, brought in its train the barbaric horrors of the late 'Barocco.' The exquisite church in which Peter of Aragon was elected by the Sicilian barons was lined with gaudy panels of coloured marbles, plastered with hideous scrolls, and adorned with obese cherubs that are not indecent only because they are impossible. The noble cathedral was degraded by the superimposition of an Italian dome, as inappropriate to its architecture as a Chinese pagoda upon Mount Sinai, and few other buildings of beauty escaped the triumphant and destroying march of corrupted taste. It is only in very recent times that some individuals have tried to reconstruct on a smaller scale the dwellings of the Saracen-Norman times, and the result is so pleasing as to make one wish that the Italians of the mainland would follow the example set by Sicilians, instead of constantly inventing new shapes of terror.

This same debasement of style in the south is witness, however, to the aggrandizement of Spain under Charles's successors. The Renascence was spontaneous in Florence and natural in Rome, but in south it was imposed by force. Venice, Lombardy, Tuscany, and Rome never submitted so long to entirely foreign domination as Naples and Sicily did, and have therefore retained something distinctly individual in their art. It is unjust to say that the south submitted because it was weaker, morally and physically, than the north; the south was better worth winning and holding, and greater armies came against it, led by greater men, from Augustus to Roger the Great Count, and from Henry the Sixth to Gonzalvo de Cordova. While the north was divided into many small states, the south was held together in a single kingdom by the strong hands of Spanish kings, and the vastness of the Spanish domination made revolt seem impossible. Even when the south was separated from Spain, the Spanish Bourbons were its kings, and the people still felt that in some way they belonged to the greater kingdom of the West, while their rulers ruled them in the same old way, and while the court still derived its elaborate manners, its corrupt customs, and its execrable taste from the mouldering remnants of what Charles the Fifth had made.

Cloister of the Moorish castle at Ravello, near Amalfi

It is all changed now, and the new influence is almost wholly commercial; but in Sicily the seed of a civilization has remained which may not be blasted by progress. There are men who are filled with a tender and discerning love for the beautiful that lies so near the surface, and their counsels are often followed; the frightful incrustations of Barocco ornament are being carefully removed from the Martorana, the noble Norman altar rail and fragments of mosaic have been unearthed from the cellars where they lay for centuries and have been carefully restored, and the original church once more appears in its true beauty. In the Palazzo dei Tribunali, whence Blanche of Navarre escaped from Cabrera on that winter's night long ago, windows of matchless grace have been found and once more opened, the light of day again falls through long-hidden traceries of stone, and the grand carved ceilings, rich with all the heraldry of knightly times, have been again uncovered. No modern hand has rudely changed the outline of the Zisa palace, and the worst of the Spanish ornaments have been effaced in the great hall of the bath, where the water still fills the little tanks in the marble floor. Everywhere throughout Sicily the artistic feeling is conservative and good, while on the mainland things go from bad to worse; and it is only here and there, as at Ravello, the lovely Moorish castle above Amalfi, that an alien hand had arrested decay and warded off improvement. In the later development of things, the mainland has not yet lost its Spanish character; but Sicily's native strength is beginning to show itself again, and if there is a resurrection in store for Italian architecture and Italian art, I venture to say that it will begin in Palermo or some Sicilian city, and not in Florence, which has become a manufactory of pretty facsimiles, nor in Rome, where art is given over to foreigners and architecture to contractors; and if any such renewal of life is to come, I think it will proceed from Saracen or Norman beginnings, and not from anything left by Charles the Fifth and the Spanish kings.

First court of the museum, Palermo

Conclusion: The Mafia

The world at large knows little of modern Sicily, but that little generally includes a word of recent origin which is closely associated with the island in the public mind, but to which no meaning is attached that is even approximately true. The word is 'Mafia.' There is another which belongs to Naples, 'Camorra,' and which is better understood because it is more easily explained, and because the thing it means is more direct in its results. Both words are of doubtful origin. Camorra means an association of persons, having for its object an illicit control of any lawful or unlawful trade, obtained by forcibly excluding other people from taking part in it. In the broad sense it means the vast organization of thieves, high and low, by which daily life in Naples is controlled, by which the city is swayed in political matters, and with the existence of which the Italian government is obliged to reckon. The social effects of the Camorra do not extend much beyond the limits of the city; politically, the whole province is affected by it. In private life, it means that all who have acted in such a way as to be considered members of the Camorra are quite safe from depredation, so that if anything is stolen from them by mistake it is at once returned; it means also that whoever is willing to help the Camorra in its ends will be helped by it. It has no regular organization, no place of meeting, no elected officers; it is everywhere and it is nowhere; its members recognize each other by their conduct rather than by signs or words, and the commands of its chiefs are given verbally and transmitted in like manner. It might be described as a society for preserving a monopoly in stealing and illicit trades, were it not that many apparently respectable officials, men of business, and tradespeople protect it, or are under its protection. So far as it can be said to be organized at all, it manages itself by a sort of natural hierarchy and affiliation; the officers of each grade are self-created, and depend on force of character for the power they exercise. It might be called a system of bullying, in which every ringleader who can impose himself upon his companions is in turn forcibly controlled by one of higher standing than himself, who again is subject to others, and so on, from the street boy who gets a living by selling the stumps of cigars, to the high official and perhaps to the member of Parliament. The real end and object of the Camorra is, I think, always profit, gained by any means, good or bad. It constrains all pickpockets, thieves, and burglars in the city to render an account of their robberies of their superiors, on pain of being at once handed over to justice; and there is no city in the world in which it is so easy to recover stolen goods, provided that application be made in the right quarter. A part of its regular practice consists of robbing all foreigners, p365both directly, when possible, and in indirectly by extortion.

The Mafia differs from the Camorra in almost every respect, and whereas the latter is based on criminal practices, the former had its foundation in lawless principles. In attempting to give some account of the power which dominates a great part of Sicily at the present time, I shall follow the interesting work of Signor Antonio Cutrera, chief of police in Palermo, published in the present year 1900, and which may be taken as a thoroughly truthful account of the present state of things by one who has spent years in a hand-to-hand fight with the evil.

Setting aside the possible ancient origin of the Mafia, its present development seems due to the great corruption which existed under the Bourbons, and especially in the police of that time, the consequence of which was a general tendency on the part of Sicilians to do justice for themselves. One of the principal functions of the Mafia is, indeed, to decide differences and dispense justice without appealing or submitting to the decision of a tribunal; and this is clearly the result a condition of things in which such an appeal was either useless or too expensive for persons of ordinary means.

Another principal element is the Sicilian character itself, which is bold, but extremely reticent, and is deeply imbued with a peculiar sense of honour for which the Sicilian language has a term of its own in the word 'Omertà.' According to this code, a man who appeals to the law against his fellow-man is not only a fool but a coward, and he who cannot take care of himself without the protection of the police is both. Evidently a profound contempt for the law is at the root of this principle, and the law is of course represented in the eyes of the people by the police and the tribunals. It is, therefore, logical that every Sicilian should do his utmost to hamper and impede the actions of both, and it is reckoned as cowardly to betray an offender to justice, even though the offence be against oneself, as it would be not to avenge an injury by violence. It is regarded as dastardly and contemptible in a wounded man to betray the name of his assailant, because if he recovers he must naturally expect to take vengeance himself. A rhymed Sicilian proverb sums up this principle, the supposed speaker being one who has been stabbed. 'If I live, I will kill thee,' it says; 'if I die, I forgive thee.'

The obligation to conceal the name of the assassin or other offender extends to all those who chance to be witnesses of the crime, and it is even considered to be their duty to hide the criminal from the police if he is pursued. The code requires an innocent man to go to penal servitude for another rather than betray the culprit, and Signor Cutrera, who should know, if any one does, states that cases are not rare in which Sicilians, though innocent, have undergone long terms of imprisonment and have even died in prison, rather than give information to the police. The Mafia would brand with 'infamy' a man who should do otherwise, and this principle makes it almost impossible to bring into court witnesses for the conviction of a Mafiuso. With regard to the injured person, the obligation of silence is the same, although the possibility of vengeance may be infinitely removed. As has been said, the derivation of the word Mafia is unknown. The word itself, in the Sicilian dialect, means the ideally perfect, and a beautiful girl, for instance, would be called 'Mafiusa,' simply on account of her looks. The word is even applied by hawkers to their wares. It was first used in its present sense by the author of a famous play, 'I Mafiusi di la Vicaria,' which was produced in 1863 and ran many nights, and which has been translated from Sicilian into Italian and has been given all over Italy. From that time the west was adopted into the Italian language to designate an uncertain combination of brigandage, 'Camorra,' and general criminality. It is not the first time that a book or a play has given a name to something which had none, and which is ill defined by it. In Sicily the word now means a condition produced by two factors only, a long reign of violence on the one hand, and that mistaken sense of honour on the other, which has been already explained.

We next come to the consideration of the results produced by this state of things, and these of course vary according to the class to which the delinquents belong, from the lowest upwards. Signor Cutrera correctly describes the appearance of a low Mafiuso of Palermo. He wears his hat upon the left side, his hair smoothed with plentiful pomatum and one lock brushed down upon his forehead, he walks with a swinging motion of the hips, a cigar in his mouth, a heavy knotted stick in his hand, and he is frequently armed with a long knife or a revolver. He stares disdainfully at every man he meets with the air of challenging each comer to speak to him if he dare. To any one who knows Palermo, this type of the lower class is familiar. He is the common 'Ricottaro,' a word which I will not translate, but which broadly indicates that the young man derives his means of support from some unfortunate woman who is in his power. It is a deplorable fact that the same mode of existence is followed by young men of the middle classes, whose plentiful leisure hours are spent in play, and who have constituted themselves the official 'claque' of the theatres, imposing themselves upon the managers as a compact body. Moreover, during elections, they can be of the utmost assistance to candidates, owing to their perfect solidarity. With the most atrocious vices, they possess the hereditary courage of the Sicilian, and will face steel or bullets with the coolness of trained soldiers; and though they will insult and even beat their women when in the humour, they will draw the knife for the least disparaging word spoken against what they regard as their property. The writer I am following observes that a considerable number of these young men end in the dissecting room or in prison, but that others mend their ways when they are thirty years of age and turn into a higher species of their kind, which may be called the real Mafiusi.

The Mafia divides itself everywhere and naturally into two parts, the one existing in Palermo and the large cities, and the other without the walls and through the open country.

The full-blown Mafiuso in the city differs from the common Ricottaro in that he works secretly and by means of moral pressure, whereas the Ricottaro boldly kills his enemy or is killed by him, without the least attempt at concealment. Statistics show that in the city of Palermo, from 1893 to 1899, both inclusive, there have been eighteen murders, twenty-eight attempts at murder, and eighty-nine stabbings, all the work of the Ricottari.

A man's position in the proper Mafia is the result of his personal influence, which derives in the first place from his reputation as a man of so-called honour, and which is afterwards increased to any extent by force of circumstances, until he becomes a 'Capo-mafia,' and one of the acknowledged chiefs. His prestige is then such that his fellow-citizens appeal to him to settle their differences, both in matters of business and interest and in questions of 'honour'; his house becomes the resort of all those who have difficulties to decide or who need the help of the 'friends,' as the Mafiusi commonly call each other. Nor are the Mafiusi the only persons who invoke the help of the Capo-mafia; strangers and even foreigners appeal to him, and as his prestige is increased in proportion to the gratitude he earns, he will take the greatest possible trouble to oblige any one who come to him for advice or assistance; and while the Mafia, as a whole, blocks the way for the law at every step, it makes itself indispensable to those who need redress and despair of getting it by legal process. We cannot call the means used by the Mafia lawful nor moral, but the scrupulous exactness with which a Capo-mafia keeps his word, and the general fairness with which he decides the cases that come before him, though he have not the smallest right to decide them, inspires great confidence in his clients and creates the sort of moral despotism on which the Mafia depends for its existence. Furthermore, the Capo-mafia may be a lawyer, and a member of the municipal or even the provincial council, or a cabinet minister, rising to the moral control of the whole society simply by his prestige and predominant will, but never by any sort of election or machinery, since the Mafia has none. Long before that he has become a rich man, because it would be practically impossible to make a contract for any public work, or to carry it out, without his intervention. Thus the vast system of patronage narrows naturally to a few chief patrons, who are of course intimately associated and who sometimes obey one head. The Mafia disposes of men of all conditions and all professions, and they are bound to it by no promises of secrecy nor oaths of obedience, but by interest and necessity on the one hand, and the strong Sicilian sense of 'honour' on the other; they are protected by it, for it can annihilate its isolated enemies, and even in criminal cases it is almost impossible to convict a Mafiuso, in the total absence of witnesses against him, so that a wise judge will generally adjourn such a case until he can find some excuse for sending it to be tried in a court on the mainland.

Old houses at Pizzo, Calabria, where Murat, King of Naples, was executed in 1815

The Mafia acknowledges no allegiance to any political party, but when it nominates a candidate his election is generally a foregone conclusion, and the successful contestant is greeted by a popular ovation. It is hard to see how a constitutional government could successfully oppose such a system. Thoughtful persons will see what Signor Cutrera has not seen, namely, that it is a complete and highly efficient form of self-government, which exists, and will continue to exist, in defiance of the constitutional monarchy under which it is supposed to live. An ancient tyrant would have destroyed it by the brutal process of massacring half the population and transplanting the rest to the mainland, but no civilized method of producing the same result seems to have occurred to statesmen. The Bourbons employed the Mafia to keep order, the present government tolerates it because it cannot be crushed; when the Mafia joined Garibaldi, the Bourbons fell, and it remains to be seen what will happen in the south when the Mafia turns against the monarchy it has called in. It is to be hoped that such a catastrophe is far removed from present possibility, and it is at least a somewhat reassuring fact that the Mafia is the very reverse of anarchic, or even socialistic; it is, indeed, one of the most highly conservative systems in the world.

Its tyranny is more outwardly visible in the country, and particularly in the rich lands that surround Palermo, than in Palermo itself, or in the other cities most infected by it. One reason of this is the great development in the cultivation of oranges and lemons during this century. The crops are relatively very valuable, and are especially tempting to thieves because immediately marketable and easily carried off; the lands are cut up into innumerable small holdings, and, without patrolling every orange grove with soldiers, which is impossible, the authorities could not possibly prevent the depredations of the fruit-stealers. The Mafia affords all who appeal to it the most thorough protection, and its despotism over the orange-growing regions is absolute; for, in return for such great advantages, landholders, whether owners or tenants, are only too glad to serve it at need and to abstain from all recourse to law.

In the first place, every landholder is obliged to maintain a 'guardiano' or watchman, in addition to the men he employs upon his land. There are, therefore, several thousands of these watchmen in the orange groves of the Golden Shell alone, and they are without exception Mafiusi, since they have the monopoly of their business and can altogether prevent the employment of strangers in their occupation. The landholder who attempts to oppose the monopoly will lose his whole crop in a night, and, if he persists, his life is not worth a year's purchase. Among the watchmen and their employers, who are often bound to them by the strongest ties of friendship as well as of interest, there are always some whose influence controls the rest, men who have killed their man in a question of 'honour' and who have shown themselves on many occasions to be thorough Mafiusi. They therefore become the Capi-mafia of the district, and they are always in communication with the Capi-mafia of the city, and thereby affiliated to the great system of patronage. All differences which the Capo-mafia in the country is not competent to decide are thus referred to the patron in the city, from whose decision there is no appeal. Any one, whether a Mafiuso or not, who refuses to obey that verdict, is killed without mercy and generally without delay, unless he can escape from the country in time. The shot is fired from behind a wall, or in a shady grove at dusk and in the total absence of witnesses the most scrupulous inquiry very rarely even leads to an arrest, and never to a conviction. It is not a fight, but an execution, approved by all the thousands of landholders and their watchmen, who manage their affairs and govern themselves in this way. It may be that the Capo-mafia's decision was perfectly fair; in any case the man knew what he risked in disobeying it, and his friends are not surprised at his death, nor do they seek to avenge it.

On the rare occasions when a Mafiuso is arrested, his friends and relatives appeal to their Capo-mafia in Palermo, and he at once institutes a most scrupulous inquiry into the man's antecedents. If it is found that the prisoner has throughout his life strictly obeyed the principles and the commands of the society, its vast machinery is instantly set in motion to secure his release or acquittal, money is spent unsparingly, though the accused be penniless, scores and sometimes hundreds of witnesses are suborned, the most eminent lawyers are secured for the defence, and the strongest arguments appear in the man's favour in the most accredited newspapers. The man is of course proved innocent, and the verdict is received with a chorus of popular approbation. If, on the other hand, the inquiry shows that the man has once failed in his duties as a Mafiuso, the Capo-mafia refuses all help, and a witness will dare to appear in his favour, and he is dealt with by the law without opposition. A stranger might think that the law has triumphed in such a case, but it has not; it has executed a verdict already given by the Mafia.

The Mafia in the country is more completely organized than that of the city, which is natural where a large body of men are employed in the same business, as watchmen of the fruit-crops. The country Capo-mafia has the privilege of disposing of all the watchmen's places in his district, the landholders or tenants pay him for his patronage, they accept the watchmen he gives them, and the terror of his name is a sufficient surety of the safety of their oranges. If they were robbed, his reputation would be endangered; if some inexperienced thief is foolish enough to attempt it, he is certain to be caught and severely beaten.

The place where Murat was shot in the castle at Pizzo

It is the business of the country Capo-mafia to make demands upon rich landholders for sums of money, when funds are needed by the Mafiusi of his district, and here lies the connecting link between the more or less innocuous Mafia and the brigandage which is the curse of Sicily. A Mafiuso, great or small, pays at once what is demanded of him for the common good; but there are many large landholders in the country who believe themselves strong enough to be independent of the Mafia, protecting their crops from thieves with a small force of armed men, and maintaining constant relations with the government's force of carbineers.

Castle at Pizzo, with the window of Murat's prison

Two hundred and nineteen letters demanding money have fallen into the hands of the police of Palermo within seven years. Signor Cutrera publishes some of these in his valuable work. Several are dated, and most of them 'Dear Sir,' or 'Dear Friend,' while they all conclude by threatening the life of the person addressed, and often the lives of all his family. The place to which the money, sometimes as much as ten thousand francs, is to be taken is always indicated with extreme clearness, and in several cases, the name of the person who is to bring it is given, and that person is generally some one in the victim's employment.

These instances, made public with a great quantity of corroboratory evidence by a chief officer of the Sicilian police, should be enough to explain the nature of the despotism exercised by the Mafia. From threatening letters to highway robbery there is but a step. Upon the road that leads from Palermo to Misilmeri there is a hamlet called Portella di Mare, which is famous for the number of attacks made upon travellers. In the whole province of Palermo the statistics show that there were one thousand and ninety-two highway robberies between the years 1893 and 1899 inclusive. When it is considered that no country in the world is so thoroughly patrolled by an efficient and courageous police, such figures show the magnitude of the difficulty with which the authorities have to contend. A further consideration of the subject would lead too far, but with regard to brigandage in Sicily it should be distinctly understood that it does not form a part of the system called the Mafia, but is often closely connected with it by the bond of common interest.

The principal reason why brigandage continues to exist is that the outlaws make themselves useful to certain great landholders, who, in return, protect the malefactors from the police. It may even be known that a whole band — supposing it to be travelling together, which rarely happens — may be concealed in the house of a rich man, and that the police may be cognizant of the fact. In order to search the house, the commander of the detachment must produce a judicial warrant authorizing him to do so. The little squad of carbineers and soldiers of the line have very probably tracked the bandits for several days through a wild and dangerous country, not having the slightest idea where they might next take refuge. It would be manifestly impossible to issue a general warrant authorizing the police to search any house in the country, for this would be regarded as an act of tyranny, and the Mafia would probably retort by bringing on a general revolution throughout the island. If the officer commanding the pursuing party sends back to his chief, therefore, for the necessary authority, the bandits, well informed of their pursuers' movements, have plenty of time to escape to another hiding-place; and if the officer at last receives the warrant, uses it, and finds no brigands in the house, the proprietor makes complaint to the heads of the Mafia, who have innumerable weapons at their command with which to make the action of the police publicly ridiculous. But if the officer, being quite sure that the brigands are in the house, takes upon himself the responsibility of searching it without a warrant, and if, as will very probably happen, the whole band escapes through a subterranean passage, such as may be found in many Sicilian houses, he is liable to an action at law, in the course of which the Mafia will spends hundreds of thousands of francs and put out its whole strength to destroy him. If by any possibility he escapes being dismissed from the service for having overstepped his authority, his only chance of life is to leave the island secretly and at once. As for a proprietor who refuses to receive the brigands or to offer them the best he has so long as they are pleased to prolong their visit, neither his property nor his life will ever be safe from that day. His crops will be burned, his orange and lemon trees hacked to pieces, his vines torn up by the roots; and if he is the possessor of great herds of cattle or flocks of sheep, the professional cattle lifters who abound in Sicily will mark him for their prey, knowing that neither the Mafia nor any band of outlaws will raise a finger to protect him. By twos and threes his cows and his oxen will disappear; with a skill that would do honour to Texas the brands on the animals will be converted into new and different ones, and before long the stolen property will be sold at a cattle fair a hundred miles away. If at the end of a year the unhappy victim is alive, he is wholly ruined, but it is far more probable that a bullet will have ended his troubles long before that time. To bring about such dire results, it is not even necessary that he should have shut his doors against the outlaws; he may receive them, entertain them, and thank them for the honour of their visit, as is customary in such cases, but if he should afterwards give the least clew to their movements, he is a doomed man as surely as if he had refused to receive them. I repeat that bandits are not necessarily Mafiusi, but in the great majority of cases they have been 'friends' before taking to the woods; and though the higher Mafia may disapprove of their proceedings, it is rarely unwilling to make exhibition of its vast power and of its contempt of the law by affording them its protection. The Mafiusi may occasionally quarrel among themselves and blood may be shed in encounters that are regarded as honourable, for it is only a man condemned by the society who is murdered without a chance for his life; the society will never interfere in the settlement of questions of so-called honour, whereas it acts as a tribunal for all disagreements which would be settled by law in a civilized country. But, owing to the strong peculiarities of the Sicilian character, violent disputes between the 'friends' are extremely rare, and the solidarity of the whole society might be an example to associations formed with a better object.

It would be unjust to Italy to leave such a subject without making two important statements. In the first place, it is quite wrong to suppose that foreigners visiting Sicily and having no interests in the island are exposed to any danger from the Mafia or from any organized band of brigands, and with ordinary precautions, if the traveller is willing to avoid a few dangerous localities, he will not be more exposed to the attacks of common thieves than in many other countries. He may go with safety where a Sicilian nobleman or a landholder hostile to the illicit powers would need the protection of a dozen mounted carbineers, and this well-known fact has been proved true in hundreds of cases. Foreigners who have been taken by brigands in Sicily and held for ransom have invariably possessed some vested interest in the country. This may be accepted as positively certain.

Secondly, as I have already said, the Camorra of Naples does not extend beyond the suburbs of the city. The southern mainland from Naples to the straits is one of the safest tracts of country in the world; it has produced no society even faintly approaching the Mafia, brigandage has been totally stamped out by the Italian government, and the entire absence of travellers who might be robbed is a sufficient reason why the evil should not break out again. The southern mountains are wild and desolate beyond description, the southern plains are lonely and thinly populated, the poverty of the lower classes everywhere is painful to see; but the country is safe from end to end, and the student, the artist, or the idler may traverse it in all directions, alone or in company, on foot or on horseback, without incurring the slightest risk. It is due to the honourable and untiring efforts of the present government to state this very clearly, and if the power which has accomplished so much on the mainland is unable to make headway against the Mafia in Sicily, the reason is that the Mafia is not an organized and tangible body which could be called to account for its actions, but is the inevitable result of many combined circumstances, involving national character, national traditions, and certain especial conditions of agriculture and wealth, none of which exist together anywhere else in the world.

My task is ended. If the curiosity of my readers is unsatisfied, let them visit the south and seek out for themselves those things which they desire to know; if they are disappointed with the story of twenty centuries, as I have told it, let them look into the fathomless archives of southern history and read in half a dozen languages and dialects the thousand tales which I have left untold. In either case, I shall not have laboured in vain. If any, after reading this book, are tempted to wander through some of the most beautiful and memorable places in the world, or if any, desiring more knowledge, are impelled to pursue the study of classic history or the romantic chronicles of Norman times, I am more than repaid for having attempted what is perhaps impossible.

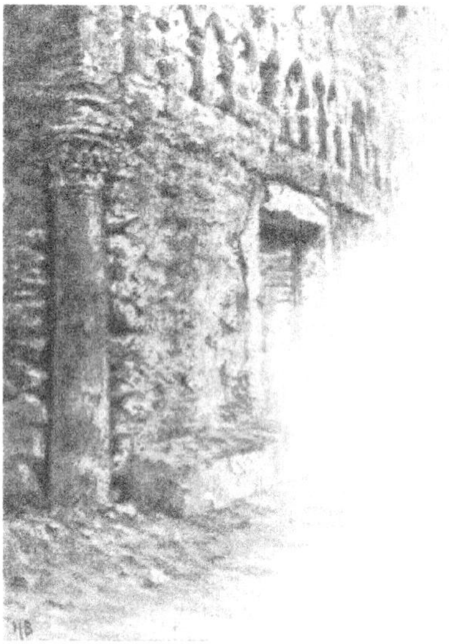

Chronology of Events
Volume I

1200 (about)	Farming developed by the Sicelians.
800 (about)	Cumae founded by the Greeks.
735	Naxos founded by the Chalcidians.
734	Syracuse founded by the Corinthians.
721	Sybaris founded by the Achaeans.
715	Crotona founded by the Achaeans.
708	Tarentum founded by Spartans, called Partheniae.
700 (about)	Catania, Leontini, and Zancle founded by Chalcidians and Ionians.
700 (about)	Megara Hyblaea founded by the Dorians.
700 (about)	Rhegium founded by the Messenians.
700 (about)	Metapontum, Poseidonia, and Terina founded by the Achaeans.
700 (about)	Selinus founded by Dorians from Megara.
690	Gela founded by Dorians from Rhodes.
648	Himera founded by Ionians.
580	Akragas founded by Dorians.
570 (about)	Pythagoras born at Samos.
485	Gelon becomes tyrant of Syracuse.
480	Hamilcar of Carthage besieges Himera.
478	Hiero succeeds Gelon as tyrant of Syracuse.
473	Pindar visits the court of Hiero.
468	Death of Hiero and accession of Thrasybulus.
467	Simonides dies at Syracuse.
465	Syracuse, Akragas, etc., become independent commonwealths.
461	Ducetius heads a rising of Sicelians.
456	Aeschylus dies at Gela.
415	Athenian expedition against Syracuse, led by Nicias, Alcibiades, and Lamachus.
413	The Syracusans, led by Gylippus the Spartan, defeat the Athenians.
409	The Carthaginians, led by the second Hannibal, take Selinus and Himera.
406	Hermocrates returns from exile, and is killed at Syracuse.
406	Hannibal dies of the plague, and Akragas surrenders to his father Himilcon.
405	Dionysius becomes tyrant of Syracuse.
397	Dionysius declares war against Carthage.
395	Dionysius defeats the Carthaginians and destroys their fleet.
367	Death of Dionysius, and accession of his son, Dionysius II.
356	Dionysius II dethroned by his brother-in-law, Dion.
353	Dion assassinated by Callippus.
346	Second tyranny of Dionysius II.
343	Timoleon deposes Dionysius II and interrupts the tyranny.

339	Timoleon defeats the Carthaginians.
337	Death of Timoleon.
317	Agathocles makes himself tyrant.
289	Death of Agathocles.
287	Archimedes born.
278	Pyrrhus, called in by the Syracusans, defeats the Carthaginians.
276	Pyrrhus leaves Sicily.
270	Hiero II made king of Syracuse.
270 (about)	Theocritus is at the court of Hiero.
265	The Mamertines appeal from Messina to Rome for aid.
264	First Punic war begins, called in Rome "the Sicilian war."
262	The Romans besiege Akragas, thenceforth known as Agrigentum.
260	First Roman fleet built.
255	The Romans, led by Regulus, are totally defeated by the Carthaginians.
254	The Romans take Drepanon, thenceforth known as Drepanum.
253	The Romans lose a fleet.
242	The Romans take Lilybaeum.
215	Hiero II dies, and is succeeded by his grandson, Hieronymus.
213	The Romans massacre the inhabitants of Henna.
212	Syracuse taken by Marcellus.
212	Archimedes slain by a common soldier after the fall of Syracuse.
210	The Romans take Agrigentum, and Sicily becomes a Roman province.
202	Scipio of Africa assembles his fleet at Lilybaeum before the battle of Zama.
139	Sicilian slaves revolt against the Romans.
132	Publius Rupilius, the consul, puts down the first servile insurrection.
104	Insurrection in Campania led by the knight Vettius.
99	Manlius Aquillius, the consul, finally crushes out the servile revolts.
79	Cicero is quaestor in Sicily.
73	Verres obtains the propraetorship of Sicily by lot.
70	Verres is tried in Rome, and retires to Marseilles.
47	Julius Caesar assembles his fleet at Lilybaeum for his African campaign.
43	Sextus Pompeius becomes master of all Sicily.
39	Treaty between Sextus Pompeius, Octavian, and Mark Antony signed at Baiae.
36	Sextus Pompeius expelled by Octavian.
21	Augustus, formerly Octavian, visits Sicily.
A.D.	
40	Saint Pancras, first bishop of Sicily, said to have been ordained by Saint Peter.
126	Hadrian visits Sicily.
164	Saint Victor and Saint Corona martyred under Marcus Aurelius.
252	Saint Agatha and three others martyred by the praetor Quintianus.
280	Syracuse plundered by roving Franks.
284	Seventy-five Christians martyred under Diocletian.

307	Saint Lucy martyred at Syracuse under Galerius.
310	Saint Nympha martyred under Galerius.
410	Alaric the Goth dies at Cosenza in Calabria.
440	Sicily laid waste by the Vandals under Genseric.
456	The Vandals defeated by the Romans near Agrigentum.
475	Peace concluded between the Vandals and Goths under Genseric and Odoacer.

Volume II

451	The Synod of Chalcedon confirms the action of the Synod of Constantinople (381), which gave the Bishop of Rome precedence over all others.
472	Ricimer the Goth, who had captured Rome, dies.
475	Romulus Augustulus created Emperor of the West.
476	Romulus Augustulus deposed by Odoacer, the Goth.
488	Theodoric the Ostrogoth invades Italy.
489	Theodoric overcomes Odoacer in battle at Verona.
493	Theodoric murders Odoacer and proclaims himself King of Italy.
500 (about)	A basilica dedicated to Saint Michael the Archangel, at Monte Gargano, in Manfredonia.
526	Theodoric puts Boethius and Symmachus to death.
526	Theodoric succeeded by his daughter Amalasuntha.
527	Justinian becomes Emperor of the East.
535	Amalasuntha assassinated, and Justinian sends Belisarius to avenge her death.
535	Belisarius takes Palermo and Naples. Sicily becomes part of the Eastern Empire.
536	Rome besieged by the Goths, who are forced to retire by Belisarius.
540	Belisarius leaves Italy.
540 (about)	Gregory the Great born.
544	Totila the Goth besieges and takes Naples.
546	Totila besieges and takes Rome, but evacuates it, and it is reoccupied by Belisarius.
549	Totila takes Reggio, crosses the straits, and ravages Sicily.
549	Belisarius returns to Constantinople, and Totila again seizes Rome.
552	Narses defeats the Goths in battle, and Totila is slain.
553	Narses expels the Goths, and Italy is again part of the Eastern Empire.
568	Italy first invaded by the Lombards.
570	Mohammed born.
590	Autharis, the Lombard, dies at Ticinum.
590	Gregory the Great becomes Pope.
610 (about)	Mohammed begins to propagate his doctrines.
622	The Hejira, or flight of Mohammed from Mecca to Medina.

652	The Mohammedans raid and despoil Sicily.
668	The Emperor Constans murdered in his bath at Syracuse by a slave.
717	The Emperor Leo the Isaurian decrees the removal of all images from churches.
766	Antiochus, governor of Sicily, martyred at Constantinople for refusing to obey the decree against images.
772	Jacob, Bishop of Catania, suffers martyrdom for the same cause.
787	The Empress Irene revokes Leo's decree against images.
826	The troops in Sicily rise against the Emperor Michael Balbus.
827	Sicily invaded by a Saracen army.
829	Mineo and Mazzara taken by the Saracens.
831	Messina taken by the Saracens.
832	Palermo taken by the Saracens after a disastrous siege.
842	Sicily ravaged by a plague of locusts.
842	Italy invaded by the Saracens, who settle at Bari.
845	The fortresses of Modica taken by the Saracens.
845	A Saracen fleet defeated by the united forces of Amalfi, Gaeta, and Sorrento, led by Duke Sergius of Naples.
846	Nine thousand Greeks slain by the Saracens before Castrogiovanni.
847	Leontini taken by the Saracens.
848	Ragusa taken by the Saracens.
848	Italy suffers from a great famine.
849	A Mohammedan army attacks Rome and is defeated by Pope Leo IV.
854	Butera besieged by the Saracens.
858	Aghlab, first Mohammedan governor of Sicily, dies at Palermo.
859	The Emir Abas, second Mohammedan governor of Sicily, overruns the country, and takes Castrogiovanni.
863 (about)	A quarrel between the Bishop of Syracuse and the Patriarch of Constantinople leads to the Schism of the East and West, which divides the Greek and Catholic churches.
870	Malta taken by the Saracens.
872	The Saracens attempt to take Salerno, but are defeated.
878	Syracuse taken and laid waste by the Saracens.
950 (about)	Ibn Haukal, an Arab traveller and writer, visits Palermo.
995 (about)	Forty Norman pilgrims rout a Saracen host outside Salerno, and on their return invite other Norman nobles to occupy Italy.
1019	The Normans, led by Raoul de Toëni, and the Lombards, under Meles, are outnumbered and defeated by the Byzantines, on Hannibal's battlefield of Cannae.
1030	Rainulf builds and fortifies Aversa, near Naples, the first Norman city in Italy.
1034	Civil war in Italy, and the Saracens ask the Greeks to intervene.
1038	An army of Greek mercenaries, and a small band of Normans, cross the

	straits, and defeat the Saracens at Messina.
1039	Guaimar, Greek Duke of Salerno, takes possession of Amalfi, and afterwards of Sorrento.
1041	The Normans defeat the Greeks in three pitched battles, in spite of heavy odds.
1042	Maniaces, the Greek General, is unable to make his soldiers face the Normans.
1043	Quarrel about the lands of Monte Cassino, between Pandolph the Wolf, Guaimar of Salerno, and Rainulf of Aversa.
1046	Apulia revolts against Constantinople.
1046	The Emperor Henry III makes Clement II Pope.
1047	The Emperor and the Pope attempt to pacify and organize Southern Italy, without success.
1052	Guaimar, Duke of Salerno, murdered by men of Amalfi.
1053	Pope Leo IX dies, and the division between the Eastern and Western Churches becomes permanent.
1053	The Normans, led by Humphrey of Apulia, Richard of Aversa, and Robert Guiscard, defeat the Germans and Lombards in battle near Monte Gargano.
1057	Robert Guiscard succeeds his brother Humphrey as Count of Apulia.
1058	Pope Nicholas II visits Apulia, and returns to Rome at the head of a Norman army.
1060	The Norman Count Roger, afterwards known as "the Great Count," with sixty knights, raids Sicily from Reggio.
1061	Count Roger, with four hundred and forty knights, captures Messina.
1061	Count Roger marries Judith, daughter of William of Evreux, at Mileto.
1062	Count Roger and his wife besieged by the Saracens at Troina.
1064	Count Roger and Robert Guiscard make a futile attempt to take Palermo.
1068	Count Roger wins a decisive battle over the Saracens at Misilmeri, near Palermo.
1068	Robert Guiscard puts down an insurrection of the Greeks in Apulia.
1071	Robert Guiscard takes Bari, after a long siege.
1072	Robert Guiscard and Count Roger besiege and take Palermo.
1073	Robert Guiscard is desperately ill, but recovers.
1083	Robert Guiscard takes an army as far as Rome, burns half the city, and routs the Emperor Henry IV.
1084	Robert Guiscard dies at Durazzo.
1085	Calabria invaded by the Arab Ben Arwet.
1086	Count Roger defeats and kills Ben Arwet at Syracuse.
1089	Judith, wife of Count Roger, dies.
1091	Noto capitulates, which completes the Norman conquest of Sicily.
1091	Count Roger takes Malta.
1094	Count Roger helps his nephew, Roger, to repress the rebellion of Grantmesnil, in Castrovillari.

1101	Roger the Great Count dies at Mileto.
1127	Roger of Sicily, son of the Great Count, takes possession of Apulia.
1130	Roger crowned King of Sicily at Palermo.
1139	King Roger takes Pope Innocent II prisoner at San Germano, and obtains investiture of Sicily, Apulia, and Capua.
1149	King Roger rescues and entertains Lewis VII of France, on his way home from the Second Crusade.
1154	King Roger succeeded by his second son, William the Bad.
1166	William the Bad succeeded by his son William II, the Good.
1189	William the Good succeeded by Tancred, a natural son of William the Bad's elder brother.
1194	Tancred dies, leaving his crown to his young son, William III.
1194	William III deposed by the Emperor Henry VI of Hohenstaufen, who claims the crown through his wife Constance, daughter of King Roger.
1194	The Emperor Frederick II, son of Henry and Constance, born at Palermo.
1197	Henry VI dies at Castrogiovanni, and his widow crowns her son Frederick King of Sicily.
1197	Queen Constance dies, leaving the Pope guardian of her son.
1208	Frederick II declared of age, and married to Constance of Aragon.
1212	Frederick goes to Germany to claim his Empire.
1220	Frederick is crowned in Rome, and returns to Sicily.
1239	Frederick establishes his Mohammedan colonists in Apulia, in the town called from them Lucera de' Saraceni.
1250	Frederick dies at Castel Fiorentino, in Apulia, and is succeeded by his second son Conrad.
1253	Pope Innocent IV names Charles of Anjou King of Sicily, Duke of Apulia, and Prince of Capua.
1254	Conrad succeeded by his son Conradin, two years old, whose guardian is his half-uncle, Manfred, a natural son of Frederick II.
1258	Manfred takes the crown of Sicily, promising to leave it to his nephew at his death.
1263	Charles of Anjou authorized by Pope Urban IV to begin the conquest of the south.
1266	Manfred slain at the battle of Benevento, and Charles of Anjou created King of Naples and Sicily by Pope Clement IV.
1268	Conradin loses the battle of Tagliacozzo, and is betrayed and sold to Charles.
1268	Conradin beheaded at Naples.
1282	Massacre of the French by the Italians, known as the Sicilian Vespers, takes place at Palermo on Easter Monday.
1282	King Peter of Aragon, husband of Constance the daughter of Manfred, summoned by the nobles, drives out Charles of Anjou, and becomes King of Sicily.

1285	Peter III of Aragon and I of Sicily leaves the latter kingdom to his second son James the Just.
1285	Charles of Anjou succeeded in his Kingdom of Naples by his son Charles II.
1291	James I, the Just, succeeds to the throne of Aragon as James II, leaving that of Sicily to his brother Frederick II.
1296	Frederick II elected king by the Sicilian Parliament after an interregnum of four years.
1309	Charles II of Naples succeeded in that kingdom by his third son, Robert the Wise.
1337	Frederick II of Sicily succeeded by his son Peter II, who is crowned during his father's lifetime.
1342	Peter II dies without male issue, and the crown of Sicily goes to Lewis, son of Peter IV of Aragon.
1343	Robert the Wise succeeded on the throne of Naples by his granddaughter, Joan I, sixteen years old, married to her cousin Andrew, brother of the King of Hungary.
1345	Andrew, consort of Queen Joan, murdered at Aversa with her connivance.
1349	The great basilica at Monte Cassino destroyed by an earthquake.
1355	Lewis of Sicily succeeded by his younger brother, Frederick III.
1377	Frederick III of Sicily succeeded by his daughter Mary, and her husband, Martin of Aragon.
1381	Charles III of Durazzo enters Naples, takes the crown, and imprisons his cousin Joan I at Muro.
1382	Joan I murdered at Muro.
1386	Charles III of Durazzo succeeded on the throne of Naples by his son Ladislaus.
1402	Mary I, Queen of Sicily, succeeded by her husband, Martin I.
1409	Martin I of Sicily dies without issue, succeeded by his father, Martin II of Sicily and I of Aragon, which reunites the two kingdoms.
1409	Martin II dies, and Blanche of Navarre, widow of Martin I, is vicar and lieutenant of Sicily, there being seven claimants to the throne.
1410	Bernardo Cabrera, Count of Modica, attempts to marry Blanche and seize the crown of Sicily.
1412	Ferdinand the Just crowned King of Sicily and Aragon, succeeding his uncle, Martin II of Sicily and I of Aragon.
1414	Ladislaus of Naples succeeded by his sister Joanna II.
1416	Saint Francis of Paola born at Paola, in Calabria.
1416	Alfonso V, the Magnanimous, succeeds his father, Ferdinand the Just, as King of Sicily and Aragon.
1435	Joanna II of Naples, last of the Durazzo line, appoints as her successor by her will René° of Anjou, Duke of Lorraine.
1442	René of Anjou, "the Good King René," expelled from Naples by Alfonso the Magnanimous, who claims the throne through the female line, and

	unites the kingdoms of Naples, Sicily, and Aragon.
1453	The Sultan Mohammed II storms Constantinople.
1458	Alfonso I, the Magnanimous, bequeaths Naples to his son Ferdinand, and Sicily to his younger brother John.
1479	John II of Sicily, Aragon, and Navarre succeeded by his son Ferdinand II of Sicily and V of Aragon, "The Catholic."
1494	Ferdinand I of Naples succeeded by his eldest son, Alfonso II, Duke of Calabria.
1495	Alfonso II abdicates in favour of his eldest son, Ferdinand II.
1495	King Charles VIII of France takes Naples.
1496	Ferdinand II succeeded by his uncle, Frederick IV.
1500	By the Treaty of Granada, Ferdinand the Catholic, of Sicily and Spain, and Lewis XII of France, agree to divide the kingdom of Naples between them.
1503	Tournament between French and Italian knights, known as the "Sfida di Barletta."
1504	Frederick IV dies of grief, and Ferdinand the Catholic becomes King of Naples and Sicily.
1515	Joan III, daughter of Ferdinand the Catholic and Isabella his wife, succeeds her father.
1516	Pope Leo X almost captured by the Barbary pirates.
1516	Joan III abdicates in favour of her son Charles IV, afterwards the Emperor Charles V.
1519	Charles V elected to the empire of Germany, for which Francis I is also a candidate.
1524	Battle of Sesia, between the French and Italians, at which the Chevalier Bayard is slain.
1525	Charles V defeats and captures Francis I of France at the battle of Pavia.
1529	Treaty of peace at Cambrai, by which Francis I abandons his claim to Italy.

Made in the USA
Middletown, DE
04 August 2022